RUFUS WRIGHT. DEL.

CITY OF DA

LITH. OF SARONY, MAJOR & KNAPP. 449 BROADWAY. N.Y.

NPORT . IOWA .

# DAVENPORT

# PAST AND PRESENT;

INCLUDING THE EARLY HISTORY, AND

**Personal and Anecdotal Reminiscences**

OF DAVENPORT;

TOGETHER WITH BIOGRAPHIES, LIKENESSES OF ITS PROMINENT MEN; COMPENDIOUS ARTICLES UPON THE PHYSICAL, INDUSTRIAL, SOCIAL AND POLITICAL CHARACTERISTICS OF THE CITY; FULL STATISTICS OF EVERY DEPARTMENT OF NOTE OR INTEREST, &C.

---

BY

**FRANC B. WILKIE.**

---

DAVENPORT:
PUBLISHING HOUSE OF LUSE, LANE & CO.

1858.

# PREFACE.

As Prefaces are in style, it is well that one should be written for the present work, although the author may not have anything particular to say, but which might as well as not be said in the body of the work. However, a few words may not be inappropriate.

The present work has been prepared under no ordinary difficulties—the data being in the first part of the work, such as were afforded by the memories of "old settlers," no two of which ever agreed exactly in relating the same circumstance. Often would the author get a glimpse of a promising fact or anecdote, and after diligently hunting it through the mazes of a half dozen memories, would discover it to be a jack o' lantern; or after finding it, having it corroborated by the "mouths of two or three witnesses," and having it printed, he would be most positively assured by some one that the thing in question was either entirely wrong, or a fable. However severe and disheartening the task has been, the author flatters himself that in almost every statement truth has been arrived at as near as is possible—for he has been careful in every case to get *all* the different versions, and to adopt the one having a majority in its favor.

There have been other difficulties no less arduous, and much more disagreeable. In a work of this kind few are without an opinion as to what the book should contain, while not a few others are of course better judges of, and much more able (in their own opinion,) to write a book than the author. In looking over the printed sheets, exceptions would be taken to this or that—one wished no anecdotes, another nothing else—a third wished simple statistics—a fourth wished it to build up this particular interest or depress that, or make it a prose song of adulation to some reigning Jupiter in the financial Olympus of Davenport. Others have ventured so far as to threaten to use their influence to suppress the work if it were not gotten up after a particular manner. Appreciating the absurdity, as well as despising such coercive measures in book making, the author aimed only to write a book for the majority, and corresponding with its title, trusting opposition would die away when its authors appreciated either its futility or unreasonableness.

The author takes pleasure in acknowledging many obligations to Hon. G. C. R. Mitchel, G. L. Davenport, Esq., James Mckintosh, Esq., D. C. Eldredge Esq., Willard Barrows, Esq., Mrs. Goldsmith, of Rock Island, Antoine LeClaire, Capt. James May, and others, who have afforded him information in regard to the early settlement of Davenport.

We would acknowledge also indebtedness to Dr. C. C. Parry for the able article upon the geological character of Davenport, to Dr. T. J. Saunders for the article upon its Medical Topography, and Scott County Medical Society, to Add H. Sanders, Esq., for a notice of Mr. Wild, the artist, and to various Clergymen for information in regard to their respective Churches.

Of the Future of Davenport, it has been thought best to spend no time in treating—a close perusal of the Past and Present will at once indicate the future.

With a hope that Davenport Past and Present will meet with the approbation of the public to an extent commensurate with the labor of getting it up, the author leaves it.

*Davenport*, April 5th, 1858.

# CONTENTS.

PAGE.

## CHAPTER VII.



## CHAPTER VIII.



## CHAPTER IX.



## CHAPTER X.



## CHAPTER XI.



## CHAPTER XII.



## CHAPTER XIII.



## CHAPTER XIV.



## CHAPTER XV.



## CHAPTER XVI.

# HISTORY OF DAVENPORT.

## CHAPTER I.

### "PAST AND PRESENT."

The province of the Historian, is less cause than effect —rather facts, than the mediate or immediate agencies of their production. Thus, in the present case, I might overstep the limits of duty by particular inquiry into the causes which have transformed the West from a wilderness to an Eden; or by discussing the probabilities of the existence of some latent "serial law" of human operations, whose result is Progression; or, less metaphysically, by inquiring whether railways, English capital, the influences of monarchial despotism, or omnipotent American enterprise, is the remote or immediate cause of these wonderful changes.

For the present let the simple facts suffice—let it be enough to know that tens of thousands of miles area have, within the memory of young men, been wrung from the grasp of luxuriant Nature by systematic Act—that forests which yesterday were growing but to decay, are now employing myriads of men in transforming them into the utilities of civilization—that the yell of marauding savages is still fresh on our ears, while its echoes are being caught up, and re-flung to the winds by the shriek of the locomotive, as the thunder of its approach heralds the advent of

Enlightened Industry—that the tomahawk yet unrusted by age, is supplanted by the plow-share—that the music of water-falls, scarcely yet dead upon the ears of forest hamadryads, is now absorbed in the busy hum of wheel and revolving saw and the clang of machinery, all ascending as the grand anthem of Progress—that echoes which yesterday slept, or drowsily repeated the hum of forest-life, are to-day sending back the ten thousand voices of many-tongued civilization. These facts—in their magnitude, in the lightning-like quickness of the transformations which they involve, and their kaleidescope beauty of results—will sufficiently interest non-philosophical readers, without a strict inquiry into their rationale.

Let one devote himself more particularly to a contemplation of the illimitable benefits conferred upon Humanity by the unlocking of such a store-house as the West—to the contemplation of *states* of acres so rich that they need but "tickling to make them laugh" in the exuberance of joyous plenty—of its vast coal beds, and lead mines—and in short its profusion in all that contributes to wealth and happiness—and where More's magnificent dream of Utopia finds its nearest possible *material* interpretation—and he will have abundant opportunity for earnest reflection, while our present history will obtain ample material for its completion.

Let us turn to them for a little, by referring to "PAST and PRESENT."

Thirty years ago there was not, save the blackened remains of a chimney at Fort Madison, a single vestige of civilization from twenty miles below Keokuk to Galena, west of the Mississippi. That part of Wisconsin, now known as Iowa, was unknown—her vast fertile prairies and rich-stocked coal-beds were unworked; and the populous, busy cities now spread over her bosom, and teeming with the vitalities of Industry, Wealth, Beauty, and Intelligence, were undreamed of by the wildest schemer of the age.

Standing upon Rock Island then, one saw opposite him, on the Wisconsin side, but a waving, irregular semicircle of bluffs, inclosing an amphitheatre of some hundreds of yards in breadth, and two miles in length. The floor or "bottom" of this amphitheatre sloped gently from the water to the foot of the bluffs, and in its quietness, and with its abrupt back-ground, whose many outlines seemed drawn by some tremulous artist-hand, against the sky, formed a pleasant and beautiful scene. Destitute of trees, covered with long prairie grass in Summer, and its snowy shroud in Winter, there was not much, however, to long interest our spectator.

But could he, as he stood there at that moment, have been imbued with the power of piercing futurity for the short space of thirty years, he would have found very much to chain his attention. He would have seen at first a straggling cabin or two—a little longer, and more of them—the rude "tavern," the insignificant store—a few new sounds indicating the travail of Labor-birth. Years hurry along—a more commodious residence supplants the cabin, a "hotel" improves upon the "tavern," more stores are erected, the bluffs are invaded, and surveyors and stakes mark the outlines of a "city." But a little longer and the rude cabins disappear, and lines of brick houses, lofty warehouses, and the church, mark the rapidity of the change.

The "thirty years" vision ends, but as it fades away a dozen lofty spires reaching high in the blue ether; palatial banks of brick and marble; and regal residences surrounded by the green of woodland foliage; massive colleges and seminaries; long, wide streets, with smooth hard bottoms, fringed by long lines of twinkling, brilliant gas-lights, and the vast white structure which spans the River, meet his view. As the sounds of his vision fade, there come upon his ear the pulsating of a score of steam-pipes, the sharp clang of a thousand hammers, the hoarse signals and deep throbs of passing steamboats, the thunders of long trains of freight and passenger cars, the scream of the locomotive, the hum of a great crowd, each member busily evolving the problem of Progression, and in short the voices, the roar, and the murmur of a GREAT CITY.

So much for "Past and Present"—for the transformations of less than thirty years—for the magical operations of the Genius of Civilization, as she waves her wand over the silent unproductiveness of Nature.

Having thus rapidly outlined a series of events, the next chapters will be devoted to developing them in detail. That the task both to reader and writer will prove pleasant, profitable, and interesting, is more than probable—it amounts to the character of a certainty.

## CHAPTER II.

Saukees and Musquakees—Black Hawk—Character, &c.—Treaties of 1804—Successive Treaties—Spirit Cave on Rock Island.

It would, perhaps, be well to devote a short space to the earlier history of this section, and collateral occurrences, before prosecuting the more direct objects of the present work. The relations of the Aborigines are so intimately interwoven with the pioneer history of every place in the West, and the character, doings and reverses of those remarkable men who once held an undisputed right to this vast continent, that a short digression, having bearing upon them, is pardonable, if not strongly desirable.

The "trail" of the Indian bearing Westward—to Poverty, Starvation—to Death—to Annihilation, runs broad and hard-beaten direct through the scenes which adjoin our homes. The funeral march of once powerful tribes has but just passed the grounds covered with the monumental masonry of the Pale Faces—and their mournful tramp is scarcely stilled yet in our ears, although filled by the shouts of a new and strange multitude.

The recent occurrence of such events, and their close alliance with this and adjacent portions of our country, give them a claim to our attention—although it must be necessarily but brief.

In 1804, the Sauks, Saukees, or Sacs,* and Musquakees or Foxes, ceded to the United States, through General Harrison, all their lands lying on Rock River, and much

* See A, end of Chapter III.

elsewhere. The principal Sac village was at the point of land between the junction of the Mississippi and Rock River—a point just below the present site of Davenport, on the Illinois side. There, according to tradition, had been a village for one hundred and fifty years. The entire country belonging to the tribes, bordered on the Mississippi, and extended about seven hundred miles down the river from the mouth of the Wisconsin, reaching very nearly to the Missouri river. In 1820, they numbered about three thousand persons in all, of whom, perhaps, six hundred were warriors.

The Sac village alluded to was commanded by the celebrated Black Hawk, *alias* the pleasant verbal agglomeration—Ma-ka-tai-me-she-kia-kiak—who, as a warrior, is as well or better known than Tecumseh, or Phillip of New England. The Musquakees, or Foxes, lived further north, and had, near the lead mines, their principal village. Still, notwithstanding the separation of the Sacs and Foxes, they were, in reality, but one tribe, as they hunted together, had similar customs, and so far as unity of purpose was concerned in their enmity to the Sioux, and other nations, they were indissoluble.

Black Hawk was the most celebrated "brave" of his nation. He had been in the service of England in 1812; had been an intimate friend of Tecumseh; was ranked among the *braves* at the early age of sixteen, and at the age of twenty, or thereabouts, succeeded his father as chief, the latter having been killed in a bloody battle with the Cherokees. With such a life—scarcely if ever defeated in battle—proud, imperious, and with a deep tinge of melancholy in his later years—venerated by his braves, and feared by his enemies, he was no common man, nor would his nature admit of such treatment as might be endured patiently by ordinary or less strongly marked men.

Of his personal appearance, the editor of the United States Literary *Gazette* thus speaks, as he saw him in Philadelphia in 1833:

"He is about sixty-five, of middling size, with a head that would excite the envy of a phrenologist—one of the finest that Heaven ever let fall on the head of an Indian.

* * * * * * *

"The son of Black Hawk is a noble specimen of physical beauty—a model for those who would embody the idea of strength. He was painted, and had his hair cut in a strange fantasy." It was remarked by many in the same city at that time, that Black Hawk's "pyramidal forehead" strongly resembled Sir Walter Scott's, while others found in its peculiar outlines a very striking similarity to those of the well-known Stephen Girard. Washington Irving, writing concerning him from Jefferson Barracks in December, 1832, says: "He has a fine head, a Roman style of face, and a prepossessing countenance." Many of our older citizens, who knew him personally, describe him as embodying in his countenance an expression of deep cunning, and as rather lacking in intellectuality. He was, however, extremely superstitious, and it is more than probable that the war in which he engaged in '31 and '2 was owing largely to the influence of a half breed Winnebago and Sac Prophet, named Wabo-kieshiek, (White Cloud,) although his constitutional hatred of the Americans, and the unwarranted aggressions of the latter in many cases, undoubtedly materially assisted precipitating the matter. In all, however, he was, with many failings, a great man—possessing a depth of character, a reach of means, energy, and patriotic feeling which, developed under the promotive and powerful influences of civilization, would have elevated him to the proud rank of those whom the world recognizes as "Great."

In regard to the treaty of 1804, there are two accounts.

One regards it as a *bona fide* transaction, whereby the lands of the Sacs and Foxes were sold by responsible men of the tribes; and that it was further ratified by a part of the tribe in a treaty with Gov. Edwards and Auguste Choteau in September 1815, and by another with the same commissioners in May 1816. These further allege, that the United States allowed the Indians to remain upon any portion of this land so long as it remained the property of the Government, and that the lands occupied by the Sac village at Rock River, had been surveyed and sold, and hence could no longer be justly occupied by the Indians.*

The other account, which is that of Black Hawk himself, states quite a different story. It is, that an American having been killed by one of Black Hawk's men, the murderer was arrested and imprisoned at St. Louis. Four Indians were dispatched by the tribe to St. Louis to release the incarcerated Indian "by paying for the person killed"—according to their custom. The return of the four is thus described by Black Hawk:

"Quash-qua-me and party remained a long time absent. They at length returned, and encamped a short distance below the village—but did not come up that day—nor did any person approach their camp! They appeared to be dressed in fine coats, and had medals. From these circumstances, we were in hopes that they had brought good news. Early the next morning the Council Lodge was crowded—Quash-qua-me and party came up, and gave the following account of their mission:

'On their arrival at St. Louis they met their American father, and explained to him their business, and urged the release of their friend. The American Chief told them he wanted land—and they had agreed to give him some on the west side of the Mississippi, and some on the Illinois

*Gov. Ford's history of Illinois.

side, opposite the Jeffreon. When the business was all arranged, they expected to have their friend released to come home with them. But about the time they were ready to start, their friend was let out of prison, who *ran a short distance, and was shot dead!* This is all they could recollect of what was said or done. They had been drunk the greater part of the time they were in St. Louis!'

"This is all myself or nation knew of the treaty of 1804. It has been explained to me since. I find, by that treaty, that all our country east of the Mississippi, and south of Jeffreon, was ceded to the United States for *one thousand dollars a year!*"

It may be questioned whether the treaty at St. Louis was one concluded by authority of the tribes—although it is not in the least doubtful that, on the part of the Commissioners, the proceeding was concluded in all fairness, and with the belief that the Indians who signed the treaty were instructed so to do by the Sacs and Foxes. Black Hawk is mistaken in some points of his statement. The treaty was signed by five Chiefs instead of four, one of whom, Pah-she-pa-ho, was a head chief among the Sacs. It was also made *before* Lieut. Pike ascended the Mississippi, instead of after, as stated by Black Hawk, as Pike did not leave St. Louis till August, 1805, on his expedition.

In September 1815, both Sacs and Foxes concluded a new treaty, wherein the treaty of St. Louis was ratified, among other matters. This treaty was held at Portage des Sioux, and was a finale to the war with England of 1812, in which a part of the tribes, headed by Black Hawk, had fought against the Americans. This treaty was not signed by Black Hawk or *his* band, although signed largely by Chiefs of both tribes, who were fully empowered so to do. In May, 1816, another treaty was held at St. Louis, in which that of 1804 was recognized, and was signed by Black Hawk.

One cannot doubt that these successive treaties were binding upon the Sacs and Foxes, although the remuneration was contemptibly small. All this rich extent of land was made over for the pittance of some two thousand dollars (in goods,) down, and an annuity of one thousand, also in goods. That such treaties should also be held among the tribes, and not a distance, is obviously no more than fair. All complaint would thereafter be prevented.

In 1816, Fort Armstrong was erected upon Rock Island. It was a measure distasteful to the Indians, for reasons which we give in Black Hawk's own words:

"We did not, however, object to their building the fort on the Island, but we were very sorry, as this was the best Island on the Mississippi, and had long been the resort of our young people during the summer. It was our garden, (like the white people have near their big villages,) which supplied us with strawberries, blackberries, plums, apples, and nuts of various kinds; and its waters supplied us with pure fish, being situated in the rapids of the river. In my early life, I spent many happy days on this Island. A good spirit had care of it, who lived in a cave in the rocks immediately under the place where the Fort now stands, and has often been seen by our people. He was white, with large wings like a *swan's*, but ten times larger. We were particular not to make much noise in that part of the island which he inhabited, for fear of disturbing him. But the noise of the Fort has since driven him away, and no doubt a *bad* spirit has taken his place!"

Not a few Davenport readers will recognize in this the base of the legend of Black Hawk's Cave, and his going thither to consult with the good Genius of the place. A fit place, truly, was it, for the dwelling of the Red man's tutelar spirit! Facing the glorious river, which, fair as the Eridanus of Elysium, rolled before it,—with the music of its flow softly filling the recesses of his retreat —with the poetry of moving waters ever dramatized before his eyes—on either side the prairie rolling back like an ocean of green, frozen to rigidity in some long, gentle swell—the shady island, with its luscious fruits, and a domain as fair as the Garden of Hesperides—with the long, winding bluffs on either side, rolling away in the distance till, uniting above and below, they walled in as glorious a landscape of plain and hill, curve, rounding outlines of surface, water, foliage and sky, as ever artist-hand sketched, or artist-brain imagined—with all these circumstances, we do not wonder that the imaginative Indian located in this peculiar spot his Guardian Genius!

## CHAPTER III.

Black Hawk Continued—Treaties—Removals—Invasions—Executive Influence and Alarm—Crossing the Mississippi—Stillman's Run—Retreat—Massacre at Bad Axe—Treaty—Close of Black Hawk's History.

In 1823, by the advice of the agent at Fort Armstrong, the larger portion of the Sacs and Foxes, headed by *KEOKUK, removed across the Mississippi. That portion of the Sac nation which, under the leadership of Black Hawk, had, by their fidelity to the British in 1812, earned the appellation of the "British Band," steadily refused to vacate the Sac village at Rock River.

It has been ascribed to a spirit of rivalry—this difference between Keokuk and Black Hawk, which prevented

* KEOKUK.—The design of the present Chapter will not allow the name of Keokuk that prominence which his character deserves. He rose from obscurity to a Chieftainship by the mere force of his talents. He was a brave warrior, a firm friend to the Americans, and an orator without a rival among the tribes of the North-West. He was a Sac, and his name denotes the "Watchful Fox." He eventually superseded Black Hawk, and was, for a long time, head chief of the Sac nation.

The following description is taken from a cotemporaneous work:

"In person, Keokuk is stout, graceful, and commanding, with fine features, and an intelligent countenance. His broad expanded chest, and muscular limbs, denote activity and physical strength; and he is known to excel in dancing, horsemanship, and all athletic exercises. * * * In point of intellect, and integrity of character, and the capacity for governing others, he is supposed to have no superior among the Indians. Bold, courageous, and skilful in war—mild, firm, and politic in peace. He has great enterprise, and active impulses, with a freshness and enthusiasm of feeling, which might readily lead him astray, but for his quick perception of human character, his uncommon prudence, and his calm sound judgment. * * * Such is Keokuk, the Watchful Fox, who prides himself upon being the friend of the white man.—*Life of Black Hawk; Cincinnati.*

LITH OF SARONY, MAJOR & KNAPP 449 BROADWAY N.Y.

KEOKUK
CHIEF OF THE SACS & FOXES.

the latter from adopting the expedient operation of the former by moving over the Mississippi. I cannot adopt this view—it may have had some influence, but it is entirely too trivial in its nature to influence the important step which Black Hawk took some few years after. Patriotism, and the love of home—of the village where his tribe had lived for more than a century, and where everything which makes life honorable or desirable had originated, had undoubtedly more influence in Black Hawk's decision than the mere desire of outvieing the rising splendor of Keokuk. He regarded the Americans as aggressors—he had fought against them in 1812—his ancestors—his father—himself had lived, hunted, fought, died, and were buried in the Sac village. He had grown old there—there slept his son; there was every endearment which could be evolved from the past, as well of the savage as the refined—and he could not bring himself to leave them. There were enough circumstances, apart from his dislike of the Americans, and their ruffianly aggressions, to explain why he left it unwillingly, and how, after leaving it, he returned with a "forlorn hope" to breast the whole force of the United States in an attempt to regain it.

By the terms of the treaty with the United States, the Indians were to retain possession of their lands until they were sold to actual settlers. Some white families, however, who probably considered an Indian's title to life, land and liberty, as merely nominal, and of no account, when measured against the "Rights" of the white man, moved on to the Sac village. Not content with thus actually stealing the land, they took advantage of Black Hawk's absence on a hunting expedition to not only fence in the Indians' cornfields, but to take possession of Black Hawk's lodge.

These whites had established themselves in direct violation of the treaty of 1804. They continued their aggressions—destroyed the Indians' corn, killed their domestic animals, and whipped their wives and children. Much against the wishes of Black Hawk, they introduced a traffic in spirituous liquor, and made drunkenness and debauchery common. The remonstrances of Black Hawk, and other chiefs, were unavailing, equally in regard to the encroachments upon their lands, or the sale of spirituous liquors. The Indians were regarded as legitimate prey by these harpies—and appeals to their sense of justice or to their reason were alike unavailing. Black Hawk, upon one occasion, even took the trouble to put in practice a modern principle of action—the Maine law—by knocking in the head of a barrel of whisky, which the owner had continued to vend in spite of the old chief's remonstrances.

This condition of things continued until 1827. In the winter of this year, while the Indians were absent on their periodical hunt, the whites devised a famous scheme for getting rid of those upon whose lands they were intruding. It was a well conceived operation—although moralists would call it rather robbery than honorable policy. It was no less than to expedite the Indians on their destination over the Mississippi, by burning their lodges! Accordingly, the torch was applied to some forty lodges, which were entirely consumed. When the Indians returned in the Spring, and required satisfaction for this unwarrantable outrage, they received only fresh insults.

The wigwam of an Indian is inconsiderable—but still so far as *right* is concerned, there was, in the burning of these lodges, as clear a case of halter-deserving arson as ever fell under the jurisdiction of judicial ermine. To apply the incendiary torch to one's lodge, and to run the plough-share through the sacred mounds of ancestral graves, are no light provocations, although committed upon the Red man. When one adds to these, the indignity of *blows* upon his own person, and worse, upon that of his wife and children, we can nearly or quite excuse him if he applies, as his remedy, the sharpest *lex talionis* at his command. Especially is such a result excusable after warning, expostulations, and appeal to higher powers, have signally and utterly failed.

There is always upon the frontier a set of reckless men, speculators, squatters, and loafers, who, devoid of principle and humanity, care less for the rights and lives of others, and especially for those of Indians, than they do for the same qualities in an irrational animal. Such men held possession of the frontiers in 1827, and such were they who had infringed upon the precincts of the Sac village.

Under the seventh article of the treaty of 1804, it was provided; "that as long as the lands which are now ceded to the United States remain their property, the Indians belonging to said tribes, shall enjoy the privilege of living and hunting upon them."

None of the lands upon Rock River were brought into market until 1829, and consequently the Indians, prior to this time, had as much right to them as if they held them in fee simple. At this time, 1829, the lands purchased in the treaty in 1804, were not offered for sale within sixty miles of this point—yet for the unjustifiable purpose of getting rid of the Indians on Rock River, the lands upon which the Sac village stood were thrown into market.

In the spring of 1830, when Black Hawk and his party returned from their winter's hunt, and commenced preparations for planting, they were notified that the land was sold, and that they must remove west of the Mississippi. Unwilling, however, to remove, he visited Malden to consult his "British Father," and returned by way of Detroit to see General Cass. Both advised him if he had not sold his land to remain quietly upon it, and he could not be disturbed. He returned late in the fall, and found his band absent upon their winter's hunt. Keokuk exerted himself strongly this winter to induce Black Hawk's followers to desert him, and to remove across the Mississippi. It was in vain. Their attachment to their village was stronger than any representations of the danger of such a course, and accordingly, in the Spring of 1831, they all returned. The agent at Rock Island immediately notified them to remove, or troops would be sent to drive them off.

In the meantime the squaws had commenced planting their corn, which the whites ploughed up. This enraged Black Hawk, and he threatened to remove the whites by force if they persisted in such proceedings. The whites became alarmed—a startling memorial was drawn up, concluding, after enumerating a long list of outrages, with the astounding outrage of the "Indians going to a house, rolling out a barrel of whisky, and knocking in its head!" Terrifying rumors were circulated of border depredations committed by "General Black Hawk" and his "British Band." The Executive of Illinois promptly ordered out *seven hundred* militia to meet this "invasion."

However, General Gaines ordered some ten companies to Rock Island, and with them proceeded there in June. A conference was held with Black Hawk, the result of which was, that he refused to leave. However, some sixteen hundred mounted militiamen having arrived, Gen. Gaines took possession of the Sac village, and Black Hawk retreated across the river. A treaty was then concluded, wherein Black Hawk agreed not to cross the river without permission.

Thus ended, for that year, this famous campaign—which, while being in reality but a squabble between Black Hawk's squaws, and the whites, about cornfields, and rights of way, was magnified by Gov. Reynolds into an actual invasion.

In the Spring of 1832, Black Hawk received information from the Prophet that not only the British, but several tribes of Indians would assist him in recovering his lands. After vainly endeavoring to persuade Keokuk to join him, he started in April from his rendezvous at Fort Madison, and, attended by his band, with their wives and children, landed at Rock River, and proceeded to ascend it. This was in violation of the treaty of the preceding year. He was ordered by Gen. Atkinson—then stationed at Fort Armstrong—to return; but he refused on the grounds of his mission being a peaceful one, as he was proceeding to a Winnebago village further up the river, there, by their invitation, to raise corn.

After reaching the Winnebago village, Black Hawk ascertained that the tribe would not assist him, although willing that he should plant corn. He then determined to return along Rock River, and recross the Mississippi, as he had by this time learned that all the promised assistance from other tribes had failed. Before returning, he determined to give a feast in honor of some Pottowatomies then visiting him.

In the meantime, Gen. Atkinson, with six hundred troops, had ascended Rock River in pursuit of Black Hawk, and at this time had arrived at Dixon's ferry, a point about half way from the Mississippi to Black Hawk's camp. There, Maj. Stillman, with some three hundred volunteers, proceeded forward on a scouting expedition. He proceeded up to Sycamore Creek, which was within a few miles of Black Hawk.

The latter hearing that troops had been seen near him, immediately sent three young men with a flag of truce, to conduct them to his camp, for the purpose of a conference. These, upon approaching the troops, were *taken prisoners, and one of them shot!* Five others were despatched by the wary old chief to mark the result. These had not proceeded far before they saw the troops coming toward them at a full gallop. Two of them were overtaken and killed, the other three reached the camp, and gave the alarm. All of Black Hawk's men were then absent, but about fifty.

These immediately charged upon the advancing troops, and completely routed the valorous three hundred! The retreat did not stop on reaching their camp, but many not even deeming Gen. Atkinson's flag a sufficient defense, kept on fifty miles farther, to their own homes!

This was the famous "battle" of "Stillman's Run," and it, perhaps, conferred a more lasting notoriety upon those engaged in it, than would have the hardest fought battle. The whole proceeding—from the firing upon the flag-bearers at the beginning, to their "turning tail" to the Indians at the end—is the most cowardly affair on record. There is not a doubt but if the flag had been respected, and a conference held, that Black Hawk would have peaceably returned to the west side of the Mississippi.

A bloody frontier war ensued. The "British Band" divided in squads, and attacked and butchered wherever they could find an opportunity. One thousand more troops were ordered out, and Gen. Scott proceeded towards the scene of action with about the same number, having been despatched by the Secretary of War. The Indians were gradually driven north, and, as they reached the Wisconsin river, they were defeated, with a bloody loss, by Gen. Dodge, the former losing some forty of their braves, the latter but one. This decisive blow ended, in reality, the war. The women and children escaping down the Wisconsin on rafts, starved, or were shot by troops stationed along the river, with but a miserably small exception.

Black Hawk, and his remaining party, attempted to reach the Mississippi by taking a direct line across the country, toward a point some forty miles above the mouth of the Wisconsin. After losing many by starvation, the flying band reached the river, and made preparations for crossing it—but the steamboat Warrior gave them another check. Regardless of a white flag, exhibited by them, the Captain let fly a six-pounder among them, and, to use his

ANTOINE LeCLAIRE'S OLD RESIDENCE.

own elegant language, "if you ever saw *straight blankets* you saw them there!"* The next morning, the whole of Gen. Atkinson's army arrived in pursuit of the Indians, and immediately attacked them. This "battle" was simply a massacre—the sharp-shooters amusing themselves by picking off the women and children, who were endeavoring to cross the river. The most who escaped by crossing the river passed from Scyllad to Charybis—for they were attacked by a party of Sioux, and were either killed or taken prisoners. The "battle" of Bad Axe was simply a victory of overpowering numbers over a starved remnant of a brave tribe, and an indiscriminate massacre of men, women and children. From the unjustifiable act of the Warrior in firing upon a flag of truce to the shooting of innocent women and harmless children, there is not much to admire.

Black Hawk escaped, but was taken by a couple of treacherous Winnebagoes, and delivered, along with the Prophet, to General Street, August 27th, at Prairie du Chien. He was sent in a few days to Rock Island, where, on the 21st September, a new treaty was concluded between the Whites and Indians. In consequence of cholera in the Fort, the treaty was held on the Wisconsin side—on the spot of ground now occupied by the Mississippi and Missouri Railroad buildings.

It was at this treaty that Keokuk made a reserve of a section of land which was made over to the wife of Antoine Le Claire, on the single condition that the latter should build his house upon the spot of ground occupied by the marquee of Gen. Scott during the treaty. The result of the treaty was, that the United States acquired from the Sacs and Foxes six millions of acres lying *west* of the Mississippi, which acquisition was known as the "Black Hawk Purchase," and subsequently as the "Iowa District."

* See B, end of Chapter III.

A reserve of forty miles square, known as "Keokuk's Reserve," was made in favor of that Chief on Iowa River.

This land was purchased for twenty thousand dollars per annum for thirty years—the payment of the debts of the tribe, and the support of a black and gun smith among them.

This ends the brief notice of prominent events in the life of Black Hawk, and the celebrated "Black Hawk War"—than which latter there is scarcely a more farcical "war" on record. Beginning in the aggressions of the whites, and lack of forbearance afterward with the less refined Indians—with bombast and cowardice, and violation of sacred pledges interspersing its sparse details of nobleness, charity and bravery, it is not one which can or should reflect particular credit upon the part of the Whites. But let it pass—every year's inquiries are revealing these facts—and posterity will yet pass a righteous verdict upon its character.

When Black Hawk passed down the river, during a visit to Rock Island in the Spring of '33, we are informed by Lieut. Mitchell that, as he passed along below Rock Island, he "cried like a child," as his eye looked upon the site of his old village. There is something peculiarly affecting in this incident, and it reveals no little of the Beautiful in the heart of the SAVAGE. He was in his sixty-fifth year—an old man. There were the rolling prairies of his beautiful village—the theatre of the great exploits of his whole life, which he was never to visit again. Expatriated, conquered, thrust down from his high position, and ignominiously treated, with the sight of boyhood and manhood's home in the possession of the stranger-enemy, and with the prospect of a distant removal in his old age, from all that he valued—why should not the aged chief weep? He died—and among all the famous events of "General Black Hawk's" history—among all his brave exploits, and magnanimous deeds, there is not one so lustrous as the aged man weeping as he passed his old home, and the graves of his kindred.

Let Posterity do him at least the justice to own that there was in his acts a single one of poetic beauty, which is paralleled only in acts giving birth to "Thoughts that breathe, and words that burn."

A. **Indian Customs.**—In closing these chapters, it may not be inappropriate to give a few of the customs, beliefs, &c., of the Sac and Fox tribes:

MARRIAGES.—Our women plant the corn, and as soon as they get done, we make a feast, and dance the *crane* dance, in which they join us, dressed in their best, and decorated with feathers. At this feast our young braves select the young woman they wish to have for a wife. He then informs his mother, who calls on the mother of the girl, when the arrangement is made, and the time appointed for him to come. He goes to the lodge when all are asleep, (or pretend to be,) lights his matches, which have been provided for the purpose, and soon finds where his intended sleeps. He then awakens her, and holds the light to his face, that she may know him—after which he places the light close to her. If she blows it out, the ceremony is ended, and he appears in the lodge the next morning, as one of the family. If she does not blow out the light, but leaves it to burn out, he retires from the lodge. The next day he places himself in full view of it, and plays his flute. The young women go out, one by one, to see who he is playing for. The tune changes, to let them know that he is not playing for them. When his intended makes her appearance at the door, he continues his *courting* tune, until she returns to the lodge. He then gives over playing, and makes another trial at night, which generally turns out favorable. During the first year they ascertain whether they can agree with each other, and can be happy—if not, they part, and each looks out again. If we were to live together, and disagree, we should be as foolish as the whites. No indiscretion can banish a woman from her parental lodge—no difference how many children she may bring home, she is always welcome—the kettle is over the fire to feed them.

DANCES.—The crane dance often lasts two or three days. When this is over, we feast again, and have our *national* dance. The large square in the village is swept and prepared for the purpose. The chiefs and old warriors, take seats on mats, which have been spread at the upper end of the square—the drummers and singers come next, and the braves and women form the sides, leaving a large space in the middle. The drums beat, and the singers commence. A warrior enters the square, keeping time with the music. He shows the manner he started on a war party—how he approached the enemy—he strikes, and describes the way he killed him. All join in applause. He then leaves the square, and another enters and takes his place. Such of our young men as have not been out in war parties, and killed an enemy, stand back ashamed—not being able to enter the square. I remember that I was ashamed to look where our young women stood, before I could take my stand in the square as a warrior.

What pleasure it is to an old warrior, to see his son come forward and relate his exploits—it makes him feel young, and induces him to enter the square, and "fight his battles o'er again."

This national dance makes our warriors. When I was traveling last summer, on a steam boat, on a large river, going from New York to Albany, I was shown the place where the Americans dance their national dance [West Point]; where the old warriors recount to their young men, what they have done, to stimulate them to go and do likewise. This surprised me, as I did not think the whites understood our way of making braves.

LABORS, WARS, FEASTS, &C.—When our national dance is over—our corn-fields hoed, and every weed dug up, and our corn about knee high, all our young men would start in a direction towards sun-down, to hunt deer and buffalo—being prepared, also, to kill Sioux, if any are found on our hunting grounds—a part of our old men and women to the lead mines to make lead—and the remainder of our people start to fish, and get mat stuff. Every one leaves the village, and remains about forty days. They then return: the hunting party bringing in dried buffalo and deer meat, and sometimes *Sioux scalps*, when they are found trespassing on our hunting grounds. At other times they are met by a party of Sioux too strong for them, and are driven in. If the Sioux have killed the Sacks last, they expect to be retaliated upon, and will fly before them, and vice versa. Each party knows that the other has a right to retaliate, which induces those who have killed last, to give way before their enemy—as neither wish to strike, except to avenge the death of their relatives. All our wars are predicated by the relatives of those killed; or by aggressions upon our hunting grounds.

The party from the lead mines bring lead, and the others dried fish, and mats for our winter lodges. Presents are now made by each party; the first, giving to the others dried buffalo and deer, and they, in exchange, presenting them with lead, dried fish and mats. This is a happy season of the year—having plenty of provisions, such as beans, squashes, and other produce, with our dried meat and fish, we continue to make feasts and visit each other, until our corn is ripe.

Some lodge in the village makes a feast daily to the Great Spirit. I cannot explain this so that the white people would comprehend me, as we have no regular standard among us. Every one makes his feast as he thinks best, to please the Great Spirit, who has the care of all beings created. Others believe in two Spirits: one good and one bad, and make feasts for the Bad Spirit, *to keep him quiet!* If they can make peace with him, the Good Spirit will not hurt them! For my part, I am of opinion, that so far as we have *reason*, we have a right to use it, in determining what is right or wrong; and should pursue that path which we believe to be right—believing, that "whatever is, is right." If the Great and Good Spirit wished us to believe and do as the whites, he could easily change our opinions, so that we would see, and think, and act as they do. We are *nothing* compared to His power, and we feel and know it. We have men among us, like the whites, who pretend to know the right path, but will not consent to show it without *pay!* I have no faith in their paths—but believe that every man must make his own path!

Origin of Corn.—I will here relate the manner in which corn first came. According to tradition, handed down to our people, a beautiful woman was seen to descend from the clouds, and alight upon the earth, by two of our ancestors, who had killed a deer, and were sitting by a fire, roasting a part of it to eat. They were astonished at seeing her, and concluded that she must be hungry, and had smelt the meat—and immediately went to her, taking with them a piece of the roasted venison. They presented it to her, and she eat—and told them to return to the spot where she was sitting, at the end of one year, and they would find a reward for their kindness and generosity. She then ascended to the clouds, and disappeared. The two men returned to their village, and explained to the nation what they had seen, done, and heard—but were laughed at by their people. When the period arrived, for them to visit this consecrated ground, where they were to find a reward for their attention to the beautiful woman of the clouds, they went with a large party, and found, where her right hand had rested on the ground, *corn* growing—and where the left hand had rested, *beans*—and immediately where she had been seated, *tobacco.*

The two first have, ever since, been cultivated by our people, as our principal provisions—and the last used for smoking. The white people have since found out the latter, and seems to relish it as much as we do—as they use it in different ways, viz: smoking, snuffing and eating!

Sports, &c.—We thank the Great Spirit for all the benefits he has conferred upon us. For myself, I never take a drink of water from a spring, without being mindful of his goodness.

We next have our great ball play—from three to five hundred on a side, play this game. We play for horses, guns, blankets, or any other kind of property we have. The successful party take the stakes, and all retire to our lodges in peace and friendship.

We next commence horse-racing, and continue our sport and feasting, until the corn is all secured. We then prepare to leave our village for our hunting grounds. The traders arrive, and give us credit for such articles as we want to clothe our families, and enable us to hunt. We first, however, hold a council with them, to ascertain the price they will give us for our skins, and what they will charge us for goods. We inform them where we intend hunting—and tell them where to build their houses. At this place, we deposit part of our corn, and leave our old people. The traders have always been kind to them, and relieved them when in want. They were always much respected by our people—and never since we have been a nation, has one of them been killed by any of our people.

We disperse, in small parties, to make our hunt, and as soon as it is over, we return to our traders' establishment, with our skins, and remain feasting, playing cards, and other pastimes, until near the close of the winter. Our young men then start on the beaver hunt; others to hunt raccoons and muskrats—and the remainder of our people go to the sugar camps to make sugar. All leave our encampment, and appoint a place to meet on the Mississippi, so that we may return to our village together, in the spring. We always spent our time pleasantly at the sugar camp. It being the season for wild fowl, we lived well, and always had plenty, when the hunters came in, that we might make a feast for them. After this is over, we return to our village, accompanied, sometimes, by our traders. In this way, the year rolled round happily. But these are times that were!

---

B.—Myself and band having no means to descend the Ouisconsin, I started, over a rugged country, to go to the Mississippi, intending to cross it, and return to my nation. Many of our people were compelled to go on foot, for want of horses, which, in consequence of their having had nothing to eat for a long time, caused our march to be very slow. At length we arrived at the Mississippi, having lost some of our old men and little children, who perished on the way with hunger.

We had been here but a little while, before we saw a steam boat (the "Warrior,") coming. I told my braves not to shoot, as I intended going on board, so that we might save our women and children. I knew the captain, (Throckmorton,) and was determined to give myself up to him. I then sent for my *white flag.* While the messenger was gone, I took a small piece of white cotton, and put it on a pole, and called to the captain of the boat, and told him to send his little canoe ashore, and let me come on board. The people on the boat asked whether we were Sacs or Winnebagoes. I told a Winnebago to tell them that we were Sacs, and wanted to give ourselves up! A Winnebago on the boat called to us "*to run and hide, that the whites were going to shoot!*" About this time one of my braves had jumped into the river, bearing a white flag to the boat—when another sprang in after him, and brought him to shore. The firing then commenced from the boat, which was returned by my braves, and continued for some time. Very few of my people were hurt after the first fire, having succeeded in getting behind old logs and trees, which shielded them from the enemy's fire.

The Winnebago, on the steam boat, must either have misunderstood what was told, or did not tell it to the captain correctly; because I am confident that he would not have fired upon us, if he had known my wishes. I have always considered him a good man, and too great a brave to fire upon an enemy when sueing for quarters.

After the boat left us, I told my people to cross, if they could, and wished: that I intended going into the Chippewa country. Some commenced crossing, and such as had determined to follow them, remained—only three lodges going with me. Next morning, at daybreak, a young man overtook me, and said that all my party had determined to cross the Mississippi—that a number had already got over safe, and that he had heard the white army last night within a few miles of them. I now began to fear that the whites would come up with my people, and kill them, before they could get across. I had determined to go and join the Chippewas; but reflecting that by this I could only save myself, I concluded to return, and die with my people, if the Great Spirit would not give us another victory! During our stay in the thicket, a party of whites came close by us, but passed on without discovering us!

Early in the morning a party of whites, being in advance of the army, came upon our people, who were attempting to cross the Mississippi. They tried to give themselves up—the whites paid no attention to their entreaties—but commenced *slaughtering* them! In a little while the whole army arrived. Our braves, but few in number, finding that the enemy paid no regard to age or sex, and seeing that they were murdering helpless women and little children, determined to *fight until they were killed!* As many women as could, commenced swimming the Mississippi, with their children on their back.s A number of them were drowned, and some shot, before they could reach the opposite shore.

One of my braves, who gave me this information, piled up some saddles before him, (when the fight commenced,) to shield himself from the enemy's fire, and killed three white men! But seeing that the whites were coming too close to him, he crawled to the bank of the river, without being perceived, and hid himself under it, until the enemy retired. He then came to me, and told me what had been done. After hearing this sorrowful news, I started, with my little party, to the Winnebago village at Prairie La Cross. On my arrival there, I entered the lodge of one of the chiefs, and told him that I wished him to go with me to his father—that I intended to give myself up to the American war chief, and *die*, if the Great Spirit saw proper! He said he would go with me. I then took my *medicine bag*, and addressed the chief. I told him that it was "the soul of the Sac nation—that it never had been dishonored in any battle—take it, it is my life—dearer than life—and give it to the American chief!" He said he would keep it, and take care of it, and if I was suffered to live, he would send it to me.

During my stay at the village, the squaws made me a white dress of deer skin. I then started, with several Winnebagoes, and went to their agent, at Prairie du Chien, and gave myself up.

On my arrival there, I found to my sorrow, that a large body of Sioux had pursued, and killed, a number of our women and children, who had got safely across the Mississippi. The whites ought not to have permitted such conduct—and none but *cowards* would ever have been guilty of such cruelty—which has always been practised on our nation by the Sioux.

The massacre, which terminated the war, lasted about two hours. Our loss in killed, was about sixty, besides a number that were drowned. The loss of the enemy could not be ascertained by my braves, exactly; but they think that they killed about *sixteen*, during the action.

We are indebted for the above details to the life of Black Hawk, dictated by himself.—Ed

## CHAPTER IV.

Meeting at Col. Davenport's—Site of Davenport—Proprietors—Survey—Cost of Pioneer Enterprises—Anecdote of a Politician—First Ball—Religious Services—Rockingham—Postmaster Appointed.

In the year 1833, there were one or two claims made upon the lands now occupied by the lower part of the city. The claim upon which the city was first laid out was contended for by a Dr. Spencer and Mr. McCloud. The matter was finally settled by Mr. LeClaire buying them both out; giving them for the quarter section *one hundred and fifty dollars!* A splendid illustration is this sale of the immense fortunes made in the West, by politic forethought, and judicious investment. This claim laid to the West of LeClaire's Reserve—the latter terminating at *Harrison* street. Below this street the city was first laid out.

Having fenced in this portion, Mr. LeClaire cultivated it until it was sold to a Company in 1835. In the Fall of this year a company was formed for the purpose of purchasing and laying out a town site. They met at the house of Col. Davenport on Rock Island to discuss the matter. The following gentlemen were present: Maj. Wm. Gordon, Antoine LeClaire, Col. Geo. Davenport, Maj. Thos. Smith, Alex. McGregor, Levi S. Colton, and Philip Hambaugh. These gentlemen, and Capt. James May, then in Pittsburg, composed the company which secured the site, and set in motion a train of circumstances, whose result is, a beautiful and flourishing city. The necessity of a town between the upper and lower rapids—the unexampled fertility of the adjacent country—the magnificent beauty of the location—its freedom from malaria-breeding marshes, and facilities for drainage, the propinquity of immense opportunity for water power, were reasons adduced for the choice of the location. Well did they choose, as the events of the last twenty years have amply established. In the Spring of the next year, the site was surveyed and laid out by Maj. Gordon, United States Surveyor, and one of the stockholders. The spot selected included the area bounded on the East by Harrison street, on the North by Seventh, West by Warren, and South by the river. It included thirty-six blocks, and six half-blocks—the latter being the portions lying adjacent to Warren, on the West.

The cost of the entire site was two thousand dollars—or two hundred and fifty dollars per share—a price which now would purchase but a very indifferent building-lot in the least valued part of it. In May the lots were offered at auction. A steamboat came up from St. Louis laden with passengers to attend the sale, and remained at the levee during its continuance, in order to afford the conveniences of lodging, edibles, and the not less essential item of drinkables. The sale continued two days, but owing to the fact that the titles were simply such as were included in a squatter's claim—and purchasers fearful that such were not particularly good—only some fifty or sixty lots were sold, and these mostly to St. Louis speculators. The lots brought from $300 to $600 each—a smaller sum than the proprietors calculated upon. The remaining portion of the site was then divided among the proprietors.

The emigration this year was but small—only some half dozen families coming in. The first Hotel or "tavern" was put up this year, and opened by Edward Powers; and is still standing on the corner of Front street and Ripley. It was put up by Messrs. Davenport and LeClaire, and was called "Davenport Hotel"—in honor of the "city"—the latter receiving its cognomen from Col. Geo. Davenport, who long previous had been a resident of the Island. In regard to its appearance, nothing need be said—all here have seen or can see it, while more distant readers are doubtlessly amply informed in regard to the appearance, character, extent, accommodations, &c., of pioneer "hotels."

The next most prominent evidence of *improvement* was erected the same year by an old sea captain, named John Litch.

It was that *vade mecum* of civilization—that cotemporary, and often pioneer of church and school-house—a drinking saloon. It was a log-shanty, and stood on Front street, below Western Avenue. It was long a favorite resort of the politician and the thirsty; and not a few grand social schemes and political intrigues were concocted beneath the genial influence of the suspiciously genuine liquids, vended by the retired and affable "Captain."

There, listening to the numerous reminiscences of Captain Litch, and growing balmy under his genial "punches" until life and its projects were roseate as the cheek of Dawn, might be seen daily many who now stand deservedly among our first citizens. The "Maine Law" then lay unevolved in the convolutions of Neal Dow's brain. "Not to drink" would then be almost, or quite, sufficient to ostracise any man from a desirable social standing; and he who did not produce the bottle and glass upon the advent of a visitor, was deemed lacking in hospitality. "Take a drink," entered then as much into a portion of social economy as "take a chair" does in the refinements of modern intercourse. The merchant preceded his customer's application by the proffer of a "smile"—all trades were prologued and finished by a resort to an imbibition—and in short, no enterprise, civil, social, religious, political, or otherwise, could well be inducted or concluded without the presence of a third party, in the shape of a dusky-visaged Bottle.

James Mackintosh opened the first store, in the latter part of October, of this year; his stock consisted of a general assortment of Dry Goods, Groceries, Hardware, Provisions, &c., to a value of about five thousand dollars; commenced business in a log house, built by A. LeClaire, near the U. S. House, corner of Ripley and third streets.

In December D. C. Eldridge also opened a large stock of Goods. Many may wonder where consumers were to be found for a "large stock of goods" in a place of less than a dozen families. It will much astonish such, as well as many others, to learn, that in the Spring of the next year (1837) the sum total of daily sales averaged ONE HUNDRED AND FIFTY DOLLARS, of which thirty-three per cent. was cash.

This apparent discrepancy of sales and buyers is explained, when it is known that from the town opposite, and a long distance up and down the river, people came here to trade.

Lumber was, at that time, brought from Cincinnati, and almost everything else from a distance. Flour at sixteen dollars per barrel, Pork at sixteen cents per pound, were brought from Cincinnati. Corn was imported from the Wabash River, and brought two dollars per bushel. The farm now occupied by Mr. McManus was bought by Dr. Hall, and paid for in this latter commodity,—the cost of the farm was five hundred bushels of corn. The Ferry also dates its existence from this year—it being a flat-bottomed craft, technically termed a "mud-boat." This in 1841 was superseded by an immense improvement in the shape of a horse-boat—which in time gave way to steam —the whole being crowned by the two magnificent and commodious steamboats constantly employed in transferring a wide deep stream of freight and passengers from shore to shore.

Our lady-readers may, perhaps, be interested in knowing that the pioneer in conjugal love, cutting teeth, chicken pox, and baby talk, in Davenport, was a son of Mr. L. S. Colton, who first looked upon the light in the Fall of this year. The feeble wail of the first baby in Davenport has been echoed not a few times since, and daily grows wider and deeper in its volume, like the tiny spring-streamlet, widening eventually into a broad river.

It will naturally be supposed that the character of social life was in some sort like the country—rather destitute of refinement. A gentleman relates a circumstance connected with a prominent politician of this State, and who has had the honor frequently of saying " Mr. Speaker" in the halls of National Legislation, that perhaps was the counterpart of a thousand others of the time. In the fall of '35 this gentleman, while passing up the Mississippi on a prospecting tour, made the acquaintance of the political gentleman at Burlington—where the latter came aboard the boat. He was at that time candidate for territorial delegate from Wisconsin. He had scarcely gotten aboard before he ostentatiously displayed a pair of pistols, and which he occupied himself in handling, loading and fixing in various shapes, at intervals, during the passage to Galena. Arriving there, he solicited our informant to land, and proceed with him to the hotel. With his wife leaning upon his arm, the latter, followed closely in the wake of the candidate for Congressional honors. As they reached the door of the stopping place, the opposition candidate happened to step out to the threshold. Our political hero confronted him in an instant, and as he drew both his pistols, he remarked, without preface—

"You are a G——d——bully, sir! Take your choice!"

The other, however, declined a choice of the extended

pistol-butts, and "made himself scarce." Both, however, relievd their irate tendencies, soon after, by a street fight, at Mineral Point, in which neither suffered according to the extent of the wishes of his antagonist. The effect upon our informant, and especially upon his wife, may easily be imagined. It may, however, be well to state, that the political gentleman alluded to is everywhere known for his courtesy and gentlemanly urbanity in every phase of his social life.

The first law office in town was opened by A. McGregor, Esquire, in April.

The first Religious discourse was delivered by Rev. Mr. Gavitt, a methodist, in the Spring, in the house of D. C. Eldridge. Preaching from an Episcopalian the same Spring.

Religious services were held semi-occasionally at the house of Mr. LeClaire, in which a priest from Galena officiated. For other amusements, our settlers had at this period, besides preachers, steamboat arrivals, which every body went down to see, horse racing at the upper end of the present site of the city, which all, from the carpenter on the roof, to the merchant behind the counter, left to witness; sleigh-rides to the neighboring places, followed by a dance, to which all went; balls at home, and wolf hunts. There was then quite as much, or more, positive enjoyment than now, for the reason that social *caste* was not there recognized, and all went in simply for enjoyment.

The pioneer ball was held in Mr. LeClaire's house, Jan. 8, 1836. Some forty couples were present, consisting of frontiersmen, officers from the Island, and others. The music was furnished by fiddles, from which no contemptible strains were occasionally drawn by Mr. LeClaire himself. Prominent among the merry dancers were G. C. R. Mitchell, A. McGregor, G. L. Davenport, Joe Conway, and last but not least, and by far the lightest dancer in the room, the now portly figure of A. LeClaire. Most of the frontiersmen wore the coarsest species of "stogy boots," "making" as our informant says, "a most infernal clatter." The dresses of the ladies were generally rather more calculated to promote comfort than ostentation. The party danced till sunrise, and then broke up—the gentlemen being, as a general thing, as genial as all the "punches" they could possibly contain, would make them. Joe Conway, eccentric in his cups as well as his actions, upon reaching the ice to cross the river, found himself unable to either stand still or walk—he very ingeniously, therefore, compromised the matter by striking a sinuous and uncertain "dog-trot" and heading for all points of the Island miscellaneously. It is mistily believed by his companions that he succeeded in reaching it—although somewhat out of his original bearings.

In the Fall of this year, Rockingham—a now deserted locality some few miles down the river—was laid out by a company, among whom were Gen. Sargent, Ebenezer Cook, Dr. Barrows, and others, of our now prominent citizens. It was thought a good locality, for the reason that it was opposite the embouchure of Rock River, which was supposed to be navigable. Gen. Sargent states that he once ascended it in a steamboat to the distance of two hundred and ten miles; and hence it was very reasonably supposed that an important junction might be formed with interior towns, and a heavy trade thereby supported.

At the time of the purchase of the Black Hawk district, it was placed under the jurisdiction of Michigan.

In 1836, Wisconsin was organized, and by an act of the Legislature (which met for the first time at Belmont,) the "Black Hawk Purchase" was divided into two counties. A line beginning at Rock Island, and extending west to the Missouri River, divided them—the north one was called Julien Township, and Dubuque county, the south one Flint Hill Township, and Des Moines county. The county seat of the former was located at Dubuque. Davenport was in the latter jurisdiction. Soon after the District was divided into counties, at which time commenced a notable spirited contest between Davenport and Rockinham for possession of the county seat. Of this we shall speak in its proper place.

In the Summer of this year, Mr. A. LeClaire was appointed P. M. Mails came once each week from the East, via Chicago; and once in two weeks from Dubuque via Davenport to Fort De Moine, (now Montrose). Postage at that time was twenty-five cents. The P. M. used to carry the mail across the river in his pocket; and his percentage for the first three months was *seventy-five cents!* The present P. M., with his two thousand boxes, and half dozen assistants, will easily recognize the difference. The mortality this year amounted to seven—the first of whom was Mrs. Tanneyhill.

In September, a treaty was held at East Davenport between Gov. Dodge, U. S. Commissioner, and the Sacs and Foxes. The object of the treaty was to secure possession of the land bordering on Iowa River, and known as "Keokuk's Reserve." About a thousand chiefs and warriors were present, and were encamped during the time just above Renwick's mill.

The land in question amounted to 256,000 acres, and was purchased for seventy-five cents per acre, or $192,000 —a very liberal price compared to what Government had heretofore paid, but "dog cheap" when we consider that in less than a year every foot of it was disposed of at ten shillings per acre.

Catlin, in his "North American Indians" thus notices this affair:

"The treaty itself, in all its forms, was a scene of interest, and *Keokuk* was the principal speaker on the occasion, being recognized as the head chief of the tribe. He is a very subtle and dignified man, and well fitted to wield the destinies of his nation. The poor dethroned monarch, old Black Hawk, was present, and looked an object of pity. With an old frock coat and brown hat on, and a cane in his hand, he stood the whole time outside of the group, and in dumb and dismal silence, with his sons by his side, and also his *quondam*, aid-de-camp Nahpope, and the Prophet. They were not allowed to speak, nor even sign the Treaty. *Nahpope* rose, however, and commenced a very earnest speech on the subject of *temperance!* but Gov. Dodge ordered him to sit down, (as being out of order,) which probably saved him from a much more *peremptory command* from Keokuk, who was rising at that moment with looks on his face that the Devil might shrink from."

The two tribes staid here nearly a fortnight, amusing themselves and others with characteristic games and dances. One amusement was "smoking horses." A party of *Ioways* came at the time, and wanted some horses of the Sacs and Foxes. Such of the latter as had horses to give away, mounted them, and commenced riding at full speed around the Ioways—then suddenly wheeling would endeavor to ride straight through them, which was prevented by using small switches against the faces of the horses. After riding a half hour or so, a Sac rider would call to an Ioway to stand out, and then passing him at full speed, he would bring upon the naked back of the other, with the full force of his arm, a heavy whip of plaited rawhide, raising a "welt" as thick as one's finger. Then immediately dismounting, he would place the bridle in the hands of the yelling victim, who was thereafter the owner of the horse. This ludicrous operation excited much sport among the spectators. It was a common custom among the Sacs and Foxes, and some other nations—the compliment being from time to time interchanged.

This Treaty was the last ever held in this vicinity.

There were seven houses in the old town limits at the

BLACK-HAWK.

LITH. OF SARONY, MAJOR & KNAPP. 449 BROADWAY, N.Y.

MA-KA-TAI-ME-SHE-KIA-KIAH.
A SAUKIE BRAVE.

close of the year. Log house of Capt. Litch, ditto of L. S. Cotton, ferryman; frame dwelling partly finished, and owned by a Mr. Shoals. It has been since known as the "Dillon House," (*of which a gentleman since Governor of the State was once hostler*). Log House of James O'Kelly—(a tailor from Detroit, Mich.)—used by James McIntosh as storehouse; log house of Wm. Allen, used for P. O.; frame building, known as Davenport Hotel, and after as United States Hotel; log house used by D. C. Eldredge as store. All these stand yet, except Dillon's and Litch's.

The events narrated above are the prominent ones of 1836. The year closed with a population of less than one hundred. Stephenson, (now Rock Island,) which had been laid out in 1834, possessed at this time a population of nearly five hundred.

## CHAPTER V.

Indian Duel—Col. Taylor's Defeat in 1820—Fight between Sacs and Foxes and Pottowatomies—Burial of the Slain—Opening of River—First Marriage—Getty's Flouring Mill—Ferry Company—Jumping Claims—Intruder Expelled—Thrashing an Indian—Sacs and Foxes—Sioux Horse Thieves—Visit to Washington—Murder of an Indian at Moscow—Escape of Murderer—Population—Scott County Organized—Elections.

In the Spring of '37, the first duel "on record," in Iowa, was fought between a couple of Winnebago Indians. A party of the tribe was here fishing, and encamped on Rock Island. A couple of young men were carousing at Stephenson, and, in a little while, commenced quarreling. The blow was passed. Too refined, by their intercourse with the whites, to avenge the blow with knife or tomahawk, they resorted to the code of honor. Unfortunately for one of them, the choice of weapons was not fully up to the prevailing principles of the code duello. One had a shot gun, the other wisely took the rifle. On the willow island, below the city, they drew up the required distance, and blazed away. The heavy lead of the cracking rifle was "too much" for the lighter pellets of its more noisy brother—the Shot Gun. The shot gun and its holder went down, and the latter was buried not far from the grave yard below the city, and upon the banks of the noble Mississippi, whose everlasting voices hymned his advent to the Spirit Land.

The Rifle hero fled to his home in Rock River country. But vengeance overtook him even there. The friends and relations of the slain clamored for the blood of the slayer —and the *sister* of the latter went for the survivor. She found him—entreated him to come back to Rock Island, and be killed, to appease the wrathful manes of the departed. Such logic was irresistable—he came—and in a canoe paddled by his own sister, he reached the Island, singing his death song. A shallow grave was dug, and kneeling upon its brink, his body tumbled into it, and his death song was hushed as the greedy knives of his executioners drank the blood of his brave heart. Can the white man show a nobler act than this, among all his bravest deeds in the arena of the duellist. The chiaro oscuro of Spartan deeds presents no more beautiful blending of heroism and duty than this—nay, verily.

This same Willow Island, whereupon the shot gun hero bit the dust, is also memorable as being a spot upon which the immortal "Rough and Ready" once received, what Santa Anna ever failed to give him, namely, a military thrashing. In 1812, Col. Taylor, with two companies of Regulars, and accompanied by a Captain Rector, with two or three companies of Rangers, was proceeding down the river. The Indians, knowing his approach, had, under the superintendence of a Mr. Graham, (a man well known by many of our citizens,) fixed a small cannon among the sand hills, on the Illinois side, which they brought to bear most effectually upon the boats. The latter, galled by the fire, steered for the Island, but here they were assailed by a volley from an ambuscade. They resolved to land and clear the Island. Rector, and his rangers, sprang ashore, and each man took "cover" to fight the Indians in their own style. Taylor landed, and formed his men immediately *in line to charge bayonets!* The thick growth of willows would hardly admit a musket, much less a company, formed in line to charge. The serried lines formed a splendid target for the concealed copper-skins, and they were not tardy in availing themselves of the opportunity. To "cover" was not in the manuel—to "about face," and "quick time, march!" to the boats, was, and in the next minute, Taylor and his regulars, were shooting down the Mississippi as fast as stout oars and lusty "elbow-grease" could carry them. The rage of Capt. Rector, when he saw Col. Taylor "countermarching" on his own advance, was boundless—his first resolution was to order his men to fire upon the regulars, who were executing such a "masterly retreat" down the river, but the necessity of saving his lead for the Indians restrained him. If Col. Taylor afterwards earned the bays at Buena Vista and Monterey, he certainly could claim no more than the *willow* in his attempt to charge bayonets in line upon an ambuscade of Indians on Willow Island.

In the Spring of this year a party of Sacs and Foxes, and another of Pottowatomie's were engaged in fishing, and were encamped in the "hollow" below Cannon's Mills. A keg of whisky induced a row, and the long knives of the belligerants soon settled it. Some dozen or more were engaged in the fight; and its expense was an unlimited quantity of ugly cuts, and two breathless braves. Face to face the two implacables were seated in the same grave, and the ground piled about them to the height of their waists, leaving their bodies, and ghastly visages, to front each other defiantly, and to present a spectacle less seemly than characteristic of the Indian. Enemies in life, they rotted as lovingly in death, as brothers, and the ghastly grin which came upon one's fleshless jaws was imitated by the other, till the whilom foes seemed to find in each other's lineaments some horrible provocative to jollity.

Some considerable alarm was felt at the time by the citizens, as the Indians, maddened by blood and whisky, went yelling through the streets, and a messenger was despatched to Montrose for assistance. The Indians, however, quieted down without doing further damage.

The river which had closed the 20th December the winter previous, opened March 23d, of 1837, and a steamboat came up the same day.

The first case of matrimony, on record, occurred in the Spring. The happy couple who first "led off" the vast hymenial dance, and pioneered the long array of wedding favors, bliss, and incipient heaven, was a Mr. WM. B. WATTS, and a niece of Antoine LeClaire. It may not be the best of logic, but still without a "first couple" there could be no second, or third, or any others—hence all who have married since, or who may hereafter, owe no small debt of gratitude to Mr. Watts and lady. Why should not the day of their marriage be marked in the calendar as a Golden one—and be set apart as a day to be crowned with orange blossoms, and sacred to the worship of Eros? The suggestion is not a studied one—still it is none the less worthy of the profound consideration of all that vast crowd who since have gone to that matrimonial bourne "whence no man returns"—a bachelor.

Mr. Watts, alluded to above, as is learned from a little reminiscence, experienced the truth of the idea, that lovers endure much tribulation. While "doing" the agreeable operation of courting, he met with a mishap, as unexpected as it was distressing and ludicrous. At the time, a Yankee teamster was employed by Mr. LeClaire, who experienced a variety of those soft, half-angelic and half-devilish feelings, yclept love, towards the lady whom Mr. Watts after married—and with his love there came jealousy toward his rival. With the latter's success, he grew revengeful; and diabolical, doubtless, were the schemes he devised, and the torments he inflicted, in imagination, upon his fortunate antagonist. One night Mr. Watts was spending the evening with the lady. The Yankee could contain his bursting indignation no longer—and he shaved the tail of Watt's horse as smooth and naked as a roll of sausage! The indecorous appearance of his steed's caudal prolongation—his entire unwillingness to bestride such an institution, may well be imagined. The transition from the low-whispered love-tales of the parlor to the clean-shaved tail of his steed, which, as Byron says, "glittered in bony whiteness, there,"—from the "airy nothings" of one to the nothing *hairy* of the other—was entirely too sudden, and too vivid in its contrasts, to afford much else than expletives more profane than elegant.

While hoping that his happiness may descend upon all, who, like him, are disposed to matrimony, yet let us wish that his mishaps will not also be en-*tailed* upon his successors.

The graceful misses of ripe twenty, and younger, whose origin is proudly claimed by Davenport, will be pleased to learn that the predecessor of their sex in the dim-remembered mysteries of being born, was a daughter of D. C. Eldredge, who pioneered her sex in May of this year. It is a pleasure to add, that she "still lives" to enjoy the honor of having preceded the hosts of fair flowers which, in connection with not a few exotics, give grace and beauty to the magnificent parterre of our goodly city.

The same gentleman who introduced the "first daughter" also introduced the first flouring mill, one of "Getty's Patent Metallic Mills." It was somewhat larger than a coffee mill, and, as our informant states, "the motive-power was horse-flesh, and it was engineered by an Irishman, a discharged soldier from the Fort, who was known, and will be remembered by all old settlers as "Joe Topin." Poor Joe has gone! a victim to misplaced confidence in a whisky jug!"

The present well-known and powerful Ferry Company dates its origin to this Spring—although not in its *present* corporate character. John Wilson bought out Mr. LeClaire for one thousand dollars, and, until 1839, teams, &c., were transported in a flat boat.

Dr. A. E. Donaldson, from Pennsylvania, came in July of this year, and was, it is said, the first resident physician. His successors, in the short space of twenty years, have increased, if not by legions, at least fully in proportion to the demand.

There was no lack of sociability among the Indians at this time. Parties would come in from the territory, encamp near the town, and spend a few days in lounging and drinking whisky, then would leave, and their place be supplied by others. That the Indian sometimes descends from his sublime stoicism to a vulgar curiosity, is illustrated in a case related by Mr. Eldredge. Having sickness in his family, it was necessary to keep a light burning all night. Indians straggling about late, to yell, dance, and walk off the effects of "fire-water," would be struck with the phenomenon of a light at such a time of night, and proportionally anxious to ascertain its cause; mingled, no doubt, with a little very natural curiosity in regard to the night-arrangement of a white man's bed room. Hearing a noise at the window, one evening, Mr. Eldredge stole noiselessly out at the back door, and passed around to the front, with a stout splinter of board in his hand. There stood a "son of the forest," upon tip-toe, peering over the window curtain, and undoubtedly cogitating upon the superior appearance of a "white squaw" *en chemisette*. A stinging pain upon a part just below his wampum belt was the first intimation he received of the indecorousness of his proceeding; while a succession of rapid blows, to which he performed an impromptu dance, not laid down in the saltatory code of the Indian, and to which he yelled an appropriate accompaniment, convinced him also that every sweet has its bitter. He made threats after, of depriving his castigator of his "har"—but the latter staid at home for a few nights, and the Indian left, doubtless, well assured of the fact, that at *bottom* there is no real enjoyment in the satisfaction of that squaw-ish trait, curiosity.

In September, a party of Sacs and Foxes came in to receive the last annuity, which was paid them at Rock Island —Gen. Street, the Government agent, soon after removing to Racoon Forks, now Fort Des Moines. While they were here, some of their scouts brought in word that a body of Sioux were in the "Timber," a place now occupied by Oakdale Cemetery. Their design was, undoubtedly, to wait until the Sacs and Foxes had received their usual annuity, and were oblivious in the "big drunk" which generally succeeded these payments, and then to steal their horses. They failed, however, for scarcely had the scouts reported their presence, before three hundred Sac and Fox braves had streaked themselves with war-paint, and followed by half the white population, were in their saddles, and after the Sioux. The Dacotahs (as the Sacs and Foxes termed the Sioux,) received notice of the approach of their intended prey, and seasonably decamped—thereby preserving intact not a few of that valuable and highly ornamental article—their scalps.

Old settlers recalling this occasion speak enthusiastically of Keokuk's eloquence—he having delivered a speech of some three hours in length, in which there was not a single repetition. When one considers that the Chief spoke almost with the velocity of lightning, it is inferable that his mental reservoir was neither shallow nor indifferently well filled.

Keokuk's eloquence on this occasion arose from the fact that Government had sent out one half their annuities in goods—instead of money—as was stipulated in the Treaty. The Indians very indignantly refused to receive them, and in consequence of this, and also in order to settle some difficulty with the Sioux, a large party of Sacs and Foxes, Whites and Sioux, went on to Washington. While in Washington a "grand talk" was held, in which the Sioux and Sacs and Foxes detailed their grievances. A Sioux chief remarked in his speech that "it was no use talking to the Sacs and Foxes—they were deaf—their ears should be bored out with a stick!" Keokuk listened to the Sioux Brave, while every vein and muscle swelled under his taunts almost to bursting. When the latter concluded he rose, and with his spear (his insignia of office,) in his hand, he said:

"It is useless to bore out the ears of the Sioux with a *stick*—their skulls are too thick. They can only be bored out with *this!*" and the indignant Brave shook his iron-headed spear fiercely in the face of the scowling Sioux.

After the return from Washington, Mr. LeClaire, G. L. Davenport, and others, started to "haul" out the goods which the Indians had refused, and which Government had decided to present to the Indians. They started for Moscow, (then a trading Station,) in Cedar county, and on the route met an Indian, who was on his way to Rock Island, to complain that one of his tribe had been murdered at Moscow by a White. Mr. LeClaire sent a man with him, and the remainder pushed on to Moscow. When they arrived, they learned the circumstances of the murder. A party of Indians had been dancing and drinking at a whisky shop in Moscow, during which, a couple of white men in amusing their refined propensities, had been betting which could *knock* a drunken Indian the farthest. One would induce an Indian to approach, by holding out some whisky, and when he approached the bait the other would strike him, and mark the distance at which he fell. Then the other empiric would try the force of his flexors and extensors, by changing places, and knocking the next Indian who came up for the whisky. The Indians, naturally enough, grew enraged at such treatment, and a row ensued. During the excitement, the stove-pipe was knocked down, which so enraged one of the whites, that he struck one of the Indians, and fractured his skull, and continued his action by kicking the Indian out doors, and then concluded his humane operations by punching the insensible body with a *rail!*

G. C. R. Mitchell was sent for, the body of the murdered brave was exhumed, an examination had, and an effort made to convict the pale-faced murderer. Moscow was, at that time, a rallying point for thieves, counterfeiters, and rogues generally—the accused sent around for his friends, and, on the day of examination, some sixty of his friends—a ruffianly, God-forsaken crowd, were present. The justice did not dare to convict him—he was released on straw-bail, and was afterwards acquitted at Dubuque, as hanging a white man for the simple offence of murdering an Indian did not enter the ethics of the age.

After his trial he returned to Moscow, and sent for the relatives of the murdered Indian—promising to pay them the usual satisfaction. They came, and agreed to accept a certain number of horses as satisfaction, which were to be paid on a certain day. The day came, as did the Indians, but the treacherous creditor, with his family, had fled to Illinois! Filled with disappointment, the Indians, on their return from Cedar River, met, on their trail, an inoffensive Methodist, itenerant, preacher, named ——— whom they unmercifully sacrificed, to appease the manes of their slaughtered brother. The thinking reader will duly consider the morality of the actors in this anecdote. Moralization is perfectly useless.

In October a notable case of *trover* occurred. It was the first trouble of note among the squatters, and it involved the last act of moment of the judicial proceedings of Dubuque county. Maj. Wilson had a claim, (which he was holding for Messrs. Davenport and LeClaire,) upon the ground now occupied by Mount Ida Female College, which was "jumped" by a man from Stephenson, named Stephens. Sheriff Cummings was sent for from Dubuque to oust the intruder, and with a posse of some fifty men, (about all in Davenport,) he proceeded to the spot, and ordered the gentleman to vacate.

But Mr. Stephens, either enjoying the superlative beauty of the prospect—or foreseeing the stately edifice which would, in time, arise upon the spot, or else actuated by simple mulishness, very firmly, not to say impolitely and profanely, refused to comply—threatening dire vengeance upon the first who should touch him, with divers fire-arms and bowie-knives, with which he had fortified his position. Sheriff Cummings, however, proved himself equal to the trying emergency, for, sending for a yoke of oxen, and a strong chain, he proceeded to put in practice a new theory of expulsion. The chain was fastened to a corner log, the cattle started, and, in a remarkably brief space of time, Mr. Stephens bolted out to prevent the consequence which might happen from falling timbers. He was shown immediately the most direct route to Stephenson, of which information he availed himself forthwith, and gave up, thereafter, the precarious employment of jumping claims in Davenport.

The posse which assisted Sheriff Cumming, at this time, was a portion of a Confederation, which was composed of the inhabitants, generally, of Davenport, Rockingham, and adjacent settlements. It was organized March, '37, had regular laws, officers, &c., and was intended for the regulation of Claims, and the settlement of disputes connected therewith. One of its laws provided that no man could hold more than half a section of land. A book was kept, in which every member registered his *claim*, his name, the locality of his claim, and with the addition of one dollar, as initiation fee, he was entitled to all the benefits and protection of the society.

The first Brick Yard was constructed this year under the auspices and ownership of our present worthy Sheriff—Harvey H. Leonard.

The religious services this year, and for some year or two after, were among Protestants, held in one place—a house belonging to D. C. Eldredge. Occasional services were held there by Clergymen from the Methodists, Presbyterian, Disciples, Congregational, and, at longer intervals, from the Episcopalian. Everybody attended these services, for the various denominations had, as yet, assumed no individuality. It cannot be stated, with certainty, whether a proportional fructification followed these labors, yet good influences were probably disseminated, which time, sooner or later, practically developed.

The population at the close of this year was about one hundred and fifty—six new houses had been erected, on the new site, making in all fifteen. The River did not close until February 13th, of 1838—a day or two before the memorable election for county seat.

The Wisconsin Legislature met in December of this year at Burlington. An act was passed at this session creating Scott county, the boundaries of which were as follows:

"Beginning at a point in the middle of the main channel of the Mississippi river, where the line dividing one and two, east of the fifth principal meridian intersects the same; thence north, with said range-line, to the line dividing township seventy-eight and seventy-nine north; thence west with said line, to the fifth principal meridian; thence north with said meridian to the line dividing townships eighty and eighty-one north; thence east with said line to a point where the said line intersects or crosses the Wapasipinica river; thence down the middle of the main channel of said river to its mouth; thence due east to the middle of the main channel to the place of beginning; shall be, and the same is hereby constituted, a separate county, to be called SCOTT."

The same act also provides for the election for county seat, between Rockingham and Davenport, which election "shall be held at H. W. Higgin's Hotel in Rockingham, John H. McGregor's Hotel in Davenport, and the house of J. A. Richards, at the house of E. Parkhurst, in Parkhurst, (above LeClaire,) on the third Monday in February of 1838." An act also provided for the election of three County Commissioners—which board of Commissioners represented the County in all suits and County business of whatever nature.

An act was also passed at this session, giving a Charter to certain persons, the authority to act as trustees of the "Davenport Manual Labor College." This scheme of a Manual Labor College was a fine one, but it never amounted to anything for two reasons—a lack of students, and a want of money. It evinced, however, a most commendable desire upon the part of those engaged in it to promote educational interests—a desire which since has been practically developed into as fine a Common School system, and other Institutes as may be found west of the most forward sea-board communities.

The number of acres in the County is two hundred and eighty thousand, five hundred and sixteen. Swamp Lands, ten thousand five hundred and sixteen acres; and the number liable to taxation, two hundred and seventy-four thousand. Davenport is thus defined: All the sections (fractional) contained in township seventy-eight, Range, three East, fifth Meridian, in all, twenty-one thousand, seven hundred and forty acres. The survey of the latter was completed in March of 1837.

Lots (which on the old site are laid out 84x150) sold during this year for from fifty to two hundred dollars—a decrease in value from the year previous.

## CHAPTER VI.

Contest for County Seat—Importation from Dubuque—Result—County Commissioners—Renewal of County Seat Contest—Newspaper Magniloquence—Death of Black Hawk—Old Burying Ground—Summary.

The act providing for an election for County Seat, to take place in February of 1838, absorbed almost everything else at the commencement of this year. The advantages occurring to the locality which should hold the seat of justice, were sufficiently important to be worthy of no small sacrifice. Appreciating this fact, the inhabitants of both places entered into the contest with a determination to win at every hazard—and the encounter, headed in each case by men of means, and keen practical sagacity, was no child's play, as will be presently seen.

The leading men on the Rockingham side were Dr. Barrows, Willard Barrows, Gen. G. B. Sargent, Ebenezer Cook, John P. Cook, a Mr. Clark, of Buffalo; Mr. Robertson, John Sullivan, and a Mr. Theller.

Under the Davenport standard were rallied G. L. Davenport, James McIntosh, Antoine LeClaire, G. C. R. Mitchell, Levi S. Colton, D. C. Eldredge, Sheriff Wilson, and Captain Fitch—although the latter is suspected by Posterity of praying "Good Lord! Good Devil!"

Readers will recognize in the above not only men of shrewd perception and indefatigable perseverance, but also in the first-named, a few who have left their first love, and who now consider Davenport as "fondly their own" as ever they did Rockingham. Headed by such men, the battle was long, sanguinary and *terrific*, if one may be allowed the latitude of moderate hyperbole.

The matter probably began by each party counting noses, and a discovery upon one side or the other that there was a deficiency. Which side first became aware of the fact, and resolved to supply it from abroad, it may be expedient not to question too closely—suffice it, that a short time before the day of election both parties were engaged in recruiting *legal voters*—Rockingham in Cedar county, and Davenport in Dubuque. An individual, named Bellows, holding a carte blanche from some seven Davenporters—who suddenly discovered that Davenport was in want of *laborers*—started to Dubuque in the capacity of recruiting Sergeant. He proved himself a most excellent one, for a day or two prior to the election he returned with *eleven sleigh-loads* of miners, who, in consideration of one dollar per diem, food and whisky, and all other expenses, had agreed to *labor* a few days in Davenport, where they had understood there was a scarcity of hands at that particular juncture. To assert that they knew anything of a pending election, were, perhaps, unwise, and, mayhap, at the same time, unjust to the worthy gentlemen who had hired them. Their arrival was the beginning of a grand carnival. Houses were illuminated, bonfires streaked the face of scowling night with roseate joy, processions were formed, gunpowder exploded, whisky gurgled everlastingly, and men with tumblers in hand, and elbows bent, were everywhere looking skyward.

The memorable nineteenth of February made its appearance—the day appointed by Legislative powers as the day of election. The town was filled with miners—roaring, patriotically drunk. They were Americans—to vote is the glorious, blood-bought, inalienable right of Americans, and so they voted. They were the fiercest, raggedest, most God-forsaken crowd under the heavens—to challenge them was useless, for to them perjury was nothing; to attempt forcible resistance were madness, and so, what could our citizens do but let them vote unchallenged and unresisted, as they wisely did?

The miners voted, and left soon after. They drank during their brief sojourn three hundred gallons of whisky, and other liquors, and cost those who brought them, for transportation, and other expenses, over $3,000! It may be well to state that $1200 of this amount was absorbed by Mr. Bellows—he having received the amount towards paying their expenses, but which he put into his own pocket, together with $300 which he received for his own services.

Upon counting votes, it appeared that Davenport was ahead—the Dubuque miners were too many for the Cedar county wood-choppers. The returns were sent to Dubuque, to the Sheriff and Commissioners, but their decision was valueless, for Dr. Barrows had visited Gov. Dodge, and made such representations of the stupendous frauds committed on the part of Davenport, that the election was annulled. So ended the first battle—with emaciated pocket-books, both parties rested on their arms. Rockingham, however, had the advantage, for the County Commissioners were elected the next month from Rockingham, and also met there.

Maj. Wilson—now of Rock Island—received the first appointment of Sheriff in Scott county.

In the Spring of this year, A. LeClaire laid out an addition to the site of two blocks in width, extending from Harrison street to Brady, and up to Seventh. It is known as LeClaire's First Addition. This addition lay upon the Reserve, and as the title was perfect, it was a desirable locality. Lots were sold on long time—in prices ranging from one hundred to five hundred dollars, with the proviso that each buyer should improve his lot, within one year, to the amount of five hundred dollars. Some thirty houses were built upon it during the year, which was the first marked improvement in the growth of the place.

It may, perhaps, be not uninteresting to give the first day's proceeding of the Board of Commissioners. It met at the store of H. W. Higgins, in Rockingham:

"Present—Benj. F. Pike, and Andrew W. Campbell.

The Board proceeded to the appointment of a Clerk.

Ordered—That Ebenezer Cook be appointed Clerk to the Board.

Ebenezer Cook having appeared in pursuance of his appointment, and taken the oath of office, entered upon his duties as Clerk.

Ordered—That the Clerk take the necessary steps to procure from the Secretary of the Territory, a seal for the use of this Board.

Ordered—That this Board do meet, at its April Session, in the town of Rockingham.

Ordered—That Benj. F. Pike be allowed three dollars for one day's service as County Commissioner.

Ordered—That Andrew W. Carter be allowed three dollars for one day's service as County Commissioner.

Ordered—That Ebenezer Cook be allowed three dollars for one day's service as Clerk.

And the Board adjourned to Session in course."

It will be seen that the largest "service" by which they claimed three dollars, was the labor of voting themselves the amount. Alfred Carter was the third Commissioner elected, but he did not participate in the laborious "services" of the first sitting.

July fourth was marked not only as the era of our National Independence, but as the day also upon which the District of Iowa was separated from Wisconsin, and became the Territory of Iowa; Robt. Lucas, of Ohio, was appointed Governor, and Wm. B. Conway, of Pennsylvania, Secretary. The Counties of Scott, Muscatine, Louisa, Slaughter and Johnson, were constituted the Second Judicial District, and were assigned to Joseph Williams. The District Court met for the first time, the "first Thursday after the first Monday in October" at Davenport. At this time, Wisconsin had thirteen counties, and 18,148 inhabitants; Iowa sixteen counties, and a population of 22,859. Scott and Clinton counties formed one election District, and elected one member to the Council, and two to the House of the Territorial Legislature.

In the Summer of this year, the first brick house was erected by D. C. Eldredge. It is still standing on the south-east corner of Main and Third streets. Nearly at the same time, the brick building, now used by the Sisters in Catholic Block, was completed as a Church. The first Presbyterian organization was completed this year.

At a special session of the Wisconsin Legislature, held in June of this year, at Burlington, an act was passed for the holding of a new election in Scott county, for the seat of justice, to be held on the third Monday of August. It provided a sixty day's residence as qualification for a voter.

Then the war began again. The most liberal inducements were held out for settlers—lots were sold at half or quarter prices, or given away to secure residents. Rockingham, which was subject to partial inundation in times of high water, was subject to many a witticism and carricature. Among the latter, was a Mr. Hedges, represented as wading the slough that surrounds the town, with his wife upon his back, and the water breast-high—this was founded upon fact. Another pictured Gen. Sargent, leading a company of men to the polls. The men hesitate upon the brink of the slough, but the General bravely plunges in, and wades to the middle. "Come on, men, its only so deep!" cries he as he turns to his company, with the water reaching close to his neck. James McIntosh, and others, commenced the work of a thorough canvass, and the "din of preparation" resounded loud and deep from both camps, prognosticating another furious struggle.

About this time, Mr. A. Logan made his appearance with materials for a printing office. There was no little strife between Rockingham and Davenport, as to which should obtain him. Extremely liberal offers were made him on both sides—such as now would gladden the heart of the printer with a joy unknown to modern supporters of these type-sticking pilgrims. Both places recognized the infinite benefit which a paper would render them in building up the towns—of the emigration it would influence, and the reputation which it would give the place abroad. Another election was impending for County Seat, and the aid of a paper would be to either side invaluable. Whether Mr. Logan was influenced mainly by the liberal offers made him, or by the superior locality of Davenport—certain it is, however, that one fourth day of August, 1838, there appeared the first number of the "Iowa *Sun* and Davenport and Rock Island *News;* which—as we learn from its salutatory—is designed "to cast its rays over the moral and political landscape, regardless of those petty interests and local considerations which might contract its beams." And in order to more readily accomplish this, we are further told that, "we have selected the *center* (Davenport,) of the system around which all our territorial interests harmoniously revolve."

The election was held, and Rockingham had a majority of fifteen votes. Mr. James McIntosh, and John Forrest, Esq., after some hard riding, and much swearing, (in a legal way of course,) secured affidavits—in many cases from the voters themselves—proving that twenty fraudulent votes were cast on the Rockingham side. These being transmitted to the Sheriff and Commissioners at Dubuque, were acted upon by them, and resulted in their declaring, on the eighth of September, that the seat of justice should be permanently located at Davenport. Rockingham, however, carried the matter before the judicial tribunals, where it remained a year or so, and where we shall meet it again in its proper place.

In dismissing the subject, until it is met again in 1840, it will not be amiss to insert a note in regard to both places, and the contest, for which we are indebted to the veteran pen of Willard Barrows, Esq.,—formerly a resident of Rockingham, but now one of Davenport's most esteemed citizens:

"Rockingham was laid out by Col. John Sullivan, of Lyonsville, Ohio, and A. H. Davenport, Esq., now of LeClaire, in this County, and although the ground upon which it was located, much of it, was low, and subject to overflow, yet its situation, directly opposite the mouth of Rock River, which, at that time, was supposed to be navigable, gave it so much importance as to attract attention—so much so, that in 1838 and '9, it contained some twenty-five or thirty houses. The early settlers of Rockingham were an enterprising and intelligent people, and noted for their hospitality and social intercourse with one-another, many of whom are now among the most respectable citizens of Davenport.

One of the most prominent causes of its downfall and decay, was the long and unsettled question of the County Seat. For several years the struggle was carried on between Rockingham and Davenport, with varied success to either party. All the ingenuity and wit of the parties were resorted to—the Law of the Territory, at that time, in regard to such questions, was anything but pointed; and great latitude was given to construe it to suit the wants of either party. At the elections held for the decision of the case between the two towns, the inhabitants of of Illinois were invited over to vote. Men were imported from Dubuque and Galena at great expense—the ballot-box was stuffed, and the poll-books showed a population that, for years after, it was hard to find. The final settlement of the question, however, was arrived at, by the citizens of Davenport agreeing to build the Court House and Jail free of expense to the County, which they did. The treaty of peace was made at Rockingham in the winter of 1840, and ratified by a ball given at the Rockingham Hotel, where not less than fifty couple were in attendance, among whom were some of our *largest* and wealthiest citizens.

During the whole of this contest, there was the utmost good feeling and gentlemanly conduct apparent in the whole transaction, and, to this time, it is often the source of much merriment among the actors of that day; and is looked upon only as the "*freaks* and *follies*" of a frontier life."

In September a stock company was formed to erect a School House—shares ten dollars. A meeting of stockholders was called the 16th to elect a building committee, &c. Some members held more than one share, and were thereby entitled to more than one vote, but some ultra-Democrat moved that all should fare alike in this particular. It was voted down, and, thereupon, the indignant Jupiter Tonans thus discoursed. For a specimen of tall traveling by such a varicose-legged apparatus as his Pegasus must have been, it is unequalled.

"That insatiable thirst for power, which is so dominant in man as well as beast, requires an Argus to watch and detect its Jinius (!) windings, and a Herculean force to destroy its hydra machinations! If that noble and magnanimous

* Mr. LeClaire.

bird, which we have adopted for our emblem, should hear such sentiments avowed, and would not eagerly part with every quill to record damnation to the principle, I would pluck her from her towering *Eriy*, and make her the companion of owls and ravens! Is there a star in the splendid galaxy which bespangles our banner, that would not blush in token of disapprobation to such sentiments, I would blot it forever from the pure etherial ether in which it shines!"

The assertion, *ex nihilo, nihil fit* seems contravened in this case—for all this burst of eloquence about that conirostral bird—the Eagle—and the bannered-star and Jinius (!) and Argus, grew from the resolution of a company of stockholders to allow a member having four shares to have four votes! Sorry is my pen that it cannot confer immortality upon the writer of the above, as cotemporaneous records make no mention of his name—nor do they even mention whether the Eagle handed over her quills, or the "star blushed," or whether either or both received the dire punishment which "Anthony"* threatened. We but know that the Eagle still roosts in the solitary grandeur of her "*Eriy*," and that the Star still waves proudly in "etherial ether" over the "land of the free and home of the brave."

The county commenced improving rapidly—roads were laid to its limits from all parts, and emigration began slowly to dot the back country with log-houses and wheat-stacks. The village for two years had passed from its ruder character, and was beginning to assume prominence abroad as a healthy, and one of the most beautiful localities on the Mississippi. A writer, in August of that year, thus says of Davenport:

"Two years ago it had but one family, now upwards of thirty, and has three large store buildings, a large hotel,

* This was the name appended to the communication.

two groceries, two forwarding and commission houses, and an elegant brick chapel has been commenced: and more than one hundred dwellings will be under contract the ensuing year. Now, as I stand here overlooking the rapid increase and improvement, (in spite of all the uncertainty of preemption titles,) I think it requires but little faith to call Davenport an embryo Cincinnati."

Keen-visioned seer! Posterity will, undoubtedly, at some future time, recognize his prophetic character.

A writer in the "Army and Navy *Register*," of that date, says: "At our feet, and on the gentle declivity between the bluff and the river, is situated the village of Davenport. The location is not exceeded by any on the Mississippi, or in the world, either for health, beauty, or the fertility of its soil." Any quantity of extracts similar in import, might be given from cotemporary papers, showing the high position which our place at once took in the public estimation, as being unequalled in the superb beauty of its location.

In regard to the fertility of the soil, the *Sun*, of Septembor, says: "We yesterday saw a Water Melon, raised about one and a half miles west of the village, which measured four feet one way, and three and a half the other—and weighed forty and a half pounds. Another gentleman has a pumpkin vine, on which, he says, he counted *sixty-eight good sized pumpkins!*" These facts speak volumes for the farming country adjacent to Davenport.

The editor of the *Sun* has not a few articles in his sheet eulogistical of the mammoth vegetables which, from time to time, were laid upon his table, by subscribers anxious for a "puff"—of the soil. He was once, however, badly sold. Mr. D. A. Burrows resolved to astonish him, and for this purpose stuck a half dozen, or more, large potatoes so nicely together with pegs, that they seemed one growth. The editor was hugely delighted with the present. It was to other potatoes what elephants are to mice—and he trumpeted the fact accordingly, defying any other soil under the sun to produce its equal. It hung in the sanctum a long time, and was a source of patriotic pride both to the worthy editor and all spectators. But one day a piece of the monster fell off—and revealed a hard woody substance protruding, which excited curiosity. A nearer examination revealed a peg, and a little more revealed the entire internal economy of the potatoe. The worthy votary of the Quill was highly incensed at the denoument, and did not puff a mammoth vegetable for three whole weeks.

At the first election, held under the new territorial law, in September, P. H. Engle, for Delegate to Congress, received three hundred and nine votes. The whole number of votes cast for Delegate was four hundred and twenty-six. J. W. Parker, for member of Council, two hundred and forty-four—for Representatives, J. A. Burchard, and G. W. Harlan received, the former, two hundred and thirty-four, the latter, two hundred and three. The District included Scott and Clinton counties.

In the next month the first District Court met. On motion of G. C. R. Mitchell, Esq., W. B. Conway, James Grant, Rufus Harvey, Simon Meredith, Edward Southwick, and J. Wilson Dewy, Esqs., were admitted. On motion of Mr. Woods, J. W. Parker was also admitted. This, from the Iowa *Sun*, is all the notice we have of the doings of this, our first District Court Organization.

We are also informed in the same paper, that the editor, "after considerable enquiry," has ascertained that "sheep do well here." This is not particularly important, save that it recalls an anecdote of that well-known gentleman, Mons. A. LeClaire—as he was termed in those days.

It seems that some one engaged in the sheep business, had secured Mr. LeClaire's service to transport a large flock of sheep across the river—as he wished to reach some point on this side ,and the only available ferriage was to be obtained here. After getting them over, the sheep driver sheared them, and was indebted to Mr. LeClaire also for pasture during the operation. Upon leaving, he presented Mr. LeClaire the fleeces as payment for his trouble, and went on. Wool was then worth some forty cents a pound, and the large pile was almost a moderate fortune to any one. But Mr. LeClaire did not then know as much of wool as he did of interpreting—it seemed simply a huge pile of refuse, utterly valueless. Accordingly he summoned his men, ordered them to pile brush on the wool, and set fire to it! It was done, and, as he traveled off, with fingers upon his nose to shut out the intolerable fume of the burning wool, he concluded that "such a cursed stench was poor pay for all his trouble!" Most readers, who have ever "smelt wollen," will join heartily in his conclusion.

D. C. Eldredge was appointed P. M. this Fall. Mails came from the East and left *via* Stephenson, Sundays; to and from the North via Dubuque, weekly; do. West via Sanbornton, weekly; and do. from South via Burlington, twice each week.

On the third of October, Black Hawk breathed his last, at his village on Des Moines River. He was buried near the banks of the river, in a sitting posture, as is customary with his tribe. His hands grasped his cane, and his body was surrounded by stakes, which united at the top. A large number of whites were present, and did honor to the occasion of his interment by their sympathy and numbers. No monument rears itself to mark the resting-place of his dust—nor does he need it. His deeds have conferred a name upon him, which will outlast a dozen granite piles—a name which will last as long as Patriotism shall be remembered as a Virtue.

The Burial place of Davenport was, at this time, on the Bluffs, near the corner of Sixth and Farnam streets, on the ground now occupied by the house and lot of Willard Barrows. DR. EMERSON, a gentleman well-known as the original owner of *Dred Scott*, was buried here. The remains have since been removed. The same spot was also the target-ground for the cannon of the Fort, before it was dismantled. Many an iron relic will yet be exhumed when the bluff is graded—if such ever will happen.

The population of the County at the close of 1838, was one thousand. The number of boats passing averaged about five per diem. The river closed December seventeenth. Wheat was worth twenty-five cents per bushel; Oats thirty-five cents; Potatoes one dollar. Pine lumber was brought from Cincinnati, and was worth from forty dollars to sixty dollars per thousand. Oak lumber was sawed in the neighborhood, and was worth thirty-five dollars per thousand. About two thousand bushels of wheat were raised in the County. The number of buildings in the village was about fifty.

The receipts of the County were four hundred ninety-seven dollars fifty three cents, and its expenses seven hundred eighty-one dollars fifty cents.

The building this year was mostly upon the Addition of A. LeClaire—the title to this was unexceptional, while purchasers were fearful of that by which the site below Harrison street was held. The number of buildings erected made it a busy year—while the tide of emigration, which was setting into, and flowing through, made money plenty, and every department of industry active. Still this activity was simply relative—in general there was not much to do, save to watch claims, and bide the effects of time. A Lyceum was started at Stephenson this winter, in which some of our citizens joined. Social enjoyment consisted mainly in discussing apple-toddies, the patriot war, and speculating upon the probabilities of Davenport's reaching a hundred thousand inhabitants.

## CHAPTER VII.

Financial Condition of County—Militia—Territorial Council—Meetings—Town of Davenport Organized—Growth of Village—Navigation of Rock River—First Church—Subscribers—Fire Department—Original Temperance Society—Schools—Death of W. B. Conway—Resolutions.

It may be a matter of curiosity to many to know the expenses and receipts, in detail, of the County, during the first year of its existence. The following is the statement for the year ending January, 1839:

RECEIPTS.

| | |
|---|---|
| For licenses to merchants and pedlars, | $120 75 |
| " " " tavern keepers, | 74 75 |
| " " " ferry " | 23 00 |
| Fine against Boile & McConnel for selling goods without a license, | 10 00 |
| Tax on John Wilson's ferry charter, | 20 00 |
| From collector of taxes, on account of tax list of 1838, | 249 03 |
| | $497 53 |

EXPENDITURES.

| | |
|---|---|
| Expenses of meeting of Commissioners, including pay of Commissioners, Clerk, Sheriff, and rent of rooms, | $138 00 |
| Expenses of laying out new roads, | 166 75 |

| | |
|---|---|
| Assessing, | 56 25 |
| Book and stationary for use of County, | 26 52 |
| Expenses of five elections, | 231 35 |
| Expenses District Court, October Term, | 115 63 |
| Extra services of Clerk, | 37 50 |
| Expenses of copies of road law, ferry law, &c., | 9 50 |
| | $781 50 |
| | 497 53 |
| Excess, | $781 50 |

The tax list for 1838, was eight hundred ninety-one dollars forty cents, of which only some two hundred forty-nine dollars three cents had been collected. If all had been, there would have remained to the County a balance of three hundred fifty-eight dollars forty cents.

This statement will give the reader a very fair idea of the financial condition of the County at that time.

An act having been passed by the Territorial Legislature to organize and discipline the Militia of the Territory, Gov. Lucas, in June, issued a general order dividing the Territory into Military districts. The counties of Scott, Cedar, and Linn, formed the first regiment, and a part of the second brigade, and were included in the third General Division. John H. Sullivan, of Scott county, was appointed one of the Aids-de-Camp to the Commander-in-Chief. Only one drill was ever had here, which will be noticed in its proper place.

The first session of the Territorial Legislature was by no means harmonious. The Governor endeavored to check the expenditures of the Legislature, which was resented by the latter; and a resolution was passed, in which they assert that the Governor "is not invested with advisatory or restraining powers over the Legislature, further than the disapproval of bills, memorials, and resolutions, presented for his signature." A committee, also, consisting of James W.

Grimes, C. Swan, Laurel Summers, and Hawkins Taylor, reported that the Governor had no right to veto certain bills of expenditure passed by the Legislature.

This Report created considerable excitement, and meetings were held everywhere to take action upon it. One was held at the house of Col. T. C. Eads, in Parkhurst, at which Gov. Lucas was cordially upheld, his patriotism eulogised, and his statesmanship, virtues, and private life, unequivocally lauded and endorsed.

The following appointments were made by the Legislature and Governor for Scott county: Willard Barrows, Notary Public; Ebenezer Cook, Judge of Probate; Adrian H. Davenport, Sheriff; Isaac A. Hedges, and John Porter, Justices of Peace for Scott county.

The town of Davenport was incorporated by this Legislature. The first election for township officers was held April first. Rodolphus Bennett was elected Mayor, Frazer Wilson Recorder, and Dr. A. C. Donaldson, D. C. Eldredge, John Forrest, Thomas Dillon, and Capt. John Litch, Trustees.

The river opened February twenty-eighth. There was, during this winter, scarcely any snow, and the whole season was more like Spring than aught else. Business opened briskly this Spring, as the following from the April number of the *Sun* shows: "Since the opening of navigation our lovely little village has been thronged with travelers and emigrants. The tide of emigration is so great to this place, that it is almost impossible to procure houses to accommodate them; although our carpenters are busily engaged in putting up houses, yet still, they are filled as fast as erected, and the demand appears to increase. The demand is so great that it requires six or eight houses to be completed weekly to supply the wants of emigrants. Forty or fifty lots have been sold the past week. Our wharves, or rather our shores, are crowded with families and merchandize.

Our farmers have sowed their spring-wheat, oats, and flax, and our prairies are in many places covered with a mantle of green, bespangled with the most beautiful flowers!"

These facts, for people in Pennsylvania, New York, and the New England States, are full of interest. Such a time, as early in April, Eastern farmers are scarcely, if ever, free from snow-banks and chilling winds, a contrast which shows the immense superiority of Iowa in geniality.

The steamboat arrivals were from one to seven each day.

The Town Council held its first Session April twentieth. James M. Boling was appointed Treasurer, Wm. Nichols Street Commissioner, and W. H. Patten Marshal.

An advertisement, in April, states that the light draught keel-boat, G. M. Searl, will start from Stephenson, and go up Rock River to Rockford. It need scarcely be added that boats do not now ascend this stream.

A company was organized about this time, which was called the "Rock River and Mississippi Steam Navigation Company." Their object is indicated in the name. Daniel G. Gornsey, G. C. R. Mitchell, and Sylvester Talcott, were Directors, Antoine LeClaire Treasurer, and Geo. Myers, Secretary. Although most of these gentlemen have now a sufficiency of the world's goods, it is not probable that they made a very large share by the navigation of Rock River.

The extensive pinerics of Wisconsin began to send their products to Davenport this year by way of rafts—and brought from thirty dollars to thirty-five dollars per thousand feet.

At the third meeting of the Town Council, in May, Dr. Donaldson resigned his seat, and Andrew F. Russel was appointed to fill the vacancy. On motion, it was Resolved, That the temporary seal of this Council be an American twenty-five cent piece.

On the twenty-third of May, St. Anthony's Church was

dedicated by Rt. Rev. Bishop Loras, of Dubuque, assisted by Very Rev. S. Muzzuchelli. The Catholic *Advocate* thus speaks of the matter, after highly complimenting the beauty of the place:

"Mr. Antoine LeClaire, a wealthy Frenchman, and a zealous and exemplary Christian, in partnership with Mr. Davenport, has generously granted to the Catholic Congregation, in the very centre of the town, a whole square, including ten lots, in the middle of which he has built, partly at his own expense, a fine brick Church, with a school-room attached. * * * In order to lay in Davenport a lasting foundation for the Catholic religion, our Bishop has purchased half a square for a hospital, and several other lots for purposes of the same kind. * * * The Church has St. Peter for its primary, and St. Anthony for its secondary patron."

The Rev. Mr. Pelamourgues, who first assumed charge of the Church, still retains it.

As this was the first Church erected in Davenport, it may not be uninteresting to publish the list of subscribers, and other matters connected with its foundation:

"At a meeting of the Catholics of Davenport and vicinity, held on the first day of December, 1839, for the purpose of regulating the Church accounts of said town, the following resolutions were unanimously adopted:

1. *Resolved*, That a Board of three Trustees be regularly elected by the Congregation, to open a subscription, collect its amounts, and pay all standing debts incurred for the purchase of the ground and for the building of St. Anthony's Church of Davenport.

2. *Resolved*, That the Trustees be elected for the term of three years, and that after said period, a new election of Trustees shall be made.

3. *Resolved*, That the Rev. John A. Pelamourgues,

Antoine LeClaire, and Geo. L. Davenport, be the Trustees of the Catholic Congregation of Davenport and vicinity, for the purpose and time above mentioned.

SAMUEL MUZZUCHELLI, *Secretary.*

---

SUBSCRIPTIONS TO PAY FOR ERECTING THE CATHOLIC CHURCH OF DAVENPORT.

| *Gentlemen.* | *Subscribed.* | *Paid.* |
|---|---|---|
| Antoine LeClaire, | $2500 00 | $3500 00 |
| Bishop M. Loras, | 150 00 | 150 00 |
| Rev. S. Muzzuchelli, | 50 00 | 20 00 |
| Rev. J. A. M. Pelamourgues, | 50 00 | 22 00 |
| Nathaniel Mitchell, | 20 00 | 20 00 |
| G. C. R. Mitchell, | 20 00 | 20 00 |
| Adam Noel, | 25 00 | |
| John Noel, | 25 00 | |
| George L. Davenport, | 25 00 | |
| George Meyers, | 25 00 | |
| David Barry, | 25 00 | |
| Richard Shial, | 25 00 | |
| C. Harold, | 25 00 | |
| W. B. Watts, | 20 00 | 10 00 |
| Otho G. M'Lain, | 15 00 | |
| Michael Riley, | 15 00 | |
| Narcisse Yerten, | 25 00 | |
| James O'Kelly, | 10 00 | |
| Patrick Fox, | 10 00 | |
| Thomas O'Kelly, | 10 00 | |
| Patrick Carrol, | 10 00 | |
| Alexis LeClaire, | 10 00 | 10 00 |
| David LeClaire, | 10 00 | 10 00 |
| James Lindsey, | 10 00 | |
| James Wicks, | 8 00 | 3 00 |

| | | |
|---|---|---|
| Harvey Sturdevant, | 5 00 | |
| Patrick Hogan, | 5 00 | |
| Louis G. Trudeau, | 5 00 | |
| John Brossard, | 5 00 | |
| John Trucks, | 15 00 | |
| *Ladies.* | *Subscribed.* | *Paid.* |
| Mrs. Margaret LeClaire, | 25 00 | 10 00 |
| Mrs. Conway, | 15 00 | 15 00 |
| Mrs. Ruth Trucks, | 10 00 | 10 00 |
| Mrs. Annie Finch, | 5 00 | |
| Miss Felicite LeClaire, | 5 00 | |
| ——Mary Trucks, | 5 00 | |
| ——Mary Long, | 5 00 | |
| ——Matilda Long, | 5 00 | |
| —— Mary Finch, | 1 00 | |
| Sarah Ann Lindsey, | 5 00 | |

EXPENSES.

| | |
|---|---|
| A Lot 320 feet square in the town of Davenport, | $2500 00 |
| Brick for building the Church, | 827 00 |
| Lumber and Shingles, | 843 25 |
| Hardware, | 167 60 |
| Glass, putty, paints, oil painting, and glazing, | 206 00 |
| Mason work, | 488 00 |
| Carpenter work, | 589 00 |
| Plastering, | 263 50 |
| A bell, | 102 00 |
| Sundry articles for the Altar, | 107 00 |
| Three Stoves, | 45 75 |
| Fuel, and two days labor, | 14 00 |

LeClaire's Second Addition was laid out in May. It extended East from Brady street, and included sixteen blocks of ten lots each. Some sixty lots were sold the first week, on all of which the purchasers bound themselves to erect dwellings in time, varying from six to twelve months.

The District Court held its second session in May. But little business was done, and there was not, we are told, a "single indictment against a resident of Scott county." Good for the morals of our worthy predecessors.

In the August election of this year, there were three tickets put in nomination. One from Davenport, another at Rockingham, and a third called the Union ticket. The Rockingham faction elected their Representatives—Laurel Summers and J. M. Robertson—two out of the three County Commissioners; Treasurer, Ira Cook; Assessor, and most of the lesser officers. Davenport elected A. F. Russel, Surveyor, and J. Work, County Commissioner.

The Davenport Ticket for Representatives were G. C. R. Mitchell and Abner Beard. The election turned mainly upon the County Seat difficulty; and it is seen that Rockingham this time was ahead. This was owing to a union with the town of LeClaire;—the latter place being induced to work against Davenport, in order to, at some future time, secure a division of the county, with LeClaire as County Seat. To assist in bringing this about was the price paid by Rockingham to LeClaire for its assistance—and most egregiously were our up-river friends of LeClaire humbugged by this promise.

The level established by the town Council, from which all grades were to be taken, was the "south door sill" of Antoine LeClaire's store on Front street. When anything was reported as being so much above or below level, it was understood to mean simply so much above or below the said door sill. The same meeting organized the first Fire Department. This consisted in obliging every man inhabiting a house to have in his possession two fire-buckets, and to use them in case of a fire.

The original Temperance Society made its appearance about this time. The Rev. Mr. Turner claims its paternity. He lectured twice so powerfully, that his total abstinance pledge received fifty-six signatures at once. The Mayor, Mr. Bennett, was its first President, upon its organization, August sixth. It commenced with some eighty members.

A "Female Seminary" was opened in September by the Misses O'Hara. The "*Davenport Forum*" also made its debut about this time. The "Rock Island Seminary" was also in existence at this time, under the care of Rev. M. Hummer. A common school was also opened about the same time by a Mr. Blood.

About the first of October, or thereabouts, a steam ferry boat was started between this place and Stephenson by John Wilson. It was a small institution, comparatively, but was infinitely superior to the flat boats which had hitherto labored between the two places.

November sixth was a dark day in the calendar of events —for it is marked as one upon which the gifted WM. B. CONWAY, Secretary of the Territory, departed from his sphere of usefulness, and from the presence of friends and admirers, "to return no more." He died at Burlington, and his body was received here on the ninth, by a Commit tee appointed for the purpose, and was conveyed to St. Anthony's Church, where the solemn services for the dead were performed by the Rev. Father Pelamorgues. A meeting was held on the morning of the ninth, whose proceedings are given in full:

PUBLIC MEETING.—At a meeting of the citizens of Davenport, convened at Davenport Hotel on Saturday, Nov. 9, 1839, to testify their respect for the memory of William B. Conway deceased, late Secretary of the Territory of Iowa, T. S. Hoge was called to the chair, and G. C. R. Mitchell appointed Secretary.

On motion, it was ordered that John H. Thorington,

Thomas S. Hoge, Duncan C. Eldredge, Ira Cook, G. C. R. Mitchell, Richard Pearce, Antoine Le Claire and John Owens, be appointed a Committee to make the necessary arrangements for the funeral of the deceased, and also to draft and report resolutions expressive of the sense of this meeting.

The committee having retired for a short time reported the following resolutions which were unanimously adopted.

*Resolved,* That this meeting has heard with the most profound regret of the death of William B. Conway, Esq. late Secretary of the Territory of Iowa. Possessing a mind richly cultivated and improved, a disposition amiable and kind, he was generous and hospitable; of manners the most bland and courteous, respected, honored and beloved by all who knew him. We feel that in his death this neighborhood has lost its brightest ornament and the Territory one of its ablest and most worthy officers and highly valued citizens.

2. *Resolved,* That this meeting sincerely condole with the family of the deceased, in their severe and deep affliction, and pray that He who tempers the blast to the shorn lamb, may support and protect them.

3. *Resolved,* That as a mark of respect for the memory of the deceased, we will wear the usual badge of mourning for thirty days.

4. *Resolved,* That the proceedings of this meeting be signed by the chairman and Secretary, and the Iowa Sun and other papers throughout the Territory be requested to publish the same.

5. *Resolved,* That Antoine LeClaire and G. C. R. Mitchell be and they are hereby appointed a committee to deliver a copy of the proceedings of this meeting to the respected Widow of the deceased.

TH. S. HOGE, *Chairman.*

G. C. R. MITCHELL, *Secretary.*

On the eleventh, a meeting of the Bar of the Territory of Iowa was held at Burlington to testify respect to the memory of the deceased, and the following was their expression.

"A distressing dispensation of Providence having deprived us of the society of one of our body, whom, during his residence among us, we had learned warmly to esteem, we feel called upon to express our deep regret for his untimely death, and of the estimation which his amiable and excellent qualities universally commanded. Therefore—

*Resolved*, That our brother, the late William B. Conway, had, by his amiable manners, unexceptionable deportment, as a member of the Bar, greatly endeared himself to his associates, the members of the Bar, of the Territory, generally.

*Resolved*, That by his death the Bar has been deprived of an able member, the Territory of a faithful officer and valuable citizen, ourselves of a devoted friend, and his wife and child of their only protector.

*Resolved*, That we take this method of expressing our deep regret at his untimely death, and of our condolence with the relatives of the deceased, and of bearing testimony to his many virtues.

*Resolved*, That we testify our respect for the memory of our deceased brother by wearing the usual badge of mourning for thirty days.

*Resolved*, That David Rorer, Esq., present these resolutions to the Supreme Court of the Territory for the purpose of having them entered on the record of the Court.

CHARLES MASON, *Chairman*.

WM. J. A. BRADFORD, *Secretary*.

*Burlington*, *Nov*. 11, 1839.

A paint shop, by Riddle & Morton, a wagon shop, by S. P. Whitney, and a drug store, by C. Lesslie, were opened this year, and were the "first" of each kind. Four churches were also organized—Congregational, Disciple, Baptist, and Catholic.

## CHAPTER VIII.

Close of 1839—Missouri War—Financial Statement of year 1839—New Election for County Seat--Result.

The celebrated "Missouri War" is ascribed to about this date. It arose from a dispute in regard to boundary—two lines having been run. The northern one cut off a strip of Iowa some six or eight miles in width, and from this portion Missouri endeavored to collect taxes. The inhabitants refused to pay them, and the Missouri authorities endeavored, by sending a Sheriff, to enforce payment. A fight ensued, and an Iowan was killed, and several taken prisoners. The news spread along the River counties and created intense excitement. War was supposed to be impending, or to have actually begun.

Col. Dodge, an individual somewhat noted as the one who, in connection with Theller, had been imprisoned by the Canadian authorities for a participation in the "Patriot War," had lately arrived here, after breaking jail in Canada. His arrival was opportune—a call for volunteers to march against Missouri was circulated, and was responded to by some three hundred men, who made Davenport their rendezvous on the proposed day of marching. A motley crowd was it! Arms were of every kind imaginable, from pitchforks to blunderbusses, and Queen Anne Muskets. One of the Colonels wore a common rusty grass scythe for a sword, while Capt. Higginson, of Company A, had been fortunate enough to find an old sword that an Indian had pawned for whisky, which he elegantly belted around him with a heavy log chain.

The Parade ground was in front of the ground now occupied by the Scott House. Refreshments were plenty, and "steam" was being rapidly developed for a start, when word came that peace was restored—Missouri having resigned her claim to the disputed ground. The army was immediately disbanded, in a style that would do honor to the palmiest revels of Bacchus. Speeches were made, toasts drunk, and a host of manœuvers, not in the military code, were performed, to the great amusement of all. Some, in the excess of patriotism and whisky, started on alone to Missouri, but lay down in the road before traveling far, and slept away their valor. A private, named Gunn, was found hacking a log, with his gun and sword bent nearly double, under the impression that the inanimate body was a Missourian.

Frequent allusions have been made, thus far, to the many "good times" had by the old settlers. It will not be inferred from it that they were dissipated or drunkards. Far from it. Some of the brightest lights now in the Church, at the Bar, and in private life, are those very men. They but complied with the character of the times, while absent from social refinements, and the elegance of older towns; almost all strangers to each other, and craving for that excitement, which now is indulged in the intercourse of hosts of friends, and friendly relations of long standing, they could not well do otherwise than they did. Mostly men from large cities, they were ennuied by the comparative quiet of a frontier life, and to vary their listless lives, resorted to stimulants, or whatever else would afford excitement.

The following was the financial condition of Scott county at the beginning of the year 1840. It will show as well, or better than anything else, the condition and growth of the county for the year past. As such facts are important, an apology is not deemed necessary for the introduction of the entire statement as made by the Commissioners.

RECEIPTS.

| | |
|---|---|
| Received for licenses to merchants, grocers, tavern keepers, ferries and pedlars, | $ 369 49 |
| Received on account of tax list of 1838, | 649 53 |
| " on account of tax list of 1839, | 1410 92 |
| " for fines and docket fees, | 149 00 |
| | $2578 94 |

EXPENDITURES.

| | |
|---|---|
| For expenses of laying out new roads, | $360 25 |
| " of meetings of Commissioners, | 196 00 |
| " rent of room for District Court for Commissioners and Clerks, | 136 50 |
| " of elections for 1838, | 12 00 |
| " extra services of Sheriff, 1838, | 30 00 |
| " " " " 1839, | 53 26 |
| " of District Court for 1838, | 21 10 |
| " " " " 1839, | 257 50 |
| " of printing, | 13 00 |
| " books, stationary, and furniture for offices, | 89 73 |
| " service of Clerk of board of Commissioners, | 163 00 |
| " of elections for 1839, | 91 10 |
| " taking and keeping prisoners, | 115 12 |
| " of assessing property, 1839, | 64 00 |
| " map of Scott county, | 10 00 |

| | |
|---|---|
| For expenses paid for support of poor, | 36 00 |
| " Attorney's Fee, | 25 00 |
| " laying out a territorial road from Davenport to County Seat of Linn county, | 113 50 |
| " amount refunded on account of excessive tax, 1838, | 30 00 |
| " amount refunded on account of excessive tax, 1839, | 8 15 |
| " amount paid treasurer for his commission for the years 1838 and 1839, | 79 42 |
| | $1804 63 |

STATEMENT OF THE FINANCES OF SCOTT COUNTY, JAN. 1, 1840.

| | |
|---|---|
| The Board of Commissioners have made allowances on sundry accounts in the years 1838 and 1839, amounting in all to | $2506 71 |
| Of which amount the Treasurer has paid | 2140 91 |
| And his vouchers have been examined and cancelled. | |
| Leaving the sum of | 365 80 |
| Yet due from the County to individuals, as appears from the books of said Commissioners. | |
| There is to be added to the above amount of $2506 71 the sum of $79 42, for amount of commission paid Treasurer, | 79 42 |
| The county has received from sundry sources in the years 1838 and 1839, as will appear from reference to the statements published, the sum of | $3076 47 |

By the above statement it will be seen that there is in the County Treasury, at this time, the sum of $856 14, and that there is yet due from the County to individuals, the sum of $365 80, leaving a balance in the County Treasury, subject to future disposition by the Commissioners, of $490 34.

JOHN WORK,
A. W. CAMPBELL,
ALFRED CARTER,
*Rockingham, Jan.* 9, 1840. *County Commissioners.*

In January a call for a meeting to organize an Agricultural Society, was put forth by A. LeClaire, G. C. R. Mitchell, and James Hall. The call was responded to, and a Society organized by appointing A. McGregor President, G. C. R. Mitchell Vice President, John Forrest Secretary, A. LeClaire Treasurer, and C. Rowe, James Hall, E. L. Davis, J. L. B. Franks, Isaac Hawley, Ira Cook, and Thomas Dillon, Directors.

The river did not close opposite Davenport until January 14th. It, however, closed above the upper rapids in December, and at Burlington January first.

The several township elections were held in April. John H. Thorington was elected Mayor, Frazer Wilson Recorder, and Geo. L. Davenport, S. F. Whiting, J. W. Parker, John Forrest, and William Nichols, Trustees.

The river opened March first, and emigrants began to arrive immediately. There were, at the time, about one hundred houses in the village.

In May of this year the land sales for the original Dubuque county were held at Dubuque. Almost the entire Claim Confederation attended, "armed to the teeth," in order to prevent operations from speculators. G. C. R. Mitchell, Esq., was appointed bidder for the Confederation, and as fast as the lots were put up they were struck off at one dollar twenty-five cents per acre. An Adjudicating Committee was appointed from the Confederation, before whom all disputes, in regard to claims, were settled, and thus the matter was speedily and harmoniously settled.

Two Patents, covering the old town limits, were given, one in 1840, and the other in 1841.

In July the Supreme Court gave its decision upon the application of certain persons in Rockingham for a writ of mandamus against the Dubuque Commissioners, commanding them to make an entry upon their minutes to the effect that Rockingham was the County Seat. The following is the order of the Court:

SUPREME COURT, IOWA TERRITORY, JULY TERM, 1840.

The United States at the relation of James H. Davenport, et al,

*versus*

The County Commissioners of Dubuque County:

And now this day came the parties, by their Attornies, and the arguments of Council being concluded, and all the premises being fully examined into, and being understood by the Court: It is ordered by the Court here, that the motion of the relators be refused, and that the defendants go hence without day, and recover of said relators the costs of the Court in this behalf expended, for which execution may issue.

I do hereby certify, that the above is a true copy of an order made in the above entitled cause, as appears on the records of the said Supreme Court.

[Seal.] In witness whereof I have hereunto set my hand and affixed the temporary seal of said Supreme Court, this tenth day of July, 1840.

THORNTON BAYLESS, Clerk,
Supreme Court, Iowa Territory.

The Court stated, in its opinion, that "we are clearly of opinion that we have no jurisdiction over the matter, and the motion for a peremptory mandamus will, of course, be denied."

A petition signed by three hundred and twenty-six inhabitants of Scott county, was immediately sent to the Legislature. It prayed for a new election. An Act was passed, in which was provided, that an election for County Seat of Scott county should be held on the fourth Monday in August, and that the electors should vote for Davenport or Rockingham, or the north-west fractional quarter of section number thirty-four, township number seventy-eight, north of range four, east of the fifth principal meridian. This latter point was at the mouth of Duck Creek, and was an unimproved portion of land of some ninety acres, which was to be donated, if it were decided that this should be the County Seat.

A bond was entered into, by many of our citizens, agreeing to give certain lots, or monies, if Davenport should be selected. Mr. LeClaire agrees in it to give certain specified lots, or three thousand dollars in money—G. Davenport certain lots, or twelve hundred dollars. A very liberal subscription of sums ranging from five to five hundred dollars, was made over to the County Treasurer in the form of a bond. To make the matter doubly sure, a bond was entered into with the County by Messrs. A. LeClaire, Geo. Davenport, A. W. McGregor, J. H. Thorington, John Owens, Harvey Leonard, James Hall, R. McIntosh, Jr., and Wm. Nichols, in which they agreed to erect the Court House and Jail free of expense to the County, upon condition that the other bond should be made over to them.

On the twenty-fourth of August the election was held. Davenport received three hundred and eighteen votes, and the point at the mouth of Duck Creek two hundred and twenty-one, giving the former a majority of ninety-seven. Rockingham voted against Davenport, with the exception of sixteen votes. This vote put a quietus on the matter, and terminated the long and spirited contest which had raged for over two years. It was not without its usefulness, for it developed the public-spiritedness of both places, and gave to all engaged in it a very memorable lesson on the philosophy of *Expenditures*. It would be a heavy sum that would give the total of monies expended, liquor drank, and *finesse* wasted in the conflict.

Party lines began to be drawn somewhat at the local election of October. A. C. Dodge, Democratic Delegate to Congress, received at the same election two hundred and sixty-two votes; Rich, the Whig candidate, received one hundred and seventy-two in the County. J. W. Parker was elected to the Council over James Grant, by a majority of four. Laurel Summers and J. M. Robertson, Representatives; A. H. Davenport, Sheriff; J. D. Evans, Recorder; Ira Cook, Treasurer; Ebenezer Cook, Judge of Probate, and E. Parkhurst, Public Administrator. It was not, however, until 1842 that separate Whig and Loco Foco tickets were put in nomination, and party lines distinctly drawn.

The subject of a Western Armory was much talked of at this time. Among other points Rock Island was prominent, as one affording facilities for the establishment of such an institution. Fuel in abundance—immense water-power, facilities for shipment of materials, the healthfulness of the location, its connection, by the Mississippi, with important places, and the seaboard, were reasons justly urged for the selection of this point. Meetings were held, the usual preamble and resolutions were passed, in all places in the West. A committee from Washington made an examination of Rock Island, and other places, but nothing ever resulted from it.

The subject of a Bank in Davenport was also much agitated, but nothing ever came of it more than speeches, memorials and resolutions.

A prominent institution of these times was the Davenport Lyceum. Every week they discussed this thing or that—including questions of every nature, social, political or moral. It was doubtless the origin of much good. It is to be inferred, however, that in course of time they descended from the high plane of purpose which they originally stood upon, for, the following notice appears in the December number of the *Sun:*

"Our Lyceum is becoming the subject of ridicule to many persons in our village. No subject, they say, can be discussed, but such as will tickle the fancy of weak females. Our Lyceum, it is true, converts what should be a hall of science, into a room to panegyrize the ladies; and, indeed, we have heard the most fulsome eulogies passed upon their character, in order to acquire the approving smiles of those present. If courtship is a science, then indeed is our Lyceum a most excellent school."

The records of all time, from the case of Adam to that of Cleopatra, and down to the Davenport Lyceum, are instinct with precedent and examples of men who have sacrificed upon the altar of feminity.

From the report of the County Commissioners, at the close of 1840, we learn that the receipts of the County were one thousand six hundred thirty-five dollars and six cents, and its expenditures two thousand one hundred twenty-one dollars and thirty-seven cents. Davenport possessed at the time a population of about six hundred. LeClaire House was finished at an expense of thirty-five thousand dollars, and was by far the finest hotel on the Upper Mississippi. Beneath it was a Reading Room, which, under the enterprise of Mr. Eldredge, afforded some thirty or forty leading papers; and a Barber Shop and Post Office. It was the grand center of attraction for everybody, and did more, perhaps, to promote the growth of intellectual intercourse than any other influence. Its capacious parlors, reading rooms, its superiority in the elegancies of life to anything else in the West, made it deservedly attractive, and highly beneficial in its influences. Mr. LeClaire deserves no little honor for the liberal plan upon which he conceived and executed LeClaire House—for its completion done more to build up the place than anything else of the day.

When it is considered that since the commencement of the town, the entire Union was staggering under the effects of the financial crisis of 1837; and that communication with the East was a long and tedious operation, the growth of Davenport is wonderful, and demonstrates most fully, that it was based entirely upon a substantial and permanent base. Had Davenport been a mere paper town, its beauty and healthfulness of location a myth, its advantages fictitious, it must, at that time, have become prostrated. On the contrary, it gradually increased—everything connected with it being so substantial and real, that capitalists everywhere confidently invested in it, and as confidently improved their possessions.

# CHAPTER IX.

1841—Finances—The Village—Duel—Court House and Jail—Davenport Gazette—Prince De Joinville—First Things—1842—Temperance—Bank—Population—Judge Williams—Bible Society—Elections—1843—Churches—Elections—Major Wm. Gordon—1844—Elections—Stage Lines—1845—Murder of Col. Davenport—Indian Ceremony.

## STATEMENTS OF THE RECEIPTS AND EXPENDITURES OF THE COUNTY OF SCOTT, FOR THE YEAR ENDING JAN. 1, 1841.

### RECEIPTS.

| | |
|---|---|
| Received for licenses to merchants, pedlars, grocers, and fines, | $571 82 |
| Received on account of tax list of 1839, | 131 81 |
| " on account of tax list of 1840, | 748 05 |
| " for fines and docket fees, | 178 50 |
| " from Sheriff, for estrays sold, | 4 88 |
| | $1635 06 |

### EXPENDITURES.

| | |
|---|---|
| For laying out County roads, | $117 50 |
| " laying out Territorial roads, | 315 31 |
| " rent of rooms for District Court, for Commissioners and Clerks, | 96 00 |
| " expenses of election 1840, | 118 50 |
| " extra services of Sheriff 1840, | 88 50 |

| | | |
|---|---|---|
| For | expenses of printing, books, stationery, and furniture for offices, | 99 17 |
| " | services of the Clerk of the Board of County Commissioners, | 186 62 |
| " | expenses of assessing 1840, | 89 00 |
| " | support of poor, | 117 40 |
| " | amount refunded for excessive tax, | 81 15 |
| " | expenses of meeting of Commissioners, | 201 50 |
| " | expenses of taking and keeping prisoners, | 197 28 |
| " | Attorney's fees, | 25 00 |
| " | costs against the County, | 125 31 |
| " | expenses of District Court 1840, | 263 12 |
| | | $2121 37 |

A. W. CAMPBELL,
JOHN G. QUINN,
JOHN WORK,
*County Commissioners.*

*Davenport, Jan.* 7, 1841.

The River opened March fourteenth. At the April election, J. W. Parker was elected Mayor, John Pope Recorder, and J. M. Witherwax, Harvey Leonard, T. K. Mills, T. McLosky, and Seth F. Whitney, Trustees.

The condition of the village, yet laboring from the effects of the "crisis" of '37, may be well understood from the following extract from an April number of the *Sun:*

"The times are hard, and business of all kinds dull. Money, even counterfeit paper, and bogus, have almost totally disappeared. (No other money having been current here since the last land sales.) Emigrants continue to pour into the Promised Land by tens, hundreds, and thousands—filling up the back country with an industrious and enterprising population.

Notwithstanding all these evils, and many others of an embarrassing nature, frame buildings are going up daily, and several brick dwellings are being erected. Our merchants are not doing so good a business as we could wish, owing to the scarcity and uncertainty of money, but still we believe that those who advertise most liberally do a respectable business.

Six hundred dollars was paid for barrels and hogshead alone, by one house, in this place, to coopers at Cincinnati, Ohio. This money would have remained amongst us if coopers had been here to perform the work, A good cooper is much wanted here. Blacksmiths are said to be also in demand. A hatter could not find a more advantageous locatton in any part of the earth than this place presents at present. There are about one thousand heads in this country to cover, and no hatter in the Territory above Burlington. Furs, and other articles for manufacturing hats, can be procured here in abundance. To be sure, coon skins have commanded an extravagant price for the last six or eight months, but as soon as the log cabin delusion subsides, we opine that coon furs will depreciate as fast as irredeemable bank paper. We, therefore, advise a hatter, a cooper, and a blacksmith, to locate in our pleasant, healthy, and thriving village."

A duel, the second on record in Iowa, and the first among white men, occurred in this year, between Messrs. Egnor and Fitch. Love, as is the case generally, was the cause of the *emeute*, and pistols alone could quell it. They met early one morning on the banks of a stream below Davenport—which stream, in consequence, has been immortalized as "Bloody Run." They fired, and returned to the city unharmed, save that Egnor's arm was bandaged, and carried in a sling. Posterity is divided in regard to the nature of the wound—a minority asserting that it was caused by a bullet, while the remainder assert that neither pistol had anything more deadly in it than powder and wadding.

Readers who have perused the account of the "First Duel," spoken of in a previous chapter, will doubtless see much more to admire in the first than in the second —although the actors in the former were the ignorant, uncivilized Indians.

The Court House and Jail were finished this year, and presented to the County, free of cost, as provided for in the bond, before noticed. Too much honor cannot be given to the gentlemen by whose liberality and enterprise these valuable privileges were conferred upon Davenport. The immense superiority of our place over every other in the county would have availed nothing, had not events been controlled by a liberal expenditure of what, at that time, was no easy thing to obtain, viz: cash.

In August the Davenport Weekly *Gazette* was started by Alfred Sanders; and it took prominence immediately in Journalism as a finely printed and ably edited sheet. It espoused Whig principles, and has occupied a leading position in politics to the present time. It eventually expanded into the Daily and Tri-weekly and weekly *Gazette*, and has undoubtedly amply remunerated its enterprising proprietor.

November fourth, Prince De Joinville and suit stopped a short time at LeClaire House, while on their travels Westward. His freedom from ostentation and aristocratic exclusiveness was the theme of general remark; and would serve besides as an exemplary model to many who unlike him lack the privileges of lofty birth, and are unduly elevated by the possession of wealth. He was strictly republican in his doings; and seemed always to be simply a gentleman.

Newhall, in 1841, thus writes in regard to Davenport:

" This town was laid out in 1835-6, on a reserve belonging to Antoine LeClaire, Esq. It is the seat of justice for Scott county, and is situated nearly opposite to the lower end of Rock Island, on a handsome elevation, with a beautiful range of sloping hills in its rear. It is about three hundred and fifty miles above St. Louis, by water, eighty miles above Burlington, and ninety-five below Dubuque. The town of Stephenson, on the opposite shore, with the glittering dome of its court house, the mouth of Rock River a few miles below, the picturesque and antiquated fortifications on Rock Island, with its beautiful villa,* the charming residence of LeClaire, the magnificent hotel overlooking the white cottages of Davenport, and the adjacent village of Rockingham—all form a combination of picturesque beauty, seldom if ever surpassed. I have approached this point from all its bearings, and whether viewed from river or bluff, it is like a beauteous picture varied in all its lights and shades. I well remember the first and lasting impression it produced upon my feelings; it was on a bright sunny morning in August, in the year 1836, the sun was fast dispelling the glittering dews, and every drooping flower was lifting its smiling crest; on the Iowa shore might be seen occasionally a gaily painted warrior of the Sacs and Foxes riding along the heights, his painted form partially exposed to view as his scarlet blanket waved to the breeze, his light feathers and gaudy trappings being in admirable contrast with the verdure-clad hills; then did I feel the utter incompetency to describe so beautiful a scene—then could I have invoked the pencil of the painter, or the pen of the poet.

The distant reader may be skeptical concerning this high-wrought description. At this I marvel not. The author is aware of the difficulty of conveying entirely correct ideas of a region to those who have never traveled beyond the threshold of home; especially in delineating *this* (in common parlance) land of the "squatters;" as if, forsooth, the

* The residence of Col. George Davenport.

land of song, of Arcadian groves, and shady bowers, must needs be in sunny Italy, or classic Greece.

I will, however, add the corroborating testimony of one or two graphic writers, to convince the reader that nature *here* has been lavish of her *beauties* as well as her bounties.

'The country around Rock Island is, in our opinion, the most charming that the eye ever beheld. Rock Island is, of itself, one of the greatest natural beauties on the Mississippi. The "old fort," not to speak of its military association, is, in truth, an object on which the eye delights to dwell. The flourishing town of Stephenson, upon the Illinois shore, adds greatly to the attractions of the scene; and Davenport, with its extended plains, its sloping lawns, and wooded bluffs, completes one of the most perfect pictures that ever delighted the eyes of man. The interior of the territory is rich, beautiful, and productive from end to end. Enterprising and industrious farmers may flock in from all quarters, and find a rich reward for moderate toil. The interior is healthy, and every section of land admits of easy cultivation.'

A correspondent of the New York *Star*, a gentleman of much taste, writing from Rock Island, says:

"There are some bright spots in this rude world which exceed our most sanguine expectations, and *this* is one of them.

"In beauty of the surrounding scenery, both on the Upper Mississippi and the Crystal Rock, I have found imaged all the charms I had pictured in my youthful imagination while reading a description of the happy valley in Rasselas, but which I never expected to see in the world of reality. The Father of Waters is a giant even here, three hundred and fifty miles above St. Louis; it is estimated to be over a mile and a quarter wide, and is one hundred miles below Dubuque, and about five hundred miles below the head of navigation, at the Falls of St. Anthony."

The location of Davenport is a healthy one. Its position, near the foot of the rapids, will cause it to become a place of commercial importance. Water-power, building stone, and bituminous coal, are convenient, and a sufficiency of timber will be found upon the bluffs and neighboring streams. It has been laid off on a liberal plan, evincing an enlightened judgment contemplating the benefits to be conferred upon future generations."

The question of a location for an Armory was again agitated this year, and a Committee from Washington gave the Island a thorough examination. Several families came on from the East with a view to a connection with its establishment, but the result, as heretofore, was simply reports, and no action.

In the Fall and Winter of this year game was abundant in the county. A respectable marksman would average two or three deer per day, while snipe and quail could be bagged by the score.

The first shoe store was opened this year by L. B. Collamer, and a butcher's stall by a Mr. Armitage. A harness shop was also opened by Jacob Lailor; and the watch-making and jewelry business was pioneered by R. L. Linbaugh. The population at the close of 1841, was about seven hundred—and about sixty thousand bushels of wheat were raised in the county, which was worth from forty-five to sixty cents per bushel.

The year 1842 seems to have improved rapidly upon its predecessors in many particulars—one of which was in the use of liquor. "Tell your readers"—says a writer in the *Gazette*—"that a passenger yesterday traveled all over your place without being able to get a glass of whisky!" The immortal Capt. Litch must have rested uneasily in his grave (if dead,) at the promulgation of such a heinous sentiment in his once powerful dominions. Powerful must have been the rush of the ball set in motion by Rev. Mr.

Turner to have so soon and effectually bowled down all the toddy-shops which stood so thickly but a short time previous.

By an act approved in February of this year, the inhabitants of Davenport were incorporated a body politic, &c., under the name of the "Mayor and Aldermen of the Town of Davenport." The town was divided into three wards, each of which elected two Aldermen. That portion west of Harrison street was the First Ward; and that lying between Brady and Harrison streets the Second, and that lying East of Brady street constituted the Third.

The Bank question was again agitated this year, and meetings were held, and reports published, but the result was the same—amounting to nothing more than simple agitation.

The population in August amounted to eight hundred and seventeen; and about one hundred thousand bushels of wheat were raised in the county. Winter wheat was raised in the county which was worth fifty cents, and Spring do. thirty cents.

Two Churches had already been built; and two more were in process of erection—Methodist and Baptist. An Episcopal society was organized—making in all six Church organizations.

Judge Williams was re-appointed as Judge of District Court. His administration was of a character calculated to excite neither particular admiration nor dislike.

The Scott County Bible Society was organized September thirteen of this year. L. L. Hoge was elected President.

The Commissioners appointed to report upon the location of a point for a Western Armory, reported in favor of *Fort Massac*—a situation on the Ohio River, in Illinois. It is needless to add that Fort Massac was *not* adopted.

In the elections for this year, R. Christie was elected to the Council, and J. M. Robertson to the House of Representatives.

The expenses of the County for '42 were two thousand one hundred thirty-one dollars forty-seven cents—the receipts were one thousand four hundred fifty-eight dollars fifty-two cents.

It will be needless to dwell minutely upon the details of each year—it is, therefore, thought best to hurry over the prominent events of several years, until one is reached remarkable as an era in the growth of Davenport. The tedious route by which emigrants reached the place, prevented a development of more than ordinary rapidity—and it was not until railroad connection with the East had been established that those marvels in the growth of the place were exhibited.

1843. Seven Churches in town, viz: One Baptist, one Catholic, one Congregationalist, one Presbyterian, one Methodist, one Episcopal, and one Disciples. G. C. R. Mitchell, for Representative, received two hundred and forty-one votes, and his opponent, James Grant, two hundred and eighteen. Jas. Thorington was elected Judge of Probate, and the whole Whig Ticket elected, with the exception of Mr. Davenport for Collector. County Receipts one thousand six hundred forty-four dollars seventy-eight cents. Expenditures, two thousand five hundred fifty dollars sixty cents.

About this year Maj. William Gordon, one of the original proprietors of Davenport, disappeared. He had proceeded from St. Louis up the Missouri River, and the last ever known of him was at a short distance beyond the frontiers. It is supposed that he was overtaken by a storm, and frozen to death. It is believed by some that he made his way to California, but this lacks confirmation. A person representing him was afterward ascertained to be another Gordon.

He was a remarkable man—a Tennesseean by birth, and a son of Capt. Gordon, who commanded a company of Spies under General Jackson in the Creek War. Major Gordon was liberally educated, and had spent several years in the Rocky Mountains, in some capacity under the American Fur Company.

He was an elegant and engaging conversationalist—spicy, original, and humorous. His fund of anecdote was endless, and of a character that always drew a crowd of interested listeners. There was a small dash of eccentricity in his character. Mr. Davenport, of LeClaire, relates, that upon one occasion he called upon Gordon. Some one asked the latter for some money to make some purchase for the company present. "Help yourself," said he, as he pointed to an inverted tub in the corner of his cabin. He lifted the tub, and revealed the Major's "pile," to the amount of some fifty or sixty dollars, lying under it! Thus he kept his money, and revealed by it his confidence in human nature, and those about him.

Some difficulty occurred between himself and another resident of Davenport named Nye. The latter suspected the Major of some attempt upon the liberality of his wife. Calling at Nye's house at one time, Nye waylaid him, and as he came out struck him down with a club, and then stabbed him. Gordon fired at Nye, but owing to dampness, and a thick coat worn by the latter, the ball did not penetrate beyond the clothing. Gordon was carried home, and lay for months unable to rise or help himself. He never used a bed, but always slept and lay, during his sickness, on some buffalo robes on the floor, with his feet to the fire.

Did space permit, many interesting incidents might be given relative to his conversational powers, his passionate nature, and originalities. At the time of his disappearance he was aged about fifty. He was unmarried till the later portion of his life, and then to one who had long lived with him in every capacity, save the title of wife. She was, however, an affectionate, and otherwise worthy woman.

1844. In August, E. Cook, Geo. B. Sargent, and James Jack, were nominated by the Whigs as candidates for the Convention to form a State Constitution. Messrs. Campbell and Grant, Democrats, and E. Cook, were elected. Campbell three hundred and eight votes, Grant two hundred and ninety-six, Cook two hundred and seventy-five. At the same election the whole Democratic ticket, with the exception of Cook, was elected. County Receipts, three thousand nine hundred fifty-three dollars seventy-seven cents—Expenditures, four thousand three hundred eight dollars sixty cents. (It will not be supposed from reports thus far given, that the County was continually falling behind; but on the contrary, the balance was in most cases in favor of the county. The seeming preponderance of expenses over receipts arose from the fact that at the time of making each report, there was always a certain amount of taxes due and unpaid. This latter amount was always large enough to leave the balance in favor of the County.

Stage lines were established this year to Dubuque and Burlington, and the contract obtained by Bennet and Lyter.

1845. River closed February fifth. Population of town one thousand. Vote upon Constitution in April two hundred and ninety-one against, and one hundred and sixty-nine for, in the county. Mr. D. C. Eldredge who had held the Post Office until July resigned, and John Forrest, Esq., was appointed his successor.

July fourth was marked as being the one upon which the

venerable Col. Davenport was most cruelly murdered. Particulars of the sad affair will be given in his Biography. He was a favorite of the Sacs and Foxes; and appended is a ceremony, which was performed over his grave. It is from the ready pen of Alfred Sanders, Esq.:

"AN INDIAN CEREMONY.—On last Friday afternoon we were witness to a strange and interesting ceremony performed by the Indians over the remains of Mr. Davenport, who was murdered at his residence on Rock Island on the 4th inst. Upon proceeding to the beautiful spot selected as his last resting place, in the rear of his mansion on Rock Island, we found the War Chief and braves of the band of Fox Indians, then encamped in the vicinity of this place, reclining on the grass around his grave, at the head of which was planted a white cedar post some seven or eight feet in height.

The ceremony began by two of the braves rising and walking to the post, upon which, with paint, they began to inscribe certain characters, while a third brave, armed with an emblematic war club, after drinking to the health of the deceased from a cup placed at the base of the post, walked three times around the grave, in an opposite direction to the course of the sun, at each revolution delivering a speech with sundry gestures and emphatic motions in the direction of the north-east. When he had ceased he passed the club to another brave, who went through the same ceremony, passing but once round the grave, and so in succession with each one of the braves. This ceremony, doubtless, would appear pantomimic to one unacquainted with the habits or language of the Indians, but after a full interpretation of their proceedings they would be found in character with this traditionary people.

In walking around the grave in a contrary direction to the course of the sun, they wished to convey the idea that the ceremony was an *original* one. In their speeches they informed the Great Spirit that Mr. Davenport was their friend, and they wished the Great Spirit to open the door to him, and to take charge of him. The enemies whom they had slain they called upon to act in capacity of waiters to Mr. Davenport in the spirit-land—they believing that they have unlimited power over the spirits of those whom they have slain in battle. Their gestures towards the north-east were made in allusion to their great enemies, the Sioux, who live in that direction. They recounted their deeds of battle, with the number that they had slain and taken prisoners. Upon the post were painted, in hieroglyphics, the number of the enemy that they had slain, those taken prisoners, together with the tribe and station of the brave. For instance, the feats of Wau-co-shaw-she, the Chief, were thus portrayed. Ten headless figures were painted, which signified that he had killed ten men. Four others were then added, one of them smaller than the others, signifying that he had taken four prisoners, one of whom was a child. A line was then run from one figure to another, terminating in a plume, signifying that all had been accomplished by a chief. A fox was then painted over the plume, which plainly told that the chief was of the Fox tribe of Indians. These characters are so expressive that if an Indian of any tribe whatsoever were to see them, he would at once understand them.

Following the sign of Pau-tau-co-to, who thus proved himself a warrior of high degree, were placed *twenty* headless figures, being the number of the Sioux that *he* had slain.

The ceremony of painting the post was followed by a feast, prepared for the occasion, which by them was certainly deemed the most agreeable part of the proceedings. Meats, vegetables, and pies, were served up in such profusion that many armsful of the fragments were carried off —it being a part of the ceremony, which is religiously observed, that all the victuals left upon such an occasion are to be taken to their homes. At a dog feast, which is frequently given by themselves, and to which white men are occasionally invited, the guest is either obliged to eat all that is placed before him, or hire some other person to do so, else it is considered a great breach of hospitality.

With the feast terminated the exercises of the afternoon, which were not only interesting but highly instructive to those who witnessed them.

## CHAPTER X.

From 1846 to 1854—Railroads—Rapids Convention—Growth of City, &c., &c.

1846. As readers familiar with the history of Iowa are aware, the State Constitution, alluded to under the year 1844, was not approved by Congress. A second Convention was held this year, and the other Constitution was limited and amended, in which form it met the approbation of the Federal Power, and in December, Iowa became a member of the confederated States.

In the August election, E. S. Wing, Democrat, was elected representative over E. Cook, by a majority of three. A. H. Davenport was elected Sheriff; James Thorington Judge of Probate over Platt Smith.

A Plow factory was started by a Mr. Bechtel. The first steam flouring mill opened by A. C. Fulton. A Board of Trustees for Iowa College was chosen.

1847. In April, James Grant was elected District Judge of the Second Judicial District, by a majority of four hundred and forty-eight. The District comprised Jackson, Delaware, Dubuque, Clayton, Scott, Muscatine, Clinton, Jones, and Cedar counties. In June the population of Davenport was, in the corporate limits, nine hundred and eighteen. A new paper, called the Democratic *Banner*, was commenced. The Banking house of Messrs. Cook & Sargent was opened this year, and was the first house of the kind in Davenport. They opened in a small house near or on the corner of Main and Second streets. The transition of the enterprising firm from the small one-storied shanty in which they made their *debut* to the magnificent four-storied marble structure in which they are now located, is no less an indication of the magnitude of their projective and executive abilities than it is of the rapid growth and high state of development reached by our city.

The preparatory department of Iowa College was this year opened.

1848. A noticeable event of this year was the death of an individual named Jas. R. Stubbs. He was born in 1797, and graduated at West Point with high honor. He was stationed at Fort Armstrong, on Rock Island, in 1822, and in 1826 he served under his brother-in-law, Judge McLean, in the Post Office Department. He afterwards removed to Cincinnati, and for some three or four years served in the Post Office and Clerk's Department of that city. While there it is supposed that he was involved in some unfortunate love-matter, for his character was thoroughly and essentially changed. He returned to Davenport in 1833, and after '37, for eight years, lived a recluse in a sort of cave excavated in a mound at East Davenport. There, with no other companion than his pets—a pig, dog, or cat, or all—he passed a rigidly secluded life. Byron, in his misanthropy, petted a bear, and Stubbs, in his, petted a pig. He would occasionally walk into town, with his family all at his heels. For some two years before his death he was induced to come forth from his hermitage. He was elected Justice of the Peace, which station he filled up to his death with an impartial and incorruptible integrity. His residence was in the small brick tenement on the north-east corner of Main and Third streets, in which he kept Bachelor's Hall. Judge Mitchell relates that upon several occasions, while passing Stubbs' house, late at night, he heard a violent clamor as if a furious altercation were being carried on within. Curiosity prompted him to open the door one evening, when the noise was at its loudest, to ascertain the cause. Instead of a half dozen persons, as he expected, about to engage in a free and deadly fight, there were only Stubbs and his cat! The latter was seated upon his knee, and listening demurely to his master, who was cursing him with every anathema in the vernacular, profane or sacred. Master Tom's offense seemed to be an amorous habit, which he had fallen into, of paying nocturnal visitations to the feline residents of the neighborhood.

Stubbs was a man of unflinching honesty, and in possession of a liberal education; and had not the unfortunate event, before alluded to, occurred to affect his life, he would undoubtedly have bequeathed his name to posterity, as a legacy honorable and respected. He died May 21st, aged about fifty-one years.

1849 was distinguished more particularly as being one in which strong efforts were made to secure the improvement of the Rapids. Two Conventions were held—one in July, and the other in October. The first was slimly attended, but in the last, four States and one Territory were represented, by about one hundred and fifty delegates.

One resolution passed, states that the improvement of the Rapids is a work which concerns the *whole universe.* The plan of improvement recommended in the report of Major Lee was endorsed, and it was urged that he should receive the appointment of prosecuting the affair. The Rapids are not yet fully improved. In another place, statistics will be given of the Rapids, the amounts appropriated for their improvement, results, &c.

The following will exhibit the commercial business of 1849, and will further act as data from which increase of business may hereafter be determined.

IMPORTS.

| | |
|---|---|
| Merchandise, | $148,500 |
| Pine and Oak Lumber, | 790,000 feet. |
| Shingles, | 1,120,000 |
| Square Timber, | 6,000 feet. |
| Reaping Machines, | 42 |
| Laths, | 310,000 |

EXPORTS.

| | |
|---|---|
| Flour, | 30,200 bbls. |
| Pork, | 1,425 " |
| Lard, | 720 " |
| Wheat, | 16,700 bush. |
| Beans, | 200 " |
| Potatoes, | 300 " |
| Onions, | 11,160 " |
| Barley, | 5,020 " |
| Flax Seed, | 120 " |
| Bran and Shorts, | 320,000 bbls. |
| Hides, | 20,400 " |
| Bacon, | 212 hhds. |

This amount of business, although since very much enlarged, was by no means small for a town possessing no railroad, or other communication beyond the high water privileges granted by the Mississippi. Improved farms, within three or four miles of Davenport, were worth about fifteen dollars per acre—seven miles out, ten dollars to twelve dollars per acre. Unimproved prairie lands, at a distance of six or seven miles out, were worth about four dollars per acre. Population of county about five thousand five hundred. Twenty-two thousand acres of land in the county were entered at the Land Office at Iowa City. In the next year twenty-two thousand forty-one were entered at the same place.

1850 may be properly deemed the year at which Davenport commenced that development which has at once given it a first rank among large cities, and excited the wonder and taxed the credulity of all cognizant of the fact. Previous to this year there had been no more to promote the growth of the location than its extraordinary healthfulness, beauty, and the possession of a rich dependent country lying adjacent. The emigrant came from the East, either by the long and expensive route afforded by a passage down the Ohio, and up the Mississippi, or else by the scarcely less dear mode of wagon emigration. Mails were infrequent and vexatious in their arrivals—the luxuries of an advanced refinement were numerically few—manufactories were undeveloped; and but little existed to induce emigration and settlement, save a fertile soil, an admirable position, and *faith* in the developments of the future.

Under such circumstances it is hardly to be supposed that Davenport would display the marvelous in its development. The year 1850, however, began a new era.

The prospect of a connection with the great cities of the East—of being a point touched by the line of commercial importance, which is always drawn westward from great maritime cities—the possession of three steam-mills, gave Davenport an impetus, whose character is equalled in but few cases.

The importance of a railroad connection with the East was duly appreciated by the inhabitants of the County. The project of a railroad to LaSalle, Illinois, connecting there with the canal to Chicago, met with so much favor that the stock (seventy-five thousand dollars,) assigned as the quota of Scott county was taken even before Rock Island county had discovered the merits of the undertaking. At the same time that the railroad question was agitated, the subject of bridging the Mississippi was also included, as was the building of the road from Davenport to Council Bluffs.

The organization for the R. I. & La Salle R. R. was completed in November. Judge Grant was elected President. Eighty-five thousand dollars in stock was taken by Scott county.

In February, 1851, a City Charter was obtained from the Legislature, and in March was adopted, by a vote of ninety-seven for, and seventy-one against. This meagre vote shows a most surprising indifference, on the part of the citizens in regard to the matter. Chas. Weston was elected Mayor, H. Leonard and A. Wygant, Aldermen First Ward; Dr. Barrows and N. Squires Second, and E. Cook, and H. Price, Third do.

Geo. B. Sargent received in April the appointment of Surveyor General in place of Gen. Booth, Democrat.

John D. Evans, H. S. Finley, and Ira Cook, were appointed deputies from Scott county.

In April, the books opened for subscription to the Chicago and Rock Island Railroad, were closed, the full amount (three hundred thousand dollars,) required by law having been subscribed. Judge Grant was chosen President of the Road.

At the August election Wm. Burris was elected County Judge, and Harvey Leonard Sheriff—which, by the way, he still remains.

January first, 1853, the Mississippi and Missouri Railroad Company was organized. Its members were John B. Jervis, Joseph E. Sheffield, Henry Farnam, John M. Wilson, N. B. Judd, Ebenezer Cook, James Grant, John P. Cook, and Hiram Price. The capital stock was six million dollars, of shares of one hundred dollars each. The corporation was to continue fifty years from date. Five per cent of subscription was to be paid down, and the remainder in instalments of not more than twenty per cent of the full amount, and at intervals of not less than three months. The highest amount of indebtedness which could be incurred was four millions of dollars. In May their first election was held. John A. Dix, of New York, was elected President.

September first, 1853, the first ground was broken on the Road. Particulars are given from the Gazette of the third inst.:

"The Railroad Jubilee.—Last Thursday was a day big with important results to Davenport. On that day the first shovel full of earth was thrown up on the Mississippi and Missouri Railroad. Or, it may be with propriety we can say, on the Atlantic and Pacific Railroad west of the Mississippi river. The act itself was trivial, but in view of the important results it heralded, 'twas thought best to accompany it with some parade that would establish the day as one to be commemorated. And inasmuch as there was some honor attached to the act of being the first man to throw up a shovel full of earth in the great enterprise, by common consent that privilege was assigned our enterprising fellow citizen, Mons. Antoine LeClaire.

About half past ten o'clock, the citizens of Davenport, Rock Island, and vicinities, assembled in front of the LeClaire Buildings, formed a procession, and proceeded to the corner of Fifth and Rock Island streets, where the great work was to be commenced. In the procession were included the two brass bands of this city, the Odd Fellows in regalia, the German Verein Society, and a large vehicle, drawn by four horses, containing Mr. Burnell, and some thirty-five or forty men who are employed at his saw-mill.

After assembling on the ground, Rev. A. Louderback, of the Episcopalian Church, offered up an excellent and appropriate prayer for the occasion, in which he beseeched the Most High to prosper the work, and to protect in health those who gave their time and services to the great undertaking.

After prayer, Hon. Jno. P. Cook ascended the stand, and entertained the audience with an extempore address of about an half hour's length, in which he spoke of the years of struggle that the citizens of Davenport had experienced to bring about this great work, how, year after year, they had petitioned Congress in vain for a grant of lands to aid them in constructing a link in the great national highway, and that finally despairing of ever accomplishing anything so long as they depended upon their federal parent for aid, they had thrown themselves upon their own resources, and now were about to reap the reward of their enterprise. Still they were indebted for their success to the fortuitous circumstance that placed in their way, and enlisted the hearty co-operation of the Railroad King in the West, Mr. Farnam, and which had now given us a Contractor in Mr. Carmichael, who was experienced in Railroad building, and able as willing to put the cars through to Iowa City in the shortest given space of time. Citizens of five or six years standing would regard the present occasion as one of deep interest, but to those who had past the last twelve or fifteen years of their lives in Davenport; those who had pitched their tents here when but few houses occupied the site so recently reclaimed from the Indians, the present must indeed be an occasion of rejoicing, one fraught with the most pleasing associations. Soon the locomotive would leave our bustling city, bear on its burden to the Capital of the State, and ere long lave itself in the waters of the Missouri. Soon a bridge would span the great Father of Waters, and a continuous line of Railroad connect us with all the great marts of the East. Our prospects are bright, the gloomiest need not despond.

It was expected that Jas. Knox, Esq., of Rock Island,

would also address the assembly on the occasion, but he not being present, Mr. Fulton, the Marshal of the day, announced the important crisis to have arrived when the soil was to be broken on the great Mississippi and Missouri Railroad route. Whereupon Mr. LeClaire descended from the stand, pulled off his coat amid the cheers of the crowd, and proceeded in a workmanlike manner to give the first touch to the great iron thoroughfare west of the Mississippi river.

During the intervals while assembled, the bands enlivened the scene by performing some of the most appropriate airs, and the members of the Verein Society sung, while a small company of artillerymen from the old country having in charge the "castiron," and stationed on a neighboring eminence, made the welkin ring.

Quite a respectable number of the citizens of Rock Island, we were pleased to observe, were on the ground, manifesting that interest which an enterprise of such great and mutual importance to the two cities was likely to beget in the minds of right-thinking men. We hope soon to reciprocate their visit, and participate with them in the celebration of the first arrival of the locomotive, through from Chicago, in their flourishing city.

We have heard the whole number of persons present estimated at two thousand. Harmoniously and quietly, at the order of the Marshal, the citizens again formed in procession, and marched to the LeClaire House, where, at two o'clock, the Messrs. Lowry served up an excellent dinner, of which from one hundred and fifty to two hundred persons partook. Thus terminated peaceably, and so far as we know, without engendering an unkind thought, the celebration of an event, that regarded with respect to the character and extent of the work it proclaimed, is the most momentous in the history of our youthful and progressive city."

A vote was taken in September in regard to the County subscribing for the road. Only three hundred and nine votes were cast, but of these only ten were opposed to subscribing. The amounts taken in all were seventy-five thousand dollars by the city, fifty thousand dollars by the county, and one hundred thousand dollars by individual subscription.

## CHAPTER XI.

Opening of Chicago and Rock Island Railroad—Bridge Opposition—Laying Corner Stone—Proceedings—Growth of City—Statistics, &c.—Letter from W. Barrows.

February 22d, 1854, was remarkable not only as the anniversary of the birth-day of Washington, but as the one upon which a connection, by railway, was completed between the Atlantic and the Mississippi. Davenport, for some reasons best known to Rock Island, was not generally invited to attend the celebration, which the occurrence gave rise to. Not behind hand in enthusiasm, a gun was brought forth, whose thunder was but a faint echo of the joy the citizens felt over the event. A splendid illumination was also gotten up at night, and quite as much or more jubilation was expressed on this as on the Rock Island side.

A few extracts from the Chicago *Press* will show the character of the initiation of the grand event:

"On Wednesday last, the 22d inst., that event looked forward to for years with so much interest by our citizens—the connection of the Mississippi with Lake Michigan by a continuous line of Railroad—was consummated. The honor of arriving first at this important goal belongs to the Chicago and Rock Island road—an honor, by the way, well worthy the Herculean efforts which have been made to achieve it. In February, 1851, the legislature chartered the company—in October of the same year the contract for its construction and equipment was taken—in April, 1852, the first estimate for work upon it was paid—and in February, 1854—three years from its charter, and twenty-two months after ground had been broken upon it—the work is completed, and cars are running daily its entire length —*one hundred and eighty-one miles!* This is certainly a proud monument to all who have been instrumental in pushing the work forward to completion, and especially so to those sagacious and energetic men who have had it in special charge—Messrs. SHEFFIELD and FARNAM.

On Wednesday morning, the 22d inst., at half past eight o'clock, the Mayor and Common Council of the City of Chicago, and a number of citizens, in all about two hundred and fifty, left the depot of the Rock Island road, in a train of six splendid passenger cars from the manufactory of A. B. Stone & Co., of this city, for an excursion to Rock Island, in honor of the completion of the road. The day was one of the most delightful of the season, and the genial sunshine, and the exhilerating atmosphere, chimed in well with the exultant spirit, which sparkled in the eye and shone in the countenance of every one of that goodly company. The train was tastefully ornamented with flags and evergreens, and its arrival at the different towns along the line was greeted with the shouts of the people, and the firing of cannons. At Joliet, Morris, Ottawa, Lasalle, Peru, Tiskilwa, Geneseo, Moline, and other places, accessions were made to our numbers, and when the train arrived at Rock Island there could not have been less than three hundred and fifty persons on it.

The reception at Rock Island was a magnificent spectacle. Thousands of people lined the streets, and crowded the doors and windows. Fair ladies waved their kerchiefs, and stout men and youths shouted exultingly, while ever and anon the thunder of Col. Swift's gun went booming across the Mississippi, arousing the echoes from the majestic bluffs. It was a glorious day for Rock Island, and for her neighboring city across the river. The citizens of those places had looked forward to it for years, some of them with fear and trembling, lest their eyes should not behold it. Hundreds of people from the contiguous country, both in Illinois and Iowa, had come in to witness the scene, and to mingle their shouts and congratulations with their city neighbors. Delegations were there from most of the river towns from Dubuque to St. Louis, and some had come from the far interior towns of Iowa, for they knew that the arrival of the iron horse upon the banks of the Mississippi was but an earnest of his speedily appearing beyond it, and stretching away on his destined course toward the Pacific. We think we are not above the mark in estimating the number present, on the arrival of the train at from five to six thousand persons.

* * * * * * *

The speeches were highly appropriate to the occasion, and elicited, throughout, enthusiastic applause from the vast concourse. While the things were transpiring within, a grand spectacle was witnessed without. The two cities of Rock Island and Davenport were most beautifully illuminated. The windows of stores, private residences, and public buildings, were lit up on both sides of the river, and the lights reflected back from the bosom of the Mississippi, were indefinitely multiplied, the whole presenting a scene of imposing grandeur. After the reading of the regular toasts, a large portion of the company, headed by the Moline brass band, marched in procession through the principal streets of the city. Others remained in the depot until a late hour, Mr. Baily, of Rock Island, presiding, where speeches and sentiments beguiled the passing hours.

We regret that our limits precluded a report of the many good things that were offered.

Much credit is due to the people of Rock Island for the handsome manner in which the celebration was gotten up and conducted, and for the hospitable manner in which private houses were thrown open to accommodate the multitude of strangers. The people of Davenport and Moline also threw open their mansions with the same hospitable spirit, and we think everybody was comfortably provided for.

* * * * * * *

In concluding our notice of the opening of this road, we wish once more to allude to the successful manner of its prosecution. The history of Railroads presents no parallel to it. Some *companies* may have built a greater number of miles of road in as short a period, but never before has individual enterprise shouldered and borne forward so rapidly to a triumphant completion such a work as this. And let it not be forgotten that a large portion of the road has been built in the face of a stringent money market. But while many companies have been compelled to hold up from this cause, Messrs. Sheffield & Farnam have moved steadily onward with their great work as though no cloud had darkened the financial sky of the country. Surely there is a triumph for which they may justly feel an honest pride.

We desire, also, to do justice to the faithful and zealous labors of William Jervis, Esq., the Chief Engineer of this road. From the beginning he has been always at his post, and to his skill and efficiency much of the credit for the admirable character of the work, and its speedy completion, is due. But we must close, without further enumeration. All honor to *all* the men who have in any way aided in the advancement of this great enterprise."

The completion of the Chicago and Rock Island Road, and the commencement of its continuation—the M. & M.

R. R.—naturally led to the adoption of means, whereby the two roads might be connected. A bridge across the Mississippi had long been foreseen as a necessity, and now as the scheme approached practical development, there was, all along the river, the most inveterate opposition.

St. Louis, which hitherto had enjoyed a monopoly in Western Commerce, was rampant in its opposition to the scheme. The Chamber of Commerce "Resolved" that a bridge was unconstitutional, an obstruction to navigation, dangerous, and that it was the duty of every Western State, river city, and town, to take immediate action to prevent the erection of such a structure. A Resolution was also passed by the City Fathers of St. Louis, instructing the Mayor of the city to apply to the Supreme Court of the United States for an injunction, restraining the building of the Bridge.

Certain old-fashioned dogmas, having origin at a time when men understood less than now the true principles of commercial industry, governed St. Louis, and other places, in their hatred to the bridge. It was a dogma founded upon the most intense selfishness, and as devoid of liberality as the system of monopoly which once disgraced the legislation of France. That Davenport, Iowa City, or Council Bluffs, had no right to be connected with Chicago and New York; and that St. Louis possessed some predominant and indisputable claim to their commerce, seemed to have been the base of action taken by the latter city. Such principles are obsolete, and it is not hazardous to assert that an iron band will yet unite the broad prairies of Illinois to the magnificent Levee of St. Louis. Stranger things than this have happened in the changes undergone by popular opinion.

The opposition of rival towns was not all the opposition experienced by the Bridge—for it had to contend against even a national, or rather Southern jealousy. Shortly after its commencement under permission from the State of Illinois, an order was issued from the War Department, commanding the Marshal, for the District of Illinois, to clear the Island of all trespassers. This was done in face of the fact that the Island had been abandoned as a military reserve by both of Davis' predecessors—Poinset and Marcy—and had been turned over to the Land Office Department for sale. Davis probably feared that the Bridge would materially interfere with the prospects of the Southern Pacific Railroad. This order, however, to clear the Island of all trespassers, was not construed as he probably intended, for it was not made applicable to the Bridge Company, and its operatives.

The corner stone of the Bridge was laid September 1st, 1854. A meeting was organized, the stone laid, and appropriate speeches made by Joseph Knox, Esq., of Rock Island, and Hon. James Grant, of Davenport. Among the sentiments of the former were some worthy of preservation, as having bearing upon the opposition hitherto extended to the Bridge. They are as follows:

"All History proves the great path of the World's Commerce to be from East to West; from India to Assyria and Egypt, from Egypt to Greece and Rome, from Rome to Spain and England, and from England to our own free America. It is certainly the duty of all wise men not to retard this Westward progress, but rather to hasten it, bearing with it, as it does, that blessed trinity, Commerce, Civilization, and Christianity; and that we regard all opposition to the workings of this great historic law as among the insanest of follies."

"*Resolved*, That in JOHN WARNER, the Contractor for the building of the Bridge, we recognize a man who, by reason of natural capacity, and long experience, is eminently fitted for the great work in his charge. We congratulate him upon his success thus far, and trust that the winds and waves and seasons may be propitious to him, until he shall have bound together the Eastern and Western halves of this great valley with an eternal clasp of oak and granite. The first Bridge across the Mississippi! It will be monumental to his memory, and perpetuate his name as long as the great river it spans flows in majesty beneath it!"

The year 1854 was distinguished as a busy one. It speaks well for the character of Davenport, that the foundations of her prosperity were never on paper, but were laid deep and permanent in the *Industry* of her inhabitants. The growth of the town has always been concomitant with the settling of the back country, the establishment of manufacturing interests, and the development of other resources. There has been at no time a retrogression, or a stand-still, indicating a fictitious progress, or an over-growth. Thus, in 1854, the population increased nearly or quite three thousand. The base of this growth was the railroad connection, *six* saw mills, turning out from twenty to thirty thousand feet of lumber each per day; two foundries and machine shops; some twenty-four run of burrs, dozens of smith and wagon shops, one wholesale plow factory, turning out one hundred plows per week, one Pork packing establishment, and a County population of about thirteen thousand. In these statistics will be recognized a solid and lasting base of prosperity, not to be quashed as a speculative bubble, or destroyed by a financial "crisis."

The following communication, from a series in the Davenport *Commercial*, by Willard Barrows, Esq., will give readers a correct idea of the city at that date:

"Davenport ranks with any other city in the West, as well in a statistical point of view, as in the beauty and natural commercial importance of its location. It contains about six thousand inhabitants; one hundred and twenty-five stores, all told; three regular Banking Houses; ten Land Agencies; six steam mills of various kinds—one of which (Burrows & Prettyman's) manufactures one hundred and seventy-five barrels of flour per day; one Foundry and Machine shop; seven Blacksmith shops; four Saddle, Harness and other leather manufacturing establishments of various kinds; nine churches; seven public houses; the Iowa College; two public school-houses; one of which cost upwards of six thousand dollars, built of stone, besides private schools; one Masonic Lodge, two Lodges of I. O. O. F., one Division of Sons of Temperance, and one Maine Law Club; fourteen Doctors, and twenty-two Lawyers; (don't be frightened at the two last items!) We have a good County Poor House, with farm attached; one tri-weekly, and four weekly newspapers.

Scott county, of which Davenport is the County Seat, is one of the best river Counties in the State, and fast settling by enterprising farmers, mostly from Pennsylvania, New York, and Ohio. Until recently we have, in common with other towns upon the Mississippi river, had to depend entirely upon steamboat navigation to carry off our surplus produce, but now a direct communication by Railroad through Chicago to New York is open, which has greatly enhanced the value of produce.

*Davenport* being situated at the foot of the upper rapids of the Mississippi river, can, with a moderate capital, bring into requisition one of the greatest water-powers in the world; and we doubt not, the time is not far distant when eastern capitalists will procure it, and take hold with energy and success. The Rock Island and Chicago Railroad terminates at Rock Island. The Mississippi and Missouri Railroad, is now in progress of construction from this place to Council Bluffs, a distance of three hundred miles, the first division of which, to Iowa City, fifty-seven miles, will be completed by the first of December, and the cars running. These two roads are to be connected at Rock Island and Davenport, by a bridge across the Mississippi river, now in course of construction. This bridge, over the main channel of the river, on the Iowa side, will be one thousand five hundred and eighty-two feet, divided into five spans of two hundred and fifty feet each in the clear; the bed of the river is rock, a good foundation. The slough, on the Illinois shore, is four hundred and seventy-four feet, also rock bottom. The bridge, on the Iowa side, is to be built with a draw for steamboat navigation; the draw to turn on a pier, or similar to a turn-table, and to be closed only for the passage of cars, upon given signals. The bridge is to be twenty-one feet above high-water mark; the estimated cost is two hundred and fifty thousand dollars, to be completed the first of December, 1855. The time now occupied by railway from Davenport to New York City is three days; to Chicago from eight A. M., to four P. M., for five dollars, and from Chicago to New York, twenty dollars. Thus, for twenty-five dollars, and *three days* time, can eastern citizens see "*Iowa as it is.*" Steamers are generally in readiness on the arrival of the cars, to convey passengers up or down the Mississippi river. Three and four trains of passenger cars per day running over the road.

Much has been said of late respecting the sale of Rock Island by the Government, to whom most of it belongs; that such will be the case, I can hardly believe. It is under the jurisdiction of the War Department, and has, till this time, been reserved from sale with a view of making it the great western depot for munitions of war: "No where (says Gen. Jessup, in his recent letter to the Secretary of War,) west of the Alleghany mountains, is there a better place for the manufacture of implements of war than Rock Island." The water power at the head of the Island is immense; the Island is high, above all overflow, and healthy, and we anticipate that in less than ten years, it will be the manufacturing place and deposit for all Government stores, requisite for our frontier, even to the Pacific Ocean.

The long and much agitated question of removing the obstructions in the rapids of the Mississippi, is now settled. Congress has made the requisite appropriations. The surveys of the channel have been made, the contracts let, and the contractors upon the ground ready to proceed when the water will permit—two hundred and fifty thousand dollars will be spent upon the rapids, and the same amount in building the bridge in the next two years, beside the railroad depots and manufacturing houses requisite to stock the Railroads of Iowa.

Have we not then some claim in point of position as a town; may we not look forward to days of prosperity? are we not on the line of the great thoroughfare across the State of Iowa to Council Bluffs, Fort Laramie, to the South Pass, Salt Lake, and to the Pacific Ocean! Is it then to be wondered at, that our town has doubled its inhabitants in the last three years, that four hundred houses were built here during the last year, and as many more anticipated; that there is not a room ten foot square to rent in the city, and that the public houses, and private boarding houses, cannot accommodate the people who are emigrating to this country? Is it surprising that real estate commands such high rates, and that money is worth twenty per cent?

Where, let me ask, are the hordes of starving Europe to find a home but in the Great West? We cannot expect in this age to wait the slow progress of the settlement of former years. Twenty years ago there were less than five thousand white inhabitants between the Lakes and the Pacific Ocean! Now there is nearly two millions. Fifteen years ago Chicago brought her breadstuffs from Eastern States; now she exports each year not less than five million bushels of grain, and one hundred and twenty thousand barrels of beef and pork.

Seventeen years ago, I was three weeks making the journey from New York, by canal and steamboat, to Davport, but now it is performed in three days, and soon will be done in two. Six years ago Chicago had not a foot of railroad completed, now there is nearly five hundred miles completed within the limits of the State, and over two thousand in process of construction. Should the fertile soil of Iowa, Illinois, or Wisconsin, be less valuable, now that it is placed within two or three days of New York, than the barren, sterile hills of the Hudson were when it took a week to reach the market! The West is still in its infancy. It has not yet become of age, not yet passed out of its *teens*. Its resources have not yet been developed. It only wants capital, and the handicraft of man to make it the *garden of the world!* Egypt, with her Nile, may do to rehearse in song, but the valley of the Mississippi, when properly developed, can never be excelled."

*Davenport, May*, 1854.

# OAK-WOOD VILLA,

RESIDENCE OF C. AUGUSTUS HAVILAND,

DAVENPORT, IOWA.

## CHAPTER XII.

Temperance—Taxable Property—August Election—Election of Gen. Sargent—Inaugural Address—Improvements—Close of 1857—History of "Past' finished—Editorial from Gazette.

That ball set in such powerful motion by the moral arm of Neal Dow, did not stop among the rocks and pines of New England, but rolled across the continent, till it leaped even that majestic cold-water institution—the Mississippi. In April, of 1855, a vote was taken upon the passage of a Prohibitory Law. In Davenport, the result would have delighted the originator of "legal suasion." In Davenport Precinct eight hundred and seventy-seven votes were cast for and against the Law, of which five hundred and seventy-one were in favor of the Law. Enos Tichenor was elected Mayor by the dominant party. LeClaire gave a majority for the law of one hundred and sixty-one. The majority in the County in favor was six hundred and thirty. The highest number of votes cast in the county was one thousand eight hundred and seventy-seven.

The Temperance ticket in August, headed by Wm. Burris, for County Judge, was, however, defeated by sixteen votes. W. L. Cook was elected Judge, and H. Leonard Sheriff. James McCosh was elected as Recorder on the Temperance ticket by a majority of thirty-three. The whole number of votes cast in the County was one thousand nine hundred and fifty-one—in the township one thousand and fifteen.

The value of taxable property in Davenport township for 1855 was—

| | |
|---|---|
| Total value of land and improvements, | $1,424,439 |
| " " town lots, | 1,859,417 |
| Capital employed in merchandize, | 258,334 |
| " " " manufactures, | 84,729 |
| Monies and Credits, | 497,138 |
| Corporation Stocks, | 86,121 |
| Furniture, | 37,944 |

This, with other property, amounted to a sum total of four million four hundred and eight thousand four hundred and thirty-three dollars.

The following statement will show the manufacturing interests of Davenport, May 1856, as compiled by a writer for the Chicago *Press*:

Hands employed five hundred and twenty-six, capital five hundred and eighty-six thousand, value of manufactures for the year past one million five hundred and twenty-two thousand five hundred and sixteen dollars. The sales of lumber amounted to seventeen million four hundred and twenty thousand one hundred and eighty-seven feet, six million four hundred and ninety-six thousand shingles, and eight million lath. Of this amount, ten million feet was manufactured here, three million five hundred thousand from Chicago, and balance rafted down the river. These statements do not include the manufactories of East Davenport—that place not being in the corporate limits of the city. Twenty thousand eight hundred hogs were packed, and four hundred and fifty-four thousand bushels of wheat bought in.

April 21st, the locomotive "Des Moines" crossed the Mississippi Bridge, being the first thing of the kind. Attempts were made to celebrate the event, but failed.

However, the era will not be forgotten, although unrecognized by the salvo of artillery, or the plaudits of enthusiasm.

May 6th, 1856, the steamboat Effie Afton, while endeavoring to pass through the draw, was struck by a wind, and driven against a pier. She took fire, and communicated to the Bridge the destructive element. A portion was burned, and the steamer was a total wreck. Allusion is made to this, because a suit was soon after commenced against the Bridge Company by the owners of the boat, in which some highly important principles were evolved. They will be spoken of in their place.

In August, 1856, the strong feeling, originating under the Kansas-Nebraska Act, materially changed the political character of the hitherto Democratic County. Timothy Davis, Republican Congressional Candidate, received one thousand four hundred and seventy-two votes in the County, and his opponent, Shepherd Leffler, ten hundred and thirty-six. W. J. Rusch was elected over G. C. S. Dow, for State Senator, by about the same majority. Rogers, Wing, and Barner, were elected Representatives over Dodge, Parkhurst, and Smallfield. J. W. Stewart was elected Prosecuting Attorney over John Johns, Jr., and J. D. Patton, County Clerk. For a convention to form a new State Constitution there was one thousand seven hundred and four votes; against eighty-nine.

In March 1857, Gen. Geo. B. Sargent was nominated as an independent candidate for the Mayoralty. B. B. Woodward was nominated to the same office by the Republicans. Gen. Sargent was elected by seventy-eight majority, together with the principal nominees of the Democratic ticket. John Johns was elected Police Magistrate by fifty-two majority. H. W. Mitchel, Marshal, E. Peck Clerk, S. Sylvester, Treasurer.

At the same election there were in the County forty-one majority for Mills, Republican candidate for District Judge

—three hundred and ninety-eight majority against licensing the sale of spiritous liquors. The Judicial District had, a short time previous, been reorganized, owing to the fact that its immense extent precluded the possibility of the Court doing one-half of the business which it engendered. The new District included Scott, Clinton, and Jackson counties. G. C. R. Mitchell, independent candidate, was elected.

The improvements projected under the new municipal *regime*, headed by Gen. Sargent, were extremely liberal. Extracts from the Mayor's Inaugural will at once express the condition of the city, and the improvements recommended:

"The Treasurer's* report of 31st ult., exhibits very clearly

*CITY TREASURER'S REPORT.

ABSTRACT OF RECEIPTS.

| | |
|---|---|
| Balance received from Treasurer last year, | $2,563 06 |
| Dividends on C. & R. I. R. R. Stock, | 5,440 00 |
| Taxes in arrear for year 1855, | 1,048 09 |
| Road fund in arrear year 1855, | 1,849 75 |
| City Clerk Licenses, Cemetery Lots, &c., | 434 45 |
| Mayor for fines, | 58 00 |
| Redemption of Lot for Taxes, | 3 00 |
| Marshal Taxes for 1856, | 14,600 39 |
| Real Estate owners on account paving Main street, | 718 25 |
| Real Estate owners macadamizing Front street, | 1,602 08 |
| Sale of ten City Bond loans of 1856, | 5,000 00 |
| Sale eighty-four shares C. & R. I. R. R. Stock, | 8,400 00 |
| Two fractional shares C. & R. I. R. R. Stock, | 100 00 |
| Dividends on M. & M. R. R. Stock, | 3,648 00 |
| | $45,465 07 |

ABSTRACT OF EXPENDITURES.

| | |
|---|---|
| Current expenses as per city orders, | $7,246 22 |
| Interest commission, and expense on C. & R. I. R. R. Bonds, | 5,025 00 |
| " " " on M. & M. R. R. Bonds, | 7,631 61 |
| Cash paid from Treasury for Road work, | 6,931 73 |
| " Street Commissioner, road fund, Mayor's order, | 1,849 75 |
| " on account paving Main street, | 2,563 00 |

the financial state of the City. It shows that the Finances are in an excellent condition.

It is a source of just pride that, thus far, in our Municipal history, we have always been able to meet our obligations promptly and fully, in consequence of which no city in the West deservedly enjoys a better reputation or credit than our own.

The Treasurer, in his report, does not include among the liabilities of the City the indebtedness to the Chicago and Rock Island Railroad, consisting of Bonds due May 1st, 1863, for fifty thousand dollars, and Bonds to Mississippi and Missouri Railroad, due August 1st, 1865, for seventy-five thousand dollars; nor among the assets of the City, five hundred shares in Chicago and Rock Island Railroad, fifty thousand dollars, and seven hundred and fifty shares,

| | |
|---|---|
| Cash paid on account Macadamizing Front street, | 2,088 62 |
| " " Brady street and steamboat landing, | 1,197 92 |
| " " Macadamizing Main street, | 510 50 |
| " Revising Ordinances, | 250 00 |
| " On account printing and binding Ordinances, | 500 00 |
| " Note and interest on account Road fund, | 1,081 67 |
| " Interest Commission and expense on Davenport Gas Stock, | 204 00 |
| | $37,081 02 |

SCHEDULE OF PROPERTY BELONGING TO THE CITY OF DAVENPORT, MARCH 31, 1857.

| | |
|---|---|
| 27 Shares C. & R. I. Railroad Stock @ $100, | $2,700 00 |
| Interest Scrip Mississippi and Missouri Railroad Company, | 54 14 |
| 40 Shares Davenport Gas Light and Coke Company, | 1,000 00 |
| 162 shares Mississippi and Missouri Railroad stock @ $100, | 16,200 00 |
| Estimated amount due from County Treasurer to Road Fund, | 4,000 00 |
| Due from Real Estate owners on Main street, | 1,845 00 |
| " " " " Front street, | 60 96 |
| Cash in the Treasury, | 8,384 05 |
| City Tax List for 1856, | 1,900 00 |
| Due from City Clerk, | 634 00 |
| | $39,778 15 |
| Deduct estimated Expenditures due and maturing, | 5,000 00 |
| Leaving nominally a balance over indebtedness, | $44,778 15 |

seventy-five thousand dollars, in the Mississippi and Missouri Railroad, for which the Bonds above alluded to were issued.

It is a source of gratification that the issuing of Bonds to these Railroad Companies has been of such vital importance to the advancement of our City, securing, as it did, the building of these roads, and thus bringing large accessions to our Municipal population, wealth and resources. During the past year, the dividends on the Chicago and Rock Island Railroad brought into the Treasury some six thousand dollars, more than enough to pay the interest on the Bonds. The liberal policy pursued towards these Railroads should be extended to other public improvements of equally essential importance to our City, and full as certain to add largely to our prosperity.

### LOAN OF FIFTY-NINE THOUSAND DOLLARS.

Of the fifty-nine thousand dollars loan, voted last year, Bonds to the amount of nine thousand dollars only have been issued. The loan was divided as follows: Twenty-five thousand dollars for filling out and grading Steam Boat Landing; less than three thousand dollars of which sum has been, as yet, expended. Mr. McCammon has a contract for grading Brady and Seventh streets, and filling up the Levee. According to the recent estimate of the City Engineer, it will not cost over twelve thousand dollars to fill between Harrison and Brady streets. The balance of the money will be subject to the order of the Council. I would urge that the Levee be Macadamized as soon as practicable, after the filling in is completed, in order to prevent damage by the action of the river current.

Ten thousand dollars were appropriated for Water works. A Committee have been making examinations for suitable grounds, who have, from time to time, reported. Although the order for this loan was made early last summer, no ground has been decided upon. It is highly important that measures should be taken immediately to secure a proper site for Water Works, and the necessary surveying and engineering done to furnish an estimate of the cost of procuring for the City a constant supply of pure water. As soon as such estimates are completed and approved by the Council, I would urge the issuing of Bonds for the amount required, and the building of said Water Works at once.

Ten thousand dollars for Fire Engines and apparatus. Of this amount five thousand five hundred dollars will have been expended (when the Fire Engines arrive here, being now on the way, via. New Orleans,) in the purchase of two Fire Engines, and necessary hose and appendages. The balance can be expended for a lot and Engine House, or towards the building of Cisterns. Either will come within the purview of the loan.

In this connection, I would urge a liberal appropriation to the Fire Department for outfit, &c., and that a lot be purchased, and an Engine House erected, as soon as practicable.

Four thousand dollars for taking stock in the "Davenport Gas Light and Coke Company." This was taken with an understanding that seventy-five street lamps were to be immediately erected. One semi-annual payment of interest has already been made, and no signs of street lamps yet appear. The Gas Company should be required, at once, to fulfil their part of this agreement. The delay that has already occurred is unjustifiable.

## PUBLIC BUILDINGS.

Among the many important matters demanding early attention, are the securing of a suitable lot for, and building thereon, a Hospital, at a cost of, at least, fifteen thousand dollars. The securing of a lot for, and building a City Prison, at a cost of about the same amount. A City

Hall, with offices for all the city officers, and a court room for the Police Magistrate, and such other judicial officers as may, from time to time, be added to the city Judiciary, with a fire proof vault or safe, for the keeping of valuable city papers, should be constructed at a cost of not less than twenty thousand dollars. In the upper story of this building could be built a large Hall, which would, if properly managed, pay at least ten per cent. on the entire cost.

I would suggest the propriety of borrowing fifty thousand dollars, on Bonds of the city, principal payable in twenty years, for this purpose.

* * * * * * *

## STREETS.

There has been an urgent necessity for the improvement of the streets, &c., in almost every part of the city. I would urge prompt action on these matters *now*, even if the necessary funds have to be borrowed on the bonds of the city, as the *best* economy and policy. Good and substantial crossings should be made in every part of the city where citizens have been taxed for sidewalks; and a contract should be made with some responsible party to keep such crossings in good passable condition during the entire season.

The principal streets in the city should be graded without delay, particularly as a large amount of Macadamizing will probably be done this season, and the road fund will be entirely inadequate. This Fund is not sufficient to make the ordinary street repairs. Other permanent improvements must be provided for by making a loan. A loan of one hundred thousand dollars for this purpose would be desirable.

Past experience has shown that the Council should never permit a single yard of dirt to be hauled upon the streets, but where they are in bad condition, they should be improved by ploughing in the gutters, and rounding up, as in almost every instance the dirt must be removed below the surface grade for permanent improvements, like that of Macadamizing. There is one idea in connection with grading of streets, to which I would call your particular attention. It is easily seen how large a quantity of land can be made by an expenditure of twelve thousand dollars on the Levee. An expenditure of fifty thousand dollars more would make enough land to pay the entire cost of making. The River is shallow in front of the city; and by extending the Levee, a better landing can be had than now; and the old landing could be cut up into lots, and sold for building purposes.

### SEWERAGE.

A general system of sewerage should be at once adopted. There is no city in the world where nature has done more towards a natural drainage than in our own; yet a judicious system of sewerage commenced now, and carried out, will add immensely to the health of the city, and save, in after years, thousands of dollars, and hundreds of lives.

### DAVENPORT.

Its situation, at the intersection of the two great arterial trade currents of the country, would alone give it consideration and importance; yet, with rivals above and below, generally competing with us for pre-eminence, we must not stay our own efforts. Although much has been done, more remains to be done. It will not do for us to rest content with the success of past exertions, nor trust our future to the natural course of events, but with combined and well directed efforts on our part, the continued success and growth of our city are beyond doubt.

Situated on the most magnificent natural highway upon

the North American continent, and on what must eventually be the main line of interoceanic communication, being the only point at which the Mississippi has been bridged, and in all probability destined for many years to be the only such point in a State that has untold wealth in its fertile soil, and commanding all its central position, there surely can be no uncertainty as to its future importance. Its past History, too, gives large promise. It has reached its present development with a rapidity unknown, except in Western experience. Its founders, and its first citizens, are yet active in our midst, and to these, whose experience has been its experience, as they look back upon its insignificant beginnings, its early struggles, its times of doubt, and remember the few short years that have sufficed for the growth and prosperity of to-day, no speculation, as to its future importance, can seem unreasonable or extravagant."

The recommendations of Mayor Sargent were not unheeded. Appropriations, for the various purposes specified, were made, and the improvement during the year was rapid beyond precedent. Over thirteen hundred Houses were erected, dating from August 1st, 1856, to the close of the year 1857, two miles of street Macadamized, four and a half miles of gas pipe laid, over two hundred and fifty street lamps erected, and thirteen miles of sidewalk laid.

This sidewalk estimate includes none above the Railroad Bridge, none in East Davenport, and none in North Davenport, except Brady street, though they are all within the city limits; these would certainly eke out the measures to twenty miles of sidewalk in the city of Davenport.

The assessed property of the city increased from one hundred thousand dollars, in 1851, to one million five hundred thousand dollars in 1854, to three million dollars in 1855, to three million five hundred and fifty thousand dollars in 1856, and for the present year amounts to five million two hundred and twenty-five thousand ninety-one dollars and ninety-one cents.

A magnificent Engine House was built at an expense of five thousand dollars, and engines, with hose carts, &c., purchased. The "Independent Fire Engine and Hose Company" had organized some time previously under a Charter from the Legislature, and to them was committed the care of the Engine House, and fixtures.

RECAPITULATION.

*The number of houses erected in Davenport during the year ending with* 1857 :

| | |
|---|---|
| Front street, eleven squares, | 39 |
| Second street, twelve squares, | 56 |
| Third street, thirty squares, | 126 |
| Fourth street, fourteen squares, | 42 |
| Fifth street, thirteen squares, | 33 |
| Sixth street, thirteen squares, | 37 |
| All in the city limits west of Warren and the bluff, to the river, except Third street, | 112 |
| Seventh, 8th, 9th, 10th, 11th, and 12th, | 111 |
| Renwick's mill to bridge avenue, | 10 |
| LeClaire's common, (laborers' cottages,) | 22 |
| Fulton's addition, | 22 |
| East Davenport, | 33 |
| Fulton and Fejary's subdivision, | 20 |
| North Davenport street, | 250 |
| Part of city bounded east by Harrison street, south by Seventh street, and north and west by city line, | 150 |
| Built outside of city line, | 106 |
| Total, | 1214 |

Number of miles of street Macadamized, 2
" " sidewalk laid, 13
" " gas pipe laid, 4½
" " street graded and not yet Macadamized, 4
" street lamps erected, 250.

Cost of twenty-one buildings erected during the past year, $511,000. Cost of one building, $75,000

At the August election, Col. Chas. Weston, Democrat, was elected County Judge, James McCosh, Republican, Recorder, and H. Leonard, Democrat, Sheriff. The vote for the new Constitution received a majority in its favor, and in all other respects, save the two above-mentioned officers, the Republican measures were victorious.

The year 1857 closed, after having, to the full, equalled its predecessors in the progress and benefits which it carried to our city. The population increased to eighteen thousand, immense improvements were projected and executed, real estate steadily rose in value, and every element of prosperity was rapid and sure in its development. The financial revulsion of the Fall, affected us somewhat, but to an extent remarkable for its meagreness. Ample facts in regard to this will be afforded hereafter.

The Winter of '57 and '8 was, up to the time of writing,* the most remarkable on record. The river was as clear of ice as it was under the sweltering influences of a July sun, while the weather was like the balmyness of Spring.

The prominent occurrence, of the early part of '58, was a difficulty between the municipal authorities and the Firemen. The former framed an Ordinance, creating certain new offices in the Fire Department, which were to be filled independently of the Firemen. The latter rebelled —refused to attend fires, and held meetings denunciatory

* February 5th, 1858.

of the action of the authorities. The Council was firm in resistance, and matters seemed likely to assume a most unpleasant aspect. Mayor Sargent, however, happened to attend a fire, when he was nearly mobbed by some Germans, indignant at some real or fancied wrong in relation to one of their Aldermanic representatives. The Firemen rallied round the Mayor, affording him a guard of honor and protection. The result was that they received their Engines again, and a satisfactory compromise effected in regard to the Fire Ordinances.

Business during the Winter was, as in all other places, dull, owing to the derangement of financial affairs, but owing to the soundness of business, there were less than half a dozen failures—a fact that challenges equality in any other place, East or West. Of these failures there were but two of consequence.

---

The "PAST" is finished—but a review of the field will not be attempted till the "PRESENT" has been minutely scanned. Then reflections, which our progress hitherto affords, will be indulged in.

As an appropriate finish, the following article, from the pen of an editorial *cofrere*, is appended. It was written May, 1857:

"Five years ago Davenport was only distinguished as the most beautiful village on the Mississippi river. Resting upon the western bank of this great river, and nestling in the bosom of a grand amphitheatre, formed by a crescent of bluffs circling around the plain, a half mile back from the river in front—the cliffs of Rock Island parting the crystal waves, and old Fort Armstrong resting upon these walls of stone—the village of Rock Island opposite, and the iver coiling off in the distance, glittering like a silver thread for miles—certainly no lovelier spot ever gladdened the eyes of man, than Davenport as a village. It then had only about seventeen hundred, or two thousand inhabitants. Now, we have a population of from fourteen to fifteen thousand people, all actively engaged in business, all intent upon developing to the utmost the great advantages of the place, all striving to continue the growth so remarkably commenced, and with every incentive to energetic action. Within five years, Davenport has changed from the village to the first city in Iowa, and she is now as remarkable for her commerce, trade and manufactures, for all the attributes of a flourishing city, as five years ago she was for her loveliness as a village. Last fall, we published a full list of the manufactures of Davenport. Our own citizens were astonished at the extent and variety of manufactures in the city, and the aggregate annual amount of manufactured articles. Since then, the list has been largely increased, and this season will mark an augmentation as remarkable as any year's increase since our village history. Upon no surer foundation for prosperity can a young city rest, than upon her manufactures—but when with these are linked so great a river and railroad, or commercial advantages, as Davenport enjoys, who can tell when or where the prosperity and progress marking our city, at this time, may cease? The people of Davenport feel justly proud of the manufactures of their city. While rival cities are depending almost entirely upon their commercial advantages, and resting their whole future upon this or that railroad enterprise, we, enjoying, probably, all their advantages of this nature, place a strong reliance upon the influence of various and extended and rapidly increasing manufactures, to carry forward that prosperity so happily begun, and so wonderfully marking our present history. We consider this no weak reliance, when we reflect upon the amount of capital invested in manufactures at this point, the number of persons engaged, and the numbers flocking here for employment, in response to the demand, the independence given us of distant communities in so many particulars, and the standard men of means who are continually coming into our midst to open new branches of mechanics. We anticipate that our list of next fall will show an increase in capital, amount of manufactures, number of hands employed, &c., of fully one-third over our last year's statistics.

Commercially, we are situated far enough on the river above St. Louis to be entirely independent of the influences of that city, and near enough to avail ourselves of its advantages as a market of demand and supply. We are at the foot of the upper Rapids, and the center of one of the richest and most thickly settled regions of country in the great Mississippi Valley. We have direct connection with Chicago by railroad, a distance of eight or nine hours travel, and through its railroad with the East, &c. With the interior we are connected by the Mississippi and Missouri Railroad, some time since finished to Iowa City, the capitol of the State, and doing an excellent business, and now fast being built to connect us with the Missouri river. This road is already a great artery of trade and travel, and every month is increasing its business, and its value to this city. Of other roads in contemplation, we have not now space to speak. At this point, the great bridge crosses the Mississippi, the only bridge spanning this vast body of water in its whole length, from St. Anthony to the Gulf. It is evident that other roads must be drawn to this point to obtain a bridge crossing. Indirectly, we consider the bridge of immense importance to our city. In itself, it is a magnificent structure, and one in which we feel a pardonable pride. We claim commercial advantages for Davenport second to those of no other point above St. Louis.

The very fact of the country, back of Davenport, being so thickly settled, farm after farm stretching out in every direction, like a vast garden, and villages dotting the prairie at every stream and grove, with the continued influx of immigrants, of the best stamina, is, in itself, perhaps, sufficient to demonstrate that the wonderful growth of our city is but the natural result of plain causes, and must continue so long as the causes exist. We have the back country, and the people in the back country, to sustain a far larger city than Davenport now is.

The population of Davenport is principally composed of the most substantial classes of Eastern people. New England is largely represented in our midst, with enough of Western leaven to add go-ahead energy to backbone! The clime is nearly assimilated to that of New England—cold dry winters, and delightful summers. At this time, there is a great deal of cash capital coming from the East to this place seeking investment. Consequent upon this, in part, there is an immense amount of property changing hands, and we have heard of no sale this season, nor do we expect to hear of one made under ordinary circumstances, in which the seller receives not a full remunerative price. Property in the city, and about the city, is steadily increasing in value, with no prospect of cessation, much less of revulsion. It is *not* above what it should be, even if our city had no prospect of future swift growth—but on the contrary, it must continue improving with the progress of the city. Property in several other upper Mississippi cities, not really so large as Davenport, is almost or quite double what it is here, and rents proportionately higher. In those places a revulsion *should* be expected. Perhaps it were better for their real prosperity that it should speedily take place, as the present condition of things is driving to other points the very men calculated most to build up a city. A portion of our daily increase of population is made up of mechanics, and others, who *cannot* go to other places if they so desire.

Thus much we have hastily sketched of our own city as it is. We have not the space to give many interesting fatcs connected with our city, or to more than barely touch upon those things in which the stranger is most interested. Davenport is healthy and prosperous. The man of capital, or the man depending upon his skill, or strong arm alone, for success, and seeking a new home, should turn his eyes to this place. Let him come and examine for himself. He will find at this point, on both sides of the river, nearly thirty thousand people, with capital and labor unitedly exerting their wonderful influence, and more capital and labor in demand. He will see evidences of prosperity and progress for which he may vainly seek among the younger or smaller cities of the East or South. Let him become one of us, and uniting his energies and industry to ours, grow and prosper with us."

# BIOGRAPHIES.

Eng^d & Print^d by Alfred Jones N.Y.

George Davenport

# CHAPTER XIII.

## COL. GEO. DAVENPORT,

ONE OF THE ORIGINAL PROPRIETORS OF DAVENPORT, AND AFTER WHOM THE CITY WAS NAMED.

George Davenport was born in the year 1783, in Lincolnshire, England, and, at the age of seventeen years, was placed with an Uncle (master of a Merchant ship) to learn the seafaring business. During the next three years, he visited many seaports on the Baltic, and of France, Spain, and Portugal. In the fall of 1803, the ship sailed with a cargo from Liverpool for St. Petersburgh, and shortly after its arrival an embargo was laid upon all the English vessels in that port—the vessels taken possession of, and their crews thrown into prison by the Russian Government. The crew of Mr. Davenport's vessel were confined in an old stone church, where they remained during a long and dreary winter, suffering very much from cold and hunger. In the Spring they were released, and their vessel restored to them. After returning home, their next voyage was from Liverpool to New York, with a cargo of goods—this was in the summer of 1804. They arrived safely at their destination, and had discharged their load, and taken in a cargo for Liverpool, and were on the eve of sailing, when an accident took place, which changed the whole course of his life. Every thing was in readiness for sailing, they had commenced to heave up the anchor, when one of the sailors was knocked overboard. Standing near the stern, at the side of the vessel, Mr. D. saw the accident, and immediately jumped into a small boat, and caught the sailor by the hair as he was going down the last time—drawing him up, and holding him until they came to his assistance. In jumping into the boat, he struck one of the seats, and fractured his leg very badly; and there being no surgeon on board, the Captain had him taken to the city, and placed in the hospital, with directions for every possible care to be taken of him. After remaining there some two months, he was advised to go into the country to recruit his health. Acting upon this advice, he went to New Jersey, and stopped at the pleasant village of Rahway, where he remained some time, and then went to Carlisle, Pennsylvania. While here, he became acquainted with a young officer, Lieut. Lawrence, who was recruiting for the army. Taking quite a liking for him, he proposed, that if he would enlist he would get him the appointment of Sergeant, which proposition was accepted, and he received the appointment of Sergeant in Capt. McLeary's Company of the First Regiment of Infantry. He then went to Harrisburg on a recruiting expeditions, and remained until they had enlisted the number of men required, after which they returned to Carlisle Barracks, and remained until the Spring of 1806, occupied in drilling, and learning all the arts of war.

They then received orders to join the army at New Orleans, under the command of Gen. Wilkinson. They walked across the mountains to Pittsburgh, and there they procured boats, and rowed down the river to New Orleans.

On their arrival at that city, they were kept constantly at work repairing and building new fortifications, and putting the place in a state of defence. During that Summer, the soldiers suffered very much from sickness. In the Fall, the troops received orders to march to Sabine River, against the Spaniards; which expedition has since been known as the "Sabine Expedition." The troops were placed in keel boats, and worked their way up the Mississippi and Red River, suffering every kind of hardship and fatigue, hot weather, bad water, and any quantity of musquitoes could afford, before they arrived at Nachetochez. During this trip, Mr. D. steered one of the boats, and came very near being drowned. In consequence of the boats sheering and swinging around, the steering oar knocked him into the river, but fortunately, as he came up, he seized hold of the blade of the oar, and held on until he was rescued. After remaining here a short time, he was sent by Gen. Wilkinson with dispatches to "Fort Adams," on the Mississippi. He took one man with him, got his provisions into a canoe, and started down Red River. When they had reached the great bend, they met with an accident, that came near losing them their lives. The canoe struck a snag; and upset them in the river, but by clinging to the drift wood, they made out to reach the shore, making a narrow escape with their lives. Losing their canoe, and all of their provisions, they were now obliged to strike across the country to the Mississippi, traveling over swamps, bayous, sloughs, having frequently to get logs together, and make rafts to cross on.

During this travel, they were nearly eaten up by musquitoes. At night they would build a fire, and make a dense smoke, to keep them off. While one of them would sleep, the other would watch, keep up the fire, and looking out for "Alligators." They were several days in reaching "Fort Adams," and were nearly worn out, living only upon what berries and wild fruit they could find.

Peace being made with the Spaniards, Gen. Wilkinson returned with the troops to New Orleans, and as soon as they arrived, they commenced to put the place in a state of defence against the "Burr Expedition," which was on its way down the river. There was great excitement in the city. The military were kept constantly on duty, and in a short time the city was declared under Martial Law. During this time, Mr. D. was on duty as "Orderly" to Gen. Wilkinson. About the middle of December, 1806, he was sent with a guard to arrest Dr. Errick Bollman, which was effected about twelve o'clock at night. They surrounded the house, posting sentinels around it to prevent any possible escape. When they knocked at the door, a person came and opened it, and enquired what they wanted. They replied "Dr. Bollman." The person stated the Doctor was not there. They, however, entered, searched the house, and found the Doctor in his room, dressing himself, when they arrested him for "Treason," taking him down to the Fort for safe keeping.

During the stay of the troops in New Orleans, they suffered dreadfully from sickness, not being accustomed to the climate. It frequently became Mr. D.'s turn to take charge of the men detailed to bury the dead. This was a dreadful duty. The graves could not be sunk more than three feet, owing to the water being so near the surface, while the men had to bail out the water as they dug the graves; and when the coffin was put in, they had to hold it down with their spades until the grave could be filled up with earth to keep the coffin from floating. The sun's scorching heat, and the intolerable stench from the shallow graves, made this the hardest duty that was possible for any one to perform, and a great many lost their lives from the effects of it. After the arrest of "Burr," and his associates, and every thing had quieted down, most of the troops were sent to Natchez, Fort Adams, and other more healthy places.

In the Spring of 1807, Mr. D. was sent with a party of troops to the Homichita River, in the Choctaw Country, where they built a Block House, and remained there until Fall, when they returned to Natchez. Mr. D. then received orders to go on a recruiting expedition to fill the regiment, which was nearly decimated by losses from sickness. He sailed from New Orleans to Philadelphia, where he enlisted quite a number of men; going from there to Baltimore, and thence to Winchester, Virginia, 1809. Here he remained until the Spring of 1810, when he was ordered West to join his regiment. They walked over the mountains to Pittsburgh. Here they procured keel boats, and proceeded down the Ohio, then up the Mississippi and Missouri to the Barracks, at Bellefontaine. He remained here until the Summer of 1812, when he went with Capt. Owens' Company, in boats, up the Mississippi, to an Island just below the mouth of the Illinois. Here they built temporary fortifications, and remained until Fall, to protect St. Louis and the settlements from being attacked by the Indians.

About this time, Gen. Howard organized an expedition to go against the Indians on the Illinois river, at Peoria Lake, where the Pottawotamies had several villages. The regular troops were ordered to proceed by water to Peoria, while the rangers and volunteers proceeded across the country. They got their keel boats in readiness, and had the "Cargo Boxes" double planked, so as to make them ball proof—made loop and port holes for musketry and light pieces of cannon. They arrived at the foot of Peoria Lake without seeing any Indians—landed their men, and commenced to build a Block House on the top of a high bank, which overlooked the prairie for some distance. After finishing this, they sunk a well to supply it with water. Having arranged things so as to draw up the water with a sweep, it was necessary to have a grape vine to attach to the pole. Mr. D. having noticed some grape vines in the woods, a short distance from the Block House, took a man with him to get one, and soon found the article in question. They cut it, and were trimming it, when an unusual sound attracted their attention. They became alarmed, and started for the Fort, and when they reached the edge of the timber he climbed a tree to reconnoiter the prairie in the direction of the Block House, and to his horror he beheld the prairie swarming with Indians, moving toward the Block House. He descended as fast as possible, and told his companion that their only chance of escape was by getting under the bank, and running for their lives along the shore of the lake, endeavoring thus to reach the Block House before the Indians discovered them. They started, but were not half way to the Fort before the battle commenced. The firing from the Block House, and the yells of the Indians on the prairie above them, increased their speed "considerable," and they made, perhaps, the fastest time ever known. When they approached near the Block House, they found it was impossible to reach it, as the Indians were nearer than they were, and their only chance now was to get to the gun boats at the lake. When they were about half way to the boats, the Indians discovered them, and commenced firing at them, and, yelling like a pack of devils, made towards the boats. This alarmed the men on board, who commenced to push out into the lake, but, fortunately, one of the boats grounded on a sand bar, which accident saved Mr. D. and his companion. They rushed into the water, and, wading to the boat, put their shoulders to the bow, and pushed it into deep water. During all this time the Indians were firing at them, and the balls kept whizing by, making it anything but comfortable. They soon got on board, and under cover. Mr. D. determined on revenge, and pointing one of the small cannon, he took good aim at the red skins, and applied the match. The gun missed fire. While hunting for a primer, some one elevated the piece too high. When he applied the match, the piece went off with a tremendous explosion, so much so that he thought the whole boat was blown up. The muzzle of the gun had been elevated above the edge of the port hole, and when it went off, the whole load struck the side of the boat. By this time the brisk fire kept up from the Block House and boats, obliged the Indians to retreat.

Nothing of any importance occurred until about the first of December, when a large party of Pottawottamies arrived with a "white flag," and sent in three of their Chiefs to the Fort, and proposed to meet the Commanding officer in Council. This was agreed to, and arrangements were made for the meeting a certain number of Chiefs and Braves in Council. A place and time were agreed upon, and when the time arrived, about forty of the principal Chiefs and Braves approached the place, dressed in their full Indian costume, headed by their principal Chief, the old Black Partridge. They were met by the Commanding officer, and all the officers of the post. After shaking hands, and passing around the Peace Pipe, the old Chief explained his business. They wished to be friends with the Americans, to stop war, and make a treaty of peace with him. The Commanding officer complimented them for the decision, and promised to send their talk to the Superintendent of Indian Affairs, Gen. Clark, at St. Louis, as he had no orders or authority to treat with them. He proposed that they should send a delegation of their Chiefs and Warriors to St. Louis, and he agreed to send some of his soldiers with them, to see them safe through the white settlements. This was agreed to. So they selected thirteen of their principal men, and one woman. The Commander ordered Mr. Davenport to select four trusty men, and take charge of the Indians, and escort them to St. Louis. This was rather an unpleasant duty, for five men to start out with a lot of hostile Indians, but it had to be done—there was nothing to be done but to obey orders, and accordingly he got a sufficient supply of provisions, and placed them aboard of a Perogue, and embarking his party, started down the Illinois river. The principal Chiefs were Gomo, Senatchwine, Shiggashack, Comas, and Black Partridge. They had traveled but one day, when the river froze up, obliging them to abandon their boat, and travel by land. Each took a small quantity of provisions, the remainder was rolled up, and placed in a hollow tree. With the provisions, they also had a small keg of whisky, and after giving each one of the party a dram, it was proposed to hide it with the provisions, so that the Indians could have it on their return, but the old Black Partridge insisted that they should drink it all then. Mr. D. told him he could not do so. He then directed them to move on, and his men to follow in the rear, while he remained to put away the keg of liquor. After they were out of sight, he took the keg and concealed it in a different place from that mentioned to the Indians, having become alarmed at their conduct, and being afraid they would return, and take the liquor, and get drunk. In that case, they were sure to have trouble, and, perhaps, lose their lives. He soon overtook the company, but all day the Old Black Partridge was very moody and discontented. At night they encamped on a point of the river; and he managed to place the Indians on the point, and his own camp behind them, so that they could not go back without his knowing it. Each had a guard to watch the other. They traveled, in this cautious manner, two or three days, when they discovered a smoke across the prairie, which alarmed the Indians. They stated that there was a large war party of Sacs out, and thought from the smoke it must be them, and if they saw them they would be killed, they could not be saved from these formidable braves. This was not very comfortable news, but they avoided the danger by avoiding the prairie, and following the timber, and making no fire at night. They traveled on for a number of days, and when they began to approach the Mississippi a new danger began to threaten the imagination of the Indians. The Rangers were ordered to scour the country as far up as the mouth of the Illinois, and there was great danger of falling in with them, and their firing on them before the Rangers discovered that there were any whites with them. When camping at night, the whites hung their hats and coats upon poles, so that in case of an approach of the Rangers, the Indians would not be fired upon.

In this way they traveled, and, after suffering very much from the inclemency of the weather, and from hunger, they arrived at St. Louis, and were very well received, and were soon called to the Council Chamber, and a treaty concluded with the Indians, who left five of their number as hostages for its fulfilment.

Gov. Clark enquired of Mr. Davenport "how it had been possible for him, and his party, to reach the white settlements without being seen by the Rangers, who were ordered to guard the frontiers from a surprise by the Indians?" Mr. Davenport replied, "that he had not seen any thing of the Rangers, nor any signs of their ever having been to the mouth of the Illinois." Some of the officers of the Rangers were present, and overheard the conversation, and when they left, they swore they would show Mr. Davenport's party whether there were rangers on the look out or not.

Gov. Clark supplied the Chiefs with presents and provisions, and directed Mr. Davenport to take the party up the river in a Perogue, and land them at the mouth of the Illinois river, on the north side, so that they might return home in safety. After getting every thing in order, they started on their return. They were obliged to keep on the Missouri side all the way up, for fear of the Rangers firing on them, as they were very angry at the statements that had been made by Mr. Davenport, and had sworn vengeance against him and his party on their return. They, however, reached home in safety.

Mr. Davenport returned to Bellefontaine, and remained there until the Spring of 1814, when the first regiment was ordered to join Gen. Brown on the Canada line. They shipped on keel boats, and went down the Mississippi, and up the Ohio to Pittsburgh. They then crossed over the mountains by forced marches, until they arrived at the town of Erie. They immediately embarked on two vessels, and sailed to Fort Erie, where they were ordered to be reviewed. They put themselves in as good order as possible, paraded, and received orders at once to march to Lundy's Lane, and arrived in time to be in the hottest part of the battle. This was very hard service, as they had just performed a long and fatiguing journey without an hour's rest. But the army was hard pressed, and had need of every man that could be brought into action during the battle. Mr. Davenport had to assist in taking one of the officers, who was severely wounded, from the field, and laid his musket down to perform the service, and when he returned it was gone. He soon found one by the side of a British soldier, which he took, and found to be one of the "Glengarian Muskets," a very excellent exchange for the one he had lost, (this old relic is still kept in the family, in memory of the war.) Mr. Davenport was in many very perilous situations during this service time, often being placed on piquet-guard duty, and during the siege of "Fort Erie," he was on duty at one of the batteries night and day, with scarcely a moment's rest. He was also on duty at Black Rock, in charge of a battery, a part of the time. At the time of the "sortie," he was one of the attacking party which drove the British from their works. After the seige was over, the troops crossed back again to Buffalo, and the First Regiment marched to Pittsburgh, and then by boats to Bellefontaine. After being there a short time, his term of service expired, and he got an honorable discharge, having given his adopted country ten years of very active duty, and of the very best part of his life. At this time, he was employed by Col. Wm. Morrison, of Kentucky, Government Contractor, as his agent to supply the troops with provisions—the Commissary Department being at that time under the management of the Contractors. He now came to St. Louis, and took charge of several keel boats, loaded with the necessary provisions. A large drove of cattle were also purchased, and driven through the country. They started up the river, and arrived at the mouth of the Des Moines River late in the Fall, and concluded to stop there for the Winter; and built a number of log huts for the men, and for storing the provisions. It being so late, it was difficult to build huts in sufficient numbers. The best he could do, was to put poles into the ground, and nail up green hides for siding and roofing, and when they got dry, they made a tolerably warm house. This Post was called "Cantonment Davis." The next year, "Fort Edwards" was built here.

In the Spring of 1816, the Eighth Regiment, and a Company of Riflemen, under the command of Col. Lawrence, (the very same officer and friend with whom Mr. Davenport had enlisted ten years before,) embarked on boats, and started up the river. They arrived at the mouth of Rock River, and examined the country for a site for a Fort, and the result was the selecting of the lower end of Rock Island as the most suitable point. They landed on Rock Island on the tenth of May, 1816. As soon as they had completed their encampment, he employed the soldiers to cut logs, and built store houses for the provisions, and had a bake house and oven put up. This was the first building ever erected on this Island. The soldiers now set to work to build the Fort, which was named "Fort Armstrong." At this time, there lived a large body of Indians in the vicinity, numbering some ten thousand, divided in three villages, one on the East side of the River, near the foot of the Island, called "Waupellow Village," and about three miles South, on the bank of Rock River, stood the famous village of "Black Hawk," and on the West side of the River stood a small village named after an old Brave, "Oskosh." Upon the first arrival of the troops on the Island, the Indians were very much dissatisfied, but the officers took great pains to gain their friendship by making them many presents, and they soon became reconciled, and were most excellent neighbors. During the first Summer they would frequently bring over supplies of sweet corn, beans, pumpkins, and such other vegetables as they raised, and present them to Mr. Davenport, and the officers, with the remark, that they had raised none, and that they themselves had plenty, invariably refusing to take any pay.

During the first Summer an incident occurred, which gave Mr. Davenport an Indian name. Some of his cattle having strayed off the Island, he took some men, and went over to look for them, in the bottom, at the mouth of Rock River, but not finding them, they were returning along the bank of the river, in front of the Indian village. When opposite some of the lodges, a party of drunken Indians came rushing out towards them—his men took to their heels, but he stood his ground; some dozen of the drunken Indians seized him by the arms, legs, and coat-tail, while another drunken fellow held a large black bottle in his hand, and would stagger up and try to hit him on the head with it, which blow would require all his strength to dodge. This manœuver was repeated a number of times, until he was nearly exhausted, and had about made up his mind that the "cursed Indian" would break his head with the bottle, when an old Indian, a friend of his, happened to see what was going on, when he cried out "Saganosh, Saganosh!" ("he is an Englishman.") These words operated like magic—they loosed holds, and commenced to shake him by the hands, and endeavored to be the cleverest fellows in the world. He was ever afterward known, by the different tribes, as "Saganosh." At this time he resided near the Fort, and continued to supply the troops with provisions, but in the second year, he built a double log cabin and store-house adjoining, about a half mile from the Fort, and where the present residence is. He now, with what little money he had saved, purchased a small stock of Indian goods, and commenced the "Indian Trader." At this time there was a large tribe of Winnebagoes, or, as the French called them, Peons, that inhabited Rock River country and the Winnebago Swamps. This tribe had a very bad name, and were always very hostile and treacherous, and they had been in the habit, for several years before, when a trader came among them with goods, to kill him, and take the goods, as the easiest way of making a short bargain, so that the French traders had been afraid, for some time, to go among them. Mr. Davenport, not knowing much about the Indians at this time, and hearing that they had large quantities of furs, and that no traders had visited them for some time, concluded that this would be the best place for him to trade in. As soon as the French Traders, (most of whom were in the employ of the American Fur Company,) heard of it, they advised him not to attempt it, as he would be killed and robbed, but he determined to try it, and fitted out five or six pack-horses, loaded them with goods, and taking two Canadians, Gokey and Degree, with him, started up Rock River. They soon reached the Winnebago encampment. He immediately got the Chiefs and principal men together, and made them a "talk." He told them he had heard that they were in want of many kind of goods, and that they had plenty of furs, so he had come up to trade with them, but that before he had started he had been told that they were a very bad people, and was advised not to go among them, but he did not believe these stories, and that he had come among them to see for himself. The Chiefs shook him by the hand, and expressed great satisfaction at the confidence he had in them, and assured him if he would trade with them, he should never have cause to complain. They then sent a cryer through the different encampments, to announce the arrival of a trader, and that they must treat him well. He now unpacked his horses, and placed his goods in one of the lodges, which was offered him. He commenced to trade, and soon sold all his goods, and had received the best kind of Furs in payment, and at very good profits. He now loaded up his horses, and started back with Gokey, leaving Degree in charge of a part of the Furs, while he returned to get another supply of goods. He now visited all the different encampments, and met with very good treatment—his trade soon increased so largely that he established several trading posts on Rock River, and maintained them for many years, making a very profitable business.

At this early time, most of the Indian goods were brought from "Mackinac" through Green Bay, then up the Fox River to the "Portage," there packed across to the Wisconsin River, then down the Mississippi in "Mackinaw Boats." He once sent an order to Mackinaw for an assortment of Indian goods, camping equipage, four hands, and a Mackinaw boat, and everything complete, was delivered to them at Rock Island.

His employees were Canadians, hired for three years, at one hundred and twenty-five dollars per year, and were very faithful hands. Shortly after he had commenced trading up Rock River he made a very narrow escape. About this time several war parties had gone to attack the settlements, one of which had been unfortunate, and had lost some of their men, so that, on their return, the relations of those that were killed felt very hostile, and determined to be revenged at the first opportunity. Not knowing anything of this state of things, Mr. Davenport packed up some goods on four or five horses, taking Gokey with him, and started up Rock River. They arrived at Prophets Town, and went immediately to their old friend, "Wetaico's Lodge." The old man met them, but seemed much alarmed. He shook them by the hand, and said he was very sorry they had come at this time; he was afraid they would be killed, as there was a war party just about to start from the upper end of the village, headed by the "Crane," who had lost some relatives, but that he would do all he could to save them. This was said to them in the Chippewa Tongue, as that was generally used by the traders. He invited them to sit down, when the yells of an approaching party of Indians was heard. He told them to keep cool, and show no signs of alarm. In a few minutes a large crowd surrounded the lodge, whooping and yelling like so many "devils.' The old man now stepped to the door of his lodge, and enquired what they wanted, (in the Winnebago language.) They replied that "they had come to kill the white men." The old man now made them a long speech, claiming the rights of hospitality, and the sacredness of his lodge. He told them they were fools! Why be in so great a hurry? That they had plenty of time, as the trader was going to encamp just below the village, and would remain three or four days to trade! This seemed reasonable, and the crowd assented to it, and retired. The old man returned, and said he could save them, but they must follow strictly his council. He then directed them to go just below the village, and pitch their tent near the bank of the river—unpack their goods, turn out their horses, and make every preparation for remaining several days, and in the meantime he would place a light canoe and paddles a little way below their tent, and as soon as it was dark, to slip away from their camp-fire, jump into the canoe, and float down the river until they were out of hearing of the village, and then to paddle for their lives, but to lay by in the high grass in the day time, as they might be pursued, and headed off across some of the bends of the river. They followed his advice strictly, put up their tent built a fire, and spanceled their horses, arranged their goods, and made preparations for cooking. Some few Indians came to them, and desired to trade, but they put them off until next day, on the score of fatigue. They did this to throw them off their guard. The hours seemed very long, but darkness came at last, and they stole away from their encampment, reached the canoe, and floated quietly down the river, and as soon as they were out of sight of the camp-fires, they began to paddle their canoe swiftly down Rock River. Several times, during the night, they saw camp-fires ahead of them, on the bank of the river, and were obliged to drift past them on the opposite side, under the shadow of the bank. As soon as it was day-light, they landed, hauled their canoe into the tall grass, and concealed themselves during the day, and when it was dark, they started again, and paddled all night. Next morning they found themselves at the mouth of Rock River, and soon reached Rock Island.

Sometime afterwards "Old Wetaico" visited Rock Island, when he gave an account of what occurred. The next morning after the escape, he said, the whole village turned out—men, women, and children, marched down to the tent, headed by the "Crane" and his war party, armed with their tomahawks, bows and arrows, and painted—singing their "war song," and beating their drums. They advanced, dancing their war dance, and surrounded the tent. But they soon found "that white man is very uncertain."

Owing to the bad feeling of this part of the tribe, he did not go among them for some time afterward. The Winnebagoes frequently came down to the Island to trade, in small parties, but they appeared very sullen and shy. They did not like to visit the Fort much. Mr. Davenport felt satisfied that if they got a good opportunity they would kill some of the whites.

In 1818, Mr. Davenport gave up the agency of supplying the troops, and turned his attention entirely to the Indian trade. He made arrangements for building him a house and store, and got the commanding officer (Col. Morgan,) to point out the place where he could build without interfering with the Forts. The place selected was the one where his late residence now stands. He put up a double log cabin, with a chimney between them. He now went to St. Louis, and purchased a supply of goods and provisions, and bought a small keel boat, ("Flying Betsey,") loaded her with them, and returned to Rock Island.

Heretofore, Mr. Davenport had confined his trade principally to the Winnebagoes, but he now commenced to trade with the Sacs and Foxes, in opposition to the "American Fur Company's" traders. During the Winter he was constantly traversing the prairies of Iowa, and visiting every encampment in person. He, in this way, selected all the best furs, while the old French traders had very little energy, and seldom left their trading post. In the Spring, he would have all his furs and skins nicely packed and prepared—feathers all sacked, bees-wax and deers tallow all barreled—then would load his boat, and go to St. Louis, and sell his cargo, which always commanded the highest market price, owing to the good condition in which everything was put up.

It was customary, with the Sac and Fox Indians, residing in this vicinity, when they had finished planting their corn, for the young men to go on a Summer hunt for Buffalo and Deer, while the old men, and most of the women, would go up to the "lead mines" in their canoes, and dig mineral, smelt it in log furnaces, and return back again about the time their corn would be fit to eat. On these occasions he would load his keel boat with provisions, and a few goods, and go up to Fever River, (or, "Mau-cau-pi-a-sepo," or Small Pox River, as the Indians called it,) and trade with the Indians for their lead. He also visited the mines on the West side of the Mississippi, (where the Dubuque mines were,) and obtained large quantities of lead of them, which branch of the trade was very valuable.

In the Fall of 1819, Mr. Davenport, and his family, came very near being massacred by the Winnebagoes. A party of twenty of whom, headed by the "Crane," arrived about sun-down, and said they wanted to trade. He told them he never opened his store after sun-down, that they would have to wait until next day. At this, they seemed to be very much dissatisfied, but he invited them into the room occupied by his men, (adjoining the room he lived in,) and gave them plenty to eat, and pipes and tobacco, and told them they could sleep on the floor, in front of the fire. At this time, he had only two men at home, Jerome, and another trader. About bed time, Jerome came into his room, and told him he did not like the conduct of the Indians, that they did not act right, that they had laid down without taking off their moccasins, or other things, and that he was afraid to sleep in the room with them, and that they intended to do some mischief. He told Jerome to bring in the other man, and their blankets, and sleep on the floor. The two rooms were divided by a chimney, with a short passage at one side, from one room to the other, with a door at each end. Jerome, and the man, came in with their blankets and guns, and laid down on the floor, with their guns beside them. Soon after, one of the Indians came in, and said he wished to sleep on the floor, as the other room was rather crowded. He secured permission to do so. As soon as the men had laid down, Mr. Davenport examined every thing, to see that the guns were all in their proper places, as he generally kept a number always loaded, standing against the wall ready, in case of an attack. He then put a sack of sweet corn against the door, (locks were scarce in those days,) and retired to bed, but not to sleep. About the middle of the night, Jerome turned over, and, in doing so, rattled his powder horn. This alarmed the Indian, who sprang to his feet, and, giving a yell, rushed into the other room. By this time, Mr. Davenport, and his men, were up, with their guns in their hands, and when the Indians, in the other room, came rushing through the narrow passage, leveled their guns at them, and told them to move back, or they would fire on them. The Indians saw that they were prepared to fire, so they retreated, and shut the door at their end of the passage, and placed every thing they could find against it, to barricade it. Mr. Davenport did the same at the other end, and, with his men, stood on guard until sun-rise, expecting every moment some kind of attack would be made on them, but during the whole time they could not hear the least noise. As soon as it was light, they began to reconnoiter, but could not see any thing of the Indians—they had gone.

Some time afterwards, Mr. Davenport learned that the party had started out with the intention of killing the whole family, and plundering the store. Their plan, at first, was to get Mr. Davenport into the store, where they intended to tomahawk him, and then kill the rest without firing a gun, for fear of alarming the Fort. Their next move was to place the Indian in the room to sleep, so that he could get up, when all was asleep, and tomahawk as many as he could, and at the same time to give a yell, as a signal that they should come to his assistance. But a "guilty conscience" frightened him, when the Frenchman moved. He thought he was going to take the start of him. Failing in this attempt, they still kept prowling about the neighborhood, watching for any straggler who might venture out alone. They at last succeeded. Two soldiers got permission to go into the woods to cut a stick for-axe helves. They were cautioned not to go far from the Fort, but at sun-down, when the roll was called, it was found they were missing, and fearing they might be lost in the woods, one of the cannon was fired off, so they might know the direction of the Fort. Next morning, Lieut. Stubbs, and a party of soldiers came up to Mr. Davenport's house, and informed him that the two men were missing. He stated that he heard, the day before, about noon, the report of two guns, and had no doubt they were killed. He then got all of his men, and with the soldiers, formed a line, and struck across the Island in the direction of the sound of the gun, and when they had reached the middle of the Island, they found their bodies. Both had been shot and scalped!

In 1822, Mr. Davenport established a trading post at Fever River, in charge of "Amos Farrar." This was a very good point, at this time, for trade with the Indians, for furs and lead. He also had trading houses at Flint Hills, mouth of the Iowa River, Waupsipinica, and Makquoketa Rivers, besides three on Rock River. To attend to them all, and have them properly supplied, kept him constantly traveling from one post to another, sometimes on foot, sometimes in a canoe, and sometimes on horseback. His principal depot was on Rock Island. Here all the furs and skins had to be collected together, and here the out-fits of goods were made up, and sent off into the different parts of the country.

In 1823, the first steamboat arrived—the "Virginia." She was loaded with provisions for Prairie du Chien, and was from Wheeling. Mr. Davenport was called upon to Pilot her over the Rapids. He took his old "Patroon Debuts" with him. They were three or four days getting over. At this time quite a number of persons went up to Fever River to work the mines. Col. Wm. Johnson, of Kentucky, had obtained permission of the government to work the mines, and passed up the river with several keel boats loaded with provisions and tools. In a short time quite a village was formed at Fever River.

Two magistrates were appointed about this time by Gov. Cass, of Michigan Territory. The following letter, written at the request of some of the inhabitants, will show the state of feeling at the idea of being in that Territory:

"ROCK ISLAND, *January*; 1825.

*Sir:* About a year ago two magistrates' commissions were forwarded by Gov. Cass, of Michigan, to two respectable inhabitants of Fever River. They were recommended by a gentleman from Michigan, then concerned in a commercial way at that place, on the presumption that it belonged to Michigan, and one of the gentlemen so appointed acted by virtue of his commission. The people were dissatisfied at the idea of being attached to a Territory so remote, and with whom, in a whole age, they could have no social intercourse. Last Spring they had the pleasure of finding that the settlements on Fever River rightfully belonged to Illinois—upon which, the magistrate acting under the authority of Michigan, declined, and since sent on a formal resignation. Of course, they are at present in an awkward situation, in the absence of civil authority, and it is the cordial wish of the permanent population of that place, that no time may be lost in appointing the persons (recommended by them some time since as magistrates,) namely, Moses Meeker, and John Connelly.

Most Respectfully, Sir, Yours,

G. DAVENPORT.

D. D. SMITH, Esq., Atlas, Pike county, Illinois.

N. B. Have the goodness to send me a prompt reply, (by the Military express, who pass through your town,) stating, circumstantially, all the forms necessary to the completion of the business, as I am much concerned in the ultimate welfare of the upper country, and you will much oblige.

I am informed that lately the Sheriff of Prairie du Chien (Crawford county, Michigan Territory,) visited the mines people, and exacted poll tax from them, some of whom were simple enough to pay, others manfully refused, and it gave umbrage to all. G. D."

The mails were carried, at this time, by express, from the Fort; the nearest Post Office was at Clarksville, Missouri. In the Spring of 1825, Mr. Davenport received the following letter:

"GENERAL POST OFFICE,
*Washington City*, 23*d April*, 1825.

*Sir:* From the information I have received, I conclude it will be agreeable to you to accept of the office of Post Master, at Rock Island, Missouri. I herewith send you a copy of the law for regulating the Post Office, a key for opening the mail, and forms, and directions conformable therewith. You will find these at the Clarksville Post Office, Missouri. After executing the bond, and taking the oath, you may proceed in the duties of the office without waiting for a commission.

I am, sir, your most obedient servant,
JOHN McLEAN.

To Mr. GEORGE DAVENPORT."

In the Fall, Mr. Davenport received his commission, but it was two or three years before he took the oath of office, as their were no officer to administer it.

In the Fall of 1826, Mr. Bostwick, Pr. agent of the "American Fur Company," arrived at Rock Island, and made an arrangement with him to become a member of that Company, purchased all his goods, trading posts, &c. Gave him the management of the trade from the mouth of the Iowa River up to Turkey River. Mr. Russel Farnam having charge of the trade below, and his main depot at "Fort Edwards." Mr. Rollette had charge of the trade above—his principal depot at "Prairie du Chien."

A few extracts from his daily record may give some idea of the "times:"

1826. Oct. 21. Thos Forsyth, Indian Agent, and Dr. Craig, left here on Capt. Culver's keel boat for St. Louis.

Oct. 30. Mr. Rollette's keel boat passed down. Mr. Ingraham on board.

" 31. Mr. Lamalease left here for Rock River to build trading house.

" " Lieut. Clarke arrived with keel boat loaded with corn for St. Peters.

Oct. 31. Brought mail. Sent mail by Lieut. Clarke for Prairie du Chien.

Nov. 1. Great fire across the river—all our hay stacks burnt.

" " Russel Farnam arrived in keel boat Oregon.

" " Mr. Burk, a Virginian, arrived, who had been lost sixteen days on Rock River.

Nov. 4. Mr. Farnam left for St. Louis.

" " Mr. Burk left for the mines—furnished him with a horse.

Nov. 5. Mr. Man's keel boat passed down from lead mines.

" " John K. Forsyth arrived from trading house on Rock River.

Nov. 6. Casnor, and my men, arrived with a canoe load of "coal" from Rock River.

Nov. 6. Keel boat "Oliver Perry" came in sight; put to, on account of the wind; arrived on the 7th.

Nov. 8. "Oliver Perry" passed up at 9 o'clock A. M.; two bark canoes arrived from the mines; laid by on account of the wind: Capt. Lowe on board.

Nov. 9. Keel boat Missouri arrived at ten o'clock, and departed at three.

Nov. 13. Boat arrived from Rock River.

Nov. 15. Winnebago Chief, Carimonne, arrived from Waupsipinica.

Nov. 20. Keel boat Missouri, Capt. Otis Reynolds, from the mines, loaded with lead, for Davenport & Co. Martin Smith, and two men, arrived, to establish a wood-yard at the mouth of Rock River.

In the Spring 1827, Mr. Davenport started on a visit to his native place in England, after an absence of twenty-three years. He remained here about a year—visited London, and all the principal cities. He returned in May, 1828, to Rock Island. During this year, the first settlements were made in this vicinity. Two families (Judge Pence and his son,) arrived on the 9th day of December, at Black Hawk's village, and moved into the Indian houses. One of them occupied Black Hawk's Lodge. Several more families came directly after, among whom were John Spencer, Jonah Case, Wm. Brasher, Kinah Wells, Joshua Vandruff, Archy Allen, Geo. Harland, Thos. Hubbard, and Jno. Danforth. On the 27th December, Mr. Davenport's daily record says: "Geo. Wells came down for provisions, he having settled on the Rapids. He makes the tenth settler in our neighborhood, and one preacher, Rev. John Kinney, who preached the first time on the Island 29th January, 1829." During the first year the settlers suffered very great hardships, and Mr. Davenport furnished many of them provisions and groceries, until they got their farms under cultivation, and raised a crop.

In the Spring of 1829, the Indians returned to their village, and found the whites occupying their houses and corn-fields. Mr. Davenport used all his influence with the Indians to induce them to remove to the West side of the Mississippi, and partly succeeded. Waupello removed his village to Muscatine Slough, and Keokuk, with part of the Sacs, removed to Iowa river; but Black Hawk, and the remainder of the Sacs, refused to go, claiming that they never had sold their lands.

In Mr. Davenport's record we find, August 5th: Steamboat Josephine, with two keel boats, arrived; purchased one thousand bushels of corn to pay the Fox Chiefs for their improvements. August 14. The Fox Chiefs refused to receive the corn, for fear of being blamed by the Sacs for selling their village.

The Indian Agent, and the commanding officer, used every argument to get Black Hawk to move West of the Mississippi, but without effect. In 1830, Mr. Davenport visited Washington City to see the President, (Gen. Jackson,) and Secretary of War, and recommended that the Government pay the Indians a few thousand dollars, (which they could well afford to do,) and that from his knowledge of their character, and customs, he felt satisfied that they would remove without any further trouble to the Government. This plan was not approved of by the President, who declared that they *should* move off.

In the Spring of 1831, the Indians again returned to their village, and shortly afterwards, Gen. Gaines, with four or five companies of Infantry, arrived. Gov. Reynolds also received a requisition for a number of companies of mounted volunteers, which were soon raised, and were on their way to Rock River, under command of Gen. Joseph Duncan. Shortly after, Gen. Gaines arrived. He notified Black Hawk to meet him in Council at the Agency, (which was half a mile from the Fort.) On the day appointed Black Hawk, and a large number of Warriors, arrived on the South side of the Island, and marched across to the Council Chamber. They were dressed in the full war costume, and most of them armed with bows and arrows, and war clubs, and what seemed singular, it was noticed that their bows were all bent, and ready for use.

Directly afterwards Gen. Gaines arrived with his Staff Officers and an Orderly, but had no guard. They entered the Council Room and arranged themselves at one end, while Black Hawk and his party occupied the other three sides and the center. Mr. Davenport noticed that they acted in very bold and defiant manner, and that the friendly Indians appeared to be much alarmed. He went to one of the officers and advised him to send the Orderly as quickly as possible to the Fort and have a strong guard sent up, which was done at once. The Council commenced by Gen. Gaines addressing them, and stating why he had come, and that they must move off or he would be compelled to use force. He made the enquiry, "who this Black Hawk was, that was giving the Government so much trouble?" This offended Black Hawk very much, and the Indians became very excited. They began to call across the room to one another, and seemed to try to increase the excitement of those on the outer side, by their yells and whooping; but fortunately the guard now came up, which fact, Mr. Davenport thought, was all that saved them from being attacked and massacred.

The first Black Hawk war now commenced, but was of short duration. When the large number of volunteers arrived in sight of the village, Black Hawk thought they were too strong to fight, and accordingly he moved to the west side of the river during the night. In the Spring of 1832 Black Hawk returned with his party, more hostile than ever. The inhabitants all flocked into the Fort with their families, for protection. Mr. Davenport fortified his house, built a stockade around it with bastions at two corners, in order to use a small swivel for protecting the sides, and had his men all well armed, and their places pointed out in case of an attack. He had been informed that the Black Hawk party had determined in council, that he and two others (Gen. Clark and the Indian Agent,) should be killed, as they had done so much to weaken their party. "Neapope" was appointed to carry out this threat; but Black Hawk having passed on up Rock River and the troop following him, the people here were not molested.

During the Black Hawk war Mr. Davenport received a commission from Gov. Reynolds, appointing him acting Quarter Master General, with the rank of Colonel. In the latter part of the Summer of 1832 the Cholera broke out among the troops on the Island, and raged fearfully for about ten days; one hundred died out of a population of four hundred; every person was dreadfully alarmed. An incident occured during this time which will show the state of feeling. Mr. Davenport, Mr. LeClaire, and a young Officer were standing together in front of the store one morning. The Officer had been giving them an account of the number of deaths, and new cases, when an Orderly came up to them with a message from Gen. Scott to Mr. LeClaire, requesting him to come down to the Fort as soon as possible. Mr. LeClaire looked at Mr. Davenport to know what excuse to make. Mr. Davenport, after a moment, replied to the Orderly to tell Gen. Scott that Mr. LeClaire could not come, as he was quite sick. The Officer and Orderly laughed heartily at Mr. Davenport and Mr. LeClaire being so much alarmed; but next morning the first news they received from the Fort, was, that these two men were dead.

At the time the cholera broke out at Fort Armstrong, there was two Fox Chiefs confined in the guard-house for killing the Menomonies at Prairie du Chien, and had been given up by their nation as the leaders, on the demand of our Government, and were awaiting their trial. Mr. Davenport interceded for them with the Commanding officer, to let them out of their prison, and give them the range of the Island, with a promise that they should be forthcoming when they were wanted. The Indians were released, and they pledged their word not to leave the Island until permitted to do so by the proper authorities. During all the time the fearful epidemic raged upon the Island, and every person was fleeing from it, that could get away, these two Chiefs remained on the Island, hunting and fishing, and when the sickness had subsided, they presented themselves at the Fort to await their trial, thus showing how binding a pledge of this kind was with this tribe of Indians. Mr. Davenport, for many years, was in the habit of crediting the Chiefs of the different villages for from fifty to sixty thousand dollars worth of goods annually, having nothing but their word pledged for the payment of them, which they always faithfully performed.

In 1833, Mr. Davenport built his late residence, and moved out of his "Old Cabin." In 1834, Rock Island county was organized, and John Spencer, John Vannatte, and Mr. Davenport, were elected the first County Commissioners of that county. The county seat was located, and the town of Stephenson laid out, (now the city of Rock Island,) and the lots sold at public sale. They established roads, and built bridges, in various parts of the county. They were re-elected several times, and their administration of the affairs of the county gave very general satisfaction to the people.

In the Fall of 1835, Mr. Davenport, Maj. Smith, Maj. Gordon, Mr. Hambaugh, Mr. McGregor, Mr. Colton, and Capt. May, purchased a claim of Mr. LeClaire (he retaining an eighth part,) upon which to lay out a town. The proprietors agreed to name it Davenport, in honor of their friend, Mr. Davenport. The town was surveyed and laid out by Major Gordon, assisted by Mr. Bennett, who were, at this time, engaged by Government to survey Mr. LeClaire's "Reserves."

In the Spring of 1836, Mr. Davenport sold the site upon which the famous "Rock Island City" was laid out, (near the mouth of Rock River,) retaining a quarter interest. In the Fall of that year, he, and some others, purchased an interest in Mr. LeClaire's Reserve at the head of the Rapids, upon which they laid out a town, which they named LeClaire, in honor of Mr. LeClaire; and about the same time he purchased an interest in the town of Port Byron, on the opposite side of the River, thus becoming interested in the rise and progress of all the towns in this vicinity.

In the Fall of 1837, Mr. Davenport accompanied Keokuk, Wapello, Poweshiek, Black Hawk, and about forty of the principal Chiefs and Braves of the Sac and Fox nation, to Washington City, and assisted Government, by his influence with the Indians, in making a very good purchase of a large portion of Iowa.

About this time, Mr. Davenport purchased an interest in Mr. LeClaire's Reserve, adjoining the town, upon which they laid out the first addition to the town of Davenport, of about twelve blocks, and the following season another addition was laid out by Mr. LeClaire, of which Mr. Davenport purchased one third interest.

In the Spring of 1838, Mr. Davenport and Mr. LeClaire bought a large stock of goods, and opened a store, under the firm of Davenport & LeClaire, on the corner of Front and Main streets; this was considered the largest store in the country for some time. Persons came a great distance to purchase their goods and provisions.

Mr. Davenport still continued the Indian trade at his store on Rock Island. The Indians came in from the Iowa, DesMoines, and Cedar Rivers, about every three months, for their supplies.

In 1838, Mr. Davenport received the following letter from one of the Proprietors of Davenport, who was sutler to the troops in Florida, which may be interesting to some of the readers of this work:

TAMPA BAY, *September* 3, 1858.

*Dear Sir:* I have no doubt you have long since concluded that a certain person, P. G. Hambaugh, is "*Co-ga-co;*" I did anticipate the pleasure of returning to your place ere this, but have been disappointed. I have no doubt but you know as much about the Florida war as I do; there will be another winter campaign, but whether on a large or small scale I am not able to say. Some gentleman in Havana has proposed furnishing "blood hounds" for the purpose of hunting down the Indians in the Hammocks, and his plan is looked upon by a majority of experienced officers as the most feasible one yet suggested. The Government will, I presume, condemn this mode of warfare, however, as being too inhuman to be practiced by a civilized nation, and it is too expensive to be undertaken by any individual.

I am told Davenport *goes ahead.* I wish to God I was there, with a few thousand dollars. What is the prospect of securing the town to the proprietors by pre-emption? I hope you and Mr. LeClaire will use every exertion to do so, and also to protect my interest while I am absent. I make this request because I shall undoubtedly (if I live,) return there, and make it my permanent residence; nothing keeps me in this infernal country but the prospect of making enough to place me in easy circumstances when I return, and another winter's campaign will do it, unless I meet with some unforseen misfortune. Write to me, and give me all the local news; tell me if Davenport is the "County Seat," and if it is to be the "Capital of Iowa;" tell me who the prominent men about Davenport are. What has become of Gordon?

Remember me to all my friends, and particularly to "Mosquakee."

Your friend,

P. G. HAMBAUGH."

In the fall of 1841, the Indian payments were made at the Agency on Des Moines River. The Indians from all the different villages gathered there to receive their annuities. Mr. Davenport, and most of the Indian traders, attended there, during the payment. Gov. Lucas, Superintendent of Indian Affairs in Iowa, made an attempt to make a treaty with the Sacs and Foxes to purchase all their lands within the State, but utterly failed. He had determined he would make a treaty with the Indians without the assistance of the Traders, and that they should have nothing to do with it. He was particularly opposed to the American Fur Company, (then Pr. Chouteauju & Co.) He ordered them to retire to their trading house, about a mile from the Agency, and posted a guard of dragoons at the house, to prevent any communication with the Indians. Among those that were placed under guard with Mr. Davenport, was Mr. LeClaire, as he was considered friendly with the Fur Company and the Indians. When he had assembled the Chiefs and Braves of the two tribes, he made them his proposition—to buy their country. The Chiefs replied, that they always consulted their old friends, whom they had known for many years, and had the greatest confidence in, and that they had understood their old Traders had been placed under guard, and not allowed to have any communication with them, they, therefore, declined making any treaty with him.

In 1842, Gov. Chambers made a treaty with the Sacs and Foxes. He took a different plan. He told the Chiefs to select any of their white friends they might choose, to assist them in making a treaty. They selected Mr. Davenport, Mr. LeClaire, Mr. Sanford, and Mr. Phelps. By this treaty the Indians sold all of their lands within the State of Iowa, and agreed to remove West of the Missouri River.

After this treaty, Mr. Davenport withdrew from the Fur Company, and gave up the Indian trade, being engaged in this business about twenty-three years, during which time he had made twenty trips to St. Louis with his keel boat. The shortest time in coming from St. Louis to Rock Island was eleven days, having a fair wind most of the time. The longest trip was forty days.

Mr. Davenport now devoted his time to the improvement of his property in Davenport and Rock Island. About this time he laid out an addition to the flourishing town of Moline.

Mr. Davenport was of a very free and generous disposition, very jovial, and very fond of company. He now, generally, spent the Winters in St. Louis or Washington City. If he traveled on a steamboat, or while at his hotel, he would always have a crowd around him, listening to his anecdotes and stories. He never sued any one in his life, and could not bear to see any one in distress without trying to relieve them. He enjoyed excellent health and spirits, and had the prospect of living many years to enjoy the comforts for which he had toiled so hard for many years, but he was struck down by the hand of one of a band of robbers, in his own home, on the fourth of July, 1845. He died aged sixty-two years.

The following lines were written by Dr. E. Keskup, who was present:

*    *    *    *    *    *    *    *    *

Hark! What that sound that makes the angler
Cast his rod aside. Hark! again; that cry,
'Tis murder!—the dreadful words are
Echoed back the woodland through, while
Consternation wild is graven deeply in the lines of every face;
The heart, first check'd, now leaps with tumultuous throe, and the warm blood,
That was wont to run its circuit mildly through, clogs the swollen vein.
'Twas a sad scene. Upon his dying bed, abused, despoil'd, lay one
Whom we (so long had he sojourned on that fair isle,) had look'd upon as portion of the spot;
His long fair hair dishevel'd by the brutal hand.
His life was ebbing fast, as flow'd the gushing heart's blood from his wound,
How chang'd the scene, that in the morn
Was joy and gladness; pity and despair or schemes of dark revenge,
Were trac'd upon each varying face,
And then with heavy heart the throng wound slow their homeward way.
The voice of love was still, and all was mute
And sad, and silent, as the grave.

In concluding the life of Col. Davenport, it may be well to add a few lines regarding his life apart from the mere incidents in which he was involved.

His life, as has been seen, was a long and active one—the position he occupied required anything but a human drone to fill it—and his whole career, from beginning to close, was replete with ceaseless activity. Although of trans-atlantic extraction, he was the true type of the American—possessing indomitable resolution, a restless desire to progress, with an invincible determination to overcome obstacles, and achieve success. Added to these qualities, was an eminent ability to read human nature, to resolve its problems, and array the prejudices, motives, hostilities, or what not, of all about him, in a manner that finally best aided his own undertakings. Especially was this last circumstance prominent in all his dealings with the Red Man. He read them as *men*, approached them as such, and by this humane and judicious procedure, received in almost all cases from them such treatment as *men* extend to each other. He was worthy of all honor for the love borne him by the savage—it is an evidence that, like the philanthropic and immortal PENN, he rose above the vulgar and inhuman prejudices of the age, and found in the Indian, if not a brother, at least a conscientious being, who could be driven to deeds of revenge and carnage by ill-treatment, or could be made a firm, reliable, honorable friend, by treating him as a MAN.

Much as Mr. Davenport's courage, perseverance, enterprise, and ability, demand admiration, there is still something more than these commanding our respect and honor—something which is more lustrous than wealth, better than position or title—it was his HUMANITY! Had men of his bias dealt with Black Hawk, and his "British Band," less gory scalp locks would have decked the belts of warring savages—less blood have been shed, and the entire fearful drama of devastation, slaughter, and carnage, which was enacted upon our frontiers a few years since, would have been wholly omitted.

Honor to his ashes —he sleeps in a grave whose proud epitaph reads—

HERE LIES A FRIEND TO HUMANITY!

Antoine Le Claire

# CHAPTER XIV.

## ANTOINE LeCLAIRE.

Antoine LeClaire was born December 15, 1797, at St. Joseph, Michigan. His father was a Canadian Frenchman, his mother the grand daughter of a Pottowottomie Chief. At this time the territory of the North-west, out of which half a dozen mighty States have been formed, was peopled almost solely by the red man, with here and there one of a different race, fearless enough to brave the perils of a frontier life, among the dusky denizens of the wilderness; the father of Antoine Le Claire was one of these.

In 1808, he established a trading post at Milwaukee, Wisconsin, exchanging manufactured articles for various kinds of furs. In 1809, he engaged more extensively in the business, in connection with John Kinsey, at Chicago, (Fort Dearborn then,) Illinois. In 1812, though surrounded with the Indian tribes with whom he was trading, and who, through the influence of British emissaries, were generally hostile to the United States, Mr. LeClaire espoused the American cause, engaged actively in the service—was in the contest at Peoria, where, with others, he was taken prisoner. The prisoners were confined at Alton, Illinois, but were released during the same year.

About this period, at the solicitation of Gov. Clarke, of Missouri, Antoine LeClaire entered the Government service, and was placed at school, that he might acquire a proper knowledge of the English language. In 1818, he acted as interpreter under Capt. Davenport, at Fort Armstrong; and the same year returned to Peoria, where, in 1820, he married the daughter of the Sac Chief, *Acoqua*, (the Kettle.) The same year he was sent to Arkansas, to watch the movements of the Indians in that locality. He was returned to Fort Armstrong in 1827, and was present as interpreter in 1832, when the treaty was made by which the United States purchased of the Sac and Fox tribes the territory West of the Mississippi River.

In consequence of cholera among the soldiers at Fort Armstrong, the treaty, which would otherwise have been held in the Fort, was transferred to the

Iowa shore opposite. Here the great Chief of the Sacs, Keokuk, made a reserve of a section of land, which he donated to Mr. LeClaire's wife, requiring, as an only condition, that Mr. LeClaire should build his house on the section, and on the spot then occupied by the marquee of Gen. Scott in making the treaty; which condition he afterwards filled to the letter. The Sacs and Foxes also gave him another section at the head of the Rapids, where LeClaire now stands. The Pottowottomies, in the treaty of Prairie du Chien, reserved two sections on the Illinois side, which they presented to Mr. LeClaire. The flourishing town of Moline is situated on this reserve.

The treaty was ratified by Congress the following Winter. In the Spring of 1833, Mr. LeClaire erected a small building, or "shanty," in the then Fox village, "Morgan," which had occupied this ground for years previous. Of the tribe having this as their head-quarters, *Maquopom* was the head warrior, and *Poweshiek* head chief. In the fall of 1834, the Sac and Fox Indians left here for the Cedar River.

In 1833, Mr. LeClaire was appointed Post Master at Davenport, and also Justice of the Peace, to settle all matters of difference between the whites and Indians. His jurisdiction extended over all the territory purchased of the Sacs and Foxes West of the Mississippi, from Dubuque, on the North, to Burlington on the South. The population of Burlington was, at this time, about two hundred, that of Dubuque about two hundred and fifty.

Mr. LeClaire is an accomplished Linguist—speaking some twelve or fourteen Indian dialects, as well as French and English, and was present as Interpreter, among other treaties, at that with the Great and Little Osages at St. Louis, 1825, with the Kansas at St. Louis, 1825, with the Chippewas at Prairie du Chien in 1829, with the Winnebagoes at the same place, in August, same year; at the same place in 1826, with Sacs and Foxes, same place with Winnebagoes in 1832, at Fort Armstrong, held on Iowa side, with Sacs and Foxes at Davenport, with Sacs and Foxes in 1836, at Washington, with same tribes in 1837, with same tribes at Sac and Fox Agency in Iowa Territory in 1842.

Mr. LeClaire was one of the proprietors of the town of Davenport, and is still one of its active business men. He is possessed of great wealth; has improved the city by a liberal expenditure of a large income, in erecting Churches, and other public buildings, at his immediate expense. The fine Church of St. Margaret—whose spire reaches from the lofty bluff till it would almost seem to touch the quiet Stars, or to mingle with the cloudy glories of a Summer's day—was built and furnished by the munificence of Mr. LeClaire. Every where over the fair city of Davenport are scattered improvements, each of which elegantly and appropriately memorializes his generosity.

His progress from the small white house, on the depot grounds, to the palatial brick mansion on the bluffs—his physical increase from the small frame of thirty years ago, to the portly embodiment of Mr. LeClaire of to-day, present a fine type, both of his increase in wealth, and the growth of the city, which he mainly founded. It is to be regretted that a history of his life, embracing its lesser details, could not have been obtained—as his whole course has been replete with stirring incident, and romantic adventure. His name, however, will not soon be forgotten—it is inscribed in the national archives, is perpetuated in a thousand forms—in spire and altar, in wall and street—in the city of his adoption, while still more enduringly than all these memorials of parchment, wood-work, and masonry, it is written upon the hearts of all who know him, the fact that he is a—PHILANTHROPIST and CHRISTIAN.

---

CORRECTION.—Mrs. LeClaire was the *grand-daughter* of Acoqua. Her father was Antoine LePage, a Canadian. (The above was not received in time to be put in its proper place.)

Geo. L. Davenport

## CHAPTER XV.

# GEO. L. DAVENPORT, ESQ.

George L. Davenport was born on Rock Island, in the Fall of 1817, and is the eldest son of Col. Geo. Davenport, and was the first white child born in this section of the country. For eight or nine years he had few playmates, but the Indian boys; he, therefore, learned to talk their language about as soon as he did the English. In 1827, he was sent to Cincinnati, and went to school one year, and then returned to the Island, and was placed in the store of the American Fur Company, where he remained until this trading post was given up, upon the removal of the Indians, in 1837, to the DesMoines River. He was, at any early age, adopted into the Fox tribe, and was called after the nation, "Mosquake," and was always a great favorite with them. He made, frequently, trips into the Indian country, with goods for the different trading posts, and attended all the Indian payments on the DesMoines River. In 1832, he made the first "claim" West of the Mississippi, and in the Fall of 1837, he accompanied the Sac and Fox delegation of Chiefs to Washington City, and also visited other large cities. On his return, he lived upon his claim, in order to secure a pre-emption. In 1838, he was in the store of Davenport & LeClaire. In 1839 he married, and commenced business for himself, and continued to attend to business very closely for sixteen years. In 1850, he, in connection with Mr. LeClaire, built the first Foundry and Machine shops in this city. They built the first steam engine, and made the first castings in this city. He continued in this business five years, when he sold out, and retired from business.

Mr. Davenport has done much toward the improvement of the city—has built a fine block, is liberal in his encouragement of enterprise, and in diffusing judiciously his ample fortune. To him, as well as Mr. LeClaire, are confided the reminiscences of pioneer life in this country, and but few lovers of the deeds and things connected with the past, have ever visited this country without being indebted to him for many courtesies, and valuable information. He is still in the prime of life, "straight as an arrow," and has before him many years of usefulness and enjoyment.

J. Mackintosh

# CHAPTER XVI.

## JAMES MACKINTOSH, ESQ.

The subject of this memoir is a native of Dundee, Scotland. His name ("Son of the First,") denotes his origin from one of the oldest, and one of the most powerful Highland Clans, whose blood has been shed for Scotland in every battle field, from the invasion of the Romans to the battle of Culloden. Almost destroyed in their efforts for the restoration of the Stuarts, in 1715, they composed a large portion of the invading army in England, and were the last to abandon the cause—fighting the last battle.

In 1745, the *Slogan* again sounded, and one thousand warriors raised their banner for Stuart; they conquered in every field, until a difference of opinion amongst the leaders led to a retreat from England, and the defeat of Culloden followed, but had all fought with the devoted bravery of *Clan Chatten*, and had their allies proved true, Cumberland could not have laid waste their country for fifty miles around, sparing neither age nor sex.

John Mackintosh, the Grandfather of Mr. Mackintosh, being in possession of a portion of the family estates, of course was in arms, and was severely wounded at Culloden. He escaped that night from a field where no quarter was given, from the horrors that followed—the burning of cottages, and slaughter helpless women and children. All was lost but honor, his estates being attainted as a follower of Stuart, the balance of his days were spent in obscurity and poverty.

The subject of this memoir remembers him well, and has often heard him describe the war of "45," and the charge of the Mackintosh division at Culloden, when Cumberland's ranks went down before them, from the centre of the line of battle, where they fought. They were victors—but not being supported by their left wing, defeat was the consequence. Five hundred of these warriors fell, as described by Campbell, in Lochiel's Warning:

"Shall Victor exult, or in death be laid low
With his back to the field, and his face to the foe,
Leaving in battle, no blot on his name,
Look proudly to Heaven, from the death bed of fame."

In the language of Ex-Governor Mackintosh, of Georgia, the legal feudal head of the race—"*we are weak and broken now, we are not what we once have been.*" The old veteran bore the mark of a sabre cut on his face, received in boarding an English vessel in the war of 1812, when a Lieutenant in the American Navy. The tear was in his eye as he spoke; before his vision passed the heroic deeds of his Ancestors, the war of 1715, when his great grandfather commanded, his death in exile, his grandfather, with the remains of his men, emigrating to Georgia, his brave defence of the Georgian frontiers against Spain, the breaking out of the Revolution, when his father, (General Laughlin Mackintosh,) and uncle, equipped a body of troops, and took the field for the Colonies; and well did they pay their oppressors for the wrongs they had done them. He thought of his brother, who fell leading the charge at Molina de la Rey, of the mountains and valleys of the Highlands. He heard the *Slogan of Clan Chattan*, when thousands of warriors would answer the call, and well might the old veteran exclaim, "we are not what we once have been," but the glory and fame of the Sons of the First will live forever.

When about eight years of age, the subject of this memoir lost his grandfather, the soldier of Culloden, and soon after, his mother, which, in some measure, broke up the family. It was then decided to emigrate to America, and his father, a carpenter, by unremitting industry for a number of years, accumulated enough for that purpose. His son James doing his part during this period, laboring in a flax factory from twelve to fifteen hours per day for five years, to attain the desired object. They arrived in Montreal in September, 1817. In the Spring following, Mr. Mackintosh selected the trade of a book-seller and book-binder, which was the first opportunity he had of acquiring an education. He had labored from early boyhood, having little time for study, in order to come to the United States, which had always been his great object. He traveled some years in the middle and Southern States. Came West in 1828, and carried on a book-bindery in Cincinnati in 1830, '31, but finding it unprofitable, sold out—went to Indianapolis, and bound the Code of Indiana for 1831. Romantic and adventurous, he then attached himself to the Oregon Expedition, then organizing in Boston, and, with Hall J. Kelly, and Captain Brown, formerly of the Greek service, endeavored to raise a company in Cincinnati to settle on the Columbia River. At one time there were nearly two thousand men ready to sail for Oregon, but it was thought necessary to introduce a bill in Congress for some encouragement and protection. This led to an inquiry as to what position the United States occupied with Great Britain regarding Oregon, which proved that neither power, by their treaty, could colonize, or take possession, without each giving to the other one year's notice. This was discouraging to the Expedition. A portion of it, however, went from Boston, taking the land route by St. Louis, under Captain Wythe, but were unfortunate, having some fighting on the route, but a portion got through; many, however, turned back. The same Spring, Mr. Mackintosh went to New Orleans, intending to go round Cape Horn, but finding no opportunity, returned to Louisville, Kentucky. Still exerting himself in the cause—having no other means of support, but what he earned at his trade; and there was not then, as there is now, such a desire to emigrate West.

In the Spring of 1833, H. J. Kelly came West, the remains of the original Expedition having sailed from New York, and again the enterprise bid fair to succeed; Mr. Mackintosh went to New Orleans. The Company had passports from Gen. Jackson, President of the U. S., and letters to Santa Anna, President of Mexico, requesting that power to give such friendly aid as either nation, by their treaty, would accord to the other, in passing through that territory. The route was by Vera Cruz, and the City of Mexico, to Accapulco, where vessels were to convey them to Oregon. So far, all had gone well, but a scheme had been laid by a portion of the men to seize the Indian goods belonging to the Company, and go to Texas, which they attempted to carry out. This led to their arrest, and confinement in the calaboose. Vexatious law suits followed, which totally broke up the Expedition. H. J. Kelly went alone through Mexico to Oregon. Mr. Mackintosh having spent his last dollar in the cause, was, for the second time, left in the midst of cholera and yellow fever. He next worked for means to move West, to St. Louis, to join the hunters, and in that way yet meet Kelly in Oregon, but it was too late. The last party had gone. Then, with two of the Company that remained with him, he crossed, on foot, the States of Illinois and Indiana, to the Ohio River. After being some months in Cincinnati, and anxious to raise means to reach Oregon, he went to Nashville, where he was profitably employed for several years. When he was traveling through Illinois and Indiana in 1833, he saw some of the volunteers from the Black Hawk War, and began to turn his attention to that region, determining to locate on the frontiers somewhere. He left Nashville in the Fall of '35, and after spending some months in St. Louis, started on horseback to examine the country. At that day, and at that time of the year, this was a trip of some interest. He traveled in company with two others as far as Warsaw, Illinois. There was nothing on the journey of particular interest; but at this point the journey had to be prosecuted alone. The promised land was in sight, but it seemed like parting with civilization. He crossed the Mississippi in the night to Keokuk, carrying his saddle and portmanteau on his back, and leaving his horse on an Island, which was brought over by some Canadians in the course of the night. On entering the only building there, a curious sight presented itself. A ball was going on, of an assemblage of half breeds, French traders, Indians, Americans, &c. There was

not much chance to rest here, besides running considerable risk of losing what he had. Having, when coming through Illinois, met with Lieutenant Lee, of Fort Armstrong, who had been with the party surveying the boundary line of the Territory, he received a description of the route to Rock Island, and letters of introduction to the officers of Fort DesMoines and Fort Armstrong. Our traveler, after spending the night with this motley party, proceeded to Fort DesMoines, now Montrose, then occupied by several companies of Dragoons, and presented his letters; was introduced to a son of Black Hawk, and his sister. The young Chief had lately received a fine sword from the officers, and was very proud of it. Both he and his sister were good looking, and dressed in good taste. He then proceeded with Col. Knapp to Fort Madison, and some time after dark, stopped a short time with Black Hawk's band of Indians, who were preparing to make sugar, and reached Fort Madison about midnight. The only house there was the Colonel's, the proprietor of the town. On coming to Skunk River, it was thought impossible to cross, but our traveler was persevering, and so he attempted it. He crossed on foot, the ice cracking under his feet, with his saddle and saddle bags on his back. His horse followed, breaking the ice before him; and he arrived at Burlington that evening. Here a town was commenced, and there were eight or ten houses. Next morning, he had to swim Flint Hill Creek, through the floating ice, as there were no ferries or bridges. He stopped that night near the Iowa River, and spent some time next morning in Black Hawk's village, where Wapello now is. He visited the old Chief's tent; the Indians were out on a hunt. He crossed the Iowa River at some risk—stopped that night at Thornton, but found no food for man or beast, and left at day-break next morning for the trading house, now Muscatine. Some miles below, a family were encamped, and they having plenty of corn, the traveler's horse was fed, and the saddle-bags filled in case of need. The family were faring sumptuously on honey, from a bee tree they had cut. An invitation was given, and gladly accepted. That was an interesting group, sitting around the stump of that tree, with chips for plates, and nothing but honey for breakfast. The next station was the trading house, and our traveler, who intended reaching Pine Creek that night, unfortunately took the wrong trail, and found himself on Cedar River, near Poweshiek village. The weather turned suddenly cold, and being wet, having waded a creek full of floating ice, the only hope left was to get to the village. But that proved impossible. The river was open, and being unacquainted with the ford, to attempt it would have been madness, and to go back was equally difficult, as the creek was to cross, the bottom wide, and the trail two feet deep in water. There was no alternative but to camp, without fire or food. Matches were not common in those days—the fire-works had been lost, and the grass was too wet to strike fire with the pistol. He made a bed of leaves and grass, wound himself in his blanket, and lay down at the foot of a stump, to which he tied his horse, who fared the best, as his supper was in the saddle bags. That was a night to "try men's souls"—the howling of the storm, and the still louder howling of the wolves, made the night terrific. Sleep was out of the question.

It froze hard enough by morning to cross the creek, or the river. He arrived at the trading house by noon, nothing the worse of his cold lodging, with a good appetite for dinner, having eaten nothing but the honey for three days and two nights. Resting there that night, he proceeded next day to Pine Creek, where the accommodation was good for that period, and the next day he arrived at Frank's Claim, below Rockingham, which he purchased. Starting next morning before breakfast, he came in sight of Fort Armstrong. At sunrise, the flag went up, the morning gun fired, and the drums beat; the air was cold and bracing, and the beautiful panoramic view that opened on the traveler's sight, was exciting. He had traveled in various climes, and seen many fair lands, but never had been so enraptured as on that morning; although in mid winter, it never looked so well as then. He exclaimed—"this is the place I have looked for, here I will set my stake!" He partook of an excellent breakfast with Antoine LeClaire, who accompanied him over to the Fort, and introduced him to Keokuk, and other Indian Chiefs, who all gave him a warm invitation to their village. But time pressed, and there was still a lonesome journey to perform to Michigan, and after spending a week or two with his brother, and making arrangements for both to locate at Davenport, he returned to his future home. Business calling him to Nashville, the favorite horse that had so nobly carried him through so many scenes, was sold to Mr. LeClaire.

He returned in September, and in October brought on a general stock of goods, amounting to some five thousand dollars, and done a fair business during the following winter. Provisions were scarce, and he made several trips to Illinois to obtain a supply. On one occasion, it nearly cost him his life. In crossing a fifteen mile prairie, one of those sudden changes took place which often occur in this climate, in which several persons were frozen to death in different parts of the country, and some lost hands and feet. He came through with hands and face badly frozen, and was incapable of doing much business the balance of the winter. The following year the great financial crisis was severely felt here, and but little business could be done. He was actively engaged in every enterprise beneficial to the town. That Summer he had the first road surveyed, and a furrow plowhed twenty-six miles on the road to Dubuque, at his own expense; laying out one night in the prairie, in a storm of thunder and rain, the horses got away, and he was obliged to pack the saddles; the nearest grove being then unsettled, was called Saddle Grove, now Long Grove. The county seat question being the all absorbing topic of the day at this time, took a large portion of his time. He was the most active of the Davenport party, until that contest was decided in 1840.

The first purchase from the Sacs and Foxes was forty miles wide, from Rock

Island. The second was made in the Fall of '37, and was twenty-six miles wide, running due West from the forty-mile post. In May, '38, General Street organized a party to examine the new purchase, and select a village site and agency for the Indians, West of the new boundary. The Sacs and Foxes were then at war with the Sioux. The party were composed of General Street, Indian Agent, George L. Davenport, Mr. Mackintosh, Louis Hebert, then an employee of the Government, H. Sturdevant, Indian Blacksmith, and W. Russel, Surveyor, and from thirty to forty Chiefs and Braves, commanded by Poweshiek, mounted on good horses, with a tent, and well armed with rifles, cutlasses, and pistols.

General Street rode in his carriage. The Indians that accompanied them from Davenport were dressed as whites, to deceive the Sioux. The party started on a bee line for the forty-mile post—encamped the first night at a small grove, south of Posten's Grove—pitched the tent—spanceled the horses, fared sumptuously on venison, and retired for the night; but their sleep was short. About midnight a storm of thunder and lightning disturbed their slumbers. The rain descended in torrents, the creek overflowed its banks, and the sleepers were roused from their watery bed. The wind had blown the tent from its fastenings, and was, for some time, held by Mackintosh and Davenport, lying on their backs in the water. The balance of that dark stormy night was spent exposed to the storm, with their blankets around them, until day dawned. After breakfast, they renewed their march, trusting to the sun to dry their clothes. All the streams were up, which they had to swim.

General Street's carriage was an incumbrance, but on one occasion helped him over the stream. It got fastened on the steep bank of the channel, the tongue resting on the opposite side, but the current was so rapid it could not stay there long. To enable the General to cross without falling in, Mr. Mackintosh and Hebert took, the water shoulder deep, each a carriage wheel, to hold against the current, and steady the steps of the timid General. Hebert, fond of a joke, several times whispered to his colleague to let go the wheel, that he might have the fun of seeing the General flounder in the stream; but he got safely over. However, Hebert had his laugh to his heart's content before night. There were more streams to swim that day, and it had to be done Indian fashion. It required considerable tact to get the provisions and arms over dry, and they frequently tied their clothes on their horses necks for that purpose. On several occasions, some of the party swimming on horseback, and the banks being steep, went over the horses heads, and had to swim down the rapid current before they could get out. On one occasion, after getting over the provisions, it was discovered that a bag of sugar was forgotten. All had crossed but Mr. Mackintosh, when Hebert proposed that he would wade into the deep water, and Mr. Mackintosh do the same, then pitch the bag to Hebert. In doing this, it did not occur, that in making the necessary effort, a reaction would follow. Hebert caught the sugar, but Mackintosh went into ten feet of water, head foremost. The current was rapid, the banks steep, and he had to swim some sixty rods before he got out. The yell of the Indians, and laugh of the whites, were general. They encamped that night at Rock Creek, and next day discovered the forty mile post. They reached Cedar River, where the General's carriage was left; the horses swam the river, and the men got over in a canoe. Then the Indians appeared in their war costume, as the white man's territory was behind—the Rubicon was crossed, and the language of "Rob Roy" came to mind—"Dinna mister or Campbell me, my foot is on my native heath, and my name is McGregor!" So felt the Indians after crossing their boundary. The surveys commenced. One of the chain carriers getting lame, it was necessary to get an Indian to take his place. The party were then entering the big woods. The Indians fearing an ambush, insisted on an advance guard, before consenting that one of their men should carry the chain. Messrs. Mackintosh and Davenport volunteered to fill the post, and the company went on in military order. They camped that night in heavy timber, the Indians carefully selecting the ground —a creek in a bend, of horse-shoe shape, high rocky banks on one side, and level ground, covered with logs and heavy standing timber, on the other. That night the Indians were unusually gloomy, and seemed to fear a surprise, and after supper, "Old Crow" told Mr. Davenport that he believed the Sioux were on their trail, that the fire must be put out, the tent struck, and they must lay on their arms all night. The fire was put out, but as four of the whites were asleep, it was thought best not to disturb them. Messrs. Mackintosh and Davenport stood guard till day-break. That night was one of interest; it was still, clear, and starry. The Indians were scattered behind logs, but could not be seen or heard. The two sentinels kept watch by the tent, going, occasionally, into the heavy timber, and attentively listening to discover an attempt at surprise, frequently being disturbed by the scream of some animal, that seemed more like an imitation than the natural sound.

Near day-break, the guard being fatigued, lay down at the opening of the tent, not intending to sleep, but were getting into a doze, when the yell of the Indians, and the firing of their rifles, aroused them. They thought that the Sioux were upon them; they were soon up, and ready for the combat, but lo, they were their friends. The night being past, the danger was over, and they commenced shouting their war song of victory.

The tents were struck, and the survey continued. At night, the Indians carefully selected the camp in the slough of the Iowa River, but their alarm still continued, and they feared the Sioux would attack their village. The General called a council of war, and through Mr. Davenport, as Interpreter, told them that the risks he had run, the exposure of his person, the undignified appearance he had often presented, when crossing the streams, leaving his comfortable quarters at Rock Island, were all for their benefit. But they were still gloomy, and fearful of the massacre of their women and children, and only four of them volunteered to remain. In the night, while fatigue overpowered the whites with sleep, they made canoes from the bark of the linn tree, and crossed the Iowa, and not a vestige of them remained at day-break, save the four volunteers.

A village site was selected that day, which was occupied by them until the next treaty, but not being satisfactory to the General, they turned their course northward, with the intention of going to Cedar Rapids, where a town of some importance has since sprung up. Through the course of the day, the reluctance of the Indians to proceed, proved they could not long be relied upon. Towards evening, they came in sight of a grove, and imagining they saw the smoke of a Sioux camp, refused to proceed. Mr. Mackintosh rode on in advance of the party, and found no cause for alarm, but there was evidence of a large party of Indians having encamped there lately. Buffalo and war trails radiated in every direction—Deer River was also in sight, where a battle had been fought the year previous. They encamped there that night, and the next morning found their volunteer Indians had gone, and for the first time the dragoon spancels had got loose from their horses, which occupied them an hour or two in finding.

The provisions were nearly out, and although some of the party desired to proceed a day or two longer, General Street ordered a return to the settlement, having only partially effected the object of the Expedition. On returning to Davenport, Mr. Mackintosh again took part in the election for county seat, having to proceed to Dubuque and Burlington, and again canvass the county. In 1840 he was one of the Commissioners appointed by act of the Legislature to lay out a road to Dubuque. During that year the most important matters that effected the welfare of the county were settled—the county seat question, the laying of roads, and the public lands coming into market; in all of which he took an active part. For years after this, financial affairs were still in a bad condition, he suffering like many others, after getting his farm in some degree of improvement. He was for some years Territorial and State Binder for Iowa, the first Public Binder for Minnesota, and established the first Book Bindery in Davenport. For the last four or five years his whole time has been occupied in developing his property.

He has expended more money in opening streets than all the proprietors put together. He has been over thirty years in the north-west and south-west, twenty-two years of which has been in Iowa and Minnesota. He is now fifty-four years of age, with robust health, and bids fair to enjoy his hard arnings to a period of life not far behind some of his ancestors. He is very social—fond of a good anecdote, which he tells or listens to with hearty good humour—is extremely liberal, and is one of Davenport's most valued citizens.

Eng^d & Print^d by Alf[illegible] N.Y.

## CHAPTER XVII.

# HON. G. C. R. MITCHELL.

Judge Mitchell was born December 3, 1803, at Dandridge, Jefferson county, East Tennessee. He was educated at East Tennessee College, (now "E. Tennessee University,") in Knoxville, Tennessee, and was a member of its first graduating class in the Fall of 1822. His parents having removed to Lawrence county, Alabama, he proceeded thither after graduating, and commenced studying law with Judge A. F. Hopkins, (now of Mobile,) and was admitted to practice in 1825. He practiced in Alabama until 1834, and spent a winter in a tour among Eastern cities, and in the Spring of 1835, came West, after visiting St. Louis, Chicago, Galena, and Dubuque.

Liking this portion of the country, and anticipating the results of its admirable location, he purchased a squatter's right—the tract of land upon which he at present resides. He erected a cabin, (which stood on Fifth street, just west of DeSoto street,) and resided in it until 1837, or two years. At that time, what now constitutes Iowa was attached to Michigan, and until Wisconsin was formed, there was neither law nor officers of any kind west of the Mississippi. For several years the principal professional business of lawyers in the territory was limited to litigation in regard to claim titles, or "Squatter's Rights." Judge Mitchell added to this species of practice, somewhat in the courts of Rock Island county, which were at that time organized.

In 1843, he was elected to the House of Representatives of the Iowa Territorial Legislature. He was nominated as Congressional Representative from the State, in 1846, but was defeated.

He was elected Mayor of Davenport in 1856, and in April, 1857, was nominated by a meeting of the Bar, and elected Judge of the Fourteenth Judicial District—composed of the counties of Scott, Clinton, and Jackson. He was elected to this office by a handsome majority, although the Republican party nominated and ran a party and opposition candidate, and had a large majority upon almost every other one of their ticket. He filled this office until the Fall of 1857, and then resigned, owing to ill health, and with a design of removing to a warmer climate.

Judge Mitchell was always a Whig, until that party dissolved, or became inducted with Free Soilism, and other of its modern characteristics; since then he has acted with the Democratic party in full faith in its nationality.

As a jurist, Judge Mitchell takes a high position—he is profoundly discriminative—a keen, careful analyst, and one whose deductions are always reliably correct. His mental processes are seemingly slow, but in reality rapid, for while others would dash to a conclusion (often the wrong one,) with an imperfect view of a few contiguous facts, he traverses the whole ground, omitting nothing, however seemingly trivial or great; and although he may be twice as long in evolving a question as another, he performs ten times the labor, and his conclusion is in the same proportion more worthy of credence. If he has one trait more prominent than another, it is his thorough *comprehensiveness*—his ability to include everything in his examination of a subject, and add to this a nice instinctive and cultivated perception of the character and weight of a fact, and one may see why he rarely goes wrong, or commits errors in conclusions.

In regard to his everyday life—that portion of a man's being which all are interested in knowing—we shall say much less than the excellence of the subject would admit. Wealthy, with cultivated literary taste, and a choice and ample library, he now enjoys life as only one surrounded by such circumstances can. Fresh, instructive, and engaging in his conversation, he takes a high rank as a social companion, and as one who can be instructive, amusing, and brilliant, without effort.

W. Barrows

# CHAPTER XVIII.

## WILLARD BARROWS, ESQ.

WILLARD BARROWS was born in Monson, Massachusetts, in 1806. At the age of ten yeras, his father removed, with his family, to New Braintree, where the subject of this notice spent most of his youthful days, enjoying the benefits of New England Common Schools, and, at the age of fifteen, was placed at the Worcester Academy. His mind, from his boyhood, seems to have been bent on travel and exploration. He loved to roam over the rocks and hills of his native land, and often, at an early age, accompanied an old mountain hunter in his night rambles after "coons," among the precipices and glens for which that county is noted. He left the paternal roof at the age of fifteen, and after spending some time in Pomfret and Thompson, in Connecticut, at school, he passed two years at Brimfield, at his Uncles, and, in 1827, located in Elizabeth Town, New Jersey. He was for many years a very acceptable teacher of youth in that place, and married there in 1832. His natural love of the "wild and beautiful" in nature, led him to select as his profession, for life, that of a surveyor and engineer. His first introduction to his profession was on a contract with the Government in 1835, to close up the public surveys of the Choctaw Indian Purchase in the cypress swamps and cane-brakes, on the Yazoo and Sunflower Rivers, in the State of Mississippi.

This expedition was full of danger, and interesting incident.

In the Winter of 1836 and '7, a sudden and unusual rise in the Mississippi cut him off from any communication with the world—his supplies grew short, and he was driven, with his party, to the severest hardships, and for many weeks they were forced to live upon short allowance. The whole country was covered with water, except the few ridges that appeared above the flood. The country was uninhabited. The larger game, by instinct, had fled the country, and for several weeks he, and his party, lived upon the fruit of the Persimmon tree, and the Oppossum. These animals being slow of locomotion, had only time to reach the higher ridges of land, and were easily taken, and then eaten, without bread or salt. Occasionally an owl or hawk was killed.

About the first of March, the water subsided, and the whole party, after many hardships and privations, reached a settlement upon the banks of the Mississippi, nearly opposite the mouth of the Arkansas River, and procuring canoes, descended the river to Vicksburg and Natchez. After making his report to the Surveyor General, at Jackson, in that State, he ascended the Mississippi to St. Louis, and hearing much of Wisconsin Territory, determined to visit the country, and then ascend the river to Galena, and return to New Jersey by way of Chicago and the Lakes. About the first of May, 1837, we find him on board the old Olive Branch Steamer, bound for Galena.

Here he first became acquainted with Col. George Davenport and D. C. Eldridge, citizens of this place. Much persuasion was used by these gentlemen to induce Mr. Barrows to stop at Davenport, and make it his home. He seems to have thought but little about it, until he found himself sailing along the shores of Scott county. "When," he says in a letter afterwards to a friend, in explanation of his object in settling in the far West,—"the beauty of the landscape, the richness of the soil, the salubrity of the climate, and, above all, the rich and rolling prairies, which seemed to me so easily cultivated, were inducements enough for me, or any one else to settle." Mr. Barrows landed at Davenport, and soon after, he, with Gen. Sargent, and two others, were mounted, and on a trip of exploration to the Cedar River, then but little known.

Mr. Barrows was so favorably struck with the beauty and prospects of the country, that he determined at once to remain for a season, and, accordingly, reported himself to the Surveyor General's office for the North West, then located at Cincinnati, and he was that Fall engaged upon the first surveys of Iowa. During that Winter he was upon the Wapsipinecon River, having left here in October, and did not return until the first of April, and lost but *three days*, during that winter, of actual labor, being in camp with nothing but a common canvas tent. "The succeeding winter," says Mr. Barrows, "was much the same in its mildness, and resembled the present winter here, (1857 and '8.")

The Indians, at this time, were his only neighbors and friends, always supplying his camp with plenty of venison, turkeys, geese and ducks, and maintaining the most friendly relations.

In the Spring of 1838, he returned to New Jersey, having been absent from his family for nearly two years, and returned with them in July of that year, and settled in Rockingham, five miles below Davenport. The most direct route at that time, from New York to the far West, was by way of the Pennsylvania canal to Pittsburgh, down the Ohio River, and up the Mississippi River to St. Louis, and thence to Rock Island. The time necessary for this trip, at that day, was four weeks.

In 1840, Mr. Barrows was engaged in the survey of the Islands of the Mississippi, from the mouth of Rock River to Quincy, Illinois.

In 1841 and '42 the public surveys being suspended, he turned his attention to farming, and being Justice of the Peace, Post Master, and Notary Public, at Rockingham, his time was occupied in discharging these duties until the Spring of 1843, when he was sent into the country lying north of the Wisconsin River, called the Kickapoo Country, to perform the surveys of that rough, broken, 'uninhabited land, where he spent most of that season,

It was, while engaged upon this work, that his depot of provisions was plundered by some straggling bands of the Winnebago Indians, and himself and party reduced almost to starvation. Mr. Barrows had left the camp in the Kickapoo River country for Prairie du Chien after provisions. Upon his return to the Kickapoo, with supplies, he found the whole country laid waste by a Tornado. The country through which he had to pass to his camp, some seventy miles, was heavily timbered, and the effects of the storm were almost utter destruction for miles in extent—the forest was torn up by its roots, trees of immense sise were twisted and hurled in every imaginable shape, and piled up in unlimited confusion. The occasion was one demanding prompt, vigorous action—and Mr. Barrows found himself equal to it. He first made the attempt to follow his old trail, and cut his way through, with the help only of a few Indians, who love anything better than work, but, after two days of hard labor, gave it up, having made only two and a half miles. His next, and only chance of reaching his men, who were fastened in by the tornado, and whom he knew to be in a starving condition, was to ascend the Kickapoo, with Indians, in canoes, until he should reach a point opposite his camp, and beyond the tornado, when he could pack out supplies through the wilderness, and reach his camp in time to save his men, if no serious obstacles opposed. The Indians took up the provisions, and Mr. Barrows went up by land, with one pack-horse only. The provisions were landed, the Indians discharged, and Mr. Barrows left alone upon the banks of the stream, just as the sun was setting. That night he carried his provisions about half a mile, into the forest, and *cached* them as well as he could, and early the next morning set out with a small bag of flour, and a little pork, on his pack-horse, upon his unknown and perilous journey, to reach his starving camp, full of intense anxiety as to the fate of his mission, and those whom he desired to save. Any one who has ever visited this portion of Wisconsin, can well imagine the difficulties to be overcome. It is the country formerly owned by the Winnebago Indians, and purchased from them by Gov. Dodge in 1834—and very correctly named the "Sugar Loaves of Wisconsin." It is almost impassable for man or beast—abounding in steep precipices, high and inaccessible points of rocks, deep ravines, and impenetrable thickets. It was through this country that the celebrated Chief, Black Hawk, led his trusty followers, after his defeat at Dixon, on Rock River, and Buffalo Grove, while on his way to Bad Axe, where he was captured. And it was among these very hills and dells, that Col. Atchison, in pursuit of Black Hawk, got entangled, and abandoned his wagons, baggage, &c., with the loss of many of his horses. No man, with pack-horses, can cut his way over five or ten miles per day. Without any trail, or even maps of the country to guide him, Mr. Barrows persevered, alone, with only his faithful horse, to accompany him, with indomitable courage and perseverance, swimming the streams that opposed his course, and resting only when darkness compelled him. On the fourth day, to his great joy, and surprise, he struck an old outward bound trail, made by himself and men, in his first entrance into the country. It was near dark, and his camp-fire was kindled, his solitary meal was eaten, and in blanket, alone in the dense wilderness, he slept again till daylight, when he was upon the trail, familiar to him, that led to the camp. He had gone but a few hundred yards among the deep glens, when, on turning an abrupt bluff, he came suddenly upon one of his men, who informed him that another of the party was a short distance behind in a starving condition, and too weak to proceed; that others of the party were left at the camp, two days previous, in dispair of receiving any help, as they supposed him murdered by the Indians, and that they had been unable to kill game of any kind, except one small pheasant; that they had eaten the two bear dogs, and boiled up the bones with nettles for soup, and that they had had nothing for six days, but such wild berries as they could chance to find. They said they had boiled coffee, of which they had plenty, and drunk quite freely at first, but its effects upon them were very unpleasant, and at times even distressing, and that they had abandoned it. They were not long in reaching the companion of the first man, to whom he soon gave, in small portions, some food, and hastened forward to the camp; here he found the rest of his men, in a pitiable condition of emaciation, and with looks of wildness and despair that was distressing to witness. They had settled down into the belief that he was either dead or hopelessly lost. They had awaited in confidence too long, without an effort to save themselves, by leaving the country, and, perhaps, not having confidence in themselves sufficient to find their way out of the wilderness.

"The camp presented a scene," says Mr. Barrows, "that I could not look upon without tears. Upon a log were stretched the skins of our bear dogs, while their bones were bleaching around the camp. Some harness had been cut up, and roasted, to eat, and many extremes resorted to to relieve them from utter destruction. The next morning we commenced our slow march back to the depot of provisions, which I had made upon the Kickapoo River. The scanty supply that I had taken with me, was now being exhausted with fearful rapidity, and we hastened our march, to reach the depot, that we might once more be fed with plenty. But what was our surprise and consternation, when we reached it, to find it plundered of its precious contents, and all carried away! Our misfortunes seemed still to hang over us, and we felt that our sufferings were not at an end. Our only chance of escape now was, to ascend the Kickapoo some twenty miles further, to a ford, the place where Black Hawk crossed in his flight to Bad Axe, where his last battle was fought. This we accomplished, and then struck across the prairie country towards Prairie du Chien. On the third day we reached a settlement, where we remained a week to recruit. There were remnants of the Winnebago tribe of Indians encamped near this place. We informed them of our loss, and instituted search through the entire camp, but found nothing. The chief of this band told us, that some Root River Indians had been on a hunt in that neighborhood, and had gone to Prairie du Chien. I pursued them, but on my arrival there, found they had left for Root River. Many articles of our clothing, that had been plundered from the depot, were found in the liquor-shops of Prairie du Chien, which had been sold by this strolling band of Indians. Our pack-horses, that strayed away at the time of the hurricane, were found some four weeks afterward, and brought into camp. Thus, by their absence, our party were compelled to eat dog instead of horse flesh!"

Up to this date, nothing definite was known of the Territory lying between the waters of the Mississippi and Missouri. The title to the lands bordering upon the Mississippi were being extinguished slowly, and in small parcels. The Winnebagoes occupied a strip running from the Mississippi River, at Prairie du Chien, to the Des Moines River, forty miles in width, called "Neutral Grounds." The Pottowattomies had removed from Rock River, Illinois, to the Western side of this State, bordering on the Missouri. But few, if any but Indians, had ever crossed this Territory to the Missouri. Trappers and hunters told many highly colored tales of the beauty of the country, of its glassy lakes, with pebled shores, the abode of vast herds of buffalo, elk, and deer; of feathered game, and of the finney tribe. The spirit of enterprise, the love of research, and of Nature's grand solitude, again prompted Mr. Barrows to shoulder his rifle and start upon the trail of the red man. He wrote to Gov. Lucas, the Secretary of State, the Surveyor General, and others, proposing to explore the country lying between the two rivers, sketch its topography, and project a map of all the country lying between these rivers, as far North as the forty-third parallel. This was accomplished in three successive years. On his first tour he experienced many hinderances and difficulties from the Winnebago Indians. He had ascended the Wabisipinica River to the boundary line of the Neutral Grounds, early in September; built him a cabin for a winter depot, but could get no communication with the Chief of that nation, until the return of the Indians from their annual payment at Prairie du Chien, which was not until the first of November.

The Chief's village was some five miles from his cabin. Mr. Barrows had furnished himself with a native youth from the Mission School at Fort Atkinson for interpreter. The arrival of the Chief, Chos-chun-ca, (Big Wave,) was at last announced, Mr. Barrows invitation presented in due form for the Chief to visit him in his cabin, which was not upon his grounds. At the time appointed, the Chief made his appearance, with some twelve of his warriors.

"He was clothed," says Mr. Barrows, "in a buffalo over-coat, a stove-pipe *hat*, and a pair of *green spectacles*. These had recently been presented by some officers and friends at the Fort. I exhibited my passport from Gov. Chambers, and told him I wished to go across his country, to make a picture of it, to show his great father, the President.

After hearing me, and examining, with much minuteness, my maps and sketches, some of which he corrected, he refused, with much earnestness, my passage into his country for any such purpose. He said that he very well knew the object his great father had in sending me there, and that he had no great respect for the "Big Captain at Washington," if he took such a course to find out the value of his land—that if I found it good and pleasant for the white man to live upon, it would be well, and his father would purchase it, but if I found it bad, he would give him but little money for it, and, therefore, I should not go."

After many entreaties and presents, Mr. Barrows found it of no use, and, leaving part of his men at the depot, he set out, with but one man, across the country, to Fort Atkinson, one hundred and twenty-five miles, on Turkey River, without any map or trail, and with full expectation of being overtaken by the Indians, and brought back. But on the first day out, a dense fog covered the prairie, and it rained in torrents for twenty-four hours, overflowing the banks of all the streams, which made it necessary to swim it themselves and horses. On the second day, near night, they came back to the first night's camp, in a small grove, having been lost in the fog and rain the whole time, and traveling at good rates. It cleared up after a snow storm, and he reached the Fort on the fifth day. The Rev. Mr. Lowry, who had charge of the Mission School, at that place, gave him a passport across the country, and wrote a letter to the Chief, which, being interpreted to him, he was allowed to proceed. Not, however, until he had made him presents of corn, pipes and tobacco.

"Barrows' New Map of Iowa, with Notes," was published in 1854, by Doolittle & Munson, Cincinnati; and was a work, at that day, of much importance. The Legislature ordered copies for each member, and for the officers of State. Many works since written on Iowa have been largely indebted to this valuable little work. It is brief, yet comprehensive, in its character, easy and vigorous, and was the cause of satisfying a wide-spread enquiry East in regard to the character and resources of Iowa.

From 1845 to '50, Mr. Barrows was engaged most of the time in the surveys of the Government, and those of the County which he had charge of for many years as County Surveyor, often making excursions into the newly settled portions of the State, examining the most prominent points of location, in many of which he has made, we believe, some very important investments. His knowledge of Iowa, as a State, is probably as extensive and correct as that of any man who ever traveled over it, and his judgment upon Real Estate investment has been of the most judicious and satisfactory character, not only to himself, but to those for whom he has operated as an agent. His present business is that of a Land Agent, and a partner in the house of Barrows & Millard of Sioux City, Iowa, and Barrows, Millard & Co., Omaha City, N. T. In the Spring of 1850, business of all kinds being dull in the West, he seized upon the opportunity to gratify his long and ardent desire to visit the plains, the Rocky Mountains, and the shores of the Pacific.

This was a project of long standing in his mind, and he entered upon it with much earnestness and vigor. Being fully equipped for such an expedition, he crossed the State of Iowa early in March, and left the Missouri River opposite Council Bluffs, in company with a California train, on the 23d of April, following the north fork of Platte River, through the present territory of Nebraska, to Fort Laramie, through the Black Hills, and thence up the Sweet-water River to the South Pass of the Rocky Mountains.

His outfit consisted of a light two-horse wagon, with five horses, and two men.

The year 1850, was one long to be remembered by those who passed over the route to California. The season was cold and backward, grass did not grow sufficient for forage until May, and for some two weeks of the early part of the journey, the animals were fed upon dry grass chopped, and rolled in wheat flour, and browsed upon shrubs and trees cut for that purpose. This misfortune, at the beginning, so reduced Mr. Barrows' horses, as well as others, that one after another of his team gave out, and either died, or was left by the way.

He left his wagon on the Humbolt, making pack-saddles for the horses that were left; and abandoning every thing but a few clothes, and his surveying instruments, he, with his men, traveled on foot upwards of four hundred miles before reaching the base of the Nevada Mountains, at which place he was left with only one horse to pass the mountains with, and which died soon after reaching California, where he arrived the 15th of July. One of his men died soon after his arrival.

A very interesting account of this trip was given by Mr. Barrows in a series of letters from California, published in the Democratic *Banner* of this city, at that time, describing, in most vivid colors, the difficulties and dangers, trials and hardships, of a journey to the Pacific. His description of the South Pass, in the mountains, so long looked upon as the great barrier to all communication with the Pacific by Railway, is the most graphic and satisfactory we ever remember to have read of this celebrated land-mark of the mountains. He details, in full, the face of the country in ascending the Platte and Sweet-Water Rivers, and at all the most prominent points, gives the latitude, longitude, and altitude, showing the feasibility of a Railroad thus far to the Pacific, which has since been fully endorsed by more scientific research. We cannot here refrain from giving a single extract from one of his letters:

"The South Pass," says Mr. Barrows, "is far different in its appearance to what I had imagined, from any description that I had ever seen. It is true, but little was known of it, and much less written. I had imagined some chasm, or deep cut in the mountains, through which we would be compelled to wind our way, or that I might, perhaps, find a pathway rent apart in the mountains by some great volcanic action, and thus we should find our perilous way through this wonderful Pass.

"But it is far different. It is a beautiful prairie country, even upon the summit level; and no one, with ordinary observation, can possibly mistake the spot, marked by Fremont as the highest point attained in the Pass.

"For days, the traveler, in his gradual assent, finds all the streams running back towards the Atlantic, and as he follows up the last rivulet to the summit, and passes over a level space of a quarter of a mile, all the little brooks and streamlets begin to run for the Pacific. Then you have passed the summit of the Rocky Mountains! I cannot describe my feelings, as I stood and gazed from the lofty eminence upon all that is good and noble in the works of Creation. A sense of solitude pervades the whole scene. Upon the right hand, away to the North, are the Wind River Mountains, with their tops covered with perpetual snow, and although some sixty miles distant, yet so clear and transparent is the atmosphere in this high altitude, we could even discern bodies of trees, and the drifted snow, as it hung over the rocky precipices. The antelope, or the mountain goat, can be seen feeding in quiet for miles distant, and the hunter is often deceived in his approach to animals of the chase. The purity of the atmosphere is such, that the traveler feels buoyed up with unusual vigor, and speeds his way with uncommon ease and rapidity. Before you lies the Great Basin, five hundred miles in extent, and as far as the eye can extend, nothing can be seen but a vast plane, sleeping amid the solitude and grandeur that has filled this desolate region since its creation.

"This Pass has derived its name, probably, from a depression of the mountain chain at this place, and is seen only when at a distance of a hundred miles. As the traveler approaches from such a distance, it has the appearance of a gap, or cut, but when in it, it is one vast space."

Mr. Barrows spent the Summer in California, traveling much of the time. As the rainy season approached, he left there for Central America, and thence to Cuba, where he spent some time, and returned to Iowa early in 1851.

From that time until the present, Mr. Barrows has resided in Davenport, busying himself in attending to his lands, Land Business, and in erecting a capacious and handsome residence. This last, is about half way up the bluffs, nearly opposite the Island, and overlooks a magnificent view of natural and architectural beauty. The house is ample, finely finished, and prejected upon a plan that marks its owner as a man of taste.

Mr. Barrows, we are happy to add, has secured, as the result of his active life, an ample fortune, which no one is better qualified than himself, by education, habit, and inclination, to enjoy.

His life has been a stirring and useful one; for, while ever laboring to secure a competence, he has at no time been unmindful of the claims o society upon each of its members, and has, therefore, at various times, given letters to the public, containing valuable scientific, and other information, while his work upon the map of Iowa has done more to disseminate a knowledge of our State than anything of the kind ever published.

In regard to his social character, Mr. Barrows takes a high rank. He possesses an illimitable fund of anecdote, pointed as to witticism, and valuable for their information; and he enjoys the sparkling *bon mot* of conversation with the fine relish of a Frenchman. His own portly form shaking with laughter over some reminiscence of the ludicrous, and a choice audience roaring with mirthfulness, is a common sight to all who have the pleasure of his acquaintance.

Liberal, charitable, a Christian, the possessor of a fortune, respected, enjoying the best of health, and with social relations, harmonious, and desirable, Mr. Barrows now rests after his eventful life, and it is the sincere wish of all who know him, that many years will yet be his portion, which may be as pleasant and happy as his early life has been laborious and active.

# CHAPTER XIX.

## CAPT. JAMES MAY.

James May was born on the 1st day of October, 1804, in Cape Girardeau county, Missouri. His father and mother went from Pittsburgh, Pennsylvania, in 1803, and, with some of their relatives, were among the "early settlers" of the now Great North West. The history of the family from the year 1798, when the Grand-father of the present James May was forced to leave Ireland, with his family, in consequence of his active participation in the cause of civil and religious liberty in his native country, with the incidents of their frontier lives in the North-west, and Texas, where some of them emigrated many years since, would make an interesting volume.

The father and family of Capt. May left St. Genevieve on a keel boat, bound for Pittsburgh, Pennsylvania, in the Spring of 1807. The crew of the keel boat, from sickness and fatigue, became unable to work the boat to Louisville. Alexander May (the father of Capt. May,) was obliged to work hard for several days to reach that point. At Louisville, the Patroon (or Captain,) of the keel boat abandoned the trip to Pittsburgh, and Mr. May was left there with his family and effects. No boat was to be obtained that was going up the River, but he determined to proceed, and for this purpose procured the best thing available—which was an old oak skiff. In this he placed his family, some six hundred pounds of lead, cooking utensils, &c., and started from Louisville up the River. His progress to Pittsburgh—a distance of *six hundred miles*—evinced that he was a man as well of nerve as of immense physical endurance. With only the help of one man for three days on the rout, he rowed the boat alone the entire distance, receiving only such assistance as his wife could render by steering the boat. The Grand-mother cared for one child, Mrs. May for the youngest with one arm, while acting as helms-*woman* with the other. Mr. May's hands were so contracted from the length of time they had been closed about the oars, that for years he could not straighten them, and they were so calloused that he could, without pain, hold red-hot coals in them. There was more heroism in this long journey than is visible at the first glance.

Capt. May commenced flat-boating on the Ohio in 1822, and continued in this business until 1827, when he obtained the mastership of the steamboat Shamrock ; and made the first voyage on her from Pittsburgh to Galena, which was the first *business* trip ever made on the Upper Mississippi, by a steam-boat—that is, from St. Louis to Galena. Steamboats had before ascended with military troops and stores, but had always after returned to *their* trade at other points.

Capt. May continued on the Upper Mississippi, as Master of a steamboat, until 1834, or a period of seven years. During this time he saw much of Indian and other life, and was personally cognizant of many scenes connected with Black Hawk, Keokuk, and the war of 1832. He brought Gen. Gaines and suite to Rock Island in 1831, at the time of the memorable interview between that officer and Black Hawk. We give an account of the affair in Capt. May's own words:

"A few hours after our arrival at Fort Armstrong, Gen. Gaines concluded to send for the Chiefs and Braves of the Band to hold a council with them, and desired me to remain with the Boat until the council could be held, which was appointed to be the next day.

"Black Hawk, with a considerable number of Chiefs and Braves, came to the council chamber, which was a log building some distance from the Fort. The Indians were all armed, each with various implements, in full preparation for war. They made bold and defiant demonstrations in the council chamber, and used even impertinent language to Gen. Gaines and his officers. (I stood by the side of an Indian trader, who interpreted to me.) Every officer and white man in the chamber knew there was imminent danger, as the Indians were all efficiently armed, and not an officer or white man in the room had a weapon.

"Mr. Antoine LeClaire was the interpreter, and did his duty on that occasion most admirably. His judicious, cautious, and conciliatory management, on that day, was, I believe, the means of saving the lives of many officers and men, as well as his own life. He, as well as all who were witnesses of the council, saw the imminent danger."

On the trip down to St. Louis, (before bringing up Gen. Gaines,) Keokuk, and several other Chiefs, accompanied by an interpreter, were passengers with Capt. May. They stopped at Yellow Banks, where Black Hawk and his Band were encamped. At the solicitation of Capt. May, and others, Keokuk landed, and made the disaffected party a most eloquent speech, advising them to avoid strife with the whites, and to quietly remove west of the Mississippi. It is needless to add that his advice was unheeded.

Keokuk was a passenger with Capt. May on another occasion. Having experienced much difficulty, at various times, in crossing the Upper and Lower Rapids, Capt. May had become impressed with the idea that, in course of time, towns must be built at the head and foot of each Rapids—in fact it may, in justice to him, be claimed that he was the *first* to suggest the location of towns on the spots now occupied by the important cities of Davenport and LeClaire. On this occasion he strenuously urged upon Keokuk the importance of reserving to his nation a portion of land thirty or forty miles square in this vicinity, when the land was purchased by Government. Keokuk seems to have disregarded his advice, however much it may have impressed him at the time.

As an illustration of Indian ingenuity, he relates that when near the mouth of Iowa River in 1831, they noticed that the surface of the Mississippi was covered with floating leaves. An Indian trader on board explained the curiosity by stating that Indians somewhere above had been ferrying their horses over the river. This was the case, for when they arrived at New Boston they found several hundred Indians and horses that had but just finished crossing. Their ferry-boats were constructed by placing half a dozen canoes side by side, six inches or a foot apart. Poles were then laid traversely across the canoes, and the whole well covered with leaves. This made a perfectly safe, and most ingenious craft.

After leaving the River in 1834, Capt. May entered in business with John Andoe, of Pittsburgh, under the firm of May & Andoe They carried on an extensive Grocery, Commission, Receiving, and Forwarding, as well as Steamboat Building business. During his business career, Capt. May superintended the building of over fifty steamboats, and more than twice as many barges, and other boats.

He was one of the original proprietors of Davenport—although not until 1847 a resident of the place. He owns largely, both here and at LeClaire, having purchased in full faith of the vast improvement which time would evolve in both places. He is now one of our wealthiest inhabitants. He is a thorough believer in the West—labors hard for its interests with tongue and pen. His nature is kind, genial, and pacific—as a superior business man, the past can amply witness.

We cannot better conclude our hasty sketch, than by giving an extract from a note sent us in reply to one soliciting the leading circumstances of his life:

"I have made many visits to this country since the year 1827, and have had familiar acquaintance with many thousands of the inhabitants during the past thirty years, and have watched with interest the progress of improvement on and near the Mississippi River. Year after year the progress seemed wonderful. Indeed, the immense increase of population, with the vast evidences of enterprise, skill, perseverance, talent, and capital, scattered over the land within the past twelve years, seems to me now more like magic than reality. Then, again, when I philosophise, in my rude way, I feel persuaded that even this wonderfully rapid and apparently magic progress cannot for many years be retarded, or if temporarily obstructed, the suspension must be of short duration, and the progress be the more rapid and permanent thereafter. This point, and say a distance of twenty miles above, is certainly the most attractive point to be found from St. Anthony Falls to the mouth of the Mississippi. I feel safe, in the assertion, that there are very few spots on the face of this earth that has many more natural advantages, in the same space, than has been conferred by Providence on this *twenty miles square.* The salubrity of the climate, depth and fertility of soil, contiguity to markets and facility for transportation and importation, are blessings pertaining peculiarly to this location on the Father of Waters.

Besides the enjoyment of all these in an eminent degree, we have tributary to this point, or on the tract, an excellent quality, and almost inexhaustable quantity, of timber, stone, stone coal, lime sand, (of superior quality for glass making,) lead, iron, &c., thus we have facilities to procure all elements and implements for manufactures on an *extensive* scale. The Valley of the Mississippi and tributaries, with the Rail and other roads, concentrating at this point, make this one of the most desirable points for judicious investment, for *extensive* operations in manufacturing establishments, that can be found in the United States.

We have, at this point, the Rapids, which are, in a low and moderate stage of the River, an impediment to Navigation, which is an advantage, as it makes an anchorage, and a portio of the year, a *terminus* at two points—Davenport and LeClaire. On this tract, consequently, those two points must, in a few years, grow to be great Commercial, Manufacturing, and Produce Depots; and with the obvious advantages presented in the intervening space, on the margin of the River, from Davenport to LeClaire, ere many years it will wear more the aspect of a Manufacturing Town than a "country place."

One fact more having bearing upon Capt. May may be added in regard to that portion of a man's character which induces him to tenaciously adhere to what he believes to be the true faith, whether religious or political. Capt. May says:

"Myself and Mr. John Andoe were in the Financial Storm of 1837, as well as for some time before and after that date, and were the only Wholesale Grocers and Commission Merchants in the city of Pittsburgh who were Anti-United States Bank Democrats, and am proud to say that we both still adhere to the same political faith."

# CHAPTER XX.

## HON. CHAS. WESTON.

JUDGE WESTON was born May, 1811, in Washington county, New York. He was the youngest son of Hon. Roswell Weston, Judge in the Court of Common Pleas. The subject of our biography graduated at an early age at the Rennsalaer Institute, of Troy, and, in 1832, commenced reading law under his father and Gen. Orville Clark—who were then in partnership. He remained with them some two years, and then transferred his studies to the office of Hon. Esek Cowen—who was afterwards one of the Justices of the Supreme Court of the State.

Several of the highest lawyers of the day were cotemporary with Judge Weston at the time—Hon. Mark Skinner, now of Chicago, and Nicholas Hill, Jr., of Albany, New York, studying in the same office, and Hon. Daniel Ullman, and Hon. Ed. Sandford, being admitted to the Bar of the Supreme Court in the same class of examination in 1836.

Judge Weston engaged for nearly a year, after his admission, in practicing law in his father's office, and then through the representations of some proprietors of the "Half Breed Tract," who resided in New York, he was induced to start for the West. The glowing enthusiasm of the owners of the "Half-Breed Tract," was, however, lost in his case, for, instead of proceeding thither' he went to Burlington. He reached that place in December, 1837, having crossed the country in the first stage (owned by the well-known *Frink*,) that ever went through from Chicago. His advent in Iowa was not as pleasant as it is now, when Steam Ferry Boats have supplanted shaky flat-boats, and precarious "dug-outs." The Mississippi was crowded with floating ice, and he nearly lost his life in crossing—he, however, succeeded, but more dead than alive.

He entered the small hotel, and after warming himself, and recovering a living amount of energy, he surveyed the company present. There were a couple of gentlemen who attracted his attention—one was a rather loose, undandified young man, with a particularly large head, and stack of hair, each member of which rose erect in proud independence of the others. His companion was a rather sharp-looking individual, and was armed *cap-a.pie*, in stout old homespun, of true Vermont origin. Both were young men—and either would have attracted considerable attention in Broadway. Judge Weston received an introduction; the first was Mr. Grimes, and the other Mr. Starr. Mr. Grimes, better known as Jas. W. Grimes, has since been Governor of Iowa, and is now United States Senator, while Mr. Starr is one of the first lawyers in the West. These were Judge Weston's first acquaintances west of the River, and both illustrated admirably the fact, that "appearances are deceiving."

He commenced the practice of law in Burlington, and continued so to do for a year or more, alternating his legal duties with trips into the back country for the purposes of health, adventure, or excitement. On one of these occasions, himself, and H. W. Starr, were spending a short time with Jerry Smith, a well known Indian trader of that time. While there, Black Hawk and his son arrived, and pitched their tents in the vicinity. He was very sociable, but most religious in his dislike of his rival, Keokuk. Starr, in order to test his feelings, said to the old Chief: "*Keokuk oc-qua-nish-a-shin?*" ("Keokuk is a good man, is he not?") Rising, with fury in his eyes, and all his bitter disappointments crowding his memory and bolstering up his wrath, the old Brave thundered out, "*Keokuk car-win, nish-a-shin!*" ("Keokuk is NOT a good man!) It is impossible to render in English the full and emphatic meaning contained in either question or reply, but more especially so in case of the latter.

Judge Weston was with W. B. Conway during his sickness and death; and soon after the occurrence of that deplorable event, he was appointed Fiscal Agent for the Territory, and exercised the duties of the Secretary of the Territory, in place of Mr. Conway.

In 1838, he was appointed Judge Advocate General, by Gov. Lucas, with the title of Colonel.

In 1839, by the death of incumbent Van Alen, he was appointed United States Attorney for the Territory, by Mr. Van Buren, which office he held until 1843.

In 1840, he removed to Davenport, and purchased a quarter section of land, which he afterward increased to a farm of several hundred acres. He was not, however, signally successful as a farmer—it generally costing him a third more to raise his own beef, butter, and wheat, than it would to have paid the cash for them. He, therefore, abandoned the pursuit of Agricultural prominence under such difficulties, married, and moved into the city, where he has since resided.

He was elected Mayor in 1851, and County Judge in 1857, which office he at present fills, in a manner at once satisfactory to his constituents, and honorable to the ermine. It may be added that none more than himself are *suaviter in modo*, and hence the difficult relations of his office are always preserved in a manner that leaves none other than pleasurable impressions—however inharmonious or antagonistic be the influences with which he may have to deal.

He is now in the enjoyment of an honorable independence, has fine tastes and means for their gratification. His progenitors are noted for longevity—his father being now eighty-seven—and he himself will probably extend the term of his life and enjoyment to an equal extent. That such may be the case, not one will otherwise wish, as his urbanity, genial sympathies, and classic tastes, have acquired for him the friendship and respect of all who know him.

# CHAPTER XXI.

## CAPT. LeROY DODGE.

Capt. Dodge was born in December, 1811, in Herkimer county, New York. His father was a farmer, and his sons received such educational opportunities as are usually given to farmer's children—hard work in the Summer, and the advantages of a District School in the Winter. Mr. Dodge made his *debut* in active life, outside of the farm, as a school teacher—which pursuit he followed some three winters. Of his success in this department, we cannot speak positively—but as he possesses a peculiarity of doing everything *well*, it can be inferred with a tolerable degree of certainty, that his endeavors to "teach the young idea to shoot" were rewarded with due and proper results.

In 1833, he started West—spent one year in Ohio, then footed it to Lake Michigan, crossing in a small schooner to Detroit, and in due time reached Chicago. He finished his pedestrian tour by footing it to Joliet, and from thence to Dubuque, at which place he obtained a situation as Clerk, with G. W. Atchison.

He remained in this situation one and a half years, and then commenced life upon the Father of Waters—the Mississippi. He started as Clerk, and fought his way by dint of perseverance and industry from the Clerk's Desk to the Wheel House, and from thence to the "Captain's Office"—evincing throughout these transformations the indisputable fact that labor is the price of success. In the Fall of the same year—1836—that he commenced on the River, he located in Rockingham, and has carried on farming in connection with steamboating ever since. In 1852, he represented Scott county in the State Legislature, as a Democrat—a character, by the way, which he has ever uncompromisingly sustained.

He was married in 1846, but subsequently lost his wife. He married again, and the same unfortunate case has again resulted—he is once more a widower.

Capt. Dodge is still engaged in steamboating, although he does not, as formerly, navigate the whole upper river—his trips being confined to running a packet between Keokuk and Davenport. His Boat—the "Ben Campbell"—is a well known and favorite institution among those who have had occasion for river transportation along that portion of the Mississippi.

Like many of our pioneers, Capt. Dodge has accumulated an ample competence, but unlike that of many others, it is in nowise the result of accident. No Genius of the Lamp erected it in a single night—no sudden and unexpected fluctuations of fortune's tide carried him where he now is. Every stone in the superstructure of his fortune was hewn and piled by his own arm—and commenced under circumstances that would have discouraged any one with less perseverance than he possesses. The most marked trait in his character is *determination*—it is seen in all his actions, and its firm unflinching character is traced in every feature and expression of his face, as though wrought in iron.

H. Price

## CHAPTER XXII.

## HIRAM PRICE, ESQ.

Mr. Price was born January, 1814, in Washington county, Pennsylvania. He removed, in 1819, to Mifflin county, Pennsylvania, in 1822 to Huntingdon county, in the same State, and in the Fall of 1844 he came to Davenport, which place has since been his residence.

His capital in business was one hundred dollars, and with this he started as a Merchant. His small pecuniary effects, however, were made up in other of his possessions—he had determined perseverance, inviolate integrity, good business tact, was temperate to the full, and keenly conscientious. With this capital he started into the work, and in a few years had erected upon it a fine fortune.

He continued in the Mercantile business until 1848. In 1847 he was elected the first School Fund Commissioner of Scott county, which office he held nine years. In 1848 he was elected Recorder and Treasurer of Scott county, which positions he filled for eight years, after which he declined being a candidate for re-election. The length of time which he was continued in these offices is a high compliment to the manner in which he filled them.

Mr. Price has always taken a decided and consistent position in favor of the cause of Temperance. He was one of those who, in February, 1848, organized the Grand Division of the Sons of Temperance for the State of Iowa, and was elected first Grand Worthy A.; and after, Grand Worthy Patriarch for the State. He has been elected every year, since the organization of the Grand Division of Iowa, as representative to the National Division of North America. In 1847 he was instrumental in organizing the present Division of Sons of Temperance in this city, and was elected the first W. P. In 1854, he was elected President of the "Maine Law Alliance" of the State; and he filled this position in a manner which, while effectual toward the end in view, invariably held the respect of its most inveterate opponents.

He was Treasurer for the Scott County Bible Society for the years 1851, '2, '6 and '7, and President for years 1854 and '5.

Mr. Price is entitled to an infinite deal of honor for the part he has taken in this section towards the construction of our Railroads. He was one of the first, West of the Mississippi, who agitated a railroad connection with the Atlantic, and it is owing as much or more to his efforts than to those of any other one, that our city and county were induced to subscribe to the project.

He also lent his exertions to the Mississippi and Missouri Railroad—which, when completed, will unite us with the Missouri River, and eventually with the Pacific. He was one of its corporators, and traveled the entire length of the line to the Missouri, procuring right of way for the road—holding meetings in the counties through which the line runs, for the purpose of securing the interests of and making friends for the M. & M. R. R., and eventually suceeeded in driving off a project for a rival road.

His present business connections are a partnership in the Publishing House of Luse, Lane & Co.; another in the Henry County Coal Company, and he is also Secretary, Cashier, and one of the Directors, of the Mississippi and Missouri Railroad.

Mr. Price is one of the few living, but much quoted, examples of what perseverance, untiring industry, and, above all, *integrity*, will accomplish. In fourteen years each dollar of his original hundred has been reproduced in a thousand; and with them all is the conviction that they are the fruit of honest industry.

His views and position upon Temperance have given him a prominence possessed by no other private citizen in the State, and yet, with this prominence, and his strong blows in warring against the serried hosts of antagonistic men and principles, there is not, we venture to say, a man of his opponents who does not respect the singular honesty of his endeavors, and his entire freedom from all effort to gain either personal or political popularity. It need not be added that he is liberal—the character we have thus far given him, fully indicates it. Added to this trait, he possesses the utmost regularity of habits—rising invariably at six o'clock, well-knowing that life is short, and its hours precious.

With an expression of regret that his fervent, philanthropic exertions upon the Temperance question have not met with the full success which their character and end deserve, and of satisfaction that his life has practically demonstrated the success of CORRECT PRINCIPLES, we leave him to the consideration of our readers.

James Thorington

# CHAPTER XXIII.

THE foregoing, although including the prominent men of Davenport, does not contain *all* who are prominent, either from long residence, the possession of ability, public spirit, or such other qualities as entitle their possessors to prominence in any community. There are others here whose biographies would confer honor upon any work—among whom are Dr. Barrows, Hon. John P. Cook, Ebenezer Cook, Hon. James Grant, Gen. Geo. B. Sargent, D. C. Eldridge, John Forrest, Andrew Logan, J. M. D. Burrows, Harvey Leonard, and not a few others. Circumstances, however, forbid a lengthened mention, however much each deserves it.

The following are the names of settlers who came to Scott county on and previous to 1840, with the year of their coming:

### SETTLERS OF 1836.

Antoine LeClaire, 1833,
George L. Davenport,
G. C. R. Mitchel, 1835,
Dr. E. S. Barrows,
James M. Bowling, 1835,
A. H. Davenport,
James McIntosh,
Capt. Leroy Dodge,
D. C. Eldridge,
Lewis L. Clark,
Charles H. Eldridge,
Wm. S. Cook,
Ebenezer Cook,
John P. Cook,
Wm. Vantuyl,
Jabez A. Burchard,
Roswell H. Spencer,
Adam Noel.
John Noel,
Henry C. Morehead,
John Armel,
Edward Rickar,
Louis Hibbert, 1831,
John Burnsides,
Sam'l. Sullivan,
Samuel Little,
James E. Burnsides,
James O'Kelly,
Wm. O. Hall,
A. E. B. Hall,
Andrew J. Hyde,
George Hyde,
E. W. H. Winfield,
Etheral Camp,
Benj. Wright,
Capt. James E. Murry,
Mrs. A. W. M'Gregor,
William Velie,
Col. T. C. Eads,
Stephen Henly,
Jesse Henly,
Foster Campbell,
John P. Cooper,
John D. Richey,
Rufus Catlin,
Robert Wilson,
Ira C. Van Tuyl,
Henry B. Armel,
Thos. H. Armel,
E. B. Armel,
Jesse Armel,
William Armel,
Jackson Armel,
James Armel,
David Barry,
John Carter,
Charles Carter,
Claudius McLafflin,
Widow John Robinson,
Joseph P. Robinson,
Perry Clark,
Andrew Ringlesby,
Strather Ringlesby,
Eph. Lane,
Wm. Lane,
Geo. W. Thorn,
Stephen Thompson,
Wm. Thompson,
G. W. Franks,

David LeClaire,
Lee I. Hall,
I. M. T. Hall,
David Sullivan,
W. R. Shoemaker,
Wade Monday, 1833,
Peter Wilson,
Henry Gabbert,
Daniel Berryman,
William Hubbard,
J. H. Sullivan,
Jules Bumberg,
Goodrich Hubbard,
Jerremiah Hubbard,
Wm. White,
James Davenport,
Henry Bumberg,

DEAD AND NON-RESIDENT.

Archer, killed at Rockingham 1837.*
Brown, J. M., Tipton, N. Y.
Baty,*
Cook, Ira, Sr., 1854,*
Cook, Ira, Jr., Fort DesMoine,
Camp, Jas. M., Linn county, Iowa,
Campbell, A. W., died in California,*
Campbell, Geo., California,
Chuver, Capt. J., St. Louis,
Camp, Wm. Mt. Vernon,
Cline, Oregon,
Carroll, John, Sr.,*
Carroll, Wm., Rock Island,
Davenport, M., 1852,*
Davenport, Jas., Illinois,
Davis, Daniel, Tipton,
Dutro, Wm., St. Louis,
Dodge, Chas., Rochester, Iowa,
Davenport, Otho, Ill.,
Gabbart, David, 1855,*
Gardner, Wm., unknown,
Giberson, Daniel, 1840,*
Hall, A. P.,*
Hall, J. H.,*
Hall, W. W.,*
Henby, Stephen J.,*
Higgins, H. W., Illinois,
Higgins, Jno. V., Illinois,
Higgins, Henry, Illinois,
Hanks, Wm., Minnesota,
Hazlett, Jas., Lyons,
Harold, C., St. Louis,
Harrison, Richard, Min. Point,
Hubbard, Asael,*
Hulse, Stephen'*
Harrison, Henry, unknown,
Heller,*
Hacker, John, drowned,*
Kale, Wm., St. Louis,
Lingo, Wm., St. Louis,
Lane, Wilcox, Oregon.
Davenport, Baily Rock Island,
Higginson, J. C., Dubuque,
Baptiste, Merchant,*
Pike, B. F., California,
Little, Frances,*
Lee, Edward, Canada,
Lingo, Edward, St. Louis,
Lingo, Thos., St. Louis,
Lindsay, Thos. came 1835, 1839,*
Lindsay, Asa, came 1835, 1839,*
McGregor, A. W., 1835, 1857,*
McLean, O. G., 1850,*
Morehead, Joseph, Insane Hospital, O.,
McLean, Reuben, St. Louis,
McCoy, J.,*
Mountain, Sam'l., St. Louis,
Mitchell,(G. C. R.'s father,)Va., 1840,*
Noel Joseph, 1839,*
Nichols,*
Parker Jonathan, Jr.,*
Powers, Moses, California,
Pope, Jno., Maquoketa,
Powers, H., Lewiston, N. Y.,
Palmer, David,*
Parkhurst, J. W.,*
Ricker, Rufus, Sr.,*
Sullivan, J. H., Ohio,
Shepherd, E. H., New York,
Sebert, Andrew, 1858,*
Sturdevant, Harvey, 1848,*
Shays, John,*
Stubbs, Jas., Captain, 1848,*
Savoy,*
Topen, Joseph, 1856,*
Tannerhill, California,
Turner, Jas., unknown,
VanAllen, 1838,
VanDyke, Amos,*
Watts, Wm. B., unknown,
Wilson, Frazier, Rock Island,
Wilcox, William, Dr., 1842,*
Wilcox, Fred., California,
Wilcox, Wm., Jr., Illinois,
White, Wm., Alton, Illinois,
White, James, Alton, Illinois.
Butler, G. H.,
Allen,
Bronson, Titus,*
Bennum, Wm., Illinois,

Gavitt, Rev. Wm., Ohio,
Sholes, Stanton,*
Wilson, James,*
Warren, Geo.,*
Wilson, John, Kansas,
Colton, L. S.,*
Gordon, Maj. Wm.,*
Emmerson, Dr., 1844,*
Bumberg, L.,*
Bumberg, Alex., Hampton, Illinois,

SETTLERS OF 1837.

Samuel Lyter,
Harvey Leonard,
Gen. G. B. Sargent,
John L. Coffin,
Willard Barrows,
John M. Lyter,
E. S. Morey,
Capt. John Coleman,
Levi Williams,
Nathaniel Squires,
John Forrest,
John F. Dillon,
Rev. J. A. Pelamorgues,
Rev. Enoch Mead,
Rodolphus Bennet,
Frank Bennet,
J. M. D. Burrows,
Mrs. Wallace,
Louis A. Macklot,
Elisha G. Burrows,
H. H. Peas,
Capt. Isaac Hawley,
George Hawley,
Daniel Hawley,
Christopher Rowe,
Louis Giberson,
John Willis,
Elihu Alvord,
C. C. Alvord,
Samuel Alford,
George Alvord,
Robert Humphrey,
John Haywood,
James Robinson,
James Mead,
James M. Leonard,
J. S. Brown,
O. F. Meyers,
John Porter,
Daniel S. Porter,
Phillip Baker,
Vincent Carter,
Caleb Dunn,
Edwin Dunn,
Alyett Dunn,
Charles Averell,
Edward Averell,
Jeremiah Hewett,
Porter McKinstry,
Noble McKinstry,
Andrew Coleman,
James Coleman,
George McCosh,
Anson Rowe,
Mrs. Finch,
Mary Trucks,
Mr. Ackerman,
David Miller,
Geo. Thorn,

DEAD AND NON-RESIDENT.

Coleman, Foster, Illinois,
Coleman, Jas., Sr., 1852,*
Coleman, Robinson, Illinois,
Dwigging, Robert, 1st, Cedar county,
Dwiggins, Robert, 2d, Cedar county,
Dwiggins, J., died '56, boiler explosion,*
Dwiggins, Andrew, Cedar county,
Dillon, Timothy,*
Dillon, Thomas,*
Dunn, John H.,*
Donaldson, A. C., California,
Davis, Garret, Camden, Ill.,
Dwiggins, Calahan, Cedar county,
Dwiggings, James, Cedar county,
Dillon, Timothy, Jr., drowned 1841,*
Eldridge, William, died in California,
Eldridge, Wm. P., died in Texas,
Easley, Milington, Wisconsin,
Easley, Franklin, Wisconsin,
Easley, William, California,
Foy, John,*
Franks, V. B., 1835, Va., Port Byron,
Matteer, George, California,
McGranahen, John, Kansas,
McGranahan, Augustus, died in Cal.,
Norris, Aaron B., Council Bluffs,
Neff, Robert, St. Louis,
Perrin, Frank, New Orleans,
Pigman, Muscatine county,
Pigman, Jeff., Muscatine county,
Quinn, John, Ohio,
Russell, A. F., Danville, Pennsylvania,
Robinson, John, killed,*
Ringlesby, Lewis, 1855,*
Ringwalt, Samuel, Downington, Pa.,
Rowe, S. Dr., Lawrence, Mich.,
Rowe, Nelson, Iowa City,
Ringlesby, John, 1855,*
Ringlesby, H., died in California 1858,
Rowe, William,*
Rowe, B. F.,*
Sheller, John S., Burlington,
Shoemaker, William R., Fort Riley,
Shepherd, S. H., N. Y.,

Finley, A. W., 1845*,
Galagher, John, Cedar county,
Gano, Aaron C.,*
Howell, H. S., Wisconsin,
Haywood, Thomas, 1850,*
Hawley, E., Philadelphia,
Mills, I. K., Fort Riley,
Davis, Edward, Pa.,
Davis, Dan., Tipton,
Hallock, J. C., Mt. Pleasant,
Brown, S. S., New York,
Colt, Geo., unknown,
Ennis, John, Philadelphia,
Ennis, Mr., Philadelphia,
Sutherland, John, St. Louis,
Chamberlain, Wm.,*
Finch, A.,*
Wade, Hampton,*
Kelly, Thomas, Mexico,
Lathrop, L., drowned,
Sibly, David, died in Wisconsin,
Sherman, Samuel, drowned,*
Smith, Capt. M.,*
Trux, Abram, 1838,*
Trux, John, 1838,
Whiting, Seth L , Elmira, New York,
Hallock, Wm., Mt. Pleasant,
Briggs, Ansel, California,
Reilly, R., Pa.,
Fipps, Chas., Dubuque,
Whiting, Stephen, California,
Knap, Eph., Minnesota,
Pierce, Wm., Dubuque,
Wilson, Dr., Wisconsin,
Hedges, Samuel,*
Hedges, Wheeler, Cincinnati,
Smith, Lionel,*
Hedges, Isaac,*
Smith, John,*
Thorn, Henry,*
Warren, Wilber,*.

SETTLERS OF 1838.

Andrew Logan,
Augustus C. Logan,
O. C. Logan,
Col. John D. Evans,
Cheeney Munger,
James McGuire,
Joseph C. Quinn,
James Quinn,
Wm. D. Quinn,
Alexander Brownlee,
James Brownlee,
Winchester Sherman,
John W. Wiley,
Sylvester Wiley,
Joseph Mounts,
Robert Christie,
John Rubey,
John Carver,
John Shuck,
Obed Donaldson,
Sam'l. Wyscowber,
Benj. Mathews,
James Baker,
William Baker,
James Grant,
Levi Moore,
Marion Moore,
Elias Moore,
Samuel Freeman,
Lemuel White,
John White,
Nathan Blackman,
John K. James,
Pat. McGuire,
George W. Fenno,
Charles Fenno,
William Fenno,
Amos Fenno,
Adam Donaldson,
Joseph Elder,
Dennis R. Fuller,
Zenas Blackman,
John Willis,
Col. Charles Weston,
George C. Havill,
Irad Noble,
James T. Carter,
Ebenezer Carver,
Levi Williams,
J. W. Williams,
John Pope,
Aug. Pope,
Abel Pope,

DEAD AND NON-RESIDENT.

Barclay, Samuel, Jr., St. Paul,
Barclay, Sam'l., Sr., 1839,*
Berryman, J. M., Ohio,
Bishop, Stephen, Canada,
Burgess, Kansas,
Burnell, Abram, 1840,*
Cooper, Henry, Dubuque,
Cooper, Austin, Dubuque,
Hutt, Hiram, Moline,
LeClaire, Alexis, 1840,*
Leech, Capt.,*
Moore, Elias,*
Mitchell, Jas., runaway,
Moss, L., 1842,*
Mounts, M , 1853,*
Mars, Samuel, Illinois,

Daily, George, Canton, Iowa,
Gill, Elias, Alton,
Gill, George, died 1839,
Hinckle, Charles, Galena,
Higginson, Samuel P., Pekin,
Hill, Irad, Michigan,
Hoge, David, 1847,*
Hutt, Abram, DeWitt,
Parkhurst, Sterling,*
Peters, A. D., 1845,*
Parr, Muscatine,
Quinn, Joseph C., Ohio,
Conley, T. J.
Dubois, John, New York,
Scott, Jonah,
White, S. H. Moline,
Bardwell, O., Galena,
Hale, Asa, Galena,
LaPage, Louis, Illinois,
Clark, Wm., uuknown,
Meredith, S.,*
Noble, Revile, Minnesota,
Noble, George, Minnesota,
Noble,*
Nichols, William,*
Nichols, F. S., Australia,
Parker, J. M., Florence,
Peters, W. H., Rhinfick, New York,
Piersol, John, Camanche,
Parkhurst, E.,*
Robertson, John, Illinois,
Sullivan, Lucien, New York,
Wright, Benjamin, Sr.,*
Warren, Alphonse, Minnesota,
Swartout, N. Illinois,
Krarger, S.,*
McCoy, James B., Mt. Morris, Ill.,
Conway, W. Wm.,*
Courtney, E., Dubuque,
Patten, Jackson, California,
Patten, Thomas, California,
Walling, Geo.,*
Walling, Wm.,*

SETTLERS OF 1839.

John Owens,
John Eldridge,
James Rumbold,
B. F. Coates,
Benj. Coates, Jr.,
William Coates,
N. M. Rambo,
James Thorington,
John Thorington,
John Morton,
L. J. Center,
James McCosh,
Samuel Parker,
J. M. Witherwax,
R. S. Craig,
Silas Glaspell,
Isaac S. Glaspell,
Barton Glaspell,
Gabriel McArthur,
Robt. Criswell,
Moses Parmalee,
Henry Parmalee,
Walter Parmalee,
John Hixon and sons,
Lewis Burrows,
David Durrows,
Christian Cober,
Leonard Cooper,
H. S. Finley,
Horace Bradley,
James Lindsey,
I. T. Lindsey,
A. A. Lindsey,
A. H. Owens,
Wm. S. Collins,
George E. W. Hoge,
Israel Hall,
John Carroll, and mother,
Wm. Carroll,
D. B. Shaw,
John Leamen,
J. H. Morton,
Coonrad Reed,
Edwin Parmalee,
Wm. Parmalee,
James Parmalee,
George F. Hall,
William Inslee,
Roderick Center,
Joshua Maw,
Wm. Newby,
Robt. Newby,
Nathan Newby,
E. A. Evans,
John Trucks,
Abram Trucks.
William Lovel,
Michael Cooper,
Raphael Cooper,
Michael Grace,
James Hale,
Osmar S. McKown,
Alibone Morton,
Wm. Todd,
Volney Warren,
Edward Burnell,
John Friday,
Montgomery Thompson,
Charles Metteer,
Charles Lesslie,
Laurel Sumners,

DEAD AND NON-RESIDENT.

Arbell, Frederick, 1842,*
Brown, Judson, Port Byron,
Little, Jas., New Orleans,
McLot, John N., 1850,*

Brown, William, 1846,*
Buck, Benjamin, drowned,*
Coleman, Charles, 1843,*
Downer, Erastus, Illinois,
Elder, C., drowned 1846,*
Fisher, Samuel, Philadelphia,
Fisher, John, San Francisco,
Fisher, James, Miniapolis,
Fitzpatrick, E., Dubuque,
Foster, Asa,*
Glaspel, Jas., Sr., died 1847,
Glaspel, Enos,*
Glaspel, Jas., Jr.,*
Gates, drowned,*
Wetmore, Wm., Ky.,
Hoge, Thomas S., New York,
Holbrook, Rev, J. C. Dubuque,
Belkin, Henry,*
Churchill, Chis., Illinois,
Boyington, Dr.,
Coody, Dr.,
Tuttle, Calvin, Wisconsin,
Squires, John, N. Y.,
Munger, W., Chicago,
Nye, died 1840,*
Owens, John, Jr., Illinois,
Owens, Jas., Illinois,*
Perrin, Aaron, California,
Perrin, John, California,
Perrin, Isaac, California,
Perrin, Theodore, 1845,*
Riddle, H. B., died 1856,*
Sherman, Abel, Alabama,
Sherman, Luke, New York,
Sherman, Samuel,*
Smith, M. Capt., drowned,
Sloper, Samuel,*
Snow, Jared,*
Thorington, Jno., Sr.,*
Shays, John, Ohio,
Squires, Isaac, St. Louis,
Moran, Wm.,
West, Narcisse Yarten,
Kingsly, Joseph, Pa.,
Taylor, Reese, Maquoketa,
Taylor, Peter, Kansas,

SETTLERS OF 1840.

R. M. Prettyman,
Alfred Sanders,
David McKown,
Gilbert McKown,
Stephen Schoolfield,
S. Burnell,
Dr. Hiram Brown,
Dr. Cyrus G. Blood,
David Buckwalter,
Henry Buchneau,
Wm. Briggs,
L. Walling and brother,
G. Tapley,
Andrew Doyle,
Andrew J. Lawes,
Thomas Kerns,
W. W. McCammon,
Alex. Wells,
Joseph Gaymon,
Yital Bucheau,
Bartholemew Wells,
Peter Trainer,
Michael McNemara,
Gibbon,
Wm. H. Gayle,
Johnson,
Sam'l. Stevens,
Thomas Wood, Sen.,
A. A. McLoskey,
John Letting,
M. G. McLoskey.
David Hawley,

DIED AND NON-RESIDENT.

Armitage, J., Canada,
Buckwalter, Joseph, 1854,*
Buckwalter, Daniel, 1847,*
Baker, Morris,*
Bronson,*
Bardwell, Doct., Linn county, Pa.,
Brophy,*
Clark, Doct., California,
Cark, Dennas, Wisconsin,
Chin, Richard, St. Louis,
Gafney, Barney, 1840,*
Grover, Erastus, Massachusetts,
Guyer, Samuels, Ohio,
Howard, M., 1843,*
Hogan, Patrick, 1856,*
Kelly, Thomas, Louisiana,
McClosky, Robert J., 1848,
Moyer, Albert, Pennsylvania,
McGranahan, Geo., Kansas,
Nichols, John, St. Louis,

*Deceased.

Coleman, Finley, Illinois,
Wood, Thomas, Jr., Ill.,
Criswell, Robert, LeClaire,
Leonard, Sam'l., LeClaire,
Grover, N. B.,
Tapley, G. Linn, Mass.,
Nichols, Wm., 1852,*

Appropriate and pertinent to the Biographies, are the proceedings of the Pioneer Settlers Association of Scott County, and their First Annual Festival, held on Monday evening of February 22d, at the Burtis House, in the city of Davenport.

At a meeting of old settlers of Scott county, who became residents prior to December 31, 1840, held in LeClaire Hall, Davenport, pursuant to a notice in the daily papers, on the evening of Saturday, January 23, 1858, some sixty persons were assembled. The meeting was called to order by Duncan C. Eldridge, Esq., whereupon Ebenezer Cook, Esq., was elected Chairman, and John Coffin, Secretary, of the meeting.

The Chairman, on taking his seat, expressed, with a few happy remarks, the pleasure which it gave him to meet so many of his old friends on this occasion, and alluded to the warm interest he had always felt in those who had stood side by side with him in the hardships and struggles incident to the early settlement of this county. He said, "that if there was anything of good about him, if he had ever been of any service to this community, and in fact for all he was at this day, he felt himself indebted to the early settlers of this county, who had always stood by him; that he had always been willing to divide the last crust of bread with any one of them that needed, and he prayed to God, that as long as he lived, he might be disposed to divide with them the last shirt on his back, if any one of them required it."

On motion of James McIntosh, Esq., a Committee of five was appointed by the Chair to draft a Preamble and Resolutions for organizing the Association.

The Chair appointed James McIntosh, Willard Barrows, John F. Dillon, D. C. Eldridge, and Edward Ricker, Esquires, said Committee.

While the Committee was absent, the meeting was entertained by Wm. McCammon, Esq., and by the Hon. John P. Cook.

The Committee then presented the following Preamble and Resolutions, which were unanimously adopted:

Whereas, it was our destiny, as American citizens, excited by a spirit of laudable enterprise, to be the pioneers in the settlement of this fair and fertile section of our State: and, whereas, it seems desirable that we should perpetuate the memory of that settlement, and from time to time recall the history of the past, so rich in incident of great and varied interest, therefore, be it—

*Resolved*, That all those who became residents of the Territory, now known as Scott county, in Iowa, prior to December 31, 1840, form themselves into a society, the object of which shall be to extend the right hand of fellowship to all those who have lived through the honorable conflict of the past to share and enjoy the prosperity of the present, and to interchange congratulations, that their early struggles and hardships have resulted in a growth and development almost without a parallel.

*Resolved*, That this Associatioe be known by the name of———

*Resolved*, That its officers shall consist of a President, ten Vice Presidents, a Secretary and Treasurer; and an Executive Committee of five members, said committee to be appointed by the President.

*Resolved*, That a committee of three members be appointed by the Chair, to draft a Constitution and By-Laws to be submitted for adoption at the next meeting.

*Resolved*, That a committee of five members be appointed to make arrangements for a festival to be held in this city, on the 22d day of February, 1858.

*Resolved*, That tickets of invitation be sent to all "Pioneer Settlers" who have since become non-residents of this county.

Considerable discussion on the subject of a name, and the word "Pioneer," having to the mids of many present a sacredness in this connection, it was moved by the Hon. Jno. P. Cook, and voted, that the blank be filled, so that the resolution as framed, stands thus:

*Resolved*, That this Association be known by the name of "The Pioneer Settlers' Association of Scott county."

The chair appointed Judge Weston, Jno. F. Dillon, and C. C. Alvord, Esquires, committee on Constitution and By-Laws; and appointed Willard Barrows A. H. Owens, James McIntosh, Geo. L. Davenport, and D. C. Eldridge, Esquires, a committee on the festival.

The Association then proceeded to elect its first officers, which resulted in the choice of the following named gentlemen:

ANTOINE LECLAIRE, *President*.

Ebenezer Cook, Esq.,
Duncan C. Eldridge, Esq.,
Willard Barrows, Esq.,
John Owens, Esq.,
Robert Christie, Esq.,
Jabez A. Burchard, Esq.,
Adrian H. Davenport, Esq.,
Alexander Brownlee, Esq.,
LeRoy Dodge, Esq.,
} *Vice Presidents*.

Dr. E. S. Barrows, *Corresponding Secretary*.
John L. Coffin, *Recording Secretary*.
Geo. B. Sargent, Esq., *Treasurer*.

John L. Coffin, *Secretary*.

Tickets having been issued, including Old Settlers, Press, Clergy, and Author and Publishers of "Davenport Past and Present," there was on Monday night of the 22nd of February, a crowded assemblage in the magnificent Halls and Parlors of the "Burtis House." A happier crowd, and one whose sympathies and affections were so freely and harmoniously developed, never, perhaps, assembled in such numbers. Formality, caste, old feuds, dislikes, and all unkindnesses, were merged, and disappeared in the joyous friendliness that filled each heart—lips were wreathed in smiles, white locks were haloed with the sunshine of the occasion—hard, stern features, that for years had scowled upon life's difficulties, lost their rigidity, and reflected only happiness. It was more, in all respects, like an assembling of loving brothers around the household hearth after long years of separation—there was the same cordial warmth of greeting, the same affectionate enquiries, and the same happy yielding to the spirit of the occasion. Not less, perhaps, than eight hundred were present—the oldest of whom was Mr. ELIHU ALVORD, who had attained the ripe old age of eighty-three.

The assembly was called to order by EBENEZER COOK, Esq., and the President, ANTOINE LECLAIRE, took his seat. After the Davenport Brass Band had discoursed a fine piece of music, a cane presentation took place. The cane was of native hickory, mounted with a costly gold head, upon which was engraved —"Pioneer Settlers' Association of Scott county, organized January, 1858." On the lower part of the head was engraved the name of the first President, Antoine LeClaire, with space for the name of all succeeding ones—as the cane is to be handed down from President to President until the last Old Settler has departed to another life. The presentation was made by JOHN F. DILLON, accompanied by a short speech in his felicitous and poetical style. He said—

MR. PRESIDENT:—I am charged with the grateful duty of presenting you with this insignia of your office. You, who were the first to pioneer the way to this lovely spot, lovelier and richer than the land "flowing with milk and honey." You, who have used the wealth it has been your good fortune to acquire, in constant endeavors to promote the growth and advance the interests of our city and country—you, who are confessed first in the esteem of all old pioneers, have been unanimously elected our first President. Happy are we, that your life has been bounteously lengthened out to behold this night. Happy that we are able to bestow upon you this testimonial of our regard.

What endeared recollections, and thronging visions this occasion must call up and inspire! Who would not fondly "give the hope of years" to enjoy the satisfaction and delight that must to-night be yours! A thousand incidents strike the electric chain of memory, and in the light of its corruscations the past comes back again, and glows vividly before you! How pleasant, at times, to retouch memories that are being moss-grown, to retint the fast fading pictures of life!

The changes you have seen, how astonishing! The like whereof will be sought for in vain, in the realities of history, and in the dreams of poetry.

Since the world began, it has never in any age or country exhibited a growth so solid, and a development so amazing as that which you yourself have witnessed. So rapid and thorough is the progress of improvement, that the memorials of our early settlement are fast passing away. Scarcely a trace or vestige of the primitive log-cabin remains; and the inquiry might be pertinently raised, not "have we a Bourbon," but "have we a log-cabin among us?" These have been succeeded by comfortable and elegant dwellings—but why specify changes when specification were endless. All, all is changed, save the unchanging sky above us, and the changeless river that rolls by us; magnificent river!

"Time writes no wrinkles on thine azure brow,

and without avouching its geological accuracy let me add—

Such as creation's dawn beheld thou rollest now."

How often in the quiet watches of the night, when I have beheld the glory of the one, reflected in and increased by that of the other, has my heart melted with gratitude, that aspiring man could not reach the heavens to cover *them* with signs and placards, or mar the beauty of earth's glorious water courses. Especially have you observed, sir, with intense interest, the growth of our fair and proud young city.

This interest has not been the indifferent interest of a mere spectator, but with you it has partaken of a warmer nature; it has claimed kindred with a paternal solicitude, and without demur has had its claim allowed.

Our feeble infancy—our slow growth—our precarious situation—our gloomy prospects awakened for awhile the most tender concern and anxious forebodings. These dark days happily have passed way, we trust, to return never more; and Davenport to-day, in size and beauty, stands peerless among rivals,—the "Queen City" of Iowa. Well may we rejoice to-night with you, in the triumphs of a faith in our destiny, that has suffered all things, endured all things, hoped all things even unto the end. But these exultant feelings, and grateful reflections come to us mingled, and tinged, and softened, and subdued with those of a sadder nature. While we have been busy, time and death have not been idle.

But I may not further indulge in reflections that crowd for utterance, save to say, that this cane, made from a stick of native growth, and skilfully fashioned by the hand of a member of our Association, is the distinctive, and we think fitting and appropriate badge of your office. As such, it is intended to be preserved with jealous care, and to be transmitted successively from President to President, until our Society shall be no more!

On it will be found engraved your own name—the name of our Association, and the date of its organization.

It affords me unfeigned pleasure, sir, in behalf of the "Pioneer Settlers' Association of Scott county," to present this ensign of office and honor to you —the *first* President, wondering, who, of those present, shall enjoy the enviable, yet melancholy distinction of being the *last*.

This effort was highly applauded, after which the President, through E. Cook, Esq., responded as follows:

"Mr. Dillon:—I receive this cane, the ensignia of my office, as President of the "Pioneer Settlers' Association of Scott County," with great pleasure, not alone because I shall take pride in its exhibition, not alone because of its beautiful and skilful workmanship, not alone for the very flattering remarks attendant upon its presentation, either of which causes would justify the feeling, but chiefly because it is, and is intended by the Association as a tangible memento of the past, and of the early history of the settlement of our country, to be handed down, I trust, to future generations, to be preserved for all time; to be exhibited to thousands upon thousands of our descendents yet unborn, as having been designed, made, and handled by their forefathers, the first settlers of Scott county.

With this cane, shall go down, I trust, the records of our Association, and if the members are faithful, and furnish, as required by the Constitution, the leading incidents of their lives, connected with their settlement and habitation in this county, to be placed upon the records, how interesting to those who come after us will be this cane, as a tangible memorial of their forefathers, long since crumbled into the dust from which they came, and whose history, to a greater or less extent, is written in the records before them.

Methinks, as I look into the far, far future, I see within the limits of our county, a noble Building, dedicated to some noble Public objects, and there, in some suitable and proper place, are deposited the records and testimonials of this Association. Within its walls is a living crowd, pressing forward, eager to see and persue the record, to see and touch the memorials handed down with it, and I hear them say, "These were sent down to us from our forefathers—here is written a history of the first settlement of this beautiful land, of the trials and hardships endured, and of the triumphs won by them. Let them be preserved forever."

Ladies and gentlemen, members of this Association, let me charge upon you that you impress upon your children, and childrens' children, that they hold it as a sacred duty, when we shall all have passed away from earth, to preserve, intact, the records and memorials of our Association, and to transmit them unimpaired to future generations.

You have been pleased, sir, to allude in very flattering terms to me, personally. If I have, in the course of a long life spent here, entitled myself to, and won the respect of my fellow men, particularly the Old Settlers of the county, I am amply repaid for any and all exertions I may have been able to make to aid in advancing the interests and prosperity of our beloved city and county.

If I have acquired wealth, it is to the settlement of the country that I am indebted for it, for of what value would have been the land on which this city and the city of LeClaire is built, except from the fact that you, gentlemen, of this Association, settled upon and improved the lands of the county, and thereby enabled us to built up a city? So that, gentlemen, we see that we are dependent, to a greater or less extent, upon one another, and when we so act as to confer a benefit upon the community, we really are benefitting ourselves.

The Association has been pleased to elect me their fi.st President. I take this, the first opportunity afforded afforded me to return my sincere and heartfelt thanks for this expression of confidence and respect. The object and aim of this organization is so eminently and apparently proper, that it is needless for me here to advert to it, other than to say that I am rejoiced that the step has been taken, and that there is the interest manifested in the subject that is apparent here to-night, and I trust that interest will be kept up and maintained by every member so long as he shall live.

This cane, made as you say, from a stick of native growth, is a fit and proper emblem of the office for which it is designed, for in the ordinary course of things it is to be presumed that your Presidents will be men advanced in years, who will require its aid and support. It is, too, a fit and proper emblem, as it will remind your future Presidents that their predecessors who have leaned upon it for support, have passed down the vale of time into eternity, whither they must soon follow, and surrender it again to aid and support some other aged man down the same path, until, at last, the last man of your Association shall grasp it, and in the performance of his sad duty, provide for it, and other memorials, a place of deposit, which we trust shall be kept sacred forever."

"After the ceremony of the Cane Presentation was concluded, the "First Annual Address" was delivered by Hon. John P. Cook. It is a splendid production, aud presents in its combinations the finest blending of philosophy, humor, wit, and pathos, that ever was delivered in Davenport. We give it entire, although it lacks the forcible expression, easy emphasis, and generally graceful oratory of the speaker:

"*Mr. President, and Ladies and Gentlemen:*

Through the politeness of the committee appointed to arrange for this occasion, it has befallen to my lot to address your association, on this the first festival of the Pioneers of Scott County.

The interest manifested in this organization, this large assembly, and the familiar nod of recognition passing from one to another, attest the perfect happiness we all feel in this union, made genial by the hardships of the past, the joy of the present, and hopes for the future.

In the West such a society is neither new nor uncommon. The first settlers of Illinois, Wisconsin, and of many of the older counties in our own beautiful Iowa, have been drawn together by that fraternal regard which is always warm in the honest heart of an "old pioneer."

If, in the excitement of business, and the duties of life, we have hitherto neglected to come together, as the pioneers of Scott county, the greater reason now exists, that we should nourish this infant association, and make it promotive of every good and noble sympathy of the heart.

Our organization is now complete, our names are enrolled, and with the exception of absentees, and such as have not yet joined, although entitled to membership, our ranks are full, and under our constitution there can be no accession to our number, other than exceptions named. With a just appreciation of the memory of the dead, you have procured the names of those who settled in this county prior to 1840, but who now no longer live, so that your records will perpetuate *their* names, who have "acted well their part," and now sleep beneath the cold clods of the valley, as ours, who have survived to consummate this organization. In thus recording the names of the dead, who were our companions in frontier life, we but open a record that will soon contain the names of all who now stand recorded as *living members* of this association.

One by one we shall pass away, and at each returning festival some familiar face will be missed at the board, some chair will be vacant, and the record of the living will be shortened to lengthen the record of the dead, while the void in our ranks can never, never be filled.

As years roll on, those of us who may be living at the end of the first decade, will realize the fearful work of death among us.

A little longer, yet a little longer, and a score of years shall have passed away, leaving but a few to cherish the memory of the departed, and to cling closely, ah! how closely, to each other.

Who shall presume to lift the veil, and name the pioneer who will then answer to the Secretary's roll call?

A little longer, and still a little longer, and the youngest among us will have reached his three score years and ten, and no one may know, until time unfolds the eternal decree, who of our number will be the last survivor of the pioneers of Scott county!

While we may not penetrate the dim future, nor name those who shall hold the last meeting, keep the last festival—though, alas! more solemn than festive it will be—and perform the last rites, ere this association ceases to exist, yet we may imagine its closing scenes, and admonish one another to prove faithful and true till the last one shall have passed from earth.

You have procured a cane, and have had inscribed thereon, "Pioneer Settlers' Association, organized January, 1858, Scott County, Iowa," and presented it to your President, with instructions that it be handed down to his last successor in office. That successor lives, and if not here with us to-day in *propria persona*, he is with us in spirit, and in well wishes, and is destined to officiate at the last act of your association.

For a moment give free scope to the imagination, and go with me to a period thirty, forty, perhaps fifty years hence, and behold here a city of two hundred thousand inhabitants, all eager to act their part in the business of life, running hither and thither, jostling each other in the crowd, some seeking the profits of commerce, some collecting the news of the day, some chasing pleasure, some bent on mischief, some bound for the station house of a balloon about to be wafted across the continent with a full load of human beings, who expect to dine in New York on the same day, some about to seat themselves in the cars of an atmospheric railway, advertised to go through to the seaboard in two hours, without change of cars, and amid the confusion, splendor and enterprise, let us, on the 22d day of that February, enter the spacious building on Twenty-Fifth street, and see congregated the last of the Scott county pioneers. There sits the President, surrounded by the survivors, numbering five, perhaps more, faithful hearts, whose whitened locks, and trembling limbs, denote them children of a century, past and gone.

They are looking back over the lost years, and with vivid recollections of the early history of our own country, are recounting many of the hardships and incidents of frontier life; they recall the first festival of the association, and mention the names, and drop tears to the memory of many assembled here to-day; they have before them the record of the association, and it tells of your annual meetings and festivals—your official doings—the names of your officers—andit faithfully preserves the history of many incidents in the existence of your association.

Some venerable patriarch selected from that little band delivers the annual address, and he wants not matters of interest, appropriate to the occasion, to talk about, and with which to hold the attention of his hearers.

With a faithful and vivid recollection of early times, and early associations, he pictures the past, and compares it with the realities about him, until

"Fond memory brings the light
Of other days around them."

Is that the last festival? Another year rolls around, and that cane supports the aged frame of the President to the Festive Hall, where he meets friends young and old; but one, a solitary one shall grasp his hand, and exclaim—

"We two alone remain, the rest are gone, all gone!"

In the ordinary course of nature, it is reasonable to suppose, that the younger members of the association will be among the last survivors of our number, and upon them will fall the duty of closing our records, and providing a depository for everything pertaining to the association.

Young man! that duty may be yours; act well your part through life, that we may have a worthy representative in closing an association so auspiciously commenced.

Teach your children to venerate the land they are to inhabit, and impress upon them the duty they owe to their native home, and their pioneer forefathers.

Leave to them as a rich legacy the pleasing duty of providing a fitting receptacle for the records and memorials of the association, that they, and their children's children, may ever find a faithful history of the early pioneers, and of the settlement of the country.

Admonish them, that when the spirit of the last one of us takes its flight from earthly scenes—the sad and interesting duty will devolve upon them, to follow the remains to their last resting place; to perform the closing scenes in our history, and to write the last chapter of our record.

To the minds of some, such an association may seem of small importance and doubtful existence; but I doubt whether a society could be organized in the West with stronger ties of friendship and sympathy than one will find among the "Old Settlers."

We have all had our strifes, our political, local, and social disagreements, and shall doubtless continue to have them; but they are soon forgiven and forgotten, and we turn to the bright side of the picture, and call to mind the early scenes in our settlement here, while the generous promptings of the heart bind us more closely together.

There is no period in man's life at which he is not more or less dependent upon his fellow man, and the experience of every day admonishes us that we should cultivate the christian virtues and neighborly kindness—and while we should manifest these towards *all* who come in contact with us, they are doubly due to those who shared our early toils and privations, and have ever been ready to lend a helping hand to the "Old Settlers."

The history of the early settlement of Scott county is replete with interesting incidents, and to those of us who first "squatted" and located our claims upon "Uncle Sam's" land, it is a satisfaction to look back to that period, and compare Scott county then with Scott county now. No one here to-day can claim a settlement anterior to that of our worthy President, and certainly no one has done more than he in aiding and encouraging the first settlers; and I may be permitted thus publicly to record the humble acknowledgments of my father's family to him, who was the first to extend his hand, to offer hospitality, and to welcome us to our prairie home. I was but a boy then, yet how well do I remember the scene when I landed one bright May morning in 1836, within four squares of the spot where we are now assembled.

The ground upon which "mine host" of the Burtis House has erected this spacious hotel, was a corn field, and two cabins below Main street constituted the improvements of the embryo "City of Davenport;" some half a dozen houses across the river in the then village of Stephenson marked the spot where now stands our twin sister city.

The booming of the morning gun from Fort Armstrong warned the red man that Uncle Sam's troops were in possession of their island home, and assured the pioneer of protection and safety. The daily movements of noble steamers upon the bosom of our majestic river told us that the way was opened to immigration; while the unclaimed acres invited the husbandman to one of the finest soils ever warmed by the sun of Heaven.

Need we wonder that the old chieftain, Black Hawk, and his noble band, refused to yield up the country to their white brethren? Can we blame them for clinging to this lovely spot, and for lingering around the graves of their dead?

"O'er the fate of the Indian,
The Great Spirit has cast
The spell of the white man,
His glory is past.

While we may not stay the arm of destiny, that is fast sweeping away the aborigines of this continent as a distinctive race, we may question the policy that would exterminate them, and should throw the broad mantle of charity over their acts.

While bounteous nature had done fully her share in making this country an inviting field for the immigrant, it required the genius and enterprise of man to develop its resources, and plant its towns and villages.

Towns in those days were laid out with reference to natural advantages presented by the Mississippi River and its tributaries, and hence every spot of ground along the river above high water mark (and some below,) was surveyed, platted, pictured, and named.

I will not undertake the task of recalling the names even of all the early cities in Scott county, but I must not pass in silence the contest for supremacy between Davenport and Rockingham. The history of this struggle for the county seat of Scott is so fresh in my memory that I can almost hear one of the "old guard" singing—

"Here we are, a happy, happy band,
On the banks of Rockingham."

Davenport claimed the seat of justice, because of her central locality, her high and dry site, her beautiful surroundings, and her many other natural advantages, which we all now concede and realize—while Rockingham expected to become the great centrepot of commerce in consequence of the rich trade that was destined (as she supposed,) to flow from the fertile valley of Rock River.

No one, in those days, expected to live long enough to see the iron horse flying over this western prairie, with its freights of human life, rich merchandize from the East, and the still more valuable products of the West.

Our ideas about traveling and commerce had not advanced beyond a light draught steamer, and John Frink's mud wagon. The wisdom and foresight of the statesmen of Illinois were directed to producing slack water navigation in Rock River, and a very decided amount of capital, energy, and enterprise, was devoted to building up Rockingham, in order that she might reap the benefit of the prosperous trade about to be opened with the Suckers in the rich valley of that river.

I think I see the steamer *Gipsey*, with the boys on board, ready to start out on an experimental trip from the port of Rockingham, bound for Fox River, with a cargo of sundries, consisting chiefly of scoo-ti-op-o, "*corn bread and common doins;*" Scoo-ti-op-o, "*chickin fixins and uncommon doins.*" Captain Gray mounts the hurricane deck, rings the bell, and gives the word to the natives on shore to "cast off the starn hawser." The old *Gipsey* moves; that ponderous pile of green oak lumber fastened to her stern slowly revolves, reminding one of the current wheels we sometimes see on the rapids of a river. Away she goes, and the crowd on her decks give us three cheers at parting, while young Rockingham returns nine yells and a *whoop.*

Such an event as opening the navigation of Rock River, with a stern-wheeler, was one of too much importance in its local bearing upon the future of corner lots, for Davenport to wish the *Gipsey* a safe trip, and the first impediment to the voyage, and the place where Davenport hopes centered, was at the rapids near Vandruf's Island.

While the "old *Gipsey*" slowly ploughed her way through the waters of Rock River, a delegation of Davenporters cut across by land to the Vandruf rapids, to witness the experiment. The old steamer pushed on, and boldly approached the rushing waters, and fearful boulders ahead, to the tune of Yankee Doodle, whistled by the wind instruments on board, with the variations. The Davenporters lay in ambush, watching the movements of the steamer, and wondering if *such* a craft could possibly ascend *such* a current. Oh, unfortunate Miss *Gipsey!* why did you run your nose between those sunken boulders, and bring everything up standing? Why destroy the precious stores laid in for the trip, by smashing up glass and stone ware, thus rendering your passengers and crew forlorn and *spiritless?* Will you give it up so? A yell from the "sepoys" in ambush decides the question. The order is given, and all hands boldly jump overboard, and never tire or faint until their craft has cleared the treacherous rocks, and is once more in smooth water.

I think I see around me some of the mariners who helped "work the ship" on that occasion, and who made the round trip, and returned wiser, if not better, fresh water coveys.

Who among you, recollecting the incidents of those stirring times, will ever forget the first county-seat question? Certainly, not the prominent actors on either side, many of whom are with us to-day? The "border ruffians" of Missouri did not originate the idea of invading an adjoining territory in order to help their friends at an important election; nor can Mr. Calhoun claim to be the first man to record names whose owners were not at the ballot box. We had a "border" and a "Delaware crossing" long before Kansas was thought of, and, to use an expression of one of my pioneer friends, there was some "tall doings" on our borders, and on our crossing.

The Suckers furnished a goodly number for both parties, but the delegations from "Snake Diggins" and Moscow, (the former headed by a two-fisted miner, and the latter by the "old bogus coon,") increased the population of Scott county in one day to a number that astonished the unsophisticated, and threatened the depopulation of some of our sister counties.

Five days before the election, both parties were certain of success, for each party supposed that it had outwitted the other in importing voters. The day of election arrived, and so did the imported parties, rejoicing in the glorious principles of "squatter sovereignty," and believing in the regulation of domestic institutions in their own way, subject only to the party that could poll the most votes, and make the returns show it.

The result of this election indicated a very respectable population in the county in point of numbers, and proved that Davenport had colonized the most votes. The returns were made to the Governor, who refused to issue a certificate, in consequence of alleged illegal voting, and the Legislature again provided for another election, and that the result should be recorded on the records of the Commissioners of Dubuque county.

The election came off, and Rockingham claimed the victory—while Davenport declared that the whole thing was illegal and void. From the popular arena the contest was transferred before the Commissioners of Dubuque county, thence to the Courts, thence to the Legislature, and finally back again to the ordeal of "popular sovereignty."

Immediate preparations were made for another struggle, and now three or four different points were brought before the people for the prize. Rockingham saw that she stood no chance in a triangular fight with her old competitor, and at once determined to form an alliance with another rival candidate, located near the mouth of Duck Creek, so that the last contest was really between Davenport and the Duck Creek cornfield.

The records of this county show that Davenport was triumphant, and the question was thus forever settled. The important incidents of this last election were not of sufficient interest to me at the time, to impress my mind with more than one idea about them. I saw something "going up," and broke for "old Cedar."

Rockingham no longer rivals Davenport, but in vindication of the truth of History, in justice to those who once inhabited the place, and in honor of two of the "old Rockingham guard," who still cling to her soil, I may be permitted to say, that she was once a great place, and *well watered.*

During the time of the contest for the county seat, an event transpired which must not be omitted, in speaking of the history of our settlement. A dispute arose between the State of Missouri, and the then Territory of Iowa as to the boundary line between them, and so determined were the authorities on both sides to exercise jurisdiction over the disputed territory, that it resulted, in what is known to the Old Settlers, as the "Missouri War."

There were warriors in those days; and I should do injustice to the patriotism of that period, if I neglected to notice the military daring of the volunteers, who rushed to the standard (and rations) of the commander-in-chief, in obedience to his call.

The Sheriff of a border county in Iowa undertook to enforce the collection of taxes in the disputed Territory. He was arrested by the authorities of Missouri. The executive of Iowa demanded his release. It was refused; and to rescue this Sheriff, Governor Lucas ordered out the militia, and called for volunteers. "My voice is now for war"—was the patriotic response of every true "Hawkeye." The county seat question was forgotten in the more important duty of driving the invaders from our soil. Davenport and Rockingham men met, embraced, buckled on their armor, and side by side shouted their war cry—"*death to the 'Pukes!'*" The officers in command held a council of war, and it was decided that Davenport should be the head quarters of the Scott County Army, in order that the troops might be inspired by the sight of old Fort Armstrong, and at the same time occupy a position so near the Fort, that a safe retreat would be at hand, in case of an attack from the enemy.

On the day appointed for the first drill, the whole country marched to the standard of the gallant Colonel in command, and Davenport witnessed one of the most *spirited* military reviews that ever took place within her limits. The line was formed on the bank of the river, fronting toward the enemy's country, the right resting against a cotton wood tree, the left in close proximity to the Ferry House. There they stood, veterans of iron nerve and dauntless courage, presenting a sight that would have daunted the most desperate foe, and assuring the women and children that they would defend their homes to the death, against the "border ruffians" from the Des Moines River.

The weapons, carried by some of these volunteer patriots, were not satisfactory to the commanding officers, and about one-fourth of the army were ordered out of the ranks, and their services dispensed with, unless they would procure others of a different character, and more in accordance with the Army regulations. The objectionable weapons consisted of a plough-colter, carried in a link of a large log-chain, which the valiant soldier had over his shoulder. Another was a sheet iron sword about six feet in length, fastened to a rope strap. Another was an old-fashioned tin sausage stuffer. Another an old musket without a lock, and the balance of like character.

The order was given for the owners of these mondescript weapons to march out of the ranks three steps. The order was obeyed. The ranks closed up, and the offending soldiers were discharged with a reprimand.

I am not prepared to say that the commanding officer was justified, in thus summarily discharging so many men, who were ready and anxious to serve their country; and the result proved, that the amount of bravery dismissed was equal to that retained; for no sooner were the discharged soldiers clear of the line of the regiment, than they formed a company of cavalry, a company of dragoons, and a company which they called the "Squad," and then, under the superior generalship of their leader, the knight of the six foot sword, they made a bold charge upon the regulars, broke their line, drove not a few of them into the river, some into, and some around the Ferry House, some into the grocery, and some out of town; thus defeating and dispersing the regular army without the loss of a man on either side.

This conflict was disastrous in its results to the regular army, and before the forces could again be collected, peace was declared and the army disbanded.

This unlooked for cessation of hostilities was a severe blow to the military aspirations of the "Hawkeyes," and disappointed the just expectations of those who had hoped to distinguish themselves in the defence of our Territorial rights. The disappointment was not felt by the army of Scott county alone. Numerous companies had been formed elsewhere, and had started for the seat of war, with supplies for the campaign.

A company of about thirty left an adjoining county, under the leadership of a chieftain, who often used to say that he could "whip his weight in wild cats," and who has since represented you in the National Congress—has been upon your Supreme Bench, and has also been Chief Justice of California.

He started out with thirty men, and six baggage wagons, well loaded with supplies for his little army, and, being determined to keep up the *spirits* of his men, he freighted five of his wagons with whisky.

The question of boundary was subsequently submitted to the Supreme Court of the United States, and the disputed Territory given to Iowa.

At the commencement of the year 1840, this county contained about twenty-five hundred inhabitants, of which number, about five hundred resided in Davenport. To-day your county boasts of a population of thirty thousand, and this city claims eighteen thousand of that number.

In 1840, at the head of the Rock Island Rapids, on the spot where now stands the city of LeClaire, with a population of twenty-five hundred, grew a dense forest.

In 1840, the fertile, beautiful prairies of old Scott were lying undisturbed by the husbandman; to-day they are teeming with industrious, happy owners of the soil.

In 1840, there was but one steam-engine in operation within the borders of your county, and that one was at Rockingham. To-day you may count them by hundreds along the bank of your river, from Buffalo to Princeton, on our prairies, and in our groves.

In 1840, every face you met was a familiar one, and the greeting a greeting of recognition. To-day the oldest inhabitant hardly knows his next door neighbor.

In 1840, it took from three to five days to go to Chicago, and thirteen to New York. To-day the lightning train puts you in Chicago in eight hours, and in New York in forty.

In 1840, the young men of this Association were happy children, sporting upon the village green, and making the welkin ring with merry laughter and innocent joy. To-day they are men aspiring to a position in life, that shall give them honor among their fellow men.

In 1840, the mothers and daughters of Scott county were happy in their cabin homes, and could pass in and out through the cabin doors. To-day the mothers and daughters occupy no more space in this open country—than the dear good creatures are entitled to.

In 1840, we were looking forward to a time when our then territory should become strong enough to add another member to the Federal Union, and convince our Eastern friends of the truth of "*Westward the star of empire takes its way.*" To-day our most sanguine expectations are far more than realized, and we regard with pride our noble State, its prospective future, and the inducements it holds out to the thousands at the East, who still cling to that "Old Fogy" three inch soil, which, with patient cultivation, yields white beans, buckwheat cakes, and pumpkin pies.

*Mr. President*—This day is the anniversary of the birth day of George Washington—our Washington—and we have chosen it as the day for our present and future festivals.

It is a day on which every true American citizen does some act in honor, or gives some thought to the memory of the father of his country. That memory is the sacred heritage of the people he established, and no generation of that people shall pass away without leaving some memento that he was indeed first in the hearts of his countrymen.

Some one has truthfully written, that "the first word of American infancy should be *mother;* the second father; the third Washington." Although it is well that we, as American citizens, should, on this his anniversary day, linger for a while at his tomb, and renew our patriotism, yet, too, it is eminently fitting, that, assembled as pioneers, with the sympathies and feelings of pioneers all aroused within us, we should go to that tomb to-day, and remember that he, too, was a pioneer, and that in him burned strongly that bold, adventurous, persevering spirit that makes the pioneer ; that he, too, endured pioneer hardships and privations, compared with which, ours sink into insignificance.

In his youth he was a pioneer surveyor in the then wilds of his native State, and many of the boundaries then established by him may be found to-day. In his early manhood he was selected by the Governor of Virginia as a pioneer envoy through the wilderness to the French Commandant on the Ohio. He was a pioneer in leading a little army against the French and Indians, in defence of the Virginia frontier, and thus early in his military career did he become known among his savage foes as the "spirit-protected man, who would be a chief of nations, for he could not die in battle." He was a pioneer in everything that tended to advance the prosperity and happiness of his native land.

He was the pioneer of freedom in our legislative halls ; on the battle-field ; through the long dark days of that terrible struggle ; through the period of doubt and confusion that succeeded ; and his wisdom and patriotism, equal to all emergencies, at last led us into the haven of rest, of peace, of prosperity.

His life is a part of his country's history; and as living he laid the corner stone of this vast confederation of States, that year by year is waxing greater among the nations of the earth, so, though dead, his maxims and example, if we adhere to the one, and imitate the other, shall produce a history more glorious than that of the past; shall nourish a greatness that time shall but add to and confirm; and the unborn generations shall rise up, and revere him as God's chosen instrument of blessing to their land. Let his wisdom and his patriotism ever pervade and guard the land he loved—let his spirit be with us to-day; and as each turning year brings round again our festival day, let us ever remember that it is also the day that marks the birth of GEORGE WASHINGTON.

## REGULAR TOASTS.

After supper, Judge Grant proceeded to read the Regular Toasts as follows:

1. *Washington!*—No nation can claim, no country can appropriate him to itself. His fame is the common property of patriots throughout the civilized world.
2. *The Early Pioneers of Scott County*—The hardships and privations of a frontier life justly entitle them to the esteem of all those who enjoy the fruits of their early struggles: their posterity shall rise up and call them blessed.

It is a matter of regret that the former, and especially the latter of these was not responded to. No toast of the evening was worthy of more eloquence than "The Early Pioneers of Scott County"—their hardships, energy, influence, and all their character and surroundings were worthy of the best oratory of the evening.

3. *The Pioneer Dead*—May their names be preserved, their hardships remembered, and memories cherished, by their survivors, by their descendants, and by all who enjoy the goodly heritage to which they led the way. Responded to by Hon. James Grant, who said—

MR. CHAIRMAN:—I cannot respond to the sentiment just uttered, without interrupting, for a moment, the current of your joyous thoughts, while I ask you to drop a tear to the memory of the dead.

Of all this numerous assembly there are few, to whom death has not come nigh, since they first encountered the privations and toils of a settlement west of the great river.

Some have lost a father or a mother, some a brother or a sister, some a husband or a wife, and many, many have seen their children wither and fade as if struck by the hand of an avenging God.

It is no exaggeration, that, since we first came here, in a single season of great calamity, incident to the exposures of every new settlement, one-tenth of our then small population was swept away.

Death, sir, is ever terrible; whether he knocks at the palace or the cottage gate, at the bridal chamber, or when the mother, for the first time feels her first-born's breath—

> The tear, the groan, the pall, the bier,
> And all we know or dread or fear
> Of agony are his.

But he came upon our departed friends when they were just entering a new world, upon the prairie land, before the spring flowers of prosperity were opened to their view; when the cabin was unthatched, and the physician, and the minister of God were far away.

They died on the spot where they were taking the place of the red man, and preparing a new theatre for civilization, arts, morals, and liberty.

Early they departed, but not till their eyes were greeted by the dawning of the day, and they beheld, in the dim mist of the morning, the budding promise of the wilderness, and friends, and sons, and daughters, to enjoy the goodly land which they had but seen.

Though too many of them the hand of angel woman ministered not in their last hour, yet the rough hand of manhood, softened by the sympathy of sorrow, was never wanted in the day of their calamity, and the pioneer, though not versed in the set phrases of cultivated society, was ever present, with gentle voice, and gentler deeds.

> "To speak the last, the parting word,
> Which, when all other sounds decay,
> Is still like distant music heard,
> That tender farewell on the shore
> Of this rude world when all is o'er."

We know not if the dead visit this earth, or take note of our actions, but if they do, their spirits are hovering over us this night, and their hearts made glad, that God is smiling upon us, that we are permitted to live, and enjoy this pleasant hour; that we have reaped the reward of those toils and sufferings under which they were doomed to fall.

No storied urn or animated bust marks the spot where the pioneers sleep their last sleep. They are buried beneath the huge oak, whose shade they never see, or under the high head-land of the Mississippi, against which the whistling winds and warring tempests are silent to them.

Their good deeds should be their monument. The glory of their fair and virtuous actions is above all the escutcheons on the tombs of the great.

Honor, then, to the memory of those brave men, and brave women, who lost their lives in fighting the battle of civilization on the frontier.

They encountered no human foes; their last acts are not stained with blood; their conquests were made with the plough and the spade, and not with the cannon and the musket; and though they fell in the beginning of the conflict, and in the heat of the day, they won the battle, and left us to enjoy the victory.

Every smiling field and green meadow; every school, every college, every church, every village, this city, with all its wealth and pomp and pride, shall be their monuments, recalling their memory, heralding their triumph, and honoring their virtues.

"How sleep the good, who sink to rest
By all their country's wishes blest
When Spring, with dewy fingers cold,
Returns to deck their hallowed mould.
She there shall dress a sweeter sod,
Than fairy's feet have ever trod.
By fairy hands, their knell is rung,
By forms unseen their dirge is sung,
There honor comes a pilgrim grey
To bless the turf that wraps their clay,
And freedom shall awhile repair
To dwell a weeping hermit there."

4. *The Star of Empire*—When in its western progress its rays of light fell upon the virgin soil of Iowa, a new destiny was conceived, which in its birth, like the "Star in the East," has brought forth its wise men to worship.

Responded to by Rev. G. F. Magoun, who, after a few introductory remarks, read the following fine Poem—the production of a young lady—Miss MARY E. MEAD—an "old settler" by birthright:

## REMINISCENCES.

As oft, at eve, by firesides bright and warm,
Some sailor group are gathered, while they tell
Of journeys far,—of conflict with the storm,—
Of dangers they have braved so long and well,—
So round this ample board we meet to-night,
And many a tale of Olden Time recite.

Once roamed the Indian all these vales among,
The deer sprung startled from his stealthy tread,
The fearful war-whoop through the forest rung,
The deadly arrow from its quiver sped;
But now we sit,—at twilight's soft decline,—
In peace beneath the shadow of the vine.

If e'er to conquering warrior has been owed
The glory of an honored, world-wide name;
If e'er on noble souls has been bestowed
That lofty homage which is truest fame;
If e'er in history's page or classic verse
Our country's Fathers have been justly praised;
In humbler strains we surely may rehearse
The deeds of those by whom our hearths were raised;
Who left their kindred to return no more,
And reared their altars on this wild-wood shore.

All are not here: Where sinks the emerald wave
In long, dull surges toward the glowing West,
Lies many a heart as noble and as brave
As e'er was laid beneath the sod to rest.
They dropped the acorn on the barren glade,—
At noon we rest beneath the oak tree's shade.

We meet again; the scattered band unite
In social converse as in days of yore;
No! Not as when, within the ruddy light
Of oak boughs blazing at the cabin door,
We sat and talked the winter night away,
Till morning streaked the Eastern hills with gray.

No more the Red Men round our dwelling prowl,
No foes lies ambushed in each leafy bower,
No more the wolf's swift spring or sudden howl
Startles the sleeper at the midnight hour;
Nor leaping flames before the rapid gale
Speed like the waves when wintry storms prevail.

From lonely ARMSTRONG'S now-dismantled fort
Down the still stream no martial strains are borne.
In stately towns where busy crowds resort,
The cheerful sounds of labor greet the morn.
From happy homes the voice of mirth floats by,
And plashing waves and laughing winds reply.

Oft have I heard the times recounted o'er,
When every cabin window was a door,
When corn was ground upon a lantern's side,
And doors by latch-strings to the timbers tied;

Small was the store a lawless horde to tempt,
From thieves and robbers happily exempt.

Howe'er that be, of this there is no doubt
In those good times the latch-strings all hung out,
And neighboring friend and stranger guest might share
The roof tree's shelter and the simple fare;
E'en now the cabin ten by twelve is seen
Where on a time 'tis said there lodged fifteen!

But mingled with these recollections gay
There wakes a sadder, gentler strain for those
Who like some castle crumbling to decay
Were doomed to ruin when the new arose.

'Tis eve, the stars with silv'ry sheen
Rise silently and slow,
The pallid moon looks out between,
The waves repose below,
And not the dipping of an oar
Breaks on the stillness of the shore.

Was it the whisper of the breeze
Sighing among the tangled grass?
Was it the moaning of the trees
When far above the storm clouds pass?
Oh no, in silence still and deep,
The tiniest flower is lulled to sleep.

But there *are* sounds,—I hear them now,
They swell along the plain;
'Tis not the murmer of the rill,
'Tis not the dash of rain,—
And can there be a foot so light
To stir the rustling leaves to night?.

There is,—along the slant hill-side,
Where darksome forests bow,
Singly the dusky figures glide,—
Look you can see them now!
Pause! 'tis a band of Indian braves—
Who come to seek their chieftains' graves.

Disturb them not, as silently
These well known paths they trace,
Not long among us may there be
Remnants of that old race.
They fade as fades the morning ray
Before the glowing eye of day.

A little time they linger here,
Uncared for and unknown,
To shed a solitary tear,
O'er comrades lost and gone.
Silent and sad they gather round
Some lonely, undistinguished mound.

Hark! all the solemn woods along,
A soft and saddened lay
As if some heart in plaintive song,
Would pour itself away.
List! while the mournful cadence swells
Clear as the tone of evening bells.

"Still roll the river waves as blue
As when we launched the bark canoe,
Or when we plied the dripping oar
Beneath the shelter of the shore,
Still sings the lark a welcome guest,
Still folds the dove her wings to rest,
Still the green arching forests spread
Their boughs as widely overhead,
But 'neath their shadow now, alas!
No more our bounding warriors pass,
Silent where once their footsteps fell,
Land of our birth, farewell, farewell!"
Soft echo answers to the trembling lay;
'Neath heavy shadows glides the group away.

Oh! kindly sun! Oh! soft benignant day!
At thy glad dawn the darkness takes its flight,
The sombre hues of twilight melt away,
And sunrise bathes the Eastern hills with light.
So smiled the morn with beauty all aglow
On this fair land some twenty years ago!
Faint the light blushes up the dewy skies,
From cot and couch the cheerful dwellers rise,
The cabin windows ope, wide fly the doors,
The frugal wife brings out her garnered stores,
The gleeful children, with their sun-browned hair,
Forsake the house and sport in open air,
While soon,—the duties of the morning done,—
Some stripling youth, with ready dog and gun,
Roams through the woods, if haply he may bring
From its far height the wild bird on the wing,
Or 'mid the rustling forest chance to hear
The short, sharp panting of the startled deer,
And proud, though weary, from the chase may bear
Back to his cot the noon and evening fare.
One seeks in pastures far the truant cow,
Another yokes the cattle to the plow,
Or marches slow the well trained pair beside;
(Plain wagon seats were then no bar to pride—
Well was the place of coach and four supplied!)
So glides the day until at eve they meet,
Children and sire, each in his 'customed seat,
While plenty smokes upon the cheerful board,
And clear cold wine the sparkling streams afford.
Well the day's ventures do the hours beguile,
The dullest face oft wears a gladsome smile.
Now blue eyed "baby" sings herself to rest,
Safe cradled in an ancient, lidless chest,
Hark, from the farthest corner "Charlie's" call
For "Pa" to make a rabbit on the wall.
Then comes the time for little hunter "Ben,"
To day he surely found a lion's den.
But closed are "Allie's" eyes, her drooping head
Finds the soft pillow of her little bed.
The hours pass cheerly till all softly creep
Away to childhood's light, unconscious sleep,—
And starlight, peeping through the half-closed door,
Kisses the sleepers on the cabin floor.

How fled the years in humble scenes like these,
With much to sadden, more, far more to please.
And who shall tell, that in this later day—
When life has grown more earnest and less gay,—
A richer pleasure through its current thrills
Than in those cots among the breezy hills?

Simple their joys, their days in quiet spent—
Hope for a watchword, for a shield content,—

Till slow at length beneath their forming blows
A garden from the wilderness arose.

Lo! As we gaze along the slender piers
Which bear aloft the lengthening arch of years,
As we retrace the first faint morning ray
And glance rejoicing to this noon-tide day,
Glad hopes, bright visions o'er our bosoms throng,
And the full heart finds utterance in song.

Oh noble WEST! Oh mighty WEST!
Oh ever bright and free,—
Thy prairies ,by the breeze caressed,
Roll wave-like as the sea.
And through the long and tangled grass
The sunbeam's golden fingers pass.

Thy streams are like the streams of Time,—
Their source we cannot see,
We only hear the water's chime
Break low and musically,
And hear the plashing waves, like rain,
Dash on the shore, then sink again.

No pilgrim comes with weary feet
O'er many a desert mile,
His prayer or promise to repeat
Beneath some sacred pile,
Nor counts the solitary hours
Beneath a city's ruined towers.

But in this world so fresh and young,
Which like the goddess from the foam
To life full grown and radiant sprung,
Lies that dear spot OUR HOME.
And round its portals Love and Truth
Shall wind the wreaths of endless youth.

---

Hushed is the song, a sadder strain were not for hours so bright,
Only the calm clear voice of Hope should whisper here to-night.

Glad faces are around us, sweet tones upon the air,
And the glance of fond affection meets our greeting everywhere.

There are blessings from the aged, kind wishes from the young,
And joy her rosy radiance has o'er our gathering flung.

We will hail the fleeting moments where the Past and Present stand,
One with a darksome cypress wreath, one with a snow-white wand.

We will hail the glorious Future with her cup of bliss untried,
We will hail the white winged maiden Hope that blushes at her side.

And the rich delicious Present shall trip rejoicing by,
As lightly as the winged wind across a Southern sky.

---

But tears are quivering on the moistened cheek,
A glance on life's receding track we cast,
Our voice is mute, our lips refuse to speak,
Ourhearts o'erflow with memories of the past.

OH! FRIENDS OF OLD! we meet again to night,
Our hopes and wishes as of yore to blend.
Thus will we keep the links of friendship bright,
Thus will we journey onward to the end.
And hand to hand in cordial greeting pressed,
We'll breathe a blessing on the glorious WEST.

5. *The History of Scott County*—When we open this book, we find inscribed on every page the gospel of both peace and plenty—proclaiming perennial blessings to all whose faith is accompanied by works.

Responded to by Mr. J. A. Birchard, of Pleasant Valley, in a brief address, in which he spoke as follows:

MR. PRESIDENT:—The history of any new country must necessarily be one of trials, hardships, and privations. The pioneers have to leave the land of their birth, the home of their childhood, the hearthstone around which centered all their early joys and sorrows—the district school-house where they received the rudiments, if not the whole of their education—the village church where they assembled weekly to worship their Creator—the friends of their youth and early manhood. These must all be left, and it is like tearing a young sapling from its mother earth.

New associations must be formd, new homes must be made, new school-houses and churches built. But, compared with the trials and hardships of the first settlers in the States east of us, if we except those of our neighbor across the river, ours are not worth talking about.

There, many of them packed their goods and little ones two or three hundred miles on horseback through an almost trackless wilderness, and were four or five weeks in making the journey. Then their difficulties with the Indians—when I tell you that I was born in the valley of the Susquehanna, in the county where the massacre of Wyoming occurred, you will believe me, sir, when I tell you that many of the tales of suffering that I have heard are too horrible to relate. Before they could raise an ear of corn they had a heavy forest to remove, that took twenty or thirty hard days work to the acre. Then they had the rocks and stumps to contend with for years. I have serious doubts whether a merciful Creator, that always does all things well, ever intended the country for the habitation of civilized and christianized man. It is the natural home of the speckled trout, the wild deer, and the Indian.

For us a bountiful Providence had provided an excellent highway to get here, and when here a prolific soil ready for the plow, and pasturage sufficient for the flocks and herds of Labon and Jacob, and their sons, for a dozen generations.

It is true, that from 1839 to '44 we thought we had some rather hard times —when it took a bushel of wheat to buy a yard of calico, and a hundred pounds of pork to pay for as many of salt. But these were very different hard times from what they have in the old country; there it is starvation times that they call hard. If we could not get the two dollars a day, we could get the roast beef, and upon the whole, we had a pretty good time of it.

I first crossed the Mississippi in a canoe, nearly where the bridge now stands. This was in July 1836. I presume there were not more than three hundred inhabitants then in the county. You, Mr. President, and your ferryman, Mr. Colton, were the only settlers in Davenport, and Mr. Eleazer Parkhurst, the only one at LeClaire.

At that time there was not, to my knowledge, a single mile of Railroad between the Mississippi River and the Alleghany Mountains.

The iron horse, except at the portage road in Pennsylvania, had never tasted the waters that flow through our noble river to the Gulf. Now the amount that he consumes daily would have floated the entire navy of the United States at the time of the revolution; and the amount of produce that he moves from this fertile valley towards a market in the same time would make a full freight for it.

The last time that I crossed the river was upon my return last fall from a visit to my friends in my native State, and I crossed at the same place, but how differently. I crossed the great father of waters as it cannot be crossed at any other point from its source to its mouth—upon a noble structure, a proud monument to the enterprise and perseverance of the inhabitants of the twin cities. To the pioneers of Davenport belongs a very large share of the credit for this truly magnificent improvement.

The train upon which I crossed was brought over by a locomotive, named after one of our prominent pioneers. We landed where, when I first crossed the river, stood the lone cabin of our worthy President. What do I find now? A young city teeming with life, and containing a larger population and more wealth than was then contained in Galena, St. Louis, and Chicago.

I think, sir, that we have proved our faith by our works, and if any man is skeptical upon the sentiment contained in the text, let him take a ride any pleasant day along the river, from Buffalo to Princeton, from thence through the prairie to Blue Grass, and he will become a convert to the "Gospel both of peace and plenty."

We have formed the new associations,—that they have been pleasant ones I have the best evidence in the world around me this evening.

We have transplanted the young sapling, it has taken deep root in a congenial soil and became a sturdy tree.

We have made the new homes, raised the new altars, built the new school-houses and churches. To do this required men; men of iron nerve, of strong arms and large hearts, and such were the pioneers of Scott county.

6. *The City of Davenport*—The Pet and the Pride of glorious "old Scott;" crown jewel of the Upper Mississippi; the rose of Sharon and the lily of the valley.

Responded to by Hon. Jas. Thorington, in whose off-hand remarks were mingled the humor and good sense which are so characteristic of the Speaker. Unfortunately, it has not been possible to obtain a copy of his remarks.

7. *The Race that occupied the land before us*—Men in physical ability, stoics in morals: They are our brothers.

Rev. Mr. Powers responded to this, and spoke as follows:

Mr. President:—It is fitting, amid the stirring, local and national associations of this hour, to remember that stern race whose fair heritage we possess. Their hunting grounds have become our harvest-fields; the sites of their wigwams are thriving settlements and industrious marts; household sounds and christian worship are heard where resounded their war cry; and on their trail the iron railway shoots toward the setting sun.

Though children of the wilderness, rude, sanguinary, and superstitious, still their savage humanity is redeemed by many heroic virtues. As magnanimous in friendship as they were implacable in revenge; as sagacious in council as dauntless in war—ever patient, intrepid, self-reliant, imperturbable in success or defeat, with their darkest traits are always blended lines of light, which reveal the nobler qualities of the man.

Indian history, sir, is not barren of pathetic incident and brilliant example. Heroes and patriots live in its exciting chronicles. And whether we contemplate the noble constancy of King Philip, the magnanimity of Massasoit, the tenderness of Pocahontas, the eloquent enthusiasm of Garangula and Red Jacket, the chivalrous heroism of Tecumseh, or the fervid patriotism of Black Hawk, we recognize types of character which claim our sympathy, and command our admiration.

Though the Indian saw, in the trophies of advancing civilization, fruitful lands and peaceful arts, the ornaments and amenities of life, still we can honor that sentiment which inspired his devotion to the rude freedom of his native wilds, and provoked resistance to the aggressive pioneer with all the arts of subtle strategy and force, even when the shadow of doom was dark upon him. Yes, we can honor him, for the land that we loved was the *land of his fathers*, and he felt that their voices spoke to him of duty and patriotism from their graves.

But the memory of this peculiar race shall not pass away, though they have left no monuments in brass and marble to plead for them from ruin and decay. It is perpetuated in the appellations of mighty waters and everlasting lands. Their legends whisper in every wind, in falling leaf, and feathery snow, and in all the cadences of the woods and shores. And while our harvests ripen under auspicious suns, while the blue rivers bear our commerce to the sea, while a grateful people enjoy the blessings of the Great Father of us all, the story of their pastimes and their prowess, shall be repeated in the homes of the happy and the free.

8. *Antoine LeClaire*—First in settlement—first in efforts to make our city peerless among rivals—first in the esteem of his fellow citizens—first President of this society; may "*his shadow never be less.*"

Responded to by E. Cook, Esq., who regretted that the reply had not been committed to abler men—a regret wholly uncalled for, as he did not fail in doing the subject full justice. His laudations of Mr. LeClaire were recognized as correct and merited.

9. *Marquette and Joliet*--The Pioneers of Pioneers. History, poetry, fiction, exhibit nowhere a heroism so lofty, a daring so noble, an ambition so pure, and faith so lovely, as may be found in the oft-neglected but simple and touching story of the first white men who trod the soil of Iowa.

Responded to by John F. Dillon, who said—

Mr. Chairman:—No sentiment has been offered to-night, to which I could more heartily respond, than to *that*. In my judgment it is eminently pertinent. I may possibly amplify, but can scarcely hope to *add to* the thoughts it concisely embraces. Its language is not that of exaggeration.

If I heard aright, Marquette and Joliet are styled "the Pioneers of Pioneers." Literally and strictly true. Beyond cavil, they were the first white men that set foot upon the soil of Iowa. Nor was the advent of the pale face so recent as we are apt to imagine. About fifty years only after the landing of the Pilgrims—nearly sixty years *prior* to the founding and settlement of Georgia by the enlightened and chivalric Oglethorpe—almost ten years before William Penn made his famous treaty with the natives, distinguished as being almost the only treaty ever made with the ill-starred race,

"Never sworn to, and never broken,"

did the illustrious Marquette and Joliet visit lovely Iowa,—the State we are proud to call our own! In strictest verity, then, they are the *Pioneers of Pioneers.*

Something, me thought I heard in the sentiment about their heroism and daring! and something about their unquestioning Faith and pure Ambition!

How gladly, under other circumstances, would I talk upon this interesting, this suggestive theme! But it would be vastly imprudent to risk an excursion to this Enchanted Ground, where one would infallibly be tempted to linger longer than the proprieties of the occasion, and the advanced hour of the night would warrant. A few words, then, and a few only, must suffice. We must be content to glance at, without entering upon, the delightful land.

The whole West, the Mississippi Valley, at the time of which I speak, was an unexplored wilderness. More than a century had elapsed since the discovery of the Mississippi by the romantic De Soto, who, though he found not gold in its sands, most fittingly found a grave beneath its waters,—yet nothing more than its bare existence was known.

No European knew where it rose or where it discharged its mighty floods. Marquette knew of it only from the reports of the natives as the "Great River" lying *somewhere* in the distant West, and whose banks were reputed to be thronged with blood-thirsty savages, and whose waters were said to abound in destructive monsters.

He felt animated to attempt its discovery; and nobly dared to brave every danger, and endure every hardship incident to the perilous undertaking.

*Why* did he seek it? and *how?*

He sought it not as thousands in our own day have sought a distant land in our own Continent, and a still more distant island in a distant ocean, *for Gold!* He sought it not for wordly fame, or worldly ends. He sought it as an humble Missionary for the purpose of proclaiming the Gospel, and erecting the standard of Christianity among the tribes that he thought to find residing upon its banks. I see in imagination, Marquette and Joliet, with but five attendants, and two guides, leave the last white settlement, and boldly pushing forward they knew not where, among hostile and unknown tribes.

Their guides can aid them no further, and the guides return. Submitting to the guidance of Providence, with their light canoes upon their backs, they at length find the Wisconsin. Unlike the streams they had left behind, *this* flowed towards the setting sun. They patiently follow its current for an entire week, when lo! the long sought for River, as magnificent then as it is to-day, burst upon their enraptured vision.

Day after day they sailed down its waters. They certainly passed, mayhaps landed at the place where our flourishing city now stands.

Near the southern boundary of our State they saw *foot prints* on the sands of the river shore. They landed,—anticipating, but not dreading, death at every step, and kept upon the trail until it led to an Indian village upon the banks of the Des Moines.

Their courage and heroism faltered not for a moment. They boldly advanced, and Marquette proclaimed to the astonished natives God and the doctrines and mysteries of the faith which he taught.

The remarks of the eloquent gentleman who responded to number seven, remind me of the first words of these natives on the banks of the Des Moines, on beholding Marquette and his companions: "*We are men*," said they. And men they were. They are our brothers. They were recognized as such by Marquette "in his labors of love."

Do the departed look down upon us? If so, with what astonishment must these early *Voyageurs* behold the miraculous growth and development of the country they were the first to point out and visit.

We love to imagine, as they trod these shores, in the majestic solitudes of nature, that they *heard* the tramp of the coming millions! and had visions of the Empires that have since arisen so marvelously upon the banks of the Great River they were the first to explore.

They founded no cities. They left no permanent monuments behind them! Yet a generous posterity will not willingly let their names perish. So far as they, or their "simple and touching story" is concerned, no "Old Mortality" is needed by the "Pioneer Settlers" assembled here to-night. So long as yon river flows, it will water their memories, and preserve them fresh and green!

10. *The Pioneer Press of Scott County.*

Mr. Andrew Logan was first called upon, and made some brief but pertinent remarks in regard to the reception and growth of the Press in Davenport. He was followed by Alfred Sanders, Esq., Senior Editor of the *Gazette*, who spoke as follows:

Mr. Chairman:—In responding to that sentiment, permit me to express my pleasure in meeting so many of my fellow citizens, those whose features and voices have so long been familiar to me. I love to look upon their smiling faces, many of which, alas! since they first were familiar to my sight, have become worn and furrowed by time, while their locks have grown thin and blanched by age. But we are *all* passing away—we that were boys and girls a few years since, are now the fathers and mothers of boys and girls, and the responsibility that devolved upon our parents now rests upon us. Another score of years and our children will be the actors in the drama of life, and we either be spectators or have retired altogether from the stage of action.

When the portals of manhood first opened to me, and the wide world lay spread out, inviting me to select a locality, I started upon a tour of over two thousand miles. I viewed many towns on my route, but the one that presented the strongest attractions, that offered the most inducements for me to return and make it my home, was the then insignificant but beautiful town of Davenport, at that time a small village of some five hundred inhabitants.

In the same year of my life I came and declared my intention of becoming a citizen, and the next year returned and brought with me my press, my partner in business—I might almost add, my partner in life, as she immediately followed—and planted my stakes for *life.*

We landed here on the 11th day of August, 1841, on one of the smallest steamers that ever ascended the Mississippi River. In crossing the Lower Rapids we had to *pole over,* the power of the engine not being sufficient to propel the little steamer against the current! We were four days thence in reaching the town of Davenport. As we landed here, the good people of the village crowded down to the wharf to see and *aid* in disembarking the new press, and so effectually did they succeed in the latter particular, that they managed before they got it ashore to bury it beneath the waves of the Father of Waters! Thus it was *baptized,* and I trust it never did discredit to the town it represented, the cause it advocated, nor—the ghostly fathers that administered the ordinance!

That we saw *hard times* for many years in the publication of the *Gazette,* every old settler from personal experience *knows* to be the fact, but being blessed with a spirit that never says die, we persevered, and the paper now stands as one of the *institutions* of the West.

With pride I say it, Mr. Chairman,—as I presume it to be the only instance on record in the West—that although we had to purchase all our paper and materials in the East, and have them brought out by the slow and tedious course of the Ohio and Mississippi rivers, and although we had our paper sunk, and burned, and delayed by every accident incident to so long a transportation, and although my assistants were sick, and I alone had to fill every department of the paper, from writing its editorials, and setting the type, to working at press, and rolling for papers, yet, during the sixteen and a half years I have controlled the *Gazette, it never has missed a single number.*

Of all those connected with the press in the State of Iowa, or in the entire region of country west of the Mississippi River, from its source to its outlet, at the time I commenced the publication of the Davenport *Gazette,* not a single *one* remains in that capacity—they are *all* gone, a few to other occupations, but the great majority of them to the bourne whence no traveler returns. I stand *alone,* and yet not alone—there are more editors this day in the city of Davenport than there were then in the entire State of Iowa, and throughout the West—who can number them?

I will but add, that if an *acccuntability* attaches to *us* old settlers, for our agency in inducing many persons to leave the comforts and luxuries of Eastern homes to take up their abode here, where they were denied those luxuries, that I will have full as much to answer for as any of you; but if I have no worse reflection to vex my last hours than the thought of my instrumentality in inducing good people to make Davenport their homes, I shall certainly depart in peace.

11. *The Pioneer Children*—They are now brave young men and fair young women; may their lives, if not as eventful, be as useful as those of their parents.

Responded to by G. W. Hoge, in a very creditable speech. He said:

One of Scott County's Earliest Born,---it is with no little pleasure, Mr. President, that I respond to this call, which recognizes me as such; and to the toast, in which we, the "children of the soil," are so kindly remembered.

There are hours, sir, in the lives of all, which, from attendant circumstances, become eras—landmarks along the pathway of life, to which memory will ever revert, with undiminished interest. Such an one will the present occasion be; and by none will it be remembered with a truer, or more lasting pleasure, than by us, the junior members of this noble family—us, "the Pioneer Children of Scott County."

Born here, many of us, at a time when but a few scattered, and lowly dwellings, marked the site of the now populous aud opulent city of Davenport —while our beauteous State, herself, was yet in embryo—our interest in Scott county has been no less deep, our affection for her no less fervent than their's who, emigrants from other States, came here to find a second home on our boundless prairies, or beside our noble river.

We, sir, had no sacred ties to sever—no happy firesides in far Eastern homes to regret—here, was our first, our only home—we knew no other, and we cared for none. To us, *the world was bounded on the East by the Mississippi, and Davenport was its Metropolis.*

Scott county, sir, has been, as it were, our twin Sister; we have grown with her growth, and strengthened with her strength—her friends are our friends, and her prosperity our "chief joy."

Here, sir, has been the theatre of all our joys, and all our sorrows. Here, cradled in the arms of Pioneer mothers, the days of our early childhood passed as one bright, unbroken dream; and as days lengthened into years, and the babe became the boy, by the side of Pioneer fathers, we have explored, to us, the unbounded expanse of the seedland, or the harvest-field; happy, though we could not work, to carry the sickle, or the hoe; and wishing that we were men, that we, too, might hold the plough, or reap the grain, or drive a prairie team.

Or we have stood, while the "sounding aisles of the dim woods rang" to the strokes of the Pioneer's axe, and watched the big chips fly, until the mighty oak reeled—tottered—and fell, with a crash that woke the woodland echoes for many a rood. How we longed to be woodsmen then!

And here, sir, on many a long, bright Summer's day, we sat in the rustic school-house, striving to comprehend the mysteries of spelling-book or primer, until released from study—gamboling in unrestrained freedom on nature's own green carpeting, spread before the door—a merry band, we shouted our delight, unrestricted by city ordinances.

And when the week slipped by, and Sabbath morning smiled, with reverence we sat in the little weather-beaten church, while, in heartfelt terms, the Pioneers praised the name of their fathers' God for this their fair inheritance, and earnestly besought his choicest blessings on their prairie homes.

Such, sir, were our joys—we had our sorrows, too. For, ever and anon, a dark cloud of gloom gathered over the little settlement, as some loved one was taken from our midst by the hand of the destroyer.

A father, perhaps—well-beloved—stricken down in the pride of his manhood; or some tender mother is gone—leaving sad and desolate, a heretofore happy hearth. Or, perchance, the prattling babe—the light and sunshine of the cottage circle—unfolded its little wings, and soared, a white-robed cherub, to its starry home. Or the merry, light-hearted child—the joyous sharer in our youthful sports—left us, with aching hearts and quivering lips, to mourn his early grave.

But this is too sad a theme—there is another—a brighter one—to which we gladly turn.

The birth-right, sir, is not alone to us of the "sterner sex"—for I can look around me here to-night, and see many a sparkling eye, whose first bright glance lit up the loneliness of a settler's cabin—many a coral lip, whose first sweet smile gladdened a Pioneer mother's heart. And the witchery of these bright glances has been round us ever. These sweet smiles—like the guerdon of the boy and man—gave zest to all our youthful pleasures, as to-night they throw enchantment round this festive scene.

And where, Mr. President—whether as now, gracing the crowded assembly, or in the home circle, filling and adorning alike the various stations of daughter, sister, wife, or all combined—*where*, I ask, *will you find a lovelier galaxy than these, the Pioneer daughters of Scott county?* And, sir, all of this gentle sisterhood are not with us on this occasion.

The snow lies lightly o'er some well-remembered forms that sleep in yonder grave-yard. Some, for a time, have left us, whom we hope, ere long, to greet again. Others—and we miss them all—on distant shrines have placed their household gods. But we feel assured, sir, that if these absent ones know of this, our social gathering, their hearts are with us in our joy; for while

"Through other scenes their footsteps roam,
Still hither must their hearts expand—
There is their loved—adopted home—
*This, this, is still their native land!*"

What wonder then, Mr. President, that we love this soil, hallowed by such associations? What wonder, that in our eyes, Scott county is the "fairest land the sun shines on?"

We *glory in this our birth-place.* We *glory in the noble stock from which we sprung.* MAY, THEY, SIR, NEVER HAVE CAUSE TO BLUSH FOR US!

12. *The City of LeClaire*—Our young and prosperous rival. Let Davenport look well to her laurels.

Mr. Laurel Summers, Esq., of LeClaire, was to have responded to this toast, but was obliged to send a letter of regret. Judge Grant made some humorous remarks in comparison of Davenport and LeClaire, bringing in some excellent puns.

13. *Woman*—The pride and ornament of the proudest palace—the joy and sunshine of the humblest cabin.

Hiram Price, Esq., responded in his usual felicitous style to this universally popular toast. He said:—

Mr. Chairman:—I am called upon to respond to the sentiment, that "Woman is the pride and ornament of the proudest Palace, and the joy and sunshine of the humblest Cabin."

Well, sir, nobody doubts that, do they? There is but one side to that subject, and consequently no chance for an argument. *Woman!* I rather like the name, it seems like coming back to first principles, and while I am well satisfied that she is justly entitled to an abler advocate, and better representative than myself, yet I am bold to assert that the declaration contained in that toast is literally and emphatically true.

You might have gone further, sir, and added to the reading, the words—"*and generally pretty hard to get ahead of*," for certain I am, that all present will agree with me, when I say that it is daily becoming a more difficult task to *get around them.*

"*The pride and ornament of the proudest Palace.*" Yes, sir, of this there can be no question, and yet what I may say upon this point, must of necessity be more the result of historical, than experimental knowledge. But, sir, when you talk of her as being the *joy and sunshine* of the humblest Cabin, I can speak from experience—on the subject of Cabins I am at home. I've been there—as boy and man I have builded them, and lived in them, and to-night memory runs back to the days of my boyhood, and calls up before my mental vision the image of my mother, as she appeared to me in those days, at once the joy and the sunshine of my cabin home.

Whether viewed from this stand point, or from one a little further down the stream of time, where with her who for near a quarter of a century has shared the lights and shades of life with me, and who accompanies me to this festive hall to-night, I commenced the battle of life in the world,—in either case, and from every point of observation, I am furnished with evidence to conclusively establish the fact, that woman is the joy and sunshine of the Cabin.

The homes of America! Yea, the homes of the World, all proclaim with united voice that Woman is not only the Pride of the Palace, but that she is emphatically the Joy and Sunshine of the Cabin.

In this world, Palaces are for the few, Cabins for the million. Among the domicils of earth, Cabins are the rule, Palaces the exception. But whether in the Palace, or in the Cabin, it is in the home circle that woman finds her proper sphere, her true element. It is from that centre that her influences radiate, revealing fountains of joy, and reservoirs of sunshine, wherever her voice is heard in the territory of christian organization, and much, very much of what the world possesses of happiness is attributable to that influence.

True, there have been occasional instances, where woman has stepped out of this sphere, and for a time has, with meteoric flashes, fixed the gaze, and attracted the attention of an astonished world. Such, for instance, as the Maid of Saragossa, Joan of Arc, and last, though not least, Florence Nightingale, the latter of whom was, and is, at once the pride of all Palaces, and the joy and sunshine of all Cabins; but these are exceptions to the rule, and only prove the rule to be that the home circle is woman's true kingdom. Without her, man would be a savage, a hairy faced, unshaven savage, for without her *smooth* and smiling face constantly before him, he would not have been sufficiently civilized to shave.

'Twas for these, among other reasons, that the declaration went forth from above, that it was not good for man to be alone. And, Mr. Chairman, it is but a few months since one of the christian powers of Europe was compelled to send out a ship load of women to one of their Island Colonies, to prevent their colonists from relapsing into barbarism. That, sir, was emphatically a ship load of joy and sunshine for the Cabins of that Colony.

It is true, sir, that without this influence,

> "Man may climb the slippery steep,
> Where wealth and honor lofty shine—
> And love of gold may tempt the deep,
> Or downward seek the Indian mine"—

but in all that enobles, all that elevates, all that raises from earth and points Heavenward, in all that feeds and fills his higher nature, he will be deficient. And even now, sir, I hear from afar the lamentation of one of earth's most favored and gifted sons, as from the exalted position to which he had climbed in search of happiness and fame, he exclaims—

> "I miss thee, my mother, in the long Winter nights,
> I remember the tales thou wouldst tell—
> The romance of wild fancy, the legend of fright—
> Ah! who could e'er tell them so well?
> Thy corner's now vacant, thy chair is removed—
> It was kind to take *that* from my eye;
> But the relics are round me, the loved and the prized
> To call up the pure and the sorrowful sigh."

This, sir, speaks of an influence deep and high. An influence upon which more than any one human agency depends the destiny of our country. It speaks in language not to be mistaken, giving tone and shape and color to the Pulpit, the Press, and the Forum. It is the power behind the Throne greater than the Throne itself.

And now to the women present—the women of Scott county. In view of the extent and importance of their influence, may I not be allowed to say, in the language of one of the gifted of their own sex—

"Up woman to thy duty! Now's
The day, and now's the hour
To use thy boasted influence—
To prove thy magic power!
Unloose thy tongue—the word of truth
That would a household save,
If spoken well, perchance may snatch
A thousand from the grave!
On in thy work with strong free heart,
Thy mission's from above!
You cannot fail if you are true,
For all the work is love!
And "God is Love;" and woman's sphere
Of love and hope was given
To draw the wanderer from his sins,
And point him up to Heaven!"

To the "Pioneer Settlers," permit me, in closing, to say, that the sincere desire of my heart is, that you may never lack pride for your Palaces, or joy and sunshine for your Cabins, and may you live to enjoy many such happy reunions as this in future time, and when all shall be numbered with the "Pioneer Dead," may you all have a brighter and a happier reunion in the land of the "Great Hereafter."

## VOLUNTEER TOASTS.

SENT BY LAUREL SUMMERS.

*Scott County*—Unsurpassed in beauty and fertility of soil; may her "Old Settlers live to enjoy their annual festivals.

Judge Grant introduced with very appropriate remarks, and a eulogy upon his subject—"*The memory of Col. Davenport,*" which was drunk standing and in silence.

Willard Barrows, Esq., was next called upon, and made a few impromtu but heartfelt and pertinent remarks. The present gathering was, he said, the fruit of long cherished hope on his part, and there never before had been a moment in his life in which such emotions possessed him as at the present. It was a blending of the brightened joys, and softened sorrows and hardships of the Past, with the serene quietness and social sympathies of the Present. They were thirsty soldiers who had met by cool waters after the hot labor of a weary campaign of years. They were victors, scarred and toilworn, but secure of the future, and save a saddened memory, as here and there an old familiar face was wanting, and thought traced its upturned lineaments upon some distant battle field, there was no cause save for rejoicing.

Mr. Barrows spoke in a similar strain for a few moments, and closed his remarks by saying that he felt to-night like one of old who *loved* her friends, and whose memorable words of affection shall live forever : " Entreat me not to leave thee or forsake thee—for whither thou goest, I will go ; thy people shall be my people, and thy God my God—where thou diest I will die, and there will I be buried !"—and when I shall have gone to that " bourne from whence no traveler returns," the greatest boon I can ask is, that my grave may be surrounded by the " Pioneer Settlers Association of Scott County !" His modest fear of saying too much, unfortunately, overcame the wishes of his auditors to listen to him longer. It is, perhaps, owing to him more than any other that the idea of an "Old Settlers" reunion became a practical fact—shaped to the fair and goodly proportions which it possessed.

All honor to his efforts, which resulted so happily, and may scores of returning Festivals afford yearly gratitude to his name as well as to those of others who labored to originate them.

By Col. T. C. Eads:

*The Old Settlers of Scott County*—Drawn together by the indissoluble ties of a common fate—a relationship stronger than than that of blood; no power, save Him who governs the world, shall sever the brotherhood till the last of the noble band shall sink into an honored grave, and leave posterity to say: He was a man.

By W. Allen :

*The Pioneer Settlers of Scott County*—May the noble spirit which prompted them to attempt the civilization of this magnificent wilderness, to mould and energize the souls of their descendants, that the Creator's grand design in the settlement of this beautiful land may be speedily accomplished, and its results be manifested by the countless spires that shall direct to heaven, from every town and village, the thoughts of a free and happy people.

By a Lady:

*Dr. J. J. Burtis*—The gentlemanly and agreeable proprietor of this palatial Hotel, may he be completely successful in his benevolent plan for public entertainment, and his brightest anticipations be more than realized.

By C. C. Alvord:

*The Sons and Daughters of the Old Settlers*—May they imitate us in perseverance, frugality and industry, and their seed not go begging bread.

*The Matrons of this Association*—Our help, comfort, and consolation in every time of need, and the fruits of their labor now follow them.

During these toasts three hearty cheers were given for Dr. Burtis, the host.

## CORRESPONDENCE.

*Bellaire, O.*, February 8, 1858.

GENTLEMEN :—I feel much complimented by your remembrance of me, and the invitation to the Festival of the "Pioneer Settlers' Association," on the 22d inst. I regret very much that I cannot be with you on that occasion—the first re-union of those, still living, who were associated in the founding of society in your county, will be an event of unusual interest. The recollections awakened by it will have some things to sadden, but more to excite gratulation. Twenty years make but a short period in the history of communities; but it is a long one in individual experience, more especially when the succession of events is a truer guage of time than the change of seasons. More than twenty years have gone by since the most of those who can be denominated the Pioneers of Scott county, settled in what was then Wisconsin Territory. Since that time what changes have come to all—what trials to many! Some have passed away; but most of those remaining are able to claim that the occurrences which have built up the prosperity of your State, have dealt kindly with their individual fortunes, and repaid them for all the hardships and sacrifices they endured in the first ten years of their pioneer experience. These are the considerations which, with greater or less intensity, according to the respective fortunes that have attended the members of your association, will more obviously link themselves with the reminiscences of the Festival. But there is a moral point of view in which the retrospection will have less of individuality, and, therefore, a higher and more refined sense of gratulation. In the migration to that country, each of us had our individual purpose to accomplish—some possibly sordid and narrow—others, doubtless, broad and elevated, with visions of enlarged usefulness and a great future for the country they had adopted. But whatever may have been our motives or dreams, the seven years of hard times which succeeded 1837, (operating with peculiar severity upon a country so isolated from market as Iowa then was,) brought everything to the grinding standard of a struggle for bare subsistence. But through all this struggle and gloom a great purpose was being accomplished:

> "There is a Providence that shapes our ends,
> Rough hew them as we will."

The very difficulties of the country were preparing it for a brighter day. Every plough-furrow—every axe-stroke were unwitting but sure agencies in the development of the country, and in advancing it towards that day of awakening—that complete and active civilization of which the Locomotive is the true representative. Twenty years elapsed, and the struggling pioneers of Iowa found themselves the fathers of a great and prosperous State.

In the spring of 1835, I settled upon the Illinois shore, where Stephenson (now Rock Island,) was afterwards located. In 1836, I removed to the west side of the Mississippi, into what was then Michigan Territory, afterwards Wisconsin, and now Iowa. In 1840, I joined you in the organization of the Chicago & Rock Island Railroad Company. These epochs tell the history of my pioneership. In them I cannot boast that I accomplished much for myself; but I thank God that I have done something—or at least I hope so—for my fellow-man.

You have placed two periods, conspicuously different in themselves, in juxtaposition upon your card—1840 and 1858,—Iowa as it was, and Iowa as it is. What a contrast the two pictures present! The rapid colonization of Obio and Kentucky were marvels in their day, but they are marvels no longer. Wisconsin may claim a parallel with Iowa; and Minnesota may boast a leap into Statehood of still greater apparent vigor; but not, when it is considered that, for the want of railroad connection with the seaboard, the first ten years of Iowa were practically lost to her.

Allow me, in conclusion, to hope that there will be many and pleasant reunions of the "Pioneer Settlers' Association."

Very truly yours, etc.,
J. H. SULLIVAN.

---

*Fruit Hill Classical Institute, Mass.,*
February 9th, 1858.

GENTLEMEN:—Your note and invitation were transmitted to me by my father. I thank you very much for your kind invitation and welcome. It is with much regret that I am obliged to inform you, that impossibilities, which cannot be surmounted, will prevent my joining you in the approaching festival. But although I cannot be present in person, still my best wishes are with you. I rejoice that I am a Hawkeye, and I feel proud of the State of my nativity—may she continue to advance as rapidly as she has for the past twenty years, till she shall become the leading State in the Union. The "Pioneer children"—may they always remain true to their native State, and never disgrace the land of their birth.

WM. B. GROVER.

---

*Foxboro*, February 15th, 1858.

GENTLEMEN:—I regret very much that circumstances are such that I cannot comply with your kind invitation to attend the first festival of the "Pioneer Settlers' Association of Scott County," Iowa; yet while absent in body, let me assure you I shall be with you in spirit. It is a long time since I lived among you, and *then* but eighteen months, yet I have always felt an interest in your prosperity, and have kept myself "posted up," by taking one of your good papers. My heart has often yearned for some of your "good things," and yet I have never felt that strong desire to be one day with you as I now do.

May the same God that has been with and highly blessed you, lead you safely through this world up to *our homes* in the skies.

Yours truly,

E. GROVER.

---

*Jacksonville, Ill.*, Feb. 15, 1858.

GENTLEMEN:—I received a letter a few days since from Mr. W. Barrows, in which was enclosed a card of invitation to a grand festival of the "old folks at home." Nothing could afford me more pleasure, than for myself and family to be present with you on the occasion mentioned—to meet with friends of former years, especially the hardy pioneers whose energy, toil and efforts have caused such wonderful developments in all that contributes to the happiness of man, would be a source of enjoyment, which would produce feelings in my heart of the most delightful character; but circumstances beyond my control will prevent my being present—and with many thanks to the committee for their invitation, I close with the following sentiment: "The pioneers of the West"—they were men of strong nerve and warm hearts; by their sacrifice, toil, and efforts, they have caused the solitary places to be glad, and the wilderness to bloom and blossom as the rose—may their memory be sacred!

H. W. HIGGINGS.

---

*Dubuque*, Feb. 1, 1858.

GENTLEMEN:—I have received an invitation from the Pioneer Settlers' Association, of Davenport, to be present at their approaching Festival, on the 22nd of February, and to respond to a toast in reference to the "Pioneer Dead." I regret that it will not be in my power to comply with the request, as my duties here will not allow me to be absent from home at that time. It would give me great pleasure to meet those who will assemble on that occasion, and to renew old acquaintanceship formed many years ago, while at the same time I should experience some pain from reminiscences of trials endured in former days, and from the absence of many former friends departed. It was at Davenport that I first trod the soil of my adopted State, about nineteen years ago. Your large and flourishing city was then but a hamlet, and no one could have rationally predicted its present prosperity from what was then visible. It is one of the most pleasant facts in my history, that I was enabled, with a few others, to found the Congregational Church, now so large and influential for good in your city. It is my sincere desire that the past success of the secular and religious enterprise of your citizens may be only a slight earnest of what is yet in store for them. With many thanks for the distinguished honor conferred upon me in assigning me a part in your anticipated exercises on the occasion referred to, I am,

Very respectfully yours,

JNO. C. HOLBROOK.

*New York*, Feb. 11, 1588.

GENTLEMEN :—Permit me to tender my grateful acknowledgment to the members of your association, for their kind remembrance of the "Absent Pioneers of Iowa."

I regret exceedingly that business will not permit my joining you on the interesting occasion of your first celebration, as it would give me intense pleasure to renew so many delightful reminiscences of the past, with those whom I have ever considered the advance-guard of your flourishing State, in her progress to her present greatness.

Although I cannot be with you in person, I shall be particularly interested in the event.

May Heaven crown your feast with gladness, and grant you a long lease of years, in which to enjoy the fruits of your early labors.

Very truly yours,

E. H. SHEPARD.

---

*LeClaire*, Feb. 20, 1858.

HON. JAMES GRANT :—*Dear Sir :* I am fearful that I shall not be able to attend the festival of the old pioneers of Scott county on the 22d inst., in your city. I have a severe cold, and am quite unwell to-day—trust, however, I shall be better on Monday. If so, I shall certainly be down. After witnessing the struggles of the "Old Settlers" for nearly twenty-one years, I feel like rejoicing when they rejoice, *feasting when they feast*, and mourning when they mourn.

In the event that I am too indisposed to come down, and there should be no person from here to respond to the twelfth regular toast, please do so yourself. I know I am safe in saying that our people would feel safe with their interests confided to your hands.

I think a good many of our old citizens will be down, but very few of them are public speakers.

I send you a volunteer toast, to be read if I cannot come.

Truly yours,

LAUREL SUMMERS.

---

*Danville, Pa.*, Feb. 15, 1858.

GENTLEMEN :—Accept my thanks for the card of invitation to the "First Festival of the Pioneer Association," and also for your kind note accompanying it.

There are no memories more cherished and fresh in my heart than those of my residence among you, from 1837 to 1841; and it would afford me great pleasure to meet with my old friends on the occasion of the Festival, but I cannot. My heart will be there, however, beating in unison with your highest aspirations for the future prosperity of your beautiful city and county, and the long life and happiness of all the pioneers.

There is not in this great country a spot more sacred to my memory than Davenport. The beauty of its situation; its salubrity; the old associates, and familiar faces of friends are always present to my thoughts, and I never fail to speak favorably for them to friends here when the West is the subject of discourse. Living, as I do, on the banks of the Susquehanna, whose waters are like crystal, and surrounded by landscapes, the grandeur and beauty of which are perhaps unsurpassed, they seem to me not comparable to the scene from the bluffs below Davenport, looking south and east, and bringing into our view the Twin Cities, the upper Rapids of the great Mississippi, embracing the beautiful Rock Island, etc.

It is a cherished purpose of my heart to visit my once home at Davenport at as early a day as possible, when I hope to renew many of my old friendships.

I have also, in the name of my wife, and daughter born in Davenport, to thank you for the invitation, and assure you that it would afford them very great happiness to visit their old home, and join the festival.

May the sun of prosperity ever shine on all of you, until "gathered as a shock of corn fully ripe."

With sincere regard,

ANDREW L. RUSSELL.

## THE CLOSE.

In response to a loud call at the close of the Festival, John P. Cook, Esq., sang "Oft, in the Stilly Night." It was finely given, and warmly applauded. The sweet voices of fair women joined in from different parts of the hall, and the effect was delightful. Finally, at 1 o'clock, "Auld-Lang-Syne" was sung in general chorus, and the "Old Settlers' Festival" was a happy memory of the past.

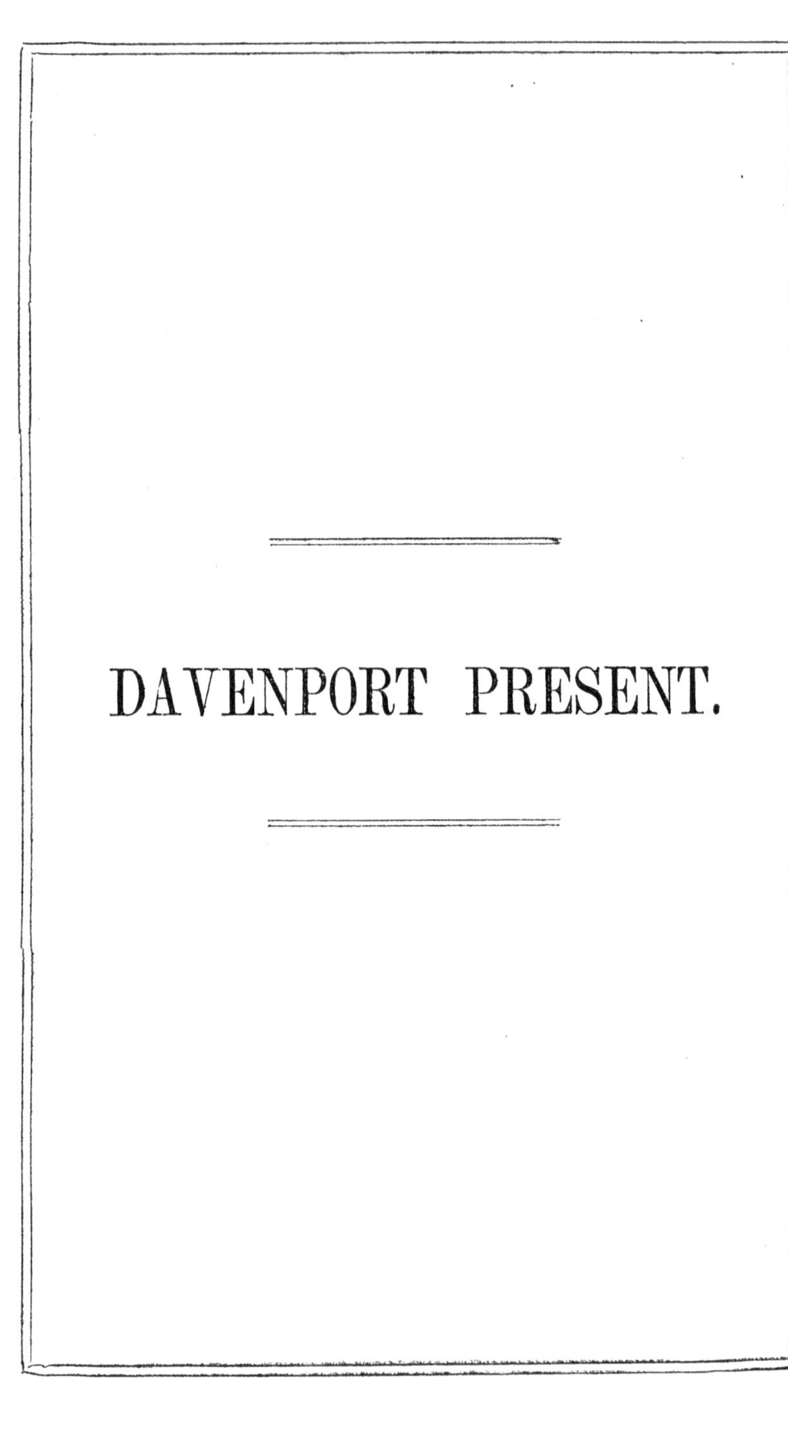

# DAVENPORT PRESENT.

# CHAPTER XXIV.

## GEOLOGICAL SKETCH OF THE CITY OF DAVENPORT.

The external features, and internal resources of any given district of country, are intimately connected with its future history. From its external features we gather in the main a knowledge of those habitable qualities which render it more or less desirable for civilized abodes. In its geographical position we learn the commercial advantages which attach to its location, as being accessible or more remote, from business centres.

From a knowledge of its internal resources, we obtain the clearest insight to its productive capacities, determining in great measure the extent and character of its future population.

Hence it is that an accurate geological view of any district, affording information, both as regards external features and internal resources, is important and useful as a key to its future history.

The Geological substratum upon which the city of Davenport is located, is a white or light gray limestone, characterized by its fossils to belong to the Hamilton group of Devonian Rocks. This limestone crops out along the river banks, of the upper portion of the city. It presents, near East Davenport, perpendicular cliffs, varying in height from 15 to 25 feet above low water mark; thence occupying the bed of the Mississippi river, it forms the lowest chain in the course of the Rock Island rapids, re-appearing again, similar in character, on Rock Island proper, and the corresponding left bank of the Mississippi. The shores of both banks of the river are here strewn with water-worn pebbles of this white limestone, variously mixed with smaller fragments of transported igneous rocks, including agates, cornelians, and numerous forms of porphyry.

This bed of limestone underlies the whole city of Davenport, appearing on or near the surface at its south-eastern border, extending from East Davenport to Perry street. Thence to the western limits of the city it is more deeply covered under alluvial deposites. This rock, together with its alluvial covering, forms a gentle ascending slope from the river bank to the irregular line of bluff hills, which here bound the valley of the Mississippi. Where this rock is largely developed in steep mural faces, as adjoining and just below

East Davenport, the bluffs approach near the river bank, leaving little or no space for bottom levels. This gives a somewhat rugged character to this locality. In following the western course of the river the limestone dips lower beneath the surface, and the bluffs recede, thus giving greater width to the valley portion of the city towards its western border.

The bluff formation, attaining an average elevation of 150 feet above the river level, presents on its outer edge abrupt slopes and rounded crests, commanding extensive views of the course of the river above and below. Extending back from the river, this formation is cut up with deeply trenched valleys, variously branched and thence emerging on the upland prairie beyond.

These several features collectively, combine a pleasing variety of external scenery, and offer grading facilities easy of application, and well suited for the purposes of drainage.

## DEVONIAN LIMESTONE FORMATION.

Referring more particularly to the special characters of the formations above alluded to, we notice the underlying limestone strata to be composed of a series of distinct beds, varying considerably in structure and composition.

First of these in a descending order is an irregular shaly bed, containing the greater part of the fossils which serve to characterize this formation. These strata are more largely developed to the south and west, being the common surface rock on both sides of the Mississippi, some eight or ten miles below the city, at and adjoining the town of New Buffalo. In this latter locality the rocks are replete with fossils easily procured, and in fine state of preservation. Within the limits of the city this bed is exposed at only one locality, formerly known as LeClaire quarry, now foot of Farnam street. The rock here crops out just at the foot of the bluff, at an elevation of about forty feet above the river level.

To this fossiliferous bed succeeds the more common surface exposure, consisting of a white or light colored rock of slatey texture, weathering on exposure into thin irregular fragments. This character of rock shows a variable thickness of from five to twenty feet, and is well exhibited at the lower point of Rock Island, forming the greater part of the exposed rocky cliff on which old Fort Armstrong was built.

To this slatey rock succeeds a more compact bed, mostly massive and heavy bedded. Its texture varies from that of a close irregular breccia of light color, and exceedingly brittle to loose strata of blue argilaceous rock, readily disintegrating on exposure to the atmosphere. Intermediate to these we generally notice several seams of a more earthy gray rock occurring in even beds, and frequently containing masses of fibrous gypsum. These latter seams furnish the best quality of building rock in this vicinity, being in fact the only rock suitable for dressing under the hammer. This seam is of very variable thickness, being in some places entirely wanting, while in adjoining localities it attains a thickness of several feet. The main bulk of the limestone quarries, being made up of the heavy bedded and irregular seamed rock, is only suitable for foundations or rough ashlar work.

Aside from building purposes this limestone contains no minerals of any economical value, occasional spangles of sulphurate of zinc or moderate sized crystals of calcareous spar being the only minerals worthy of note. The slatey surface layers are employed for conversion into quick-lime, but the product is of rather indifferent quality.

One peculiarity of this limestone formation deserves more than a passing notice, both from its singularity and also its connexion with the subterranean distribution of water. This peculiarity consists in the frequent occurrence of fissures filled in with clay, evidently infiltrated from above. These fissures or clay seams may be frequently noticed in the perpendicular face of quarries, here they are seen interrupting the regular series of rock strata with masses of grayish, very adhesive clay. These seams vary in width from a few inches to several feet, and are frequently bottle-shaped, narrowing above and bulging out below. Prof. Hall, State Geologist, is inclined to the opinion that this clay is cotemporaneous with the underlying fire-clay of adjoining coal measures, and that these fissures were filled up at the same period that coal was in process of formation. These clay seams are frequently met with in digging wells or deep cellar foundations, in which situations they are often accompanied with living springs of water. From such sources are evidently derived the supplies of water from artesian borings, which have been made with partial success in various parts of the city.

## BLUFF FORMATION.

The bluff formation constitutes a well marked step in the series of quarternary deposites, succeeding the drift or boulder era, and anterior to the recent surface alluvium. This formation, generally of considerable thickness, corresponding to the height of the bluff hills, forms the substratum of the upland prairies. It is composed of a great variety of earthy materials, including finely pulverulent marls, beds of coarse sand and gravel, aggregations resembling hard-pan or pudding-stone, overlaid by a variable layer of yellow clay, and gradually blending with the present surface soil. These several features indicate this formation as resulting from the deposition of extensive fresh water lakes, having variable currents and mostly shallow waters. Not unfrequently well excavations bring to view a buried soil of rich vegetable mould now covered up by twenty feet or more of lacustrine deposites, containing fresh water shells. This earlier surface soil supported a rank arborescent vegetation, and is proved by buried remains, to have been the roaming places of the now extinct tribes of the gigantic Mastodon and Northern Elephant. The upper clay in the bluff series, is everywhere extensively used for the manufacture of brick.

A fine sectional view of the general features of this bluff formation may be seen in the cutting along the west side of Harrison street, opposite Sixth street.

## COAL.

It would be interesting, did space allow to present some facts, in regard to the supply of coal in this district, but this must be left for another occasion. It will be sufficient here to state, that the only reliable supply of coal for this section of country, is to be obtained from the Rock River coal basin. This has been recently opened to market by two Railroads, and is successfully worked by three distinct mining companies. The present facilities are sufficient to meet the local demand, and the source of supply is ample for all future wants.

## CHAPTER XXV.

### MEDICAL TOPOGRAPHY OF DAVENPORT.

Ever since the influx of the white population commenced, Davenport has been noted for the healthiness of its location. Situated in latitude 41½° north it has a climate which partakes neither of the extreme severity of the higher regions, nor of the lassitude incident to more southern situations. At appropriate seasons of the year it is decidedly cold or warm, and is not subject to such intermediate weather as characterizes so much of the country near the seaboard, and which is so prolific in the elimination of disease in its various forms. The country on both sides of the Mississippi, at the commencement of the Upper Rapids and where the great Bridge spans the stream, is marked by high bluffs of gradual ascent. Below, these elevations recede from the river, and above they hug it more closely. On the Iowa side a large fan-like plateau is formed, varying from a few hundred yards to perhaps a mile in width, gradually rising to the base of the hills, none of it subject to inundation, and every foot of which is susceptible of the most complete drainage. Upon this the business portion of the city is situated. It is rarely, if ever, the case that stagnant pools are to be found anywhere upon this surface. Hence, miasmatic diseases are seldom encountered in their epidemic form. Added to this, on account of the city being situated on an east and west reach of the river which soon inclines to the southward after leaving the town, the prevailing winds come from a dry and healthy quarter, in fact, almost directly from the rolling prairie. Having reached the crest of the bluffs, the country northward gently undulates to a stream called Duck Creek, about one and a half or two miles from the river, and running parallel with it the length of the city bounds. This creek empties into the Mississippi about five miles above the bridge, and possesses the peculiarity of seeking its estuary up the Rapids. That portion of the promontory (if it may be so called,) formed by the streams, and which is enclosed within the municipal limits, is being rapidly covered with handsome residences, more than one hundred feet above the water, and made accessible by means of streets. Some of the finest and healthiest spots which the lover of ease and retirement could desire, are to be found between LeClaire's residence and East Davenport, spread over the sloping hill-sides. In winter shielded from the blast of the north, and in summer accessible to the refreshing breezes of the west, with no marshes or superabundance of decaying vegetable matter to inspire dread, with a full view of the busy river and overlooking, withal, the Twin-Cities, this portion of Davenport has always seemed as though calculated to satisfy the most fastidious, and is destined to become the resort of many seeking a permanent, desirable, and beautiful home. Irregularities in living, unnecessary exposure, or any want of proper care as regards health, will, in the very best climate, produce disease. Hence, medical men are in demand the world over. But, the fact is asserted, that Davenport during the probation of a full generation, has proved its claim to being situated in one of the most salubrious atmospheres of which our country can boast. The mortality of the place is uncommonly small, and the type of disease in its development, undergoes such modification as is agreeable alike to patient and practitioner. An accomplished physician, of long standing, has been known to state, that he never knew of an original case of phthisis pulmonalis in the city, and that all persons affected in that way, by residing in this locality, have had their unpleasant symptoms mitigated and their lives prolonged. The population is composed of persons of regular habits, as a general rule; and this fact assists materially in giving to Davenport its wide-spread reputation for healthiness. In former times, when only a rural village on the Upper Mississippi, the place would be crowded throughout the summer months by families from St. Louis, seeking relaxation and enjoyment. The advent of a dense population has deprived the spot of a certain charm for sportsmen, but has in nowise diminished the invigorating breezes which gave so much zest to their expeditions in fishing and fowling, and which, after all, contributed the most to the enjoyment of life.

# CHAPTER XXVI.

## SCOTT COUNTY MEDICAL SOCIETY.

Notice having been given through the public prints, that a meeting would be held for the purpose of organizing a Medical Society for the County of Scott, nine regular members of the profession met at the office of Drs. Witherwax and Carter, (Third street, west of Brady,) on the 18th of October, 1856. Dr. Jas. Thistle presided, and Dr. Tomson acted as Secretary. Committees were appointed to report upon the several subjects of Constitution and By-Laws, Code of Ethics, and Fee Bill, and the meeting adjourned to meet ten days subsequently. On the 28th of October, thirteen physicians met at the office of Drs. Fountain and Adler, (Second street, between Brady and Main,) received the reports of the respective Committees, adopted a Constitution and By-Laws, as well as the Code of Ethics recommended by the American Medical Association, and proceeded to elect the following permanent officers, to serve for one year;

*President*, Dr. Egbert S. Barrows; *Vice President*, Dr. Lyman Carpenter; *Secretary*, Dr. J. J. Tomson; *Treasurer*, Dr. James Thistle, and *Censors*, Drs. T. J. Saunders, Jno. M. Adler, and J. W. H. Baker.

Although regular meetings four times a year had been agreed upon, calling this the Anniversary, yet the necessity seemed to exist for a special meeting, and the members agreed to meet again in two weeks. The Society convened in the Young Mens' Literary Association Hall, (Post Office Building,) on the 11th of November, Dr. Carpenter, Vice President, occupying the Chair. At this meeting a Fee Bill was adopted, and the members generally signed the Constitution. January 27th, 1857, the first regular quarterly meeting took place at the office of Drs. Fountain and Adler, the President taking the Chair. A resolution was adopted, and a committee appointed relative to forming a union with the Rock Island County Medical Society. Drs. Barrows and Saunders were elected delegates to the American Medical Association, to convene in Nashville, Tenn., the succeeding May. The second quarterly meeting took place in the Council Chamber, at the corner of Brady and Third streets, April 28th, the President filling the Chair. The members of the Rock Island Medical Society were admitted as Honorary members, and entitled to all privileges, save voting. Dr. Patrick Gregg, former and first President of that Association, read an eloquent and instructive address, by special invitation. Dr. Baker was appointed to deliver an essay at the next, or a future meeting. Drs. Fountain, Thistle, Carter, Pelton, and Barrows, were appointed delegates to the State Society, to meet at Iowa City the following June. The third quarterly meeting met at the Council Chamber, July 28th, the Vice President in the Chair. The annual meeting convened at the same place, October 27th, Dr. C. C. Parry presiding at the morning, and the Vice President at the afternoon session. Resolutions were adopted, making the annual meeting to occur the last Tuesday in January, and postponing the election of officers until that period, and continuing the existing organization. A committee, consisting of Drs. Carter, Thistle, and Adler, was appointed to revise the Constitution and By-Laws. The annual meeting assembled at the same place January 26th, 1858, Dr. Fountain presiding. The afternoon session was held at the office of Dr. Baker, the same gentleman in the Chair. Officers for the year were elected as follows :

*President*, Dr. Th. J. Saunders ; *Vice President*, Dr. James Thistle ; *Secretary*, Dr. A. H. Ames ; *Treasurer*, Dr. J. J. Tomson ; *Censors*, Drs. J. W. H. Baker, E. J. Fountain, and Jno. M. Adler. Dr. Baker read an Essay, agreeably to appointment. Dr. C. C. Parry was appointed Essayist for the next meeting.

The number of members at the present time is about twenty, three-fourths of whom reside in the city of Davenport. The object of the Society is "to promote the diffusion of true Medical Science among its members, and to elevate the character of the profession in the community." At the various meetings many interesting cases have been brought forward and discussed, calculated to impart instruction, and a general basis of action has been instituted, the effect of which will be, to define the rights and duties of practitioners agreeably to the rules and regulations laid down by the highest medical authority of the country. Among a newly settled people, baneful irregularities are apt to be imputed to the profession generally, unless there is an organization, zealous in its guardianship of the portals of Medicine. Without there is a charmed line over which mere empirics cannot pass, and which is constantly kept visible to the public eye, the votaries of Science have to suffer depreciation by being classed with irresponsible practitioners, noted only for the excess of their ignorance, and the audacity of their pretensions. Already are the effects to be seen, of a close combination on the part of those properly qualified for taking upon themselves the responsibility for practising the healing art. Uniformity of action, courteous relations, and a keen desire to promote the general welfare, are apparent among the members, and the prospect now is, that the medical corps of Davenport and vicinity will stand at no distant day pre-eminent in the valley of the Upper Mississippi.

DAVENPORT'S BLOCK.

CORNER MAIN AND SECOND STREETS.

# CHAPTER XXVII.

## MANUFACTURES AND INDUSTRIAL PRODUCTS.

### ARCHITECTS.

W. L. Carroll, in Grigg's Block.—Mr. Carroll has designed some of the finest public and private structures in the city, among which are Iowa College, Engine House, Grigg's Block, Haviland's and H. H. Smith's residences, School Houses in Districts 4 and 7; besides a host of School and Court Houses, Churches, and Private Dwellings in various parts of the Country. His claims to superiority are scarcely questioned in the West.

J. L. Cochrane.—Among Mr. Cochrane's best efforts are Metropolitan Hall; Lambrite's residence; St. Luke's church, superintended by Squires; and Willard Barrows' residence.

Octave Roberts.—Nickolls' Block.

### BAKERIES.

"Philadelphia Bakery," Schricker & Matthes.—Brady street, between Front and Second streets.

"Union Bakery," J. Metzger.—No. 18 Second street.—Capital, $3.000. Raw Material per year, $6.000. Value manufactures per year, $10.000. Established 1854.

D. Moore.—20 Front st.—Capital, $5.000. Raw material per year, $8.000. Established 1842. This was the first one of the sort, of note, established in Davenport. The old house was lately burned, but is being rebuilt.

F. Zahrrer.—149 Fourth street.—Five hands.

W. Pape's "Pacific Bakery.—Harrison street.

There are several smaller Bakeries in town, not enumerated.

## BARRELS.

Jones, Chapin & Co.—Corner Fifth and Fillmore streets.—Employ twenty hands, and turns out from 1000 to 1200 per week.

J. M. D. Burrows.—On Telegraph Road.—Twenty-eight men turn out about 75,000 flour barrels per year, besides a large amount of pork cooperage.

Wilson, Perry & Co.—Corner of Bridge Avenue and Front streets.—Run a twelve horse power engine. Employs fifteen to twenty hands at $3 per diem. Capital $5,000. Use in raw material per year $20.000. Value of manufactures per year $35.000. Established 1857.

There are three other Cooper Shops in the city besides the foregoing, and also one patent Wash-Tub and a Chair Factory.

## BLACKSMITHS.

H. A. Kent.—Alley opposite Post Office.—A carriage shop attached by John Murphey.

Some dozen shops in town.

## BOOTS AND SHOES.

Moore & Garrett.—43 Brady street.—Capital $1,500. Raw material per year $3 500. Product $10.000. Established 1854.

F. H. Griggs & Co.—25 Brady street.—Capital $1 500. Value of raw material per year $3.500. Product $10.000. Employ ten hands at the aggregate cost of $3.500 per annum. Mr. Griggs deserves honorable mention for the use he has made of his capital. He has invested it liberally in city improvements, among which are some fine brick buildings, known as "Griggs Block." His investments have all tended to build up and ornament the city, and to contribute materially to its permanent prosperity.

D. B. Carleton.—96 Brady street.

C. Stahl.—Harrison street.

T. O. Russell.—Main street.

A. Galleu.—54 Perry street.

H. Fuhlendorff.—Main street near Second.

J. M. Sellen.—Corner Second and Harrison streets.—Employs 14 hands.

J. C. Todd.—84 Brady street.

Ashton & Freeman.—Brady street, above Post Office.

Fuller & Hubbard.—Second street, near Metropolitan Block.—This firm has the reputation of doing as good work, and of possessing as much, or more enterprise in their peculiar department, than any other firm in the West. Their work is of the very best order, and afforded at prices which will compare honorably with the best Eastern establishments.

There are many other establishments of this kind in town.

## BREWERIES.

Matthias Frahm.—Harrison street.—Capital, $30.000. Use yearly 10,000 bushels Barley, and 8,000 pounds Hops. Brew 4,000 barrels Beer, worth $36.000. Established 1851. The first year the establishment brewed 150 barrels Beer, and used only some 350 bushels Barley. It is one of the largest Breweries in this State.

Dr. T. Dreis.—Main street, above seventh.

Thos. B. Carter's Ale and Porter Brewery.—Near East Davenport.

## BRICK YARDS.

Baker & Clark.—Harrison street, between seventh and eighth streets.—Capital $3.000. Employ twenty men. Made 130,000 last year, worth $9.200. Use Hall & Adams Press, a decided improvement on the old system. Intend to double their operations this year.

There are three yards in the western part of the town, in rear of J. M. D. Burrows' residence, and employ from fifty to sixty hands.

Jno. Rocke.—Gaines street.—Made 140,000 last year. Twenty hands.

Harvey Leonard commenced making Bricks in Davenport, in June 1837, made about 300,000; in 1838 made about 500,000; in 1839 made about 500,000; in 1840 made about 800,000; in 1841 made about 500,000; in 1842 made about 500,000; in 1843 made about 100,000; in 1844 made about 200,000; in 1845 made about 200,000; in 1846 made about 500,000; in 1847 made about 600,000; in 1848 made about 600,000; in 1849 made about 600,000; in 1850 made about 300,000.—Leonard & Hebert in 1851 made about 1,400,000; in 1852 made about 1,500,000; in 1853 made about 1,500,000.—Leonard in 1854 made about 1,200,000; in 1855 made about 1,200,000.—Leonard & Hebert in 1856 made about 1,300,000; in 1857 made about 1,300,000.—Commenced in 1838 laying brick; in 1839, Eldrid & Leonard Brick Laying and Plastering. 1840 making, laying, and plastering. During that period burned very nearly all the lime used in the city. The number of hands employed ranges from six to sixty; common laborers wages by the month from twenty to thirty dollars; brick layers wages ranging from two to three dollars per day. The first brick building in the city was built by Leonard, in 1838, on the corner of third and Main streets; the second brick building (the Catholic church) built by Adam, John, and Joseph Noel. During the first six years of the time Mr. Leonard did all the brick work done in the city, among which were the Court House, Jail, LeClaire House, and Macklot and Webb's dwellings. Leonard & Hebert's brick yard is now situated on James McIntosh's land, west of Scott street and north of eighth street, within the city limits.

H. Delfs.—Fourteen men. Makes about 90,000 per year.

## CARPENTRY.

D. T. Young.—Second street, above Rock Island street.—Capital $6.000. Value of manufactures per year $12.000. Employs fifteen men at $10 to $15 per week.

John A. Nirrau.—Corner Fourth and Gaines sts.—Value of manufactures per year $4.000.

Davis, Bro. & Fraser.—On Perry street above Fourth.—This firm, although lately come to Davenport, have established a wide reputation for excellence in their craft; particularly in the difficult department of stair-building, in which they have no rivals. All are practical and excellent draughtsmen, and possess in connection with their practical skill, in wood-work a thorough scientific knowledge of architecture. One of the best specimens of their work may be seen in a counter at the Banking House of Messrs. Hill, Allen & Co., which is by far the best specimen of fine workmanship in the West.

James Crawford.—Corner Iowa and Second street.

E. T. & E. L. Johnson.—Second street, between Rock Island and Perry.

Orndorf Brothers.—Carpenters and Builders, on Main street between Fifth and Sixth.

Jacob Kenton.—On Main street, in rear of Judge Grant's Block.

J. Rumbold, Jr.—On alley rear of Congregational church.

I. N Field & Sanders.—On Perry street, between Second and Third sts.—This firm have done some very fine Jobs, one of which is the counter in Jacoby's Drug Store.

Coates & Patchen.—Alley between Fifth and Sixth, and between Brady and Perry streets.

John Hawley.—Corner Main and Park streets.

W. S. Collins.—Opposite Trinity Church, Rock Island street.

F. H. McClelland.—Corner Rock Island and Second streets.

John Hornby.—On Bluffs, Sixth street, between Main and Brady streets.

G. W. Hall.—Third street, between Ripley and Scott streets.

P. X. Fitzpatrick.—Near Jail, on Fifth street.

H. & J. Gundaker.—On Iowa street, between Second and Third streets.

N. Squiers.—Oldest Builder in Davenport, and Superintendent of St. Luke's Church.

Noel & Marget.—Corner Harrison and Front streets.

J. B. Davis.—Sixth street, between Rock Island and Perry streets.

L. R. Allen.—Boards at "Pennsylvania House."

## CARRIAGE AND WAGON MAKING.

Andrews & Burr.—Fourth street, between Brady and Perry.—Large first class eastern establishment, with heavy branch establishment on Second street, between Rock Island and Iowa streets.

G. HAGER & Co.—Third street near Harrison.—Capital $7.000. Employ twelve hands at $1.50 per diem. Raw material per year $1.000. Value of product $10.000.

SADDLER & HORSEMAN.—Corner Gaines and Front streets.

A. & G. WOEBER.—Corner Harrison and Third streets.—Among the best, if not the best, workmen in the West in every department of their trade. Their work will bear comparison with the finest ever turned out from eastern workshops. Capital $8000. Eighteen hands, at $1.50 per day. Produced last year $40.000. Established 1854.

KRUSE & ECKHARDT.—Corner Second and Gaines streets.

GOOS & LEISNER.—Gaines street, north of Third.

SCHMIDT & RODLER.—Second street, near Scott.

RHODE & FINKE.—Harrison street, below Second.

C. STELTING.—Scott street, near Second.

## CIGARS.

H. HAAK & Co.—Second street between Harrison and Ripley.

NICHOLAS KUHNEN.—34 Second street, and also one corner Main and Second streets.—Manufactures $12,000 worth per year.

JEFFREY & CARMICHAEL.—42 Second street.—Manufacture yearly 1,200,000 Cigars, at $25 per thousand. Brand 50,000 papers Smoking Tobacco, and brand 5,000 cases Chewing Tobacco a year.

KASTEN.—Main street, between Front and Second.

There are many other shops in town, of whom space will not allow us to particularize.

## CONFECTIONERY.

DR. C. PIERRUCCI.—60 Brady street.

E. BAILY.—86 Brady street.

## DAGUERREOTYPES.

ADAMS—Photographist, Ambrotypist, and Daguerrean, on Brady street near Third.—This is one of the best establishments west of Buffalo. Mr. Adams Photographed the Portraits for this work. They speak for themselves.

TAYLOR'S Gallery.—Davenport's Block.

W. A. NESBIT.—Corner of Brady and Second streets.—Sphereotypist and Daguerrean.

SCHULER'S Daguerrean Rooms.—On Main street, next to Nickolls' Block.

## DENTISTS.

CHAS. GOODRICH, Dental Surgeon.—On Brady st., two doors below Third.—Dr. Goodrich has taken high rank in his profession as a careful and skilful operator. He has undergone the test of many years experience, and has in all cases, thus far, proved himself superior in all matters relating to operative Dentistry.

James Morrow.—On Fourth st., near Main.—Dr. Morrow is of an inventive mind, artistic in his taste, and prepared to execute everything in a superior manner.

Julius Chesebrough.—In Merwin's Block.

R. D. Myers.—On Second street near Perry street.

C. H. Bartlett.—Corner Brady and Fourth streets.

## DRUGS AND MEDICINES.

Francis Jacoby.—Corner Perry and Fourth streets.—Mr. Jacoby has one of the finest Drug Stores in town, and the elegant external and internal character of his establishment, together with a skilful Prescriptionist, indicates fully the fact, that his arrangements are all of a superior order.

Taylor & Ballord.—LeClaire Block.

W. W. McCammon & Co., "Union Drug Store."—On Brady street, between Second and Third.—This is a first class establishment, and is under the superintendence of Mr. Reger, whose ripe skill in putting up prescriptions is the result of long and close experience.

Stephenson & Carnahan.—LeClaire Block.

Allison & McBride.—On Second street, next to Cook & Sargent's Bank.

Ditzen & Co.—97 Second street.

## FLOUR MILLS.

J. M. D. Burrows, "Albion Mills."—Corner Front and Perry sts.—Engine 140 horse power. Established in 1847, and commenced January 1848, with a capacity of manufacturing 1200 barrels per week. In 1855 it was remodled and rebuilt, with a capacity of turning out 2500 barrels per week. Manufactured the past year 80,000 barrels flour, at an average value of $4.50 per barrel. Hiram Johnson, head miller.

D. A. Burrows.—On River, foot of Mound st.—Engine sixty horse power. Capital $65.000. Raw material per year $300.000. Employ twenty-eight hands at $1 50 per day.

Gillet, Green & Co.—Front street below Ripley.—Capital $16.000. Grind per year 50.000 bushels. Established 1854. Two engines, sixty horse power.

Graham & Kepner.—On River, foot of Mound street.—Engine fifty horse power. Ten hands. Cost of wheat, coal, barrels, hands, &c., per year $99.300. Turn out 30,000 barrels flour per year, $120.000. Value of bran, shorts, &c., $13.000.

"Hawkeye Mills," by Jacob Weaver.—Corner Perry and Third streets.—Engine twenty horse power. Capital $6.000. Turn out 200 barrels a week.

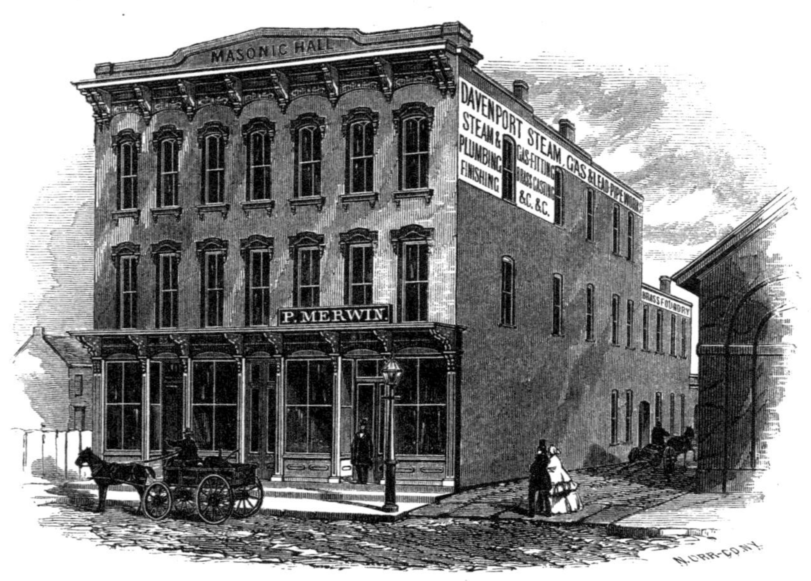


MERWIN'S BLOCK.

## FURNITURE.

John Collins.—Front street, east of Perry.—Engine ten horse power. Capital $9.000 Raw material per year $20.000. Value of manufactures per year $40.000. Eighteen hands, at $1.50 to $2.50 per day.

Knostman, Timpke & Co.—Corner Housel and Second streets.—Engine six horse power. Capital $3.000. Raw material per year $6.000. Employ seven hands at $1 to $1.50 per day. Building, three rooms, and contemplate enlarging soon. All of the firm are practical mechanics.

Wm. Campbell, Cabinet and Jobbing Shop.—In alley opposite Post Office.

J. B. Riches, Prospect Turning Shop.—Gaines street, corner of Seventh.—Engine six horse power.

P. P. Sumons.—On River, near foot of Bridge Avenue.—Manufactures "Excelsior Mattress Material." Engine ten horse power.

John Wierum, Turning Shop.—Gaines street, between Third and Fourth.—Engine fifteen horse power.

J. K. Mills & Co.—Corner Farnam and Third streets.—Employ forty men. Wages per year $22.000, at $1.75 per day, per hand. Capital $40.000. Value of furniture per year, $16.000. Planing, $7.700. Sash, blinds, and doors, $11.000. Job work, $2.800. Total value of manufactures, per year, $37.000. Engine twenty-five horse power. Their Agencies at Iowa City and Rock Island, sell also a large amount flooring, siding, and other lumber. Machinery, one engine lathe, three turning lathes, one scroll saw, moulding machine, three plowers, sticking machine, split saw, six circular saws, two tenanting saws; two morticing, two boring, and one dovetailing machine; screw cutter and turning machine.

McNeil & Bro.—Corner Second and Perry streets.

## FURRIERS.

Julius Koch.—Harrison street.

M. H. Heidenheimer.—11 Main street.

## HATS AND CAPS.

A. B. Alston.—Davenport Block, Second street.

C. W. Verder.—Second street, near Brady.

## IRON WORKS AND MACHINERY.

"Davenport Steam Gas and Lead Pipe Works, and Brass Foundry," by P. Merwin.—81 and 83 Perry street.—Gas and Steam Fitting, Plumbing, &c., in all its various branches; Brass Goods of every description manufactured to order. Also, on hand and ready to be just put up at short notice, Chandaliers, Pendants, Shower Baths, Wash Basins, Brackets, Glass Globes, Bath Tubs, Water Tanks, &c. The attention of Machinists, Engine, and Boiler

Builders, is invited to the large assortment of Brass and Iron Fitting constantly on hand, such as Safety Valves, Steam Guages, Water Guages, Guage Cocks, Globe Valves, Oil Valves, Heaters, Boiler Pumps, Oil Cups, Regulator Valves, Check Valves, Whistles, &c. Wrought Iron Pipe, with all kinds of Fittings for connecting Boilers, Engines, Pumps, &c., fitted to order and sent to any part of the country ready to connect. Pipe and Fittings supplied to the trade on reasonable terms.—Mr. Merwin deserves honorable notice for the enterprise he has exhibited. He is but a young man, has invested in a fine brick building, and furnished it as noticed above. This establishment is the only one of the kind in the State, and is in all respects of a high character.

F. B. ABBOTT, Machine Shop, and manufacturer of Carter's Patent Oscillating Engine Pumps.--LeClaire street, near Third.—Double engine, six horse power. Capital $15.000. Mostly a Repairing and Jobbing Shop.

"Excelsior Agricultural Works, and Machine Shop," JOHN HERRMAN.—Gaines street, between Third and Fourth sts.—Capital $1.000. Manufactures Agricultural Implements principally. Mowing and Reaping Machines, Straw and Stalk Cutters, Corn Shellers, &c.

DAVIS, WATSON & Co., "Washington Machine Works."—Corner Third street, near Railroad Bridge.—Capital $25.000. Raw material used per year, $16.000. Manufactures $40.000. Employ twenty hands, at $2 per day. Engine twenty-four horse power. Pitts' Patent Thrashing Machine, turn out two to three per week.

JOHN ANNABLE & SON, Screw Bolt Manufactory.—LeClaire st., near Third.—Make from 2000 to 3000 Bolts per day, besides Jobbing. Business for last year $2.000. Not much capital required in the business.

JEMME, DONNELLY & LEA, "Davenport Iron Works."—Rock Island street, near Second.—Engine twenty horse power. Do a large business in heavy machinery and house building castings. Capital $18.000. Raw material per year $15.000. Value of manufacturies, per year. $100.000. Employ fifty-five hands. Established 1856. Attached to the establishment are a Blacksmith Shop, Brass Foundry, and Pattern Shop. One of the heaviest establishments of the kind in the State.

S. MILLER, Machine, Jobbing, and Repairing Shop.—Gaines st., near Second.

TOWNSEND, SMITH & Co.—Fourth street, opposite Catholic Cemetery.—Engine eight horse power. Make Oscillating Engines, &c.

"Mississippi & Missouri Railroad Locomotive Works and Car Factory."—At Railroad Depot.—Engine sixty horse power. A. Kimball, Foreman of Machine Works; M. Wright, Foreman of Smithry; and S. W. Remer, Foreman of Car Works. Capital $54.000. Raw material, per year, $10.000. Established 1856.

"LeClaire Machine Works," corner Front and Scott streets.—This is the oldest Foundry in town; was built by LeClaire & Davenport in 1851, and owned by them until 1856, when it was bought by Mr. Donahue, its present proprietor. The Machine Shop is leased by Townsend, Hays & Co., while the Foundry is carried on by Mr. Donahue. Capital $50.000, Forty hand at $30.000 per annum. Manufactures per year $150.000. Raw material per year $30.000. Engine thirty horse power.

W. Skinner & Co., "Davenport Plow Factory."—Corner Rock Island and Third streets.—Engine twenty horse power. This establishment was started in 1846 by John Bechtel, better known as "*Honest John.*" It is now the largest establishment in the State, and has established a wide reputation for the superiority of its workmanship, aud the excellence of many improvements introduced by the inventive genius of Mr. Skinner. He has made many remarkable and decided improvements in his line of business. Capital $25.000. Raw material, per annum, $20.000. Value of manufactures, per year, $45.000. Thirty hands, at $2 per day. Made last year, 3,500 Plows, 200 Cultivators, 200 double and single Shovel Plows, Harrows Horse-rakes, &c.

J. Whitson & Co., "Massillion Machine Works."—Front st., near Farnam. Engine 20 horse power. Makers of Massillon Threshing Machines, &c.

## LIVERY AND SALE BUSINESS.

Parker & Spearing.—13 Second street, opposite LeClaire Row.—Forty horses, with proportionate number of vehicles. Run two Omnibusses and one four horse Hack to DeWitt to connect C. I. & N. R. R. This is by far the largest Livery establishment in the city, and possesses accommodations in its line of the very first character. They have some of the finest carriages, sleighs, and the most elegant turnouts in the West. It is a pleasure to notice the fact, that their efforts to obtain excellence in their department are fully appreciated by the public, as is evinced in the amount of business done by them.

High & Co.—Harrison street, next to Scott House.—Twenty-five horses and other accommodations to match. The Messrs. High & Co. have heretofore deservedly reaped a large amount of public patronage, from the fact, that they never fail in their efforts to give satisfaction. Their "rigs" are unexceptionable, and their drivers the *ne plus ultra* of the Jehu-ic stamp. For a tramp or a hunting tour across the glorious prairie-country back of our city, there is no better companion, *bon vivant*, or careful driver, than either of the gentlemen of the firm, as the author's experience can testify.

H. Smith.—Alley opposite Post Office.—Twenty horses.

Thomson & Hill.—55 Second street.—Fifteen horses, three carriages, six buggies, and two riding horses.

J. J. Somers & Co.—Main street, between Third and Fourth.—Six horses, two open and two top buggies, and one carriage.

J. H. Camp & Co.—Harrison street, between Second and Third.—Fourteen horses, and eight carriages.

There is also a Livery and Sale stable in the Alley in rear of LeClaire House, besides one other stable in town.

This business is perhaps one of the best paying in the West. Prices range from three to five dollars per day, for single horse and carriage, without drivers; and six to ten dollars with driver. Double teams are from five to ten dollars per day, with or without driver.

## LUMBER BUSINESS.

S. T. Allen, Saw Mill with Lath Machine.—Corner Warren and Front sts.—Engine forty horse power. Lately burned down.

Burnell, Gillet & Co., Saw Mill, Sash, Door, and Blind Factory, with Lath and Shingle Machine attached.—Corner Scott and Front streets.—Two engines, one-hundred horse power. Capital $125.000. Manufacture yearly 6,000,000 feet Lumber, 3,000,000 Lath, 4,000,000 Shingles, at a total value of $160.000. Doors, Sash, and Blinds, per year, $15.000. Employ ninety hands, at an average of $1.65 per day. Established 1850. Machinery, two upright and two rotary saws; can saw 50,000 feet per day, of twelve hours.

Cannon & French, Saw and Plaining Mill, Sash, Door, and Blind Factory.—On River near Myrtle street.—Engine eighty horse power. Capital $75.000. Employ eighty hands, three Salesmen, and one Bookkeeper. Real Estate $50.000. Cost of logs for past year (4,014,770 feet,) $43.635. Labor for year, $18.000. Value of product from April 4th, 1857, to December 19th, 1857, $91.045. Sales for past year $112.202.88. Manufactured from April 4th, '57, to December 19th, 1857, 1,721,100 Lath; sawed Shingles, 1,019,500; shaved Shingles, 695,000; Pickets sawed, 25,400. Machinery, one Muley, one Rotary, one Lathing, and one Slab Saw; Shingle Machine; Norcross' Patent Planing Mill, for dressing Flooring; one Siding Saw, and Farwis' Patent Planing Mill for two inch lumber.

Cotes & Davies, Lumber Dealers and Manufacturers of Sash, Doors, Blinds, and dressed Lumber.—Corner Harrison and Fourth streets.—Established 1851. Capital $75.000. Thirty hands, at $1.50 per day. Value of product for 1857, $61.715.28. Sale of lumber, same year, $112.286.25. Engine twenty-five horse power.

N. Kendall & Co., Saw Mill and Lath Machine.—Corner Front and Warren streets.—Engine thirty horse power. Capital $50.000. Raw material used per year, $40.000. Value of manufactures $70,000. Labor $11.000. Thirty-five hands.

Renwick & Son, Saw Mill, with Lath, Shingle, and Stave Machines attached.—On River above Railroad Bridge.—Engine forty horse power. Capital $50.000. Raw material, per year, $25.000. Thirty hands, at $1.25, per day. Manufacture per year 3,000,000 feet Lumber, 2,000,000 Lath, 2,000,000 Shingles, 1,000,000 barrel staves, 1,000,000 barrel heads. Machinery, nine Saws, one Heading Machine, one Jointing Machine, one Stave Machine, one Shingle

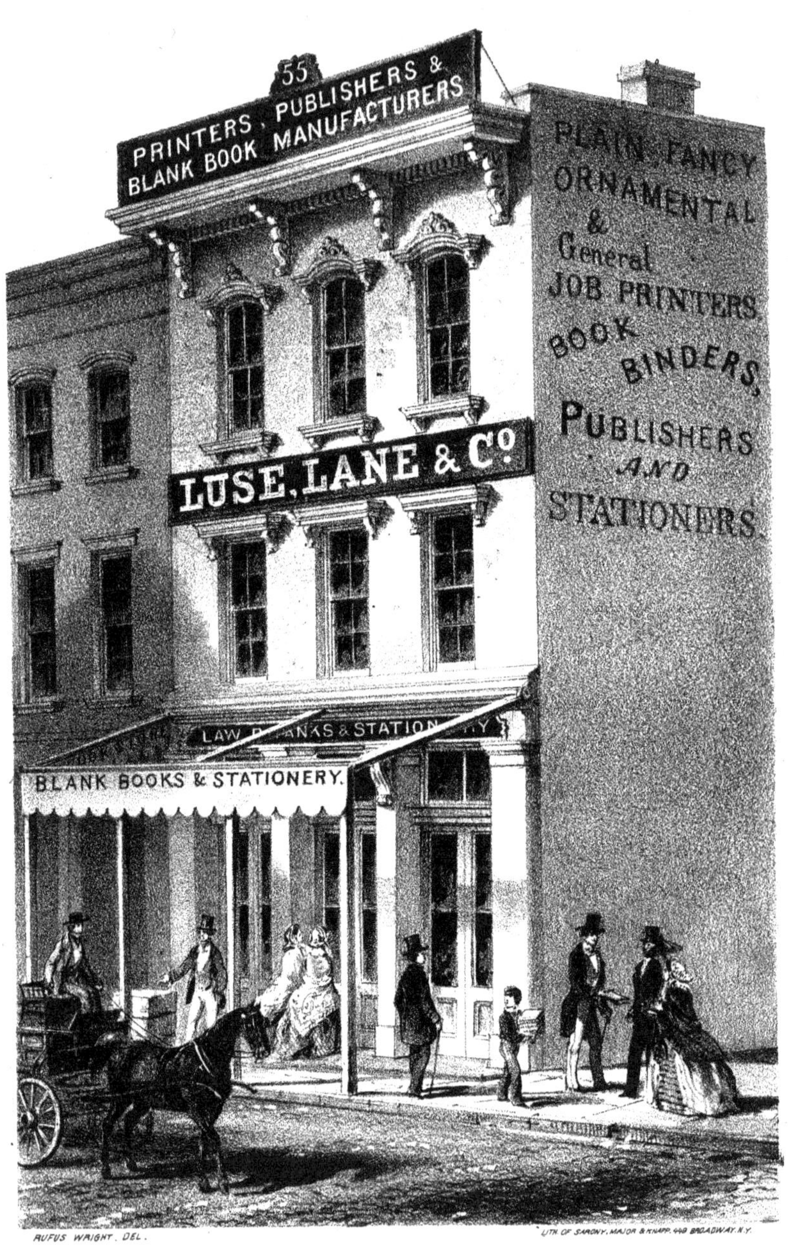


RUFUS WRIGHT. DEL.

LITH. OF SARONY, MAJOR & KNAPP. 449 BROADWAY. N.Y.

*PUBLISHING HOUSE OF*
**LUSE, LANE & Co.**

Machine. Established 1854. Use no fuel but saw dust. Value of product per year $60.000.

SAMUEL STANCHFIELD, Saw and Plaining Mill, Lath and Shingle Factory.—Main street, East Davenport.—Capital $20.000. Sawed last year 2,500,000 feet, valued $20.000. Has a Planing Mill attached.

S. FULLER'S Lumber Yard.—Corner Iowa and Fourth sts.—Capital $10.000. Aggregate sales of sawed Lumber, per year, $25.000. Established 1856.

## MARBLE WORKS.

JOHN DAVIS.—Perry street, north of Second.

B. WATHAN.—Main street, near Second.

W. H. GUTHRIE.—Main street, between Front and Second.—Makes Mantles, Cemetry Work, such as Monuments, Grave Stones, Cenotaphes, Spires, Tablets, &c., in the best style of the art. Mr. Guthrie's work has deservedly given him a wide reputation throughout the West. Employs six men

## MILLINERY AND DRESS MAKING.

MRS. JONES.—Corner Second and Brady.

WELLAN & BAKER.—Corner Brady and Second, over Crampton's Store.

MR. TYLER.—No. 6, Forrest Block.

A. A. CRAMPTON.—Corner Brady and Second streets.

E. A. MOORE.—No. 19 Second Street.

MRS. R. RENWICK.—No. 90 Brady street.

## NUSERIES.

H. S. FINLEY.—On Second street, west end of the city.--Mr. Finley commenced this business in 1839, and after Herculean efforts has succeeded in establishing one of the finest and largest nurseries in the West.

## PIANO FORTES.

JOHN ZIMMERMAN.—Sixth street, between Iowa and LeClaire streets.—First class establishment, and only one in city. Just completed a splendid instrument for A. LeClaire, at a cost of $1,000.

## PRINTERS AND PUBLISHERS.

LUSE, LANE & CO.—No. 55 Perry street.—The only Book Publishing House in the State. Capital $30.000. Business for last year, $28.000. Employ 20 to 25 hands; viz.: in Bindery twelve, Composing Room five, Press Room three, Store three. The size of this Establishment, and its enterprise in having pioneered book-publishing in Iowa, deserves a particular notice. They own and occupy a building, three stories, twenty feet front by ninety-six deep. Their

Press Room is furnished with a Chronometer Engine of two horse power, one Medium Hoe Press, one Adams Press, one Adams Card Press, and two Hand Presses. The Composing Room contains 412 founts of Type, 260 of which are placed in a Revolving Rack, a most ingenious and room-saving invention by Mr. Chester Barney, the Foreman of the Printing Office. The Bindery has two Standing Presses, (made by S. O. Shorey, of Davenport,) two Hikock's Ruling Machines, one Paging Machine, seven Hand Presses, and one Stabbing Machine.—They have published during the past year the Debates of the Constitutional Convention, in two large sized oct. volumes of 600 pages each, and also the Iowa Form Book; besides a multitude of Blank Books for nearly every County in the State, and for many of adjacent States. They have ample facilities for doing every kind of work as well and cheap as it can be done East. A large Store Room is on the lower floor, amply supplied with Stationery, Law Blanks, and in short everything pertaining to the business. Established 1854.

Sanders & Bro., *Gazette Office*. See article on "Press."

John Johns, Jr., & Co., *News Office*. See article on "Press."

Richardson & West, *Democrat Office*. See article on "Press."

Lischer & Co., *Der Demokrat*. See article on "Press."

## SIGN PAINTING.

E. S. Moore.—Third street near Ripley.

Rufus Wright.—Post Office Building, up stairs.—Mr. Wright has done much to confer honor upon himself apart from excellence in his Sign Painting. He is a fine artist, and has executed some Portraits and Landscapes of high excellence. Among his best works are a magnificent view of Davenport, (now being lithographed,) the "Banished Lord," "Rest at Eve," and the "Lost Children." Mr. Wright is still a young man, and possesses a most promising future.

A. D. Jewell, House, Sign, and Ornamental Painter.—Third street, one door east of Brady.

C. D. Glime.—Third street, near Brady.

Cook & Hopkins.—Main street, back of LeClaire House.

Willard, dealer in Sash, Doors and Blinds, and Sign and House Painter.—Corner Second and Harrison streets.

## SOAP AND CANDLES.

E. Arndt & Ruehe.—Foot of Ainsworth street.

H. Ruggs.—On Second, near Ainsworth street.—$8.000 per annum.

Thomas Winkless.—On River, foot of Bridge Avenue.

John C. Matthes.—On River, below City Cemetry.—$25.000 per annum. Employs five men.

## SODA WATER.

John F. Miller.—Second street, near Gaines.—Manufactures 300 bottles per day.

## TAILORING AND CLOTHING.

R. H. Parks & Co.—Metropolitan Block.

J. S. Drake & Co., dealers in Clothing and Gents' Furnishing Goods.—22 West Second street.

T. S. Gilbert, Draper and Tailor.—5 Franklin Block.

R. Krause & Co.—McManus' Block, Second street.—Employs six men.

N. Husen.—119 Second street.

F. Schnabel.—Harrison street.

P. L. Cone.—Employs nine men.

Latimer.—Corner Brady and Third streets.

Mrs. Stoddart.—32 Perry street.

## TANNERS.

H. Winch.—On Rockingham Road.—$10,000 per year.

Only one in town.

## TIN SHOPS.

Smith & Remington.—39 Second street.—Capital $3.000. Raw Material per year $10,000. This firm has done an increasing business for the year past, nearly doubling, notwithstanding the hardness of the times.

Graham & Early.—22 Front street.—Manufacture $5,000 worth per annum.

Brunner & Cassel.—67 Harrison street.—Manufacturers of Smoke Stacks, Mill and Engine Machinery, and general Tin Jobbery.

Wickersham & Williams.—4 Burrows' Block.—Capital $5,000. Product per year $12,000.

## UNDERTAKER.

I. Hall.—Brady street, near Third.—Only one in town, and eminently fitted for the position.

## UPHOLSTERY.

John Betts.—Second street, between Rock Island and Third.

L. Waepfner.—Second street.

J. Ledermeier.—Third street.

## VINEGAR MAKERS.

Antoine Iten.—Corner Front and Brown streets.—1000 barrels per annum.

## WATCHES AND JEWELRY.

A. C. Billon & Co.—8 LeClaire Row.

W. R. Lindsey.—Brady street.—Engraver, Repairer, &c.

J. Grevsmuehl.—Second street, near Harrison.

Wallace & Ingalls, dealers in Musical Instruments, Watches, &c.—24 Second street.

Wm. Effey.--Second street, near Ripley.

H. Langmack.—Second street, between Main and Harrison.

R. & J. Nelson.—60 Brady street.

Appropriate to the present article is the Report of the Board of Trade, made at the close of 1857, which sums up the various matters of business, expressed in detail by the foregoing.

### REPORT OF THE DAVENPORT BOARD OF TRADE, FOR 1857.

The footings in some of the principal branches of trade for the year ending December 31st, 1857, show an aggregate for the business in the same of $14,435,812.24. Of this amount $8,539,744.28 has been Banking and Exchange; $2,628,602.57 sales of Merchandise; $1,158,000.00 sales of Grain and Provisions; $353,000.00 sales of Consignments and Forwarding; $751,030.00 Manufacturing not estimated in sales; $450,029.00 Freight and Cartage; $555,406.39 Lumber, Doors, Sash, &c.

The Banking department shows an aggregate of $6,616,737.34 for Exchange, and $1,923,006.94 for Discounts.

The sales of Merchandise, together with the stock on hand, show as follows:

| | SALES. | STOCKS. |
|---|---|---|
| Agricultural Implements, | $ 25,000 00 | $ 12,000 00 |
| Boots and Shoes, | 72,000 00 | 34,000 00 |
| Books, Wall Paper, etc., | 34,000 00 | 12,000 00 |
| Bakery, Confectionery, etc., | 8,000 00 | 3,000 00 |
| Clothing, | 164,700 00 | 61,000 00 |
| Dry Goods, | 600,902 57 | 164,500 00 |
| Furniture, Matrasses, Carpeting, | 89,000 00 | 44,300 00 |
| Groceries, | 771,800 00 | 163,000 00 |
| Hardware, Iron, and Nails, | 264,500 00 | 120,500 00 |
| Hats, Caps, and Fur, | 34,000 00 | 14,000 00 |
| Jewelry, Watches, etc., | 27,000 00 | 18,500 00 |
| Leather and Saddlery Hardware, | 87,000 00 | 24,200 00 |
| Millinery, | 42,000 00 | 12,700 00 |
| Drugs, Paints, Oils, etc., | 70,000 00 | 35,300 00 |
| Queensware, | 25,000 00 | 18,000 00 |
| Stoves, House Furnishing, etc., | 125,000 00 | 44,000 00 |
| Assorted Merchandise, | 116,200 00 | 16,700 00 |
| Tobacco and Cigars, | 59,000 00 | 14,000 00 |
| Wines and Liquors, | 13,500 00 | 7,000 00 |
| Total Stock on hand, | | $818,700 00 |

Owing to the monetary difficulties, which came down upon us so suddenly in October, there has been a falling off in all branches of trade. In no department have the figures been so affected as in the Banking. During sixty of the last ninety days, Exchange has not been procurable at any price, or under any circumstances, except in very small sums. Notwithstanding this, our local business has suffered far less diminution than was at first apprehended.

With an encouraging activity in their affairs and operations, our merchants have slowly, but steadily, met their liabilities at home and abroad, with a manifestation of promptness that, under the circumstances, has received the hearty approbation of their correspondents, and preserved intact the high standing they have previously maintained.

Careful inquiries have developed the fact beyond dispute that, during the last few months, we have had important accessions to our trade, from various sections of the country hitherto tributary to other points. It is presuming very little to say, that the acquaintances thus formed, cannot but result mutually advantageous. Whether the first introduction was the result of purely superior inducements in stock and prices, which our merchants are ever ready to offer, or more directly the effect of the local currency, that has been so exclusively the agent of our transactions, is not left for decision here, and indeed it is no matter, having gained so much of a point, it only remains to retain it.

The high price of exchange has operated more manifestly upon the stocks of grocers, in the articles of coffee, sugar, and molasses, and has maintained the price of these articles, at quotations much above the ordinary margin between this and Eastern and Southern markets. The indications being favorable for a speedy equalization of funds, we may reasonably hope for an improvement in these articles, and a corresponding increase of sales of the same.

The estimates of Grain and Provisions exhibit as follows:

| | | VALUE. |
|---|---|---|
| Bushels Wheat, | 1,019,000 | $509,000 |
| Bushels Barley, | 34,000 | 13,600 |
| Barrels Flour, | 175,800 | 879,000 |
| Tons shipped stuff, etc., | 8,610 | 129,600 |
| Bushels Potatoes, | 20,000 | 5,000 |
| Bushels Onions, | 25,000 | 12,500 |
| Barrels Pork, | 3,500 | 52,000 |
| Tierces Bacon, | 1,280 | 32,000 |

Of the wheat received during the comprised period, there was manufactured into flour eight hundred and seventy-nine thousand bushels.

The number of Hogs packed at this point was thirteen thousand.

The estimated value for the same, after allowing for the wheat, etc., manufactured, is $1,158,000.

The Commission and Forwarding Business, with an aggregate of $353,000, shows an advance of freight and charges of $150,000.

The following list of different branches of manufacture shows for

| | |
|---|---|
| Agricultural Implements, | $ 49,000 |
| Boots and Shoes, | 20,000 |
| Book Binding, Printing, etc., | 108,000 |
| Bakeries and Confectionary, | 25,000 |
| Clothing, | 28,000 |
| Carriages, Wagons, etc., | 87,000 |
| Furniture and Matrasses, | 67,000 |
| Plows, Castings, and Iron Work, | 205,000 |
| Paints, Oils, etc., | 4,000 |
| Stove Furnishing, etc., | 10,000 |
| Cooperage, | 105,130 |
| Lumber, Sash, etc., | 235,154 |
| Flour, Feed, etc., | 957,000 |
| Hog Product, | 113,715 |
| Sundry Manufactures, | 32,909 |

In no year have the crops of the country been more abundant than the present, yet owing to the great falling off in price, as compared with the former years, the receipts have fallen far short of the amount due. During the early months of the year, prices ranged at a point that offered great inducements to the producer, and large quantities of seed were planted.

The exuberant crop, with a falling off in demand, followed by the financial troubles, created such a sudden and heavy diminution of price, as to induce growers of grains to sell no more than they were compelled to do.

The opening year, however, offering no assurance of an improvement, there has been an increased disposition to sell, and consequently a marked improvement in receipts.

There are few points in the West where the manufacture of flour is more largely engaged in.

The value of this department alone approximates one million dollars, while the brands of the different mills enjoy an enviable reputation in foreign markets.

The crop of barley promised a great abundance, but the result of heavy rains at the period of early harvest was a bitter disappointment and loss to the farmers, and a greatly deteriorated quality of grain. Much of the gathering has been grown or dampened, so that the prices have ranged from the low quotation of twenty cents per bushel to fifty cents per bushel.

In common with other sections of the country, there has been an extensive disease among Neoshannock potatoes. Pinkeyes appearing the most healthy, have been most sought after. Large quantities have been exported, but stimulated by the excessive prices of last spring, the crop was heavy. There are many held in the country, in the hopes of advanced prices upon the resumption of navigation in the spring.

An important and distinctive feature in our list of productions, is the culture of onions. The annual crop is largely in excess of any other point in the West, and indeed enters creditably into competition with the great district of Wethersfield, so long famous for onions. In no soil is the crop grown more easily, profitably, or satisfactorily. The average price for the year has been fifty cents per bushel, with a total receipt of twenty-five thousand bushels. The shipments have been liberal with a fair stock on hand.

The Hog crop at this point has never assumed the importance that has characterized the same at other places of some less size. Operatious have been confined to a few dealers, so that competition has never been sufficient to raise prices, or invite a supply exceeding the demand. There is no State better adapted for the raising of stock and culture of the necessary food than our own. Fertile, well watered, with almost limitless extent of natural pastures, and a soil responding generously to the rudest advances of cultivation, but a few years will elapse before we will assume that importance in this particular we are eminently qualified to maintain; it is but little to anticipate

HARDWARE
BLOCK

that the superiority of our position and advantages will largely identify us with such a result and make this city an extensive depot of provisions.

The Commission and Forwarding Business, which this year shows an aggregate of over one-third of a million, is rapidly increasing in importance. As the Mississippi and Missouri Railroad is extended, so will our products increase, and the same, whether seeking an Eastern or Southern market, must, on transhipment here, give employment to a large amount of labor and means.

## MANUFACTURES.

The solid growth and importance of a city is admitted by all political economists to be based upon the manufacturing interest contained therein—and while we are deficient in none of the elements necessary for the growth and success of a great mart, it is mostly upon our unequalled facilities for manufactures that our anticipations of the future are based.

Favored as we are by nature in our location, with every advantage for the convenient association of the different agencies required in the transformation of raw material into the necessaries of society, it requires only the most casual observation to discern our future importance; scarcely one stranger passes without being impressed with this great fact, while to those who give more attention to the subject, favorable results geometrically increase.

Already we have attained importance; already we have arrested and given employment to capital seeking profitable investments. The success that has attended efforts already begun, connected with the facility of furnishing the raw material—be it Lead from our own borders, Copper from Superior, Iron from Missouri, Lumber from Wisconsin or Michigan, Hard Wood from Indiana, Cotton from Southern States, all of which can be brought to our door without reshipment, added to Coal for fuel from meadows and fields whereon we raise abundant supplies of food for the thousands whose labor is transforming the crude materials we gather—cannot fail to favorably attract the attention of the capitalist and citizen, and induce to a citizenship among us, a portion of the best talent and energy of the country. Already are we conceded the superiority of manufacturing facilities, and already is a wide area of territory dependent upon us for those supplies we can more economically produce than import. Every mile of Railroad that is completed to the West, as well as every acre of raw prairie that is broken for cultivation, increases our manufacturing importance; in no age has the march of emigration been more rapid and continual, and in no case has a larger percentage of population accumulated than in our own State; legitimate causes produce legitimate results. No city has had a more rapid, vigorous, and continued improvement than our own, and no improvement has been founded upon a more permanent basis, viz:—manufactures.

There is scarcely a branch of this class of industry that might not be entered into successfully. Mills, machine shops, etc., are already established, yet these can be duplicated and the supply not exceed the demand. Cotton and woolen mills, paper manufacturers, foundries, shops for agricultural implements, and all the various kinds of handicraft will meet a welcome and a support upon the occasion of their advent.

Here the expense of living is moderate, and the price of real estate governed by its value for actual use; for the proprietor, unequalled sites of residence present themselves, while the mechanic and laborer can find abundant places for a home, at terms to suit the most limited means; for the purposes of business no city has a site superior, while few can equal our own.

The estimate for Lumber, shows the following aggregates:

| | |
|---|---|
| The receipts have been in feet | 22.213,216 |
| The number of Lath received and manufactured, | 6.795.000 |
| The number Shingles received and manufactured | 5,2 4,750 |
| The number Pickets manufactured, | 31,463 |

Of the receipts fourteen million seven hundred and seventy-five thousand two hundred and sixteen feet have been by river, and seven million four hundred and thirty-eight thousand feet by railroad.

The amount of freight and charges paid here for the year have been $450,029.00. Of this the amount of railroad charges was $401,470.00. And the amount of river charges was $48,559.00.

The aggregate exports and imports for the same time have been, as nearly as can be ascertained, ninety-three thousand six hundred and eighty-three tons. Of this amount forty thousand five hundred and eighty-four tons are exports, and fifty-three thousand and ninety-nine tons imports. Of the exports thirty-four thousand one hundred and fifty-seven tons were by railroad, and six thousand four hundred and twenty-seven by river. Of the imports forty-seven thousand and twenty-nine tons were by railroad, and six thousand and seventy tons by river. Total river tonnage, twelve thousand four hundred and ninety seven. Total railroad tonnage, eighty-one thousand one hundred and eighty-six.

The whole number of steamboat arrivals and departures have been one thousand five hundred and eighty seven. Of this number nine hundred and sixty have been boats running to this point exclusively, and six hundred and twenty-seven transient boats.

The number of boats that have passed the railroad bridge is one thousand and sixty-seven; and the number of rafts six hundred. The number of collisions of boats with the bridge has been twenty five; of which eight sustained injury, and seventeen sustained no injury. The number of rafts colliding with the bridge has been thirty; of which about two-thirds sustained injury, and one-third no injury. In no case was the injury sustained serious, with the exception of a few rafts.

The river opened on Thursday, February 26th, the ice moving slightly. It again became gorged on the 28th, and remained stationary until March 25th, when it again broke loose, and permitted boats to reach the landing The first boat of the season was the Fire Canoe, and half an hour later the Conewago. The first boat that passed the bridge was the Conewago, bound up; and the last boat the Cremonia on the 25th of December, bound down. On the 25th of March the ferry commenced regular trips for the season.

Up to the time of closing this report, the river has not frozen over at this point.

The first raft passed down the 18th of March, and the last one the 18th of November.

Of the rafts passing down the bridge more than one-half were manufactured lumber.

It is a matter of interest to note the comparative magnitude of the river and railroad business of the city, and the statements assume greater interest, in connection with the strong influence that has been exerted for the removal of this important connection between great Eastern and Western overland thoroughfares.

St. Louis, with a greatly preponderating river over railroad business, attributes to this bridge, the greatest injury her business has received. The admission calls attention to the fact, that an immense interest has found a more favorable and profitable accommodation than before; an interest that is daily increasing, and if not at present, soon will become of greater importance than the inconveniences presented to any opposing interest. In this view, and aside from any local benefits that may accrue, it would seem to any but the most selfish prejudice, a retrogressive policy that would disturb so great a general good.

There has been received here during the year by railroad:

| | |
|---|---|
| Lumber, in feet | 7,438,000 |
| Shingles, | 3,370,000 |
| Railroad Iron tons | 1,593 |
| Coal, tons, | 13,095 |
| Oats, bushels | 33,843 |
| Barley, bushels | 4,688 |
| Corn, bushels, | 75,834 |
| Wheat, bushels | 183,297 |
| Pork, lbs. | 342,385 |
| Pork, bbls., | 3,956 |
| Machinery, lbs. | 183,436 |
| Barrels of Flour, | 4,410 |
| Wool, lbs., | 18,306 |

Of the above the entire estimates for Lumber, Shingles, Railroad Iron, Coal, and Corn were received by the Chicago and Rock Island Railroad. And the entire amount of Wheat, Pork, Flour, and Wool, was received by the Mississippi and Missouri Railroad. The remainder was received as follows: By Chicago and Rock Island Railroad, Oats 29,380 bushels, Barley 2 316 bushels. By Mississippi and Missouri Railroad, Oats 4,463 bushels, Barley 2,372 bushels.

In addition to this there has been passed over the Mississippi and Missouri Railroad:

| | |
|---|---|
| Barrels of Flour | 29,302 |
| Bushels of Potatoes, | 2,996 |
| Bushels of Oats | 4 830 |
| Bushels of Corn | 46,258 |
| Bushels of Wheat | 235,217 |
| Pounds of Wool, | 25,416 |

The total number of pounds passed over this road, for the year, has been one hundred and thirty million six hundred and ninety-five thousand five hundred and sixty-six pounds.

While the receipts by river have been large and interesting, no reliable records of the different articles exist upon which tables can be founded. The amount of Lumber received in feet has been fourteen million seven hundred and seventy-five thousand two hundred and sixteen.

The following is a list of a portion of the exports by river and railroad:

| | RIVER. | RAILROAD. | TOTAL. |
|---|---|---|---|
| Bushels Wheat | 80,072 | 57,936 | 94.008 |
| Bushels Barley | 18,388 | 2,279 | 20,667 |
| Barrels Flour | 19,819 | 86.5[illegible]9 | 106.319 |
| Tons Coal | | 5,647 | 5,647 |
| Feet Lumber | 9,000 | 16,039,112 | 16,048.112 |
| Shingles | | 5,890,000 | 5,890,000 |

In addition to the above, there has been shipped from this port as follows:

| | |
|---|---|
| Bushels Onions | 18,520 |
| Bushels Barley | 16,372 |
| Bushels Corn Meal | 1,400 |
| Bushels Oats | 376 |
| Tons Ship Stuff | 976 |
| Barrels Lard | 297 |
| Packages Butter | 138 |
| Tierces Bacon | 1,280 |
| Barrels Pork | 1,372 |
| Hides | 1,713 |
| Wagons and Carriages | 26 |
| Barrels Fruit | 32 |
| Packages Furniture | 961 |
| Packages Merchandise | 1,565 |
| Packages Groceries | 860 |
| Packages Queensware | 63 |
| Packages Hardware | 659 |
| Packages Plows | 567 |
| Packages Agricultural Implements | 520 |
| Bundles Sash | 90 |
| Pork Barrels | 254 |
| Sack Seeds | 100 |
| Sack Wool | 11 |
| Bales Gunnies | 291 |

I. P. COATES,
*Secretary of Board of Trade.*

DAVENPORT, IOWA, January 1st, 1858.

BURTIS HOUSE

# CHAPTER XXVIII.

# HOTELS.

## BURTIS HOUSE.

Located on corner of Iowa and Fifth streets.—Dr. J. J. BURTIS, Proprietor.

This house is by far the best Hotel in the West, and in deed contradiction is challenged, when it is asserted, that the "Burtis House" for elegance, accommodation, beauty of structure, and in all its details, is inferior to no House in the United States. For this last reason a particular description will not be deemed amiss, and will furthermore fully evidence the assertion of its superiority.

The "Burtis House" is a simple Dining Room, surrounded on three sides by Parlors, Halls, Bedrooms, Closets, &c., rising to the height of five stories, including basement. The whole structure is 118 feet on Fifth street, and 109 feet on Iowa street. The Dining Room is 39 by 81 feet, supported by iron columns, and magnificently frescoed by Messrs. Patterson & Hildebrand.

In the Basement there is the Engine Room, containing an engine of thirty-five horse power, which, in connection with one of Worthington's pumps, forces the water to a tank in the fifth story, from which in hot and cold jets it is distributed to every Hall in the house. The boiler in this room was made by Walworth, Hubbard & Co., of Chicago. The boiler, steam and gas fitting, and plumbing, was made by Mr. Merwin of this city. There are also upon this floor a Laundry Room, veined by steam pipes; a Restaurant, Billiard Room, Bar Room, Smoking Room, Barber Shop, Bath Room, and three Store Rooms, together with a multiplicity of smaller rooms, closets, &c., unnecessary to mention.

On the first floor is found the Rotunda, a marble-floored, lofty, and roomy arrangement, with trumpets, bells, &c., beautifully frescoed, together with three imposing stair cases, leading respectively to the Ladies, Gents, and other rooms above. It communicates by wide Halls with the Ladies and Gents' Parlors on this floor, with external entrances, and with the stairways above alluded to. Upon this floor are also the Dining Room (by far the most splendid specimen of architectural beauty in the West,) Reading Room, Ladies Parlors with folding doors, Wash and Private rooms, the latter projected in all particulars similar to those of St. Nicholas Hotel, New York City.

Passing from this floor to the second, by either of the beautifully constructed staircases, one is compelled to admire the work of Mr. Walker, one of the best Stairway Builders in the West. On the second floor are Parlors, with bedrooms attached. Linen closets, suits of bed-rooms and parlors attached for the use of several families. The servants rooms are detached from other parts of the house, and like every other room in the house, are well warmed and ventilated. Each room is warmed by steam, and cooking is done by the same means. Every room is lofty, and from most of them magnificent views of Bluff or River scenery are obtainable. The Dining Room, occupying as it does the centre of the house, is lighted from front, rear and skylight. Its being located in the precise spot it is, makes it a vast improvement over everything else of the kind. The Rotunda is in all respects a fine specimen of design and finish, and successfully challenges comparison.

There are 150 sleeping rooms in the house; basement 18 rooms; first floor 18, exclusive of the Rotunda; and the remainder of the rooms are distributed on the floors above. The House itself is on the Railroad, and but a few steps from the Depot, thus saving to travelers the expense of Omnibus bill.

In concluding the notice of the "Burtis House," it is but justice to the excellence of the parties to state, that the head builder is Mr. Wm. Poole; the plasterers Messrs. Rambo & Crimp; J. H. Morton, Painter; John Hillar, Stone Mason; McManus & Wilkinson, Brick Masons; the marble flooring by Ed. Wathan; and the Iron Castings by Jamme, Donnelly & Lea. The whole superstructure was designed by Dr. Burtis, assisted in part by Messrs. Underwood & Cochrane, and "last, but not least," by Mr. Carroll.

In regard to Dr. Burtis but little need be said—as former Lessee of "LeClaire House," and of the house in Lexington, Mo., he gained a reputation for management in the Hotel business, which no eulogy can heighten. There is but a small share of western travel for a few years back, that has not been indebted to Dr. Burtis for those gentlemanly and hospitable attentions that tend so much to lessen the discomforts of travel, and to ameliorate the hardships of absence from home.

The Furniture, which is of the very best quality, was furnished in New York. Mattrasses, Linen, Bedding, Carpets, &c., of A. T. Stewart; Table Furniture from Haughout & Co., 488 Broadway, New York; and the other articles from various other establishments.

The whole house is lighted by Gas, and in every respect superior to any other in the United States.

To omit adding that Dr. Burtis possesses as his assistant Frank Kendrick, would be to leave unsaid one of the most valuable facts in regard to the "Burtis House." To all who know him, nothing need be said, in regard to his qualifications—to others it need merely be said, that he is—a gentleman.

## LeCLAIRE HOUSE.

This House is so well known to the traveling community, that any notice of it is almost superfluous. It was built in 1839, at a cost of $35,000, by Antoine LeClaire, and was at the time a marvel of beauty and magnitude; and was not excelled anywhere in the Mississippi Valley. It was for a time Davenport proper,—inasmuch as it was the rallying point for all residents of the city, and during the Summer was a resort for visitors from St. Louis and other southern cities, who came here with their families to ruralize, hunt, escape warm weather and yellow fever.

It was first taken by Mr. Hulse, then Chapman, next Miller, then Dr. Burtis, (the present proprietor of the late finished Burtis House,) and is now kept by Messrs. Batteman, Swits & Schuyler.

The arrivals for the past year have averaged thirty-five per day, and the average of regular boarders has been about seventy.

## WORDEN HOUSE.

On Third Street, between Rock Island and Perry streets.

This House, now a very popular one, has undergone some remarkable transformations. It was originally a Nunnery, then a dwelling, a third rate hotel, and finally under the enterprising management of its present proprietor, A. H. Cole, Esq., it has assumed the proportions, comforts, and appurtenances of a first-class House. Number of boarders forty five. Number of rooms sixty.

## NEW PENNSYLVANIA HOUSE.

C. Davis, Proprietor.

This House on the corner of Iowa and Fourth streets, has lately been largely increased in size. It is built of stone and its dimensions are sixty-four feet front, one hundred and thirty feet deep and five stories in height, and contains one hundred and two rooms. Number of boarders one hundred and twenty. It has one of the best wells attached to it in the city, being cut through solid rock to the depth of 150 feet, at a cost of $1,000. The gentlemanly proprietor, Mr. Davis, is a veteran in the business, and has long been identified with the business of Hotel Keeping in Davenport. He is one of the oldest settlers, and deservedly enjoys a large amount of public patronage. Attached to the basement is a Billiard and Refreshment Saloon.

## FARMERS' HOTEL.

William Anderson, Proprietor.—76 Second street.

## DENTON HOUSE.

Corner Third and Iowa streets.—Benj. Denton, Proprietor.

Size fifty-seven by sixty-four. Forty rooms, and accommodation for one hundred boarders. This popular house is kept on Temperance principles,—has a barber-shop attached. Mr. Denton is from Poughkeepsie, N. Y., and is deservedly liked by his many friends.

## IOWA HOUSE.

E. L. Lindley, Proprietor.—68 Second street.

## MECHANICS' HOTEL.

William Egbert, Proprietor.—Rock Island, between Fifth and Sixth streets.

## KEYSTONE HOUSE.

J. K. Rhodes, Proprietor.—On Harrison street, between Front and Second. Sixteen rooms. Boarders average forty.

## CHICAGO HOUSE.

F. Steiner, Proprietor.—Corner Main and Front streets.

Sixteen rooms. Can accommodate thirty boarders.

## OLD PENNSYLVANIA HOUSE.

Second street, between Main and Harrison.—W. Davis, Proprietor.

Sixteen rooms. Can accommodate twenty-five boarders.

## MERRITT HOUSE.

Jas. Merritt, Proprietor.—Main street between Second and Third.

Twelve rooms. Average fifteen boarders.

## HOTEL HAISCH.

F. Haisch, Proprietor.—Front street, between Harrison and Main.

Sixteen rooms. Average thirty boarders.

## UNION HOUSE.

Jos. Luderscher, Proprietor.—On Front street, between Main and Brady.

Eighteen rooms. Average thirty boarders.

## STEFFEN'S BOARDING HOUSE.

Corner Second street and Washington Square.

## SCOTT HOUSE.

Corner Harrison and Front streets.—J. J. Humphrey, Proprietor.

Size 50 by 100 feet, four stories high, one hundred rooms. Average sixty boarders. This house has one of the finest locations in the city. It fronts the River and commands a view of Rock Island City, the Island, Fort Armstrong, Mississippi Bridge, and a long stretch of beautiful scenery up and down the River. It is the nearest point to the Steamboat Landing, and possesses in its elegant structure, fine view, excellent accommodation, and worthy landlord, high claims to the patronage of the public. Board $1.50 per day for transient, and $6.00 to $8.00 per week for permanent boarders.

# CHAPTER XXIX.

## RELIGIOUS.

### FIRST PRESBYTERIAN CHURCH.

Established in the Spring of 1838; Pastor, James D. Mason; Members, one hundred and ninety; Church, forty-five by seventy feet, with basement; Sunday School, about one hundred pupils; Volumes in Library, eight hundred and forty-one.

### DAVENPORT CONGREGATIONAL CHURCH.

This Church was organized on the 30th day of July, 1839, by Rev. Albert Hale, now pastor of a Presbyterian Church in Springfield, Illinois, and then Agent of the "American Home Missionary Society." Two Congregational Churches then existed in the Territory of Iowa, those of Denmark and Danville. The same year a Congregational Church was formed in Fairfield, and the next year one at Farmington. These are the five oldest Congregational Churches in the State. The original members of this Church were twelve in number. All brought letters from other Churches—two from the First Congregational Church in Quincy, Illinois; three from the First Congregational Church in Brattleboro,' Vermont; four from the First Presbyterian Church in Galesburg, Illinois, and three from the First Presbyterian Church in Davenport. Missionary explorers had reported a town here of "five hundred" people, and that "*Stephenson*," in Illinois, had "six hundred." Those who united in the new Church organization were, at the time, sustaining a Sabbath School and a Prayer Meeting. "Principles, By Laws, Articles of Faith, and a Covenant," were adopted, (Mr. Hale in the Chair,) and two deacons elected. In all these things the pattern of the Orthodox Puritan Churches of New England was followed. At first, sermons were read by one of the deacons, on the Sabbath, in a room hired for public worship. The first ordained minister who preached to them was Rev. J. P Stuart, of Stephenson. Mr S. was commissioned by the American Home Missionary Society for "Stephenson and vicinity" in August 1839, and preached in Davenport, as part of that "vicinity," from July, 1840, to the beginning of winter. In September, 1841, a call was extended to the Rev. Reuben Gaylord, since pastor at Danville, now at Omaha City, N. T., which was not accepted. The same month, Rev A. B. Hitchcock, from the Theological Department of Yale College, was invited to minister to the Church, and commissioned by the American Home Missionary Society as a missionary for this place. The Church then numbered fifteen or eighteen members. Mr. Hitchcock remained till September 1843, when he accepted an invitation to take charge of a Church at Moline. During his ministry thirty-two members were received. In 1844, Rev. Ephraim Adams, of Mount Pleasant, was invited to minister to the Church, and commissioned in November of that year. Mr. Adams was installed some time in the summer of 1847 as pastor,—the first pastor. The Church was aided by the American Home Missionary Society in sustaining its minister till November, 1852. Mr. Adams continued pastor till 1855. During his ministry one hundred and seventy-eight persons were added to the Church, forty-seven of whom united at the communion in March 1855, the last preceding Mr. Adam's resignation.

The present pastor commenced his labors in June, 1855, was called to the pastorship in November of that year, and installed January 2d, 1856. During his ministry one hundred and thirty-two persons have been received to the Church. It now numbers two hundred and forty members.

Others, besides those mentioned above, have ministered to the Church for shorter periods of time; among them Rev. Oliver Emerson, Jr., for many years since pastor at Sabula, during a number of months in 1841.

The place of worship has been several times changed. The Church was organized in the small school building on the west side of Main street, near Fourth, and opposite St. Anthony's, Catholic Church. Afterward, Sabbath service was held at the foot of Harrison street, on the Levee, then at the foot of Brady, then on Harrison, near Fourth, and then in the Main Street School House again. The present Church building, on Fifth street, was erected in 1844. It has been enlarged twice—in 1852, and in 1855. Its original dimensions were twenty-eight feet by thirty-eight; present size, forty by sixty-two feet.

The Church owns three contiguous lots on the corner of Fifth and Main street—on one of which the place of worship now stands—extending, in all, one hundred and ninety-two feet on Fifth street, by one hundred and fifty feet on Main street. The corner lot on Main street was purchased in August, 1855, with a view to the erection of a larger house of worship. The present edifice is altogether insufficient for the wants of the congregation.

The regular Sabbath services are held in the morning and evening; and the afternoon of the Sabbath is devoted to the Sabbath School. The Monthly Concert of Prayer for the conversion of the world is held on the first Monday evening of each month, and on other Monday evenings a Young People's meeting. Prayer meetings (for ladies) on Wednesday afternoon, and (for all) on Thursday evening. Social meetings to promote personal acquaintance are occasionally held.

The present officers of the Church are as follows:

*Pastor*, Rev. George F. Magoun; *Deacons*, David Gower, F. B. Abbott, Charles S. Shelton; *Sunday School Superintendents*, Charles S. Shelton, E. Alden; *Librarian*, Jerome C. Lambrite; *Church Committee*, John L. Davies, J. R. Shepherd, J. B. Sutton; *Clerk*, J. Smith Connor; *Treasurer*, H. L. Bullen.

The Sabbath School numbers something over two hundred scholars; library three hundred volumes; Church library one hundred and fifty-one volumes. There is a Young People's Association for doing good, of forty members. The benevolent contributions of the Church last year were three thousand six hundred and thirty-two dollars.

## PROTESTANT EPISCOPAL.

The organization of the Protestant Episcopal Church in the Diocese of Iowa was effected at Muscatine in August 1853: but the election of a Bishop did not take place until the first of June, 1854. The Convention sat in Davenport, in the basement-room of the First Presbyterian Church, Trinity not being ready for use. The Rt. Rev. Dr. Kemper, Missionary Bishop of the North-west, presided. The balloting resulted in the election of the Rev. Henry W. Lee, D. D., then Rector of St. Luke's Church, Rochester, N. Y. The Bishop-elect was consecrated in Rochester in October of the same year, and soon entered upon his new duties. Having made his first visitation to the Diocese, he selected Davenport as his place of residence, it being, in his judgment, the most eligible and convenient point with reference to his duties. The Diocese of Iowa includes the entire State; and from thirteen parishes, and eight clergymen in 1854, it has increased to thirty parishes and twenty-five clergymen in January, 1858. Bishop Lee, at the present time, has also the Episcopal charge of the Territory of Nebraska; this being, however, but a temporary arrangement.

## TRINITY CHURCH.

The first and regular services of the Protestant Episcopal Church were commenced in Davenport on Thursday, the 14th day of October, 1841, by the Rev. Z. H. Goldsmith, who was appointed as a Missionary to the Station by the Domestic Committee of the Board of Missions of the Protestant Episcopal Church—his time being divided at intervals between Davenport and Rockingham, which latter place, at the time, promised to be of the most importance. A Parish was regularly organized at Davenport on Thursday, the 4th of November, 1841, by the name and title of "Trinity Church Parish;" and a

Vestry was elected, resulting in the following choice: Ira Cook, J. W. Parker, W. W. Dodge, Ebenezer Cook, H. S. Finley.

The regular meetings of the Parish for public worship were held during a succession of years, and until November of 1853, in the small frame building still standing on the west side of Main street, between Fourth and Fifth streets, occupying the middle lot of that half block, when it was abandoned as no longer tenantable. Divine services were held during the same winter of 1853, and until April of 1854, in the store room at the north-east corner of Rock Island and Second streets, and from April, until the completion and occupancy of the new edifice of Trinity church, in August of 1854, in the house of the present Rector, Rev. A. Louderback, known as the Emerson House, on Second street, between Rock Island and Perry streets.

The incumbency of the Rev. Z. H. Goldsmith continued until the spring of 1849, when, in the following year, he was displaced from the ministry, and continued to reside here until his death, which occurred in the summer of 1853. The resignation of the Rev. Z. H. Goldsmith, which occurred on the first of April, 1849, was followed by the call and settlement of the present Rector, Rev. Alfred Louderback, as Rector and Missionary, on the 5th of May following, making a vacancy of one month in the Parish—since which time he has continued in uninterrupted charge of the Church. When he assumed the charge of the Parish and Station, at a salary of two hundred dollars per annum, with a like sum from the Domestic Committee, he found the Parish in debt some seven hundred dollars—or twice the amount of what the church lot and building were then considered worth—with about nine communicants in all, and an immense and increasing prejudice against the Church, and with but little prospect of its permanent and successful establishment. Patient, continued, and persevering efforts, however, amidst no ordinary discouragements, have met with success. For, frequently, after careful preparation for the duties of the pulpit, there would not be over ten or fifteen persons present to join in the services, and listen to the sermon; while, at the same time, the Parish was without a Surplice, or Communion set, a Melodeon, a Sunday School library, or any of those external appliances and aids so necessary to give effect and interest to the public services, because the poverty of the congregation would not admit of procuring them. At the expiration of the second year these necessary aids were obtained, and also a complete set of plans from Mr. Frank Wills, of New York city, who generously furnished them at a trifling cost. A subscription was, at the same time, started with a view to building the present edifice of Trinity Church, and on the 5th of May, 1852, just three years from the time the present Rector assumed charge, the corner-stone was laid by the Right Rev. Bishop Kemper, D. D., then in Episcopal charge of Iowa, as yet unorganized into a Diocese. The walls rose to their proper height during that year, and remained bare the following winter, until the spring of 1853, when the roof was put on, and the building plastered and floored, and the windows roughly closed up, in which condition it stood until the spring of

1854, w en it was determined to finish it off. Contracts were made accordingly, and its occupation entered upon by the congregation on Sunday, the 20th day of August, of the same year, 1854. The original cost of the two lots in 1851, and now owned by the Parish, was five hundred dollars—the cost of the edifice about ten thousaud dollars—the organ, one of Erben's build, of New York city, and the generous gift of Gen. George B. Sargent, seven hundred dollars--in addition to which, the Parish holds about eight or nine acres of ground, being a part of the "Pine Hill Cemetery," as a burial ground for their dead—being, in all, a property worth, at the lowest estimate, over twenty thousand dollars, and all in a perfectly safe condition. In conducting the Parish to this gratifying state of outward, temporal prosperity, much credit and praise are due to the untiring interest, generosity, and zeal of Mr. Ebenezer Cook, who has been the constant friend and liberal supporter of the Parish throughout its entire history, without mentioning what is due to the efforts of the Rector.

The whole number of communicants, which have been connected with the Parish, at various times, is about one hundred and forty. Number of baptisms—adults, twenty-two; infants, one hundred and nineteen; making in all one hundred and forty-one. Confirmations, thirty-four; marriages, thirty-eight; burials, eighty-one; present number of communicants about sixty-five. Size of the Church at present, about seventy-five feet long, by thirty-five feet broad, in the clear, exclusive of chancel recess, with a view to enlargement, at a future day, by the addition of transcepts, so as to make a cruci-form building, Capable of seating about three hundred persons at present; when enlarged, as plans call for, affording sittings for about one thousand persons. Parochial Library, for the reading of the congregation, mostly imported English works, of near four hundred volumes, the generous gift of Ebenezer Cook. Sunday School Library of about one hundred and forty volumes. Sunday School scholars, about sixty; teachers, six; Rector, superintendent. "Parochial Association" meets the first and third Tuesday evenings in every month, except during Lent, at the houses of Parishoners, with a view to promoting acquaintance, and sociality among the members of the congregation, and exciting a deeper interest in the welfare of the Parish. Church chairs purchased, from the avails of that association, at a cost of about one hundred and seventy-five dollars, being the contribution of one dime per month from members, with one dime, also, as entrance fee.

On the 2d of April, 1856, canonical consent being asked for the organization of a new Parish by a few families formerly connected with Trinity Church, and others uniting, the requisite leave was granted, whic resulted in the existence of St. Luke's Parish, without any detriment to the old organization.

## ST. LUKE'S CHURCH.

Established April 4th, 1856; Pastor, Horatio N. Powers; Number of members, forty; Size of Church one hundred and twelve feet by forty-five, with basement fourteen feet high, containing five rooms. Size of Sunday School, thirty scholars.

## METHODIST EPISCOPAL CHURCH.

Established June 1st, 1842; Pastor, Geo. Dixon Bowen; Members, three hundred and seventy five; Church, forty-four by sixty-eight feet, with basement; Sunday School, one hundred and seventy-five pupils; Volumes in Library, three hundred.

At the organization of this Church, in June, 1842, the society consisted of about twenty members, and were possessed of no Church property of any kind. Since which time, another Church has been formed from it, to wit, "Wesley Chapel," and the old organized Church now numbers three hundred and seventy-five members, with a neat and comfortable Church, forty-four by sixty-eight feet, with end galery, and class rooms and lecture room below, the whole Church, above and below, lighted with gas.

There is also a Parsonage building on the same lot, twenty-four by forty-five feet, two stories, with basement, and also on rear of same lot, a neat and comfortable house for the use of the Sexton.

The entire Church property is vested in Trustees, and is clear of debt.

## WESLEY CHAPEL.

Established 1856; Pastor, D. C. Worts; Members, sixty; Church, forty by sixty feet; Sunday School, ninety pupils; Volumes in Library, two hundred and fifty.

Rev. J. P. Linderman organized the Society, and was its first pastor.

## FIRST ENGLISH EVANGELICAL LUTHERAN CHURCH.

Established November 25th, 1855; Pastor, Jacob Steck; Members, twenty-five; Sunday School, seventy-five scholars; Volumes in Library, three hundred.

This Society has yet no Church edifice, but has one in contemplation, which will be finished next Summer.

## FIRST ASSOCIATE REFORMED PRESBYTERIAN CHURCH.

This Church is situated on the south-east corner of Scott and Eleventh streets, on a lot of ground donated by Mr. James McIntosh. It is a neat, plain frame building, thirty-five by forty-five feet, and calculated to seat between three and four hundred persons. It was founded A. D. 1856.

The congregation numbers about sixty members, and is under the Pastoral care of Rev. Samuel M. Hutchison. They have a Sabbath School of thirty-one scholars, and six teachers, with a library of one hundred and seventy-five volumes.

It may be observed that this Church is in its infancy, and is the only one of the kind in Davenport. It belongs to a large and influential branch of the Presbyterian family, which originated in a union of Associate Presbyterians and Reformed Presbyterians, who came from Scotland and Ireland, as Missionaries, prior to the revolution, and in the year 1782, they united together, and retaining their primitive names in one, have since been known by the name of Associate Reformed Presbyterians. An effort has been made to unite this body with the Associate Presbyterians—if this proves successful, it may change the name of this Church to United or Union Presbyterian.

## SECOND PRESBYTERIAN CHURCH, N. S.

Established May 4, 1857; Pastor, D. F. Packard; Members, twenty-one; number of Congregation, one hundred; Sunday School, twenty-five pupils; Volumes in Library, two hundred and fifty.

## SECOND BAPTIST CHURCH.

Established Oct. 7, 1851; Pastor, I. Butterfield; Members, three hundred; size of Church, forty-four by eighty-six feet; Sunday School, two hundred and twenty-five pupils; Teachers, twenty-three; (Mission School, one hundred pupils; Teachers, ten;) Volumes in Library, five hundred; Mission School, three hundred.

This Church was organized Oct. 7th, 1851, with sixteen members. They had no Pastor, or place of worship.

Their first Pastor, Rev. E. Miles, commenced his labors the first of the following June, and closed them June 1st, 1857, leaving the Church with one hundred and fifty members, and a well constructed house of worship, forty-four by eighty-six feet.

Their present Pastor, Rev. I. Butterfield, commenced his labors June 1st, 1857, since which time the congregation has more than doubled. They have also a Mission School of one hundred scholars, ten teachers, and a Library of three hundred volumes.

## FIRST BAPTIST CHURCH.

Established 1839; Pastor, N. S. Bastion; Members, eighty; Church, forty-five by seventy-five feet—brick, on stone foundation; Elizabethan architecture. Sunday School, seventy scholars; Volumes in Library, six hundred.

Church erected in 1855—corner Main and Sixth streets

## KUNIGUNDA CHURCH.

Established 1855; Pastor, Jean Baptiste Baumgartner; Members, about three hundred and thirty-three; Church between Fifth and Sixth streets; Sunday School in the Church. No Library.

## ST. MARGARET'S (ROMAN CATHOLIC) CHURCH.

Established October 1856; Pastor, H. Cosgrove; Members, about one thousand; Church, forty by eighty feet; Sunday School, sixty children; Volumes in Library, four hundred and sixty.

This Church was built by Mr. A. LeClaire, and the block on which it stands was given by the same.

## ST. ANTHONY'S CHURCH.

Established 1838; Pastor, J. A. M. Pelamourgues; Members, three thousand; Church, forty-four by eighty-four feet; School, four hundred pupils; Volumes in Library, five hundred.

## GERMAN CONGREGATION.

Established July 19, 1857; Pastor, A. Frowein; Members, nineteen; Church, twenty-five by forty feet; Sunday School, thirty pupils; Volumes in Library, forty.

## "CHURCH OF CHRIST," OR DISCIPLES' CHURCH.

Established July 28th, 1839; Pastor, Eli Regal; Members, one hundred and sixty-seven; Church, forty by seventy-five feet, with basement; Sunday School, fifty-five scholars; Volumes in Library, two hundred.

This Church was organized at an early day, and with but few members, and although for many years without a preacher, yet it has steadily increased in numbers. Since its organization, no serious cause for disagreement has arisen among the members, but disclaiming human creeds and traditions, and acknowledging the Bible as the only rule of faith and practice, all differences being thus referred, have been speedily and most satisfactorily settled. The Church is now in a healthy and highly prosperous condition.

## FREE-THINKERS' ASSOCIATION.

On Sunday, March 14, 1858, a "Society of Free Inquirers" was organized, in the Court House—Jonathan Parker in the Chair, and Th. Guelich Secretary. Dr. Hall, Robt. McIntosh, and Th. Guelich, were appointed a committee on Constitution, &c.

## SCOTT COUNTY BIBLE SOCIETY.

The Scott County Bible Society, auxiliary to the American Bible Society, was organized in the city of Davenport on the 13th day of September, A. D. 1842, at which time a Constitution was formed and adopted, which continued without material alteration or amendment until the present time.

The officers elected at the organization were—

Rev. D. Worthington, President; Charles Leslie, Secretary.

And at the subsequent anniversary meetings the minutes of the Society show the following election of officers:

In 1843, Rev. Z. H. Goldsmith, President; Rev. D. Worthington, Secretary; Wm. L. Cook, Treasurer.

Who continued until 1847, when—

Rev. Z. H. Goldsmith was elected President; Rev. Ephraim Adams, Secretary; Wm. L. Cook, Treasurer.

In 1848, Rev. Ephraim Adams, President; Asa Prescott, Secretary; Alfred Saunders, Treasurer.

In 1849, Rev. Ephraim Adams, President; Asa Prescott, Secretary; Rufus Ricker, Treasurer.

In 1850, Rev, J. D. Mason, President; Rev. Asa Prescott, Secretary; Rufus Ricker, Treasurer.

In 1851, Rev. J. D. Mason, President; H. Price, Treasurer; Rev. H. L. Bullen, Secretary.

In 1852, Rev. J. D. Mason, President; H. Price, Treasurer; Rev. H. L. Bullen, Secretary.

In 1853, Rev. J. D. Mason, President; Prof. D. S. Sheldon, Secretary; Jno. H. Morton, Treasurer.

In 1854, H. Price, President; Rev. J. D. Mason, Secretary; James L. Dalzell, Treasurer.

In 1855, H. Price, President; Rev. J. D. Mason, Secretary, Jas. M. Dalzell, Treasurer.

In 1856, Strong Burnell, President; Rev. J. D. Mason, Secretary; H. Price, Treasurer.

In 1857, H. T. Slaymaker, President; Rev. J. D. Mason, Secretary; H. Price, Treasurer.

And the Treasurer's books show also that the aggregate receipts have been eleven hundred and one dollars and forty-seven cents. The receips for the first year were nine dollars and thirty-seven cents, and for the last year three hundred and forty-eight dollars, showing a steady increase in the collections of the Society, equal if not exceeding the increase in wealth and population of the county.

This money has all been expended in the purchase of bibles and testaments in different languages, which have been distributed (except some which are now on hand,) among the inhabitants of this city and county, without any distinction of sect or party.

The Depository of this Society is at present at the Publishing House of Luse, Lane & Co., No. 55 Perry street, between Second and Third streets, Davenport. The names of persons contributing to the funds of the Society are registered on the Treasurer's book, and thereby become members of the Society.

Recapitulation.—Church Members, 5,700; Sunday School Pupils, 1,096; Sunday School Libraries, 3,819 volumes.

# CHAPTER XXX.

## EDUCATIONAL.

The State of Iowa possesses a liberal Educational system—having obtained from Congress a grant of five hundred thousand acres of land, whose proceeds are devoted entirely to the support of Common and Academic Schools. While the State has taken such a high position in the encouragement of Education, Davenport is in nowise behind. Schools are ample in number, and first in character; and this is equally applicable to both public and private institutions. The buildings belonging to the public schools are almost without exception, costly and commodious structures, which combine at once elegance, consideration of health and convenience.

### PUBLIC SCHOOLS.

School District No. 2.—There are in this District nine hundred and seventy-six children entitled to school privileges, and an average attendance of two hundred and fifty.

The District was organized 1853, and the same year a stone house was erected corner of Perry and Seventh streets, at a cost of eight thousand dollars. It is two stories in height, with a basement residence for the Principal, and will comfortably accommodate five hundred scholars.

The School is graded—having Private, Intermediate, and Grammar School Departments. There are included in the branches taught, besides the common, Higher Mathematics, Philosophy, Chemistry, Astronomy, Physiology, History, Drawing, Book Keeping, &c.

J. H. Bowers, Principal; Miss Sarah Bradley, Assistant in Grammar School; Miss Julia Humphrey, Intermediate Department; Misses Mary Slater and Elizabeth Bowers, Primary Department.

School District No. 17.—District organized, and brick school house sufficient for ninety scholars—erected in 1855—on Sixteenth street, between Main and Harrison street. There are now in the District three hundred and ninety-three school children.

This winter the school-house accommodations were found to be entirely insufficient, and three schools were, therefore, opened as follows:

*First School*—(in brick school house,) average attendance, one hundred and twenty. Frank M'Clellan, Teacher; Miss A. M. Lindsley, Assistant.

*Second School*—On Brady street, north of Locust. Average attendance, forty-nine. Peter Van Ornam, Teacher.

*Third School*—Corner of Rock Island and Locust street. Average attendance, thirty. Miss E. J. Kelly, Teacher.

SCHOOL DISTRICT No. 5.—This District returns three hundred and three school children, with ninety as the average attendance.

There is a fine two story stone school-house, forty by twenty-five feet, and capable of accommodating about one hundred and twenty scholars; corner of Second and Pine streets; it was erected in 1855, and enlarged in 1857—cost three thousand dollars.

The District was organized in 1850. J. S. Coates, Teacher; Mrs. A. W.Reed, Assistant.

This District embraces the Third street West End settlement, and extends beyond the city limits.

SCHOOL DISTRICT No. 7.—Organized in 1850. There are now twelve hundred school children, with an average attendance in the public school of three hundred and eighty. In 1857, a large, and handsome brick school-house, 42 by 62 feet, and three stories, (with grounds for calisthenic exercises attached,) was erected, at a cost of about sixteen thousand dollars; corner of Warren and Sixth streets.

The school is thoroughly graded, and in addition to common studies, embraces all the higher branches of a complete English education.

A. S. Kissell, Principal; Miss M. A. Scofield, Assistant in Grammar School; Miss M. M. Townley, Secondary Department; Miss Helen Lusk, Secondary Department; Miss M. M. Lyon, first Assistant in Primary Department; Miss Sarah E. Washburn, and Miss C. E. Williams, Primary Department.

SCHOOL DISTRICT No. 10.—Organized in 1854. Children in District, two hundred and thirty-seven; average attendance, sixty-eight.

There is a respectable frame school-house, capable of accommodating eighty scholars, on Main street, west of Mound, (East Davenport.)

A. M. Geiger, Teacher; Miss Cornelia M'Carn, Assistant.

## SELECT AND OTHER SCHOOLS.

GERMAN AND ENGLISH SCHOOL.—Established in 1857, in the St. Kunigunda Catholic Church; has sixty scholars. Henry Koehler, Teacher.

CATHOLIC SCHOOL.—Large two story frame school-house on Church Square, rear of St. Anthony's Church, erected in 1856; which was, however, only an addition to other school buildings near at hand. This school was first opened in [illegible], by Rev. J. A. M. Pelamourgues. There are now about forty-seven scholars in attendance.

Rev. J. A. M. Pelamourgues, Principal; J. D. Smith, and Mrs. Sullivan, Assistants in Male Department.

Eight Sisters conduct the Female Department.

German School.—Brick school-house, corner Warren and Fourth streets. Established in 1853; sixty-two scholars. John H. True, Teacher.

Select Schools.—L. C. Burwell, in Grigg's Hall block—thirty-two scholars.

Miss Byron, in Forrest's block—fifteen scholars.

Misses Lyon & Munn, corner Perry and Fifth streets—thirty-five scholars.

Misses Severance & Bennett, in Bailey's Hall.

Mrs. Stevens, on Main street, above Eighth—eighteen scholars.

W. Wier, on Main street, opposite Catholic Church—twelve scholars.

Mrs. N. Crockett, Young's Block, Brady street—twenty scholars.

German and American Institute—On Scott street, between Third and Fourth. W. Riepe and Louise Riepe, teachers—thirty scholars. Ladies' and Boys' Departments.

Davenport Commercial College—In Jacoby's new building, corner of Third and Perry streets. The course embraces Double Entry Book-keeping, as applicable to every branch of Trade, viz: Wholesale, Retail, Forwarding and Commission, Banking, Steam Boating, Joint Stock and Compound Company Business, both Individual and Partnership, and as comprehensive as at any similar Institution in the United States.

Commercial Calculations and Correspondence form a part of the course, together with a course of Lectures on Commercial Law, by an able lecturer. There is in connection with the Institution, and under the immediate supervision of the Principals, a Ladies Department, in which Book-keeping and Penmanship will be thoroughly taught. Every facility will be afforded to pupils to enable them to complete the course in the shortest possible time. J. C. Lopez, Principal; W. H. Pratt, Assistant Principal.

Mount Ida Female College.—This Institution was organized in Davenport, and commenced its first Session on the 7th day of September, 1857, under the direction of Rev. M. McKendree Tooke, A. M., and Lady, through whose instrumentality the "Mount Ida College Association" has recently been organized, and under whose auspices this College is placed.

The principal object of this Association is the promotion of the higher educational interests of the Young Ladies of the West.

The unfinished building, formerly designated as the "Ladies College," which was commenced and prosecuted with commendable energy for a time, by Mr. T. H. Codding, has recently been purchased, and is now being fitted up in the most approved style of Eastern Colleges. The Boarding Hall, (now neatly

finished,) and dormitories, are sufficiently commodious to accommodate one hundred Young Ladies as boarders. The Session Rooms have just been furnished with the nicest styles of Boston furniture, diagonally arranged, and the three commodious parlors have been neatly papered, grained, carpeted, and furnished with new and elegant pianos, &c., for the accommodation of the Musical and Ornamental Department.

The building itself, is a substantial brick edifice, four stories high, and when enlarged and completed, as now designed, with two wings, each fronting the river on Third street thirty-five feet, and extending northward, parallel with Bridge and College avenues, eighty feet, making in all a front of one hundred and thirty feet by eighty, rear, and finished with appropriate embellishments, verandahs, observatory, &c., with grounds beautifully laid out, and newly fenced—will cost, it is thought, inclusive of the beautiful plat of four acres of ground upon which it is situated, between seventy-five and one hundred thousand dollars, and will accommodate from three to five hundred students.

The College is situated on a delightful eminence in the eastern part of the city, surrounded by a beautiful grove, overlooking the main part of the city of Davenport, with her sister cities of Rock Island and Moline in full view, and commands a most enchanting view of the celebrated "Father of Waters" for a distance of nearly sixteen miles, with its life-like steamers passing and repassing almost every hour.

This combines most charmingly for educational purposes, all the advantages both of country and city location, and in general healthfulness, purity of moral atmosphere, sublimity and beauty of scenery, is not excelled, it is thought, by that of any similar Institution of this nation. The central position also of this enterprise, will always render it easy of access from all points of compass—from North and South, by the palace-like Packets upon the Mississippi; and from east and west, by the Chicago and Rock Island Railroad, which crosses the Mississippi upon the magnificent Railroad Bridge near Fort Armstrong, in full view of the College edifice, and the Mississippi and Missouri Railroad passing on Westward through the interior of Iowa, intersected by various railroad branches.

Four Departments are established in this Institution, viz:

1. A Model School for Misses.
2. An Academic Department, preparatory to entering the Collegiate.
3. A Collegiate Department, embracing substantially the Scientific and Classical course recently established for Female Colleges, by a Convention of Presidents of Colleges held at Cincinnati, Ohio.
4. A Musical and Ornamental Department.

This College being incorporated with the highest collegiate powers, full and formal Diplomas conferring appropriate literary degrees, are awarded to those Young Ladies who sustain a satisfactory examination in the prescribed course of study, or such other branches as may by the Faculty and Curators be deemed an equivalent.

FACULTY.—Rev. M. McKendree Tooke, A. M., President, Prof. of Intellectual and Moral Science, and Belles Lettres.

Rev. D. R. Carrier, A. M., Prof. of Ancient Languages and Mathematics.

Mrs. L. P. Tooke, M. P. L., Adj. Prin., Prof. of Modern Languages, and Ornamental Branches.

Mrs. D. R. Carrier, M. P. L., Teacher of Natural Science and higher English branches.

Miss Matie J. Tooke, Teacher of Vocal and Instrumental Music.

Mrs. Mary A. Soule, Assistant Teacher in Academic and Model School Department.

Miss Lucia A. Crandall, Assistant Teacher on Piano Forte and Guitar.

Rev. Justus Soule, Steward, and Financial Agent.

A large and intelligent Board of Council and Visitors, have been selected from this and adjacent cities. The following gentlemen have been already chosen as Directors or Curators in the College Association:

Col. Adrian H. Davenport, of LeClaire; George McCullough, Esq., of Iowa City; Hon. Judge Cook, Willard Barrows, Esq., Prof. J. Dial, and Rev. M. M. Tooke, of Davenport.

Additional Directors are hereafter to be chosen in this Association.

## THE EDUCATION OF OUR DAUGHTERS.*

While it is true that the improvement of our city, and the development of the county are important and desirable, yet they are not more important than the improvement of the minds and morals of our children. And although the attention of many of our Western people has been largely centered upon trade and speculation, and the development of the physical resources of the country, yet the time has now come when our citizens are beginning to recognize their responsibility in reference to the proper education of their children. Large and commodious buildings have been erected in this city, for the advancement of our public schools. A college for young gentlemen has also been established in this city, by the Congregational Church, and efforts are now being made for the establishment of a first class Female College also in this place, to which we shall refer in the sequel. That "woman is the *ornament of the palace, and the sunshine of the cabin*" in every country where she is properly educated, is a truth generally conceded. And if it be true that society in all its forms, is to a large extent dependent upon and indebted to the influence of woman for its elevation and success, how appropriate in anticipating the interests of society in the future, that we now encourage the proper education of the Young Ladies of our country.

We have no hesitation in affirming, that a thorough education is the *richest patrimony* that parents can possibly confer upon their daughters. And what

*Contributed by M. M. Tooke.

we mean by a thorough education is not merely to enable them to read, write, and cipher a little, as was thought quite sufficient for our grandmothers in olden times, not a little smattering in a few of the more fashionable accomplishments merely, nor is it to become mere "book worms," and look down with polite horror upon the appropriate duties of the "true woman" in domestic life, but a *solid, thorough,* and *useful* education *of body, mind,* and *heart,* such as will fit them for the sober realities and high responsibilities of life. Such an education will be to them emphatically a *fortune* in person, which they can never lose, but which will raise them to positions of honor, influence, and usefulness in the midst of the most elevated state of society. Let me whisper in every parent's ear, and suggest to him that "*it will pay,*" thus to educate his daughter. Suppose you look at this subject a moment in the light simply of pecuniary gain—of mere dollars and cents—(the only *sense* through which many are capable of seeing with clea ness in this age of speculation and investment·) Suppose that daughter of thine should be thrown out upon her own resources for a livelihood. Under such circumstances, with ordinary capacity of miud, and health of body, she could earn say one hundrod dollars a year at ordinary service without an educatiou. But with a thorough education, as an accomplished Instructor, she can earn from three to five hundred dollars a year. Subtracting the one hundred say from four hundred, we have an annual income to be credited to education of three hundred dollars. Now suppose it costs to educate that daughter, in tuition books, and extra expenses, exclusive of board, (for these she must have whether she attends school or not,) say four hundred dollars. We have then an annual income upon the capital actually invested in her education of seventy-five per cent—a much better interest you see than is realized on most bank or railroad stock in these days! Besides, this is a permanent and imperishable investment. Ordinary investments in the mere perishable may "take to themselves wings and fly away," but this we believe will not only be permanent and available here in this life, but to some good extent when this mortal shall put on immortality. But may we not come to fathers and brothers on this subject with a nobler motive for the education of their daughters and sisters, than the assurance that it "will pay" in dollars and cents? Can you in the pride and manliness of your hearts, look upon those beloved *family jewels*, sparkling even in their uncultivated beauty, and deny them this heaven-sent boon? Nay! would you not rather use your influence to polish those "gems of immortality," and fit them not only to shine as lights in the world below, but as radiant and still brightning stars in the coronet of Angels and of God, in brighter worlds on high!

Pause a moment, and gaze upon the nature of mind itself. See those powers of thought—of genius—those towering susceptibilities and lofty aspirations of soul longing for activity, yearning for appropriate exercise and development—and will you lend your influence to cripple their energies? or will you *allow* them to become stultified or dwarfed by inactivity or neglect in youth? How many painful regrets have been scattered along the pathway of thousands, in after years, because of such early neglects! Suppose you give that blooming daughter a *farm*, or thousands in bank stock, instead of an education, she will feel and lament her deficiencies and inferiority as long as she lives, and regret in vain that a large portion of that dowery had not been expended in her education, which would have been worth more to her than ten thousand times the same amount of earthly treasures.

Looking away from the benefits which the subjects of female education themselves shall realize, to the influence which female refinement would exert upon the *young men* of our country, in stimulating them to greater mental activity and laudable emulation, we find a prominent reason for its promotion. Besides it would obviate the necessity of our educated sons of promise becoming associated with companions of no mental culture, whose tastes and peculiarities must almost necessarily produce a disparity and alienation of feeling between them, destructive of domestic peace and happiness, and promotive of drunkenness and dissipation. Already is it intimated that because of a want of opportunity for mental culture on the part of the young ladies of the West the young men, in a similar ratio, are relaxing their mental energies, and but few are aspiring to graduation in any of our colleges. Be this as it may, the masses of our citizens in this rich and fertile country are destined to be wealthy, and ere long these noble bluffs and beautiful prairies will be dotted over with lovely mansions and palatial dwellings, and to become the regulators, the ornaments, the "sunshine," the "joy," of these mansions and palaces, the daughters of the West should be enlightened and refined. Indeed, all the circumstances of this beautiful West, and of the age in which we live, require the constant elevation of the female mind. Our new States are now demanding thousands of teachers for our primary schools. And as in the older States, the larger proportion of the education of our youth has been most honorably conducted by females, so also must the daughters of the West be trained for this great work if we would ever properly educate the masses.

The *progressive character of the age* in which we live requires a more thorough education of the female mind among us. The education of the past will not answer for the future, and those who would keep up with the world's progress, and help to mould its character, and hasten and consumate its brightness, by the ushering in of that auspicious period, long echoed by ancient Prophets, when "Wisdom and knowledge shall be the stability of our times, and strength of salvation," must encourage the educators of the race.

The signs of the times are beckoning onward the determined, the energetic, the noble spirited daughters of the West to higher attainments. The wealth of the country is rapidly increasing, educational institutions are being multiplied among us—expenses are diminished—parents are waking up to the importance of female education, and will do anything in their power to encourage and aid a beloved daughter longing for improvement, and struggling for an education. Mount Ida Female College, recently organized in this place, an account of which we have just given, is destined at no distant day, we trust, to become not only the Queen of the "Queen City," but the Queen of the West itself, and constitute an efficient instrumentality in the accomplishment of this great and glorious work. And it is hoped that all our citizens, friendly to the cause of female education in the West, will in some substantial manner bid her "God speed" in this labor of love.

## LADIES' EDUCATION SOCIETY.

Febuary 5th, 1858, a number of ladies met at the residence of Charles E. Putnam, Esq., and organized the "Ladies' Education Society, of Davenport, Iowa." Art. 1, of their Constitution reads as follows: "This association shall be called 'The Ladies' Education Society,' the object of which shall be to assist promising and suitable young ladies in obtaining an Education." Mrs. R. Christie, President; Mrs. S. Burwell, Vice President; Mrs. Dr. Shelton, Secretary; Mrs. Chas. E. Putnam, Treasuress. There is also a Board of thirteen Directresses.

## IOWA COLLEGE.

The first movements toward the establishment of a College in Iowa, according to what is known as the "New England plan"—the plan of Harvard, Yale, Brown, Bowdoin, Dartmouth, Amherst, &c., &c.,—were made in the years 1841–'4. In the Spring of 1844, a called meeting was held at Denmark, Lee county. Those who attended it were principally Congregational and Presbyterian ministers, and christians of those denominations, with some others. The first plan was to secure a township of land, and College colony. A gentleman in Kesauqua offered a tract in Buchanan county, with a water power on the Wapsipinecon River for the purpose. A committee (Rev. J. A. Reed, of Fairfield, Seth Richards, Esq., of Bentonsport, and Jonas Houghton, Esq., of Farmington,) were appointed to examine locations. This committee called a meeting in April, 1844, to report. Thirteen persons were present, who then formed the "Iowa College Association." The committee made a favorable report, an agent was appointed to collect funds in the East, with which to enter the land, and certain regulations were adopted. At the East, however, the agent was discouraged, and prevented from collecting funds, and this part of the plan was given up in accordance with the suggestions of a meeting of friends of Western Education, held in the city of Boston, May 28 and 29, 1844. It was decided first to get a location, when the institution itself could commence operations, and then attempt to secure an endowment. After several meetings, it was concluded (1846) to locate at Davenport; "provided the citizens would raise $1500 for buildings, and furnish certain specified grounds for a site." At a meeting held Jan. 20, 1847, it was voted, notwithstanding the conditions were not fully complied with, to commence operations at Davenport, with the understanding that the subscriptions should be increased as much as possible. The members of the Association had pledged themselves to "raise $100 each" in the State, and "through private friends in the East." Some of them made great efforts and sacrifices to do this. Christian ladies, living in different parts of the State, did nobly in the work. With these funds, and those secured in the town. the first building was erected, (near Western Avenue, between Sixth and Seventh streets—now the residence of S. S. Gillet, Esq.) It was a small one story brick edifice, with a plain cupola. About this time twelve trustees were elected by the Association, two of them residents of Davenport. The trustees were incorporated under the Statute, June 4, 1847. The threatened deficiency in the funds was provided for at a meeting of the original "College Association," and "trustees" held conjointly that day, by a resolution binding those present to pay the same within one year from date, "provided the amount does not exceed $600," (not an inconsiderable sum at that stage of the history of the Territory.) The Institution was opened November, 1848, with one teacher, Rev. Prof. Ripley. The first College Class was formed in 1850. Since that time instruction has been sustained, though much interrupted in 1844–'5, by the abandonment of the old site, on account of the contemplated cutting of streets through it.

Seven young men have graduated with the degree of Bachelor of Arts, the first class of two in the year 1854. The Institution generally has about a hundred students—of whom ten are in the College proper. During the last year young ladies have been admitted to the advanced classes. About twenty have been in attendance.

Candidates for admission to the Freshman Class must be fourteen years of age, present adequate testimonials of good moral character, and sustain a satisfactory examination in English Grammar, Geography, Arithmetic, Algebra, (through Simple Equations,) Latin Grammar, Cæsar's Commentaries, Cicero's Select Orations, Virgil, Greek Grammar, and the Anabasis—or their equivalents.

The stated times for the examination of candidates are—the day before the close of the Summer Term, and the day before the commencement of the Fall Term.

Candidates for admission to advanced standing, in addition to the above, must sustain an examination in those studies to which the class they propose to enter has attended; and if from another College, a certificate of their good standing in the same must be presented to the Faculty.

The studies pursued in the College proper are those required in the first Institutions of the East. An elevated grade of scholarship is aimed at, rather than the securing of the attendance of large numbers. The instructors are all liberally educated men, of first rate competency and experience in their profession.

The new site—of ten acres—between Brady and Harrison streets, above Tenth—was purchased in March, 1854—and the Boarding House erected thereon that year. The present College edifice was erected in 1855, at a cost of $22,000. W. L. Carroll, architect. It crowns the highest point of land in the city limits, and commands an extensive view of the river, the neighboring region of Illinois, and the country for miles back of Davenport. Travelers pronounced the prospect from the observatory unsurpassed. The building itself is one of the finest structures in the State.

It is built of limestone; three stories high, with a basement; and contains a large room for the use of the Preparatory and English Departments, which, for the present, will also be used for a Chapel; a Laboratory; rooms for Library, Cabinet, Apparatus, Literary Societies, and Recitations; and in the third story, twelve rooms for Students.

With these enlarged facilities for Educational purposes at their command, the Trustees of the College are confident in the expectation that they can fully meet the wants of our rapidly increasing population, and furnish, on our own soil, at a reasonable expense, the means of a thorough and complete Education.

The Library of the College contains upwards of 1800 volumes, and is open to all the Departments.

The Chrestomathian Society has also a Library of its own, of some 500 volumes; for most of which they are indebted to recent donations from their friends.

The Apparatus is sufficient to illustrate the principles of Natural Philosophy, Chemistry and Astronomy.

Collections have been made in Mineralogy, Zoology, and Botany.

Commencement is held on Wednesday, the last day of the third term. (In 1858, on Wednesday, July 14.) There are three College terms in the year, two of thirteen, and one of fourteen weeks.

The government of the College is intended to secure the best moral influence. Besides the daily religious exercises for all, the students from abroad are expected to attend some place of religious worship on the Sabbath, designated by their parents or guardians.

The Institution is not under the control of any religious denomination, but of its own board of trustees. They are as follows:

Rev. Asa Turner, Denmark; Rev. John C. Holbrook, Dubuque; Rev. Julius A. Reed, Davenport; Rev. Harvey Adams, Farmington; Rev. Alden B. Robbins, Muscatine; Rev. Ephraim Adams, Dacorah; Rev. William Salter, Burlington; Rev. O. Emerson, Dewitt; H. Q. Jennison, Esq., Muscatine; James McManus, Esq., Davenport; Charles Atkinson, Esq., Moline; Rev. J. B. Grinnell, Grinnell; Rev. J. Guernsey, Dubuque; F. H. Stone, Esq., Muscatine; Joseph Lambrite, Esq., Davenport; Jacob Butler, Esq., Muscatine; Gen. Geo. B. Sargent, Davenport; Rev. Geo. F. Magoun, Davenport.

The officers of the Board are—Rev. A. B. Robbins, President; Rev. Geo. F. Magoun, Clerk; Joseph Lambrite, Esq., Treasurer; Rev. Julius A. Reed, Financial Agent; Prof. H. L. Bullen, Librarian.

Faculty.—Rev. Erastus Ripley, Carter Professor of Ancient Languages;

Rev. H. L. Bullen, Professor Mathematics and Natural Philosophy; D. S. Sheldon, M. A., Professor of Chemistry and Natural Science; Rev. D. Lane, M. A., Professor of Mental and Moral Philosophy.

The partial endowment of the College has been obtained from charitable persons in this and other States. Peley W. Carter, Esq., of Waterbury, Connecticut, gave, in 1853, $5,000 towards the Classical Professorship. One other professorship is partially endowed. A benevolent gentleman in the State contemplates the endowment of Chairs of Practical Science. Within the last year, Hon. Geo. B. Sargent has established a medal fund, from which one gold and two silver medals are awarded—for scholarship—in the manner designated by the donor—each commencement.

The prospects of the Institution have been much impaired of late by the proposed extension of one of the streets of the city through the centre of its beautiful grounds. If carried out, this plan will oblige a second removal to some site not liable to encroachment.

# CHAPTER XXXI.

## MILITARY.

The first permanent organization in Davenport was that of the Davenport Rifle Corps—a German Company. They now number forty men, Capt. Haupt; First Lieutant, Scherer; Orderly Sergeant, Winegardner.

The next Company organized was an American Company—the Davenport City Artillery. It was organized June, 1857, under the auspices of Capt. Schuyler—whose indefatigable exertions have more than anything else brought the Company to its present character.

OFFICERS.—C. N. Schuyler, Captain ; W. W. Gallaer, 1st Lieutenant ; 2nd do., Chas. C. Harris ; 3d do., John Johns. Forty men and two six pounders.

Davenport City Guards (German.) The officers of this Company are mostly old soldiors from Schleswig-Holstein. Organized Feb., 1858. Captain, F. Unrow ; 1st Lieutenant, Steward ; 2nd Lieutenant, John Hempel ; Orderly Sergeant, D. Hempel. Forty men.

Davenport Sarsfield Guards, (Irish.) Not organized fully.

## FIRE DEPARTMENT.

The Fire Department of Davenport never assumed prominence for efficient service until the matter was taken in hand by R. M. Littler, formerly of Cincinnati. Through his efforts a Company was organized July 26, 1856, and two of Honeyman's best Engines purchased, which arrived May, 1857. The Company organized was the "Independent Fire Engine and Hose Company, No. 1." R. M. Littler was elected President. In February, 1858, the Fire Department was reorganized, and in March R. M. Littler was elected Chief Engineer over

O. S. McNiel by a majority of twenty. The entire vote was two hundred and fifty-four. Christian Mueller was unanimously elected First Assistant, and E. A. Tellibine, Second, over D. Moore.

The organization now consists of—

"Independent Fire Engine and Hose Company, No. 1."—Two Engines, two Hose Carts. Fifteen hundred feet of Hose. Cost $6500. Chris. Buckholter and Isaac Cummings, Foremen of Engines, and John Gundaker Foremen of Hose. One hundred and twenty-five sets of equipments, and one hundred and twenty members. Engine House on Brady street, near Fifth. Cost $6,000.

"Fire King Company, No. 2."—Organized 1857. Smith's Engine, and eight hundred feet of hose. Marsh Noe, Foreman. House in Davenport's Block. One hundred and nineteen men.

"Pioneer Hook and Ladder Company, No. 1."—Organized December, 1857. Ninety men. Chas. Eyser and H. La Franz, Foremen. House on Third street, near Washington Square.

"Engine Company No. 3."—House with Pioneer No. 1, Hook and Ladder—sixty-four men. Officers to be elected 2d Monday in April.

# CHAPTER XXXII.

## MUSICAL.

Davenport, among its other excellencies, possesses its quota of musical talent—albeit its development is not particularly marked, as a general thing, among our Church choirs. In fact, save a few sopranos like Mrs. Davie, Misses Sylvester and Scarborough, and in *basso* and *tenore* the brothers Davis, and Mr. Davie, and a few others of all classes, the bulk of musical ability, both vocal and instrumental, rests with our German population. Strausser, as a violinist, and Braeunlich and Schlegel, as pianists, take a front rank among amateur musicians. In the department of vocal music we have the Philharmonic Society, formed 5th of August, 1856, and its first meeting, for the practice of vocal music, held 12th of August, 1856.

Its object is the improvement of the members (male and female) in the culture of vocal music.

During the first winter of its existence it gave six performances. During the present winter ('57 and '58,) it will probably give four or five; one of which will be Handel's Oratorio of the "Messiah," with orchestral accompaniments, the vocal parts given by about fifty voices; the instrumental parts by a band of seventeen performers.

The Society's regular meetings are held every Tuesday evening, during the winter, at the old St. Luke's Church, Brady street, at 7 o'clock. When necessary, rehearsals are also held on Friday evenings.

The number of performing members is about forty, and is increasing. There is also a body of subscribing or non-performing members.

The officers elected 2d March, 1858, are—

President, General Geo. B. Sargent; Vice President, S. W. Barber; Treasurer, J. C. Wallace; Secretary, J. J. Ingalls; Finance Committee, S. W. Barber; Wm. Morehouse, S. M. Harley; Musical Director, Chas. H. Davie.

## GERMAN MAENNER CHOR.

This Society was organized June, 1851, under the following officers: A. F. Mast, President; G. Schlegel, Secretary; Aug. Smallfield, Cashier, and G. Wiehle, Musical Director.

In June, 1854, a flag was presented to the Society by the Ladies of Davenport, as a compliment to their efforts and success. At the "Western Singing Festival," held at Chicago in June, 1857, the Maenner Chor took the second prize, and we believe intend *Da Capo* in future cases. It now has music and instruments worth one thousand dollars, and has at present twenty-two active and thirty-four honorary members. The following are its officers:

A. Miedke, President; A. Bruns, Vice President; T. Holm, Recording Secretary; R. Krouse, Corresponding Secretary; A. G. Smallfield, Cashier; G. G. Schlegel, Musical Director.

## GESANG-CHOR DER TURNGEMEINDE.

Twenty members. Riepe, Director. This is a branch of the "Turner Society." Practice twice a week.

## DAVENPORT MUSICAL INSTITUTE.

Founded March 9th, 1858. Asa Hull, President; Chas. Burr, Secretary.

This Society numbers some twenty-five members, and is a sort of succession of a Society formerly under the charge of Mr. Hull. It possesses the elements of a good Musical Institution, which time will develope into no second-rate character.

## DEUTSCHER SAENGER-BUND.

Glee Club—twenty-five members. Practice two nights in each week. Jacob Strasser, Director.

## GRUETLI VEREIN.

Swiss Glee Club meets once each week. Twenty members. Albert Snhnyder, Leader.

## INSTRUMEMTAL.

"Majo's String Band."—First and Second Violins, Bass Viol, Cornet a Piston and Picolo.

"German Rifle Band."—Storm, Leader. Three Altos, Tenor Horn, Baritone, Tuber, and two Drums.

"White's Cotillion Band."—First and Second Violins, Clarionet, Flute, Cornet, First and Second Trumpet, First and Second French Horns, First Baritone and Contra Bass.

"White's Brass Band"—First and Second E♭, First and Second B♭, two Tenors, two Baritones, First and Second Bass, two Altos, and two Drums.

"Independent Brass Band."—Ten Sax Horns, and two Drums.

---

## ARTISTIC.

Hanging high upon the wall of a city parlor, is a *living memory* of the village of Davenport, just as it is limned and lined and colored in the recollections of "old settlers." It is a paint and canvass memory, and though the hand that thus in form and color faithfully reflected what the eye saw, has long since mouldered in the dust, yet its writing on the wall is as a memory to all who peruse it, of the surpassing village grace and loveliness which in olden times distinguished Davenport. It is well that he whose skill has left us this undying memory of our village life, should have a page in this book as a memoir of himself. When the tongues which may tell us of the olden times are silenced forever, and the men who lived in those days have passed away, it may be that from some wall, browned with age, shall creep the mouldy forms and colorings of a far-back memory, brushing away the dust and cobwebs of intervening space, and revealing grass-robed plains and tree-covered bluffs, clustering white houses on the river's graveled beach, gray cliffs rising from the dark-flowing waters and up-bearing the old fort ruins, and the thousand physical details of what was once literal life and reality. And it may be, that a yellow and faded leaf from this book, shall then summon a phantom memory of one whose eye saw all this, even as we now trust it gazes upon scenes of celestial beauty, and the cunning of whose hand in faithful shades and shadows mirrored the vision upon canvass.

When we recollect how distinguished was Davenport in its village days for remarkable loveliness, and the number of strangers who summer after summer came here to revel among its surrounding beauties, it seems strange that but this single painting, and a few lithograph copies of it, are all we have as a record of the physical appearance of this place before its hundreds of people became thousands, and the village had swelled into a city. We may well imagine that the skill of amateur artists was often tasked to delineate upon paper or canvass the glowing scenery and beautiful towns which at this point found intimate connection with historical associations. But whatever their trials and their success, only a single painting and its copies now exist, to the knowledge of the writer, by which the stranger in the new city may form a correct idea of the long time past appearance of Davenport, and assuming which as data he may judge of our subsequent progress. Probably it is from this fact, that we set a higher value upon the artist to whom we feel a debt of gratitude for this painting.

Among the strangers from St. Louis who visited Davenport in the Spring of 1845, was John Casper Wild, a gentleman of considerable reputation as a landscape and portrait painter, and lithographbist. He was a tall spare man of about forty years; with long raven black hair, whiskers and moustache, and restless brown eyes. He had, at times, a worn and haggard look, the result, doubtless, of ill health, and a life-long battle with the world for the bare means of subsistence. He was uncommunicative as to his own life, but it i an impression of the writer's that he was born in poverty, reared among the trials of indigence, from which, unaided, he sought to emerge, and in his maturity, a good artist, but poor financier, so that his history was a continued struggle. It is but little wonder then, that through the clouds which so constantly surrounded him, he could see but little sunshine. On his arrival here, he was totally dependent upon his talent. He soon commenced work, and produced this painting of Davenport and Rock Island, as one picture. From this a limited number of beautifully colored lithograph copies were taken, for those who would buy. Alas! poor Wild—the pictures which now would bring their weight in gold, had then a dull and weary sale. This view was not only faithful in its details, and beautiful as a picture, but it proved Mr. Wild an artist of high talent.

It is worthy of mention, that the artist lithographed his own picture in stone, and made and colored the impressions himself. It has been remarked, that so fine a specimen of lithographing cannot now be done in the metropolis of the country.

Mr. Wild afterwards commenced a second painting of Davenport, viewed from another point, but it was never finished. The same summer he made paintings, from which lithograph copies were taken, of Dubuque, Galena, Muscatine and Moline. All these sketches were distinguished for their correctness and beauty. He worked rapidly but well, and a practical knowledge of lithography was useful in securing correct copies of his works. The writer of this accompanied Mr. Wild on a trip to the Falls of St. Anthony, in 1846, in which excursion he made a number of small sketches, but they never were reproduced on canvass. The painting of Davenport and Rock Island truly represents the young cities as they slept in 1845, upon the green banks of the great river, before the rushing winds and waves of progress had broken their slumbers. There are but few copies of this painting now in the possession of our citizens, and it is needless to say that the lapse of time, and the intervening wonderful changes in the aspect of our city, render these pictures invaluable to their owners.

In 1846, Mr. Wild, who continued residing in Davenport, painted a fancy sketch, of which it may be right to make a particular note, as it was the nearest approach to an *artistical smile* of which Mr. Wild was ever known to be guilty. He had neither humor of his own, nor an appreciation of humor in others. He looked tragedy, thought tragedy, and his conversation outside of business and art, was never much more cheerful than tragedy. This little oil sketch represented three notable characters of the village, each of whom, at that time, was personally known to almost every man, woman and child in the place. They were collected at the well-remembered ferry-house, and near the equally well-remembered old bell-post. The bell there suspended was then furiously jingled, and often with disagreeable pertinacity, by those who wished to call the old ferryman, Mr. John Wilson, from the opposite side. The ringer was generally considered under personal obligation to stand to his *post* some time, in company with his horse and vehicle, if he had any to cross over, so that the ferryman might with proper deliberation determine whether the skiff or horse-ferry-boat were required by the nature of the cargo. The large person of Mr. LeClaire sits in a buggy, to which is attached the notable old white horse that used to drag his master about the place. Close by stands Mr. Gilbert McKown, whose store was on Front street, a few steps distance, but whose burly figure and good humored face, seen on any street, seemed a part and parcel of the town, and directly identified with its corporate existence. The third figure is Sam Fisher, as he was familiarly called by every acquaintance. He then lived in the house now owned and occupied by Mr. Geo. L. Davenport, at the corner of Brady and Third streets. Sam Fisher was the *best* fisher in the town, a good story-teller, and had a most marvellous memory of past times and incidents, of facts and dates, which united to some peculiar eccentricities of character, exclusively and honestly his own, made him a conspicuous character. One of his smaller eccentricities is shown in the picture. He is standing with his pants drawn up to the top of one boot, and down to the sole of the other—using a favorite gesture, and evidently doing the *talking*, of course. These three persons are now alive, and two of them continue residents of Davenport. The picture is in the possession of Hon. G. C. R. Mitchell, who, by the way, ought to have figured in the painting.

Mr. Wild was a native of Zurich, Switzerland. He went to Paris when young, where he resided fifteen years, and then emigrated to the United States. He lived several years in Philadelphia, where he finished some views for Atkinson's Casket, a Panorama of Philadelphia, and a view of Napoleon's Marshals on horse-back. In the Spring of 1841, he went to St. Louis, and remained there till he removed here. At St. Louis, he commenced a periodical called "The Valley of the Mississippi Illustrated"—edited by Louis Faulk Thomas, the views by Mr. Wild. Only ten numbers were issued. Mr. Wild died in Davenport, in the year 1846. When sick, he was kindly taken to the residence of Mrs. Webb, now occupied by Mr. Henry, where he received the attentions of a son during the long illness which preceded his death. While thus lying on his death-bed, the home of his boyhood seemed a beautiful picture before his eyes, and he expressed a longing desire to die at Zurich. This was not granted him, but kind hands softened the last shadowy pencilings of his life, and laid him gently among the Summer flowers.

Mr. R. Wright has been spoken of heretofore. In addition to him we have Mrs. Codding, whose principal work is a painting of Davenport, which, for fidelity. is scarcely excelled.

Mr. Wolfe, a former resident of Davenport, displayed much genius in several performances in Landscape and Portrait Painting.

# CHAPTER XXXIII.

## THE PRESS.

It is a telling indication of the enterprise and good sense of the pioneers of the County, that one of their earliest movements was to secure the benefits of that omnipresent Americanism—a NEWSPAPER. They were fortunate in securing the very man they did to undertake the enterprise—one who possessed the peculiarity of having a deal of *practical* good sense, and one who was neither scholar enough to play the *role* of a pedantic essayist, or philosophical enough to treat his readers to a hebdominal dish of metaphysics, as is not unfrequently the case of those handling the Quill Editorial at the present day. Such was ANDREW LOGAN, who in August, 1838, issued the first number of the "*Iowa Sun, and Davenport and Rock Island News*,"—a title as lengthy as significant. Right well did the *Sun* battle for the interests of the City, County, and State; and we do its editor no more than justice, when it is asserted that his share towards building up Davenport, and inducing hither many a rich freight of immigration, was none of the least felt or important. The *Sun* was a weekly, democratic, underwent one enlargement, and was continued until 1841, when it was succeeded by the

### DAVENPORT WEEKLY GAZETTE.

The *Gazette* was started as a Weekly, imperial size (22 by 32,) six columns, by ALFRED SANDERS. In 1848 it was enlarged to a seven column paper. August 1st, 1853, the *Tri-Weekly Gazette* was commenced, and was succeeded by the *Daily Gazette* in October, 1854. The Weekly and Daily are still published, and are of the largest size. It was edited by Alfred Sanders up to 1857, and published by him until 1843, when he associated with him Mr. Davis. The latter gentleman continued until January 1st, 1857, a member of the firm, and was then succeeded by Add. H. Sanders, brother of the principal proprietor, and former editor of the *Evansville* (*Ind.*) *Journal*. The firm now—editorial and publishing—is SANDERS & BRO.

The *Gazette* has now been an institution of the country for some seventeen years,—a length of existence that sufficiently guarantees its permanency. The Senior, Alfred Sanders, is of scholarly attainments, particularly in Natural History, and has thus far been thoroughly identified, both with the West and Journalism. He has never missed issuing a number of the *Gazette* since its beginning, and has often achieved this, under circumstances which would have daunted men of less energy, or of less pride in their profession. As a writer he is less brilliant than solid, rather shy of ornament, and prefers generally to present facts in *puris naturalibus*. He writes earnestly, and will in many cases carry conviction simply from the deep air of conviction—of faith—which his articles present. Did space permit, we might allude more at length both to his character as a writer, and his efforts, enterprise, preseverance, and sagacity, in developing the interests both of his party and Davenport. We need not dwell upon these points, however well deserving they are of eulogy, as he is well enough known to render either panegyric or particular notice superfluous.

His brother, Add. H. Sanders, has acquired no unenviable reputation as a ready, sparkling, and piquant writer. He is largely imaginative has a keen appreciation of the humourous, notices instinctively the ludicrous both in men and things, and possesses the rare faculty of easy and graceful *expression*. Many of the best waifs of anecdotal literature, which periodically appear and disappear upon the waves of Journalism, owe to him their existence. We cannot but regret that he has not entirely turned his attention to description and other departments having origin in the possession of a ready pen, active fancy, and much imagination.

We are happy to be able to add that the long and arduous labors of the proprietors of the *Gazette* have not been unrewarded. Their present establishment consists of two editors, three carriers, and some eighteen compositors, pressmen, &c. They use a Steam Engine of six horse power, Taylors' Steam Press, Hoe's Card, Ruggles' Card, American Steam, two Hand Diamond Job, and Wells' Power Job Presses.

## THE WEEKLY BANNER.

This sheet was started by Alexander Montgomery in 1848, as a Democratic sheet. In the winter of 1848 and 1849 it fell under the charge and ownership of R. Smithem, and in the Spring of 1849 it was transferred to T. D. Eagal, who held it until 1851. J. W. Wheeler then took charge of it, but soon after sold out to Austin Corbin, who in 1852 was bought out by R. S. Millar. He sold to T. D. Eagal in 1853, who continued its publication until 1855, when it was bought by Messrs. Hildreth, Richardson & West, and was changed to the *Iowa State Democrat*, under which name it is still published. Of the influence and character of the *Banner* we cannot speak from observation,—it, however, done much undoubtedly towards preserving an efficient organization of the party whose interest is advocated.

## THE TEMPERANCE ORGAN.

This sheet was established November 1855, by H. Price and others. It was published by A. P. Luse & Co.

The Organ did good services for its party for about one year, and was then discontinued.

## THE WEEKLY UNION.

This sheet was published for a few months in the Fall of 1856, with a view to aid the election of Millard Fillmore to the Presidency. It was edited by the well known Col. Wm. Brown.

## IOWA STATE DEMOCRAT.

Notice has been taken before of the origin of this paper in 1855. The Daily was commenced in October 1856, enlarged from seven to eight columns in April, 1857, to nine in October 1857. The *Democrat* was started with a Hand Press, and a debt of some $1500. It now is printed by Steam, and has amply remunerated its enterprising proprietors. The establishment has one Washington Hand Press, a Steam Cylinder Press, Hoe's Medium Large Cylinder Press, Ruggles' Rotary Circular and Card Press, and some twelve hands, besides an ample stock of other material. A Weekly is also published.

The *Democrat* is now conducted by Messrs. Richardson & West, than whom the editorial and publishing fraternities, posses no more enterprising, gentlemanly, or reliable members. They have achieved a success on their paper, which at once indicates their energy and the character of the West.

Mr. Hildreth died in September of 1857. The following obituary is taken from the *State Democrat:*

"Mr. Hildreth was born in Johnstown, Fulton county, N. Y., September 12th, A. D. 1809, which would make him just 48 years old to-day. Mr. Hildreth was a son of Matthias B. Hildreth, Esq., formerly Attorney General of the State of New York. His life has been an eventful one, filled with the lights and shades of prosperity and adversity. He was left an orphan at the age of fifteen, and inherited a large fortune. He was a graduate of Union College of that State, after which he engaged in the wholesale dry goods and jobbing trade in Albany, N. Y. After a few years he became embarrassed in business and failed, and lost his entire fortune in the failure. He then removed to Johnstown, N. Y., and was there elected a magistrate and Master in Chancery.

Previous to his engaging in business in Albany, he received the appointment by commission, of Major in the Staff of Gov. Troup.

He was married in Johnstown, in 1839, to Mrs. A. E. J. West, who survives to mourn his loss.

From Johnstown he removed to Kenosha, Wisconsin, in 1843, where he was universally beloved and esteemed, and was there elected to many offices of honor and trust, which he filled to the entire satisfaction of all parties. He moved to Peoria, State of Illinois, in 1853, and became associated in the publication of a journal called the *Daily Morning News*. From Peoria he moved to Davenport in October, 1855, and in company with Messrs. Richardson and West, purchased the old *Banner* newspaper of T. D. Eagal, Esq., and with them commenced the publication of the *Daily Iowa State Democrat*, of which he was the Senior Editor until his lamented decease.

Mr. Hildreth was a man of most generous impulses, and had a faculty of making and retaining friends. He was a fast and reliable friend, a kind husband, and an Old School Jeffersonian Democrat. He was uncompromising in his political views, but he never allowed politics to intrude into his social or business relations. All who knew him, esteemed him for his generous heart. In his death his family has lost a valuable friend, the public a generous hearted citizen, and the Democratic party one of its strong pillars."

## EVENING NEWS.

This sheet, Daily and Weekly, was started by Harrington & Wilkie, September 1856. It continued in their possession over a year, and was then purchased by John Johns, Jr., & Co. The *News* is Administration Democratic, and takes a leading position in Journalism. It is edited by John Johns, Jr., Edward L. Kerr, and Chas. C. Harris. All are good writers,—the first two in political discussions and essays, and the last as a perpetrator of "good things," ludicrous, witty, and otherwise.

The *News* has a good Job Office, containing a Guernsey's Power Press, Hand Presses, and ample other material appertaining to such a department.

## DER DEMOKRAT, (German.)

Republican—Daily, Tri-Weekly, and Weekly. Started 1851, by T. Guelich, and now published by H. Lischer & Co. Edited by Theo. Olshausen.

## REAL ESTATE REGISTER.

Monthly, by Allen & Clark. This sheet takes a first class position among papers of its kind. Its Financial articles during the past winter have been of the ablest character, and have done much towards sustaining the credit and advancing the interests of Davenport abroad. Started Mai, 1857.

# CHAPTER XXXIV.

## BENEVOLENT ORDERS.

### MASONIC.

TUSCAN LODGE, No. 57, of F. & A. Masons, was organized under a charter issued by the M. W. Grand Lodge of Iowa, June 6th, 1855.

D. H. Wheeler was W. Master for 1855 and '6—H. W. Mitchell was W. Master for 1856 and '7.

The Present officers of the Lodge are—

O. S. McNeil, W. M.; Edwin Smith, S. W.; Sam'l. Perry, J. W.; M. H. Hall, Sec'y.; R. D. Myers, Treas.; H. D. Neely, S. D.; John Monath, J. D.; G. W. Jones, Tyler.

The Lodge meets every Friday evening in their Hall, LeClaire Block, corner of Second and Brady streets. Regular meetings the Friday on or before the full moon in each month. Members eighty-seven.

DAVENPORT LODGE No. 37, of Free and Accepted Masons, was organized under a charter issued by the Most Worshipful Grand Lodge of the State of Iowa, June 8th, A. D. 1853. A. L. 5853.

Austin Corbin was Worshipful Master for 1853–4. Wm. L. Cook was Worshipful Master for 1854–55. Jno. A. Boyde was Worshipful Master for 1855–56. Wm. B. Barnes was Worshipful Master for 1856–57.

The present officers of the Lodge are—

C. Stewart Ells, W. Master; Wm. S. Minier, S. W.; Chas. E. Fuller, J. W.; A. Walker, Sec'y.; P. Merwin, Treas.; J. D. Kelly, S. D.; Jno. Granlees, J. D.; J. Johnson, Tyler. Lodge meets every Monday evening at their Hall, Merwin's Building, Perry street. Regular communications on every Monday evening before full moon. Number of members, seventy-six.

## I. O. of O. F.

Davenport Lodge, No. 7, instituted April 23, 1847, by D. D. G. Sine, John G. Potts. Charter members, Jas. Thorington, Ste. Schofield, Thos. V. Blakemore, S. McCormick, V. M. Firor.

First officers—N. G., Jas. Thornington; V. G., S. McCormick; R. Sec., T. V. Blakemore; T., V. M. Firor.

July 1st—N. G., Jas. Thorington; V. G., L. J. Centre; R. S., Jas. McManus; T., V. M. Firor.

January 1st. 1848—N. G., L. J. Center; V. G., Jas. McManus; R. S., John Pope; T., Lewis Hamilton.

July 1st, 1848—N. G., Jas. McManus; V. G., John Pope; R. S., M. D. Westlake; P. S., Jas. Thorington; T., Lewis Hamilton.

January 1st, 1849—N. G., John Pope; V. G., Chas. Weston; R. S., H. Brewster; P. S., Jas. Thorington; T., Geo. B. Sargent.

July 1st—N. G., Chas. Weston; V. G., H. Brewster; R. S., Jno. D. Evans; P. S., Jas. Thorington; T., Jno. H. Morton.

January 1st, 1850—N. G., A. Sawyer; V. G., M. D. Westlake; R. S., C. Weston; P. S., Jas. Thorington; T., John H. Morton.

July 1st—N. G., M. D. Westlake; V. G., A. S. Nugent; R. S., H. Price; P. S., N. M. Rambo; T., Jno. H. Morton.

January 1st, 1851—N. G., A. S. Nugent; V. G, H. Price; R. S., A. Sawyer; P. S., N. M. Rambo; T. Jno. H. Morton.

July 1st—N. G., H. Price; V. G., N. M. Rambo; R. S., Willard Barrows; P. S., Job M. Woodward; T., Jno. H. Morton.

January 1st, 1852—N. G., N. M. Rambo; V. G., Willard Barrows, R. S., Thos. S. Arrison; P. S., A. Sawyer; T., Jno. H. Morton.

July 1st—N. G., Willard Barrows; V. G., Thos. S. Arrison; R. S., B. B. Woodward; P. S., J. M. Woodward; T., Jno. H. Morton.

January 1st, 1853—N. G., Thos. S. Arrison; V. G., B. B. Woodward; R. S., N. M. Rambo, P. S., J. M. Woodward; T., Jno. H. Morton.

July 1st—N. G., B. B. Woodward; V. G., Hiram Johnson; R. S., H. J. Hughes; P. S., Jno. Bechtel; T., Jno. H. Morton.

January 1st, 1854—N. G., Hiram Johnson; V. G., H. J. Hughes; R. S., J. C. Fuller; P. S., Jas. Thorington; T., Jno. H. Morton.

July 1st—N. G., H. J. Hughes; V. G., J. C. Fuller; R. S., J. H. Dumont; P. S., B. B., Woodward; T., Israel Hall.

January 1st, 1855—N. G., J. C. Fuller; V. G., John Hornby; R. S., Jas. Wickersham; P. S., B. B. Woodward; T., I. Hall;

July 1st—N. G., Jno. Hornby; V. G., Thos. Allum; R. S., J. D. Patton; P. S., B. B. Woodward; T., I. Hall.

January 1st, 1856—N. G., Thos. Allum; V. G., J. H. Dumont; R. S., M. D. Snyder; P. S., B. B. Woodward; T., I. Hall.

July 1st—N. G., J. H. Dumont; V. G., M. D. Snyder; R. S., A. H. Barrow; P. S., B. B. Woodward; T., I. Hall.

January 1st, 1857—N. G., M. D. Snyder; V. G., A. H. Barrow; R. S., J. W. Danah; P. S., B. B. Woodward; T., I. Hall.

July 1st—N. G., A. H. Barrow; V. G., J. W. Danah; R. S., Jno. H. Bell; P. S., B. B. Woodward; T., I. Hall.

January 1st, 1858—N. G., J. W. Danah; V. G., Jno. H. Bell; R. S., J. B. Leake; P. S., B. B. Woodward; T., I. Hall. One hundred and seventy-five members.

STATE ENCAMPMENT, No. 3, I. O. O. F., was instituted April 22d, 1848, by D. D. G. Sire, John G. Potts. Charter members, James Thorington, R. M. Prettyman, John H. Morton, Thos. V. Blakemore, Lewis Hamilton, M. D. Westlake, L. J. Center.

Officers—C. P., James Thorington; H. P., Jno. H. Morton; S. W., T. V. Blakemore; J. W., L. J. Center; S., R. M. Prettyman; T., Lewis Hamilton.

January 1st., 1849—C. P., Chas. Weston; H. P., Geo. B. Sargent; S. W., A. Nugent; J. W., R. M. Prettyman; S., Jas. Thorington; T., Jno. H. Morton.

July 1st.—C. P., Jno. D. Evans; H. H., L J. Center; S. W., John Pope; J. W., R. M. Prettyman; S., Jas. Thorington; T., Jno. H. Morton.

January 1st., 1850—C. P., Thos. V. Blakemore; H. P., Lewis Hamilton; S. W., R. M. Prettyman; J. W., Chas. Weston; S., Geo. B. Sargent; T., Jno. H. Morton.

July 1st.—C. P, Aaron S. Nugent; H. P., M. D. Westlake; S. W., N. M. Rambo; J. W., Abijah Sawyer; S., Jas. Thorington; T., Jno. H. Morton.

January 1st, 1851—C. P., Nathan M. Rambo; H. P., C. M. Peck; S. W., A. Sawyer; J. W., L. J. Center; S., M. D. Westlake; T., Jno. H. Morton.

August, 1851, the State Encampment renewed its Charter, and on the 1st day of October, 1855, reclaimed it again.

Officers January 1st, 1856—C. P., A. H. Barrow; H. P., C. M. Peck; S. W., William Pool; J. W., S. N. Stevens; S., B. B. Woodward; T., L. C. Dessaint.

July 1st—C. P., William Pool; H. P., B. B. Woodward; S. W., M. D. Snyder; J. W., S. N. Stevens; S., S. K. Barkley; T., L. C. Dessaint.

Sanuary 1st, 1857—C. P., M. D. Snyder; H. P., Wm. Pool; S. W., Marsh Noe; J. W., L. S. Johnson; S., M. Dalzell; T., L. C. Dessaint.

July 1st—C. P., B. B. Woodward; H. P., A. H. Barrow; S. W., J. W. Darrah; J. W., J. J. Humphrey; S., Jno. H. Bell; T., Wm. Pool.

January 1st, 1858—C. P., J. W. Darrah; H. P., Wm. B. Kerns; S. W., Jno. H. Bell; J. W., Jac Metzger; S., L. S. Johnson; T., Wm. Pool. Thirty-three members.

SCOTT LODGE, No. 37, I. O. O. F., instituted January 13, 1852, by James Thornington, D. D. G. M. Charter members, Thos. V. Blakemore, Jr., Jno. A. Boyd, Wm. Howard, Wm. Sims, Wm. H. White, Geo. G. Arndt, R. Roberts, A. Smallfiald, and Thos. V. Blakemore, Sr.

Officers—N G., Wm Sims; V G., Wm Howard; R S., Wm H White; T., Jno A Boyd.

July 1st, 1852—N G., Wm Howard; V G., H S Finley; P S., H Reichenbach, T., Jno A Boyd.

January 1st, 1853—N G., H S Finley; V G., John Weeks; R S., Geo G. Arndt; P S., T V Blakemore; T., Jno A Boyd.

July 1st—N G., Wm P Bailey; V G., Geo G Arndt; R S., Jno Hornby; P S., T V Blakemore; T., Jno A Boyd.

January 1st, 1854—N G, Geo G Arndt; V G, Ephraim T Johnson; R S, Edward L Johnson; P S, T V Blakemore; T, Jno A Boyd.

July 1st—N G, A Smallfield; V G, E T Johnston; R S, E L Johnston; P S, T V Blakemore; T, Jno A Boyd.

January 1st, 1855—N G, E T Johnston; V G, E L Johnston; R S, John A Rode; P S, Isaac Maas; T, John A Boyd.

July 1st—N G, E L Johnston; V G, Isaac Maas; R S, A Smallfield; T, Jno A Boyd.

January 1st, 1856—N G, J A Rhode; V G, L W Steinberg; R S, F Mahuke; P S, A Smallfield; T, F Dittmer.

July 1st—N G, L W Steinberg; V G, F Mahuke; R S, C J H Eyser; P S, A Smallfield; T, F Dittmer.

January 1st, 1857—N G, F Mahuke; V G, F Dittmer; R S, H Seifiert; P S, L W Steinberg; T, Claus Wulff.

July 1st—N G, F Dittmer; V G, C Wulff; R S, Jac Metzger; P S, L W Steinberg; T, H Rhode.

January 1st, 1858—N G, Claus Wulff; V G, Jac Metzger; R S, Chas A Wodz; P S, F Dittmer; T, H Rhode.

Twin City Degree Lodge. No, 1, I O. O. F., instituted March 21st, 1856. Charter members, Jas. Thorington, A. H. Barrow, H. Price, Wm. Pool, B. B. Woodward, J. D. Patton, Geo. W. Arndt.

Officers—D M, Wm Pool; D D M, L W Steinberg; A D M, Geo G Ardnt; S, B B Woodward; T, A H Barrow.

July 1st—D M, Wm Pool; D D M, L W Steinberg; A D M, Geo W Hall; S, B B Woodward; T, J W Danah.

January 5th, 1857—D M, Wm Pool; D D M, L W Steinberg; A D M, Wm B Kerns; S, B B Woodward; T, J W Danah.

July 1st—D M, B B Woodward; D D M, L W Steinberg; A D M, Wm Pool; S, John H Bell; T, J W Danah.

January 1st, 1858—D M, Wm B Kerns; D D M, L W Steinberg; A D M, Wm Pool; S, Jno H Bell; T, J W Danah.

# SONS OF TEMPERANCE.

The order of the Sons of Temperance was established in Davenport, on the 5th day of October, 1847, by the organization of Scott Division, No. 1.

The organization was effected by a dispensation of the National Division of North America to T. S. Battelle, the then acting Deputy for the State of Iowa.

At the institution of this Division, H. Price was elected W. P., and Enos Tichenor, W. A., and operations were commenced in the loft of an old school house, with a membership of eleven.

The prejudice existing in the minds of many good men against Secret Societies, has exerted an influence unfavorable to the success of this Society, but notwithstanding the opposition from this and various other sources, Scott Division has continued to increase in numbers and in interest, having during the time that has elapsed since her organization, enrolled the names of hundreds among her members and marshaled them to the contest against the great enemy of the human race.

It is worthy of remark that the first prohibitory Liquor Law of the State of Iowa was drawn up by a member of this Division, and the printing and speaking, and writing, and lobbying necessary to secure its passage through the Legislature, was done by members of this Division.

The meeting nights of this Division from the commencement has been Friday, and whether the *place* has been attractive or otherwise, the *time* has been strictly observed and no omission suffered to mar the record.

This Division has furnished three G. W. P.'s and two G. Scribes; but the brightest feature connected with her history is the fact that at the present time there are many men included in her membership who have been literally taken from the gutter and restored to their families, to usefulness and respectability, and who but for this organization would be filling dishonored graves, or, if living, be a disgrace and a curse to themselves and the community.

At the present time the Division occupies a splendid room on Brady between Front and Second streets; is free from debt, and has money in her Treasury.

## CENSUS OF THE CITY OF DAVENPORT, TAKEN MARCH 1858.

| OCCUPATIONS. | 1st Ward. | 2nd Ward. | 3rd Ward. | 4th Ward. | 5th Ward. | 6th Ward. | Total. |
|---|---|---|---|---|---|---|---|
| Accountants, | | | 1 | | | | 1 |
| Agents, | | 3 | 2 | 5 | | | 10 |
| Auction and Commission, | | | | 2 | | | 2 |
| Architects, | | | 1 | 1 | 1 | | 3 |
| Auctioneers, | | | 1 | | | | 1 |
| Artists, | | | 1 | | | 1 | 2 |
| Agricultural Implement Dealers, | | | 1 | | | | 1 |
| Baggage Master, | | | 1 | | | | 1 |
| Barbers, | | 3 | 3 | 2 | 1 | 1 | 10 |
| Bankers, | | | 5 | 10 | 1 | | 16 |
| Bakers, | 15 | | 8 | 6 | 1 | | 30 |
| Bar Keepers, | | | 3 | 2 | | | 5 |
| Bell Hanger, | | | | 1 | | | 1 |
| Basket Makers, | | | 1 | | 1 | | 2 |
| Builders, | | | | 6 | 1 | 1 | 8 |
| Bishop, | | | | 1 | | | 1 |
| Bill Broker, | | | | 1 | | | 1 |
| Blacksmiths, | 5 | 24 | 20 | 13 | 10 | 4 | 76 |
| Book Keeper, | 1 | 1 | 5 | 9 | | | 16 |
| Book Binders, | | | 2 | 3 | | | 5 |
| Boatmen, | 1 | | 4 | 4 | 1 | | 10 |
| Boarding House Keepers, | 2 | 5 | 4 | 3 | | 2 | 16 |
| Book Seller, | 1 | 1 | 3 | | | | 5 |
| Boat Builders, | | 1 | 1 | | | | 2 |
| Boiler Makers, | | | | | 1 | 1 | 2 |
| Brick Makers, | 12 | 3 | 2 | | 4 | 1 | 22 |
| Brakesmen, | | | | 6 | | | 6 |
| Brick-layers, | 2 | 5 | 16 | 3 | 6 | 3 | 35 |
| Bridge Builders, | | | | 1 | | | 1 |
| Butchers, | 13 | 18 | 6 | 4 | 2 | 1 | 44 |
| Brewers, | 2 | 5 | 4 | 1 | | 2 | 14 |
| Carpenters, | 155 | 109 | 152 | 50 | 51 | 22 | 539 |
| Carpet Dealers, | | | | 1 | | | 1 |
| Cabinet Makers, | | 4 | 8 | 4 | 4 | 7 | 27 |
| Carriage Trimmer, | | | 2 | | | | 2 |
| Carriage and wagon maker, | 4 | 21 | 16 | 3 | 1 | 1 | 46 |
| Cement Roofer, | | | 1 | 2 | | | 3 |
| Chair makers, | | 1 | | 1 | 3 | | 5 |
| Car makers, | | | | | 1 | | 1 |

## CENSUS CONTINUED.

| OCCUPATIONS. | 1st Ward. | 2nd Ward. | 3rd Ward. | 4th Ward. | 5th Ward. | 6th Ward. | Total. |
|---|---|---|---|---|---|---|---|
| Civil Engineers, | | | 1 | 1 | | | 2 |
| City Treasurer, | | | | 1 | | | 1 |
| " Marshal, | | | 1 | | | | 1 |
| " Clerk, | | | 1 | | | | 1 |
| Clerks, | 4 | 20 | 66 | 44 | 11 | 2 | 147 |
| Clerk of Courts, | | | | | 1 | | 1 |
| Clothiers, | | | 13 | | | | 13 |
| Cashiers, | | | 1 | | | | 1 |
| Contractors, | | 2 | | 4 | 1 | | 7 |
| Conductors, | | | 6 | 5 | 1 | | 12 |
| Coopers, | 38 | 45 | 6 | 2 | 5 | 5 | 96 |
| Confectioners, | | 1 | 1 | 2 | | | 4 |
| Commission Merchants, | | 1 | 2 | 1 | 1 | | 5 |
| County Surveyor, | | | 1 | | | | 1 |
| " Commissioner, | | 1 | | | | | 1 |
| Coachmen, | | | 1 | | | | 1 |
| Coal Dealers, | | | 2 | | | | 2 |
| Constables, | | | 1 | | | | 1 |
| Comedian, | | 2 | | | 3 | | 5 |
| Cotton Spinner, | | 1 | | | | | 1 |
| Collectors, | | | | 1 | 1 | | 2 |
| Cutters, | | | | 4 | | | 4 |
| Crockery Dealers, | | | 2 | | | | 2 |
| Clergymen, | 2 | 1 | 7 | 2 | 3 | 1 | 16 |
| Dentists, | | | 2 | 5 | | | 7 |
| Daguerreans, | | | 3 | 2 | 1 | | 6 |
| Draymen, | 3 | 3 | 4 | 9 | 9 | | 28 |
| Dressmakers, | | 1 | | 5 | 1 | | 7 |
| Druggists, | | | 5 | 1 | | | 6 |
| Deputy Sheriff, | | | 1 | | | | 1 |
| Dyer, | | | 1 | | | | 1 |
| Editors, | | 2 | 4 | 2 | | | 8 |
| Engineers, | 4 | | 6 | 8 | 7 | 3 | 28 |
| Engraver, | | | | | 1 | | 1 |
| Express Agent, | | | | 1 | | | 1 |
| Farriers, | 2 | 5 | 2 | 1 | | | 10 |
| Farmers, | 18 | 11 | 12 | 21 | 13 | 5 | 80 |
| Firemen, | | 5 | 1 | 5 | | 3 | 14 |
| Flour Dealer, | | | 1 | | | | 1 |
| Fruit Dealers, | | 5 | 1 | 2 | | | 8 |
| Fur Dealer, | | | 1 | | | | 1 |
| Furniture Dealers, | | | 5 | 2 | 1 | | 8 |
| Gas Fixtures, | | 1 | | 4 | 1 | | 6 |
| Gardners, | | 2 | | | 1 | 1 | 4 |
| Gentlemen, | | | 6 | | | | 6 |
| Glaziers, | | 1 | 1 | | | | 2 |

## CENSUS (CONTINUED.)

| OCCUPATIONS. | 1st Ward. | 2nd Ward. | 3rd Ward. | 4th Ward. | 5th Ward. | 6th Ward. | Total. |
|---|---|---|---|---|---|---|---|
| Grocers, | 14 | 10 | 20 | 25 | 2 | 2 | 73 |
| Gunsmiths, | | 2 | 2 | 1 | | | 5 |
| Hat and Cap Dealers, | | | 2 | | 1 | | 3 |
| Hardware Dealers, | | | 7 | 3 | | | 10 |
| Hatter, | | | 1 | | | | 1 |
| Horn Worker, | | | 1 | | | | 1 |
| Hotel Keepers, | | 1 | 10 | 5 | 1 | | 17 |
| Ice Dealers, | 1 | 1 | | | | 1 | [illegible] |
| Insurance Agents, | | | 1 | 2 | | | 4 |
| Iron Dealer, | | | | | 1 | | 1 |
| Iron Manufacturers, | | | 1 | | | | 1 |
| "Jack of all Trades," | | | 2 | | | | 2 |
| Jewelers, | | 1 | 7 | | | | 8 |
| Justices of the Peace, | | | 1 | | | | 1 |
| Judges, | | | | 1 | | | 1 |
| Lamplighters, | | | | 1 | 1 | | 2 |
| Land Agents, | | | 4 | 2 | 1 | | 7 |
| Laborers, | 426 | 386 | 116 | 91 | 215 | 67 | 1301 |
| Law Students, | | | | 1 | | | 1 |
| Loafers, | | 1 | 3 | 1 | | | 5 |
| Land Holder, (A. LeClaire,) | | | | | 1 | | 1 |
| Leather Dealers, | | 1 | | 1 | | | 2 |
| Lime Makers, | | | 1 | | | 2 | 3 |
| Livery Men, | | | 12 | 5 | | 3 | 21 |
| Lawyers, | 2 | 5 | 24 | 14 | 10 | 2 | 57 |
| Locksmiths, | 2 | | | | | | 2 |
| Lumber Dealers, | | 2 | 3 | 2 | 5 | 1 | 13 |
| Masons, | 12 | 26 | 14 | 11 | 7 | 8 | 78 |
| Marble Workers, | | | 1 | 2 | | | 3 |
| Machinists, | 7 | 12 | 6 | 7 | 9 | 2 | 43 |
| Manufacturers, | 3 | 2 | | 2 | 3 | 2 | 12 |
| Mattress Maker, | | | | | 1 | | 1 |
| Master Mechanic, | | | | | 1 | | 1 |
| Machine Peddler, | | | 1 | | | | 1 |
| Messenger, | | | 1 | | | | 1 |
| Musicians, | 1 | 14 | 1 | | | | 16 |
| Missionary, | | | 1 | | | | 1 |
| Mineralogist, | | | | 1 | | | 1 |
| Merchants, | | 12 | 30 | 34 | 6 | | 82 |
| Medical Students, | | | | 1 | | | 1 |
| Merchant Tailors, | | | 2 | 2 | 1 | | 5 |
| Milliners, | | 1 | 2 | 6 | | | 9 |
| Mill Wrights, | | | | 1 | 2 | 1 | 4 |
| Millers, | 2 | 1 | 3 | 13 | 2 | 7 | 27 |
| Music Teachers, | | | | 3 | 1 | | 5 |
| Moulders, | 7 | 1 | 3 | 1 | 1 | | 13 |

## CENSUS (CONTINUED.)

| OCCUPATIONS. | 1st Ward. | 2nd Ward. | 3rd Ward. | 4th Ward. | 5th Ward. | 6th Ward. | Total. |
|---|---|---|---|---|---|---|---|
| News Dealer, | | | 1 | | | | 1 |
| Notaries Public, | | 2 | | | | | 2 |
| Nurserymen, | 1 | | | | | | 1 |
| Overseer Poor, | | | | | 1 | | 1 |
| Painters, | 12 | 9 | 28 | 22 | 6 | 1 | 78 |
| Pattern Makers, | 1 | 1 | 3 | 1 | 1 | | 7 |
| Paper Carriers, | | | 2 | | | | 2 |
| Peddlers, | 4 | 2 | 5 | | | | 11 |
| Plasterers, | 14 | 16 | 13 | 13 | 3 | 1 | 70 |
| Plumber, | | | 1 | | | 1 | 2 |
| Physicians, | 1 | 4 | 8 | 11 | 3 | 1 | 28 |
| Paper Hanger, | | 1 | | | | | 1 |
| Piano Maker, | | | | | 1 | | 1 |
| Piano Mender, | | | | | 1 | | 1 |
| Pilots, | | | | | 5 | 1 | 6 |
| Plow Makers, | | | | 2 | | | 2 |
| Post Master, | | | | 1 | | | 1 |
| Policemen, | 1 | 3 | 2 | 2 | | 1 | 9 |
| Pork Packers, | 1 | | | | | 1 | 2 |
| Professor Mathematics, | | | 1 | | | | 1 |
| Professor Book-keeping, | | | 1 | 1 | | | 2 |
| Professor Languages, | | | 1 | | | | 1 |
| Prof. Mental and Moral Philoso'y, | | | 1 | | | | 1 |
| Printers, | | 3 | 7 | 16 | 3 | | 29 |
| Publishers, | | | | 3 | | | 3 |
| Pump Makers, | | 1 | | | | | 1 |
| Raftsmen, | | | 1 | | | | 1 |
| Real Estate Dealers, | | | | 1 | | | 1 |
| Recorder, | | | | 1 | | | 1 |
| Road Master, | | | 1 | 1 | | | 2 |
| R. R. Repairers, | | | 1 | 1 | | | 2 |
| R. R. Superintendent, | | | 1 | | | | 1 |
| Roofer, | | | 1 | | | | 1 |
| Salesmen, | | 2 | 1 | 1 | | | 4 |
| Saloon Keepers, | 6 | 18 | 18 | 14 | 7 | 2 | 65 |
| Sash and Blind Makers, | | | 3 | 1 | 2 | | 6 |
| Sawers, | | 6 | | | | 3 | 9 |
| Segar Makers, | 1 | 9 | 6 | 1 | 1 | | 18 |
| Sempstresses, | 1 | 7 | 4 | 4 | 1 | | 17 |
| Sexton, | | | 3 | 1 | | | 4 |
| Sailors, | | | | 1 | | | 1 |
| Secretary Railroad, | | | | 1 | | | 1 |
| Segar Peddler, | | | 1 | | | | 1 |
| Sausage Maker, | 1 | | | | | | 1 |
| Saddle and Harness Makers, | 1 | 3 | 9 | 3 | 4 | | 20 |
| Silver Plater, | | | 1 | | | | 1 |
| Shingle Maker, | 4 | 1 | | | | | 5 |

CENSUS (CONTINUED.)

| OCCUPATIONS. | 1st Ward. | 2nd Ward. | 3rd Ward. | 4th Ward. | 5th Ward. | 6th Ward. | Total. |
|---|---|---|---|---|---|---|---|
| Shoemakers, | 12 | 31 | 32 | 20 | 5 | 6 | 106 |
| Shoe Dealers, | | | 6 | 5 | | | 11 |
| Sheriff, | | | 1 | | | | 1 |
| Shoe Cutters, | | | 1 | | | | 1 |
| Sculptors, | | 1 | | | | | 1 |
| Soap Makers, | 7 | | | | | | 7 |
| Speculators, | 1 | 2 | 6 | 7 | 2 | | 18 |
| Straw Goods Makers, | | | | 1 | | | 1 |
| Stove Dealers, | | | 1 | 1 | | | 2 |
| Students, | | 2 | 8 | 5 | | 11 | 26 |
| Starch Makers, | | | | 1 | | | 1 |
| Stair Builders, | | | 1 | | | | 1 |
| Steamboat Captains, | | | | | 1 | | 1 |
| Stone Cutter, | | | | | 1 | | 1 |
| Steam Fitters, | | | 2 | | | | 2 |
| Surveyors, | | | 1 | 1 | | | 2 |
| Switch Tenders, | 1 | | | | | | 1 |
| Tailors, | 13 | 31 | 16 | 10 | 3 | 1 | 74 |
| Tailoresses, | | | | 4 | 2 | | 6 |
| Tanners, | 1 | 1 | 1 | 4 | 1 | | 8 |
| Teamsters, | 39 | 36 | 37 | 14 | 6 | 13 | 145 |
| Teachers, | | 3 | 15 | 3 | | 5 | 26 |
| Tellers, | | | | 2 | | | 2 |
| Tinners, | | 1 | 1 | 6 | | | 8 |
| Tobacconists, | | 2 | 5 | 1 | | | 8 |
| Traveling Agents, | | | 1 | 1 | | | 2 |
| Traders, | | 1 | 1 | | | | 2 |
| Trunk Makers, | | 1 | | | | | 1 |
| Umbrella Makers, | | | 1 | | | | 1 |
| Undertakers, | | | | 1 | | | 1 |
| Upholsters, | | 2 | 2 | 2 | | | 6 |
| Varnishers, | | | 1 | | 1 | | 2 |
| Varnish Makers, | | | 1 | | | | 1 |
| Vegetable Dealers, | | | 1 | 2 | | | 3 |
| Washerwomen, | 8 | 14 | 8 | 2 | 9 | 1 | 42 |
| Watchmen, | | 2 | | 1 | | | 3 |
| Watch-makers, | | 5 | 4 | | | | 9 |
| Well Diggers, | 1 | 3 | | 3 | | | 7 |
| Weighers, | | | | 1 | | | 1 |
| Wheat Buyers, | | | 4 | | | | 4 |
| Wood Buyers, | | | | 1 | 1 | | 2 |
| Wood Sawyers, | | | 1 | | | | 1 |
| Writers, | | | 1 | | | | 1 |

## CENSUS (CONTINUED.)

| NATIVITIES. | 1st Ward. | 2nd Ward. | 3rd Ward. | 4th Ward. | 5th Ward. | 6th Ward. | Total. |
|---|---|---|---|---|---|---|---|
| America, | 915 | 1174 | 1928 | 1738 | 782 | 486 | 7023 |
| Ireland, | 327 | 325 | 296 | 442 | 488 | 83 | 1961 |
| England, | 17 | 40 | 59 | 60 | 30 | 34 | 240 |
| Germany, | 16 | 437 | 622 | 133 | 35 | 4 | 1277 |
| Holstein, | 459 | 626 | 1 | | | 82 | 1268 |
| Mecklenburg, | 88 | 110 | | | | 2 | 210 |
| Bavaria, | 48 | 32 | 13 | | | | 93 |
| Wurtemberg, | 17 | 24 | | | | 6 | 47 |
| Hessia, | 12 | 35 | | | | 14 | 61 |
| Saxe Coburg, | | 6 | | | | | 6 |
| Scotland, | 4 | 10 | 23 | 20 | 15 | 8 | 80 |
| Hungary, | 8 | 8 | 7 | 2 | | | 25 |
| Canada, | 19 | 11 | 13 | 5 | 19 | 4 | 71 |
| Wales, | | | 13 | 2 | 1 | | 16 |
| France, | 11 | 10 | 3 | 10 | | | 54 |
| Italy, | | | 3 | 2 | | | 5 |
| Sweden, | | | | 2 | 1 | | 11 |
| West India, | | | 4 | 1 | | | 1 |
| Negroes, | 12 | 7 | | 2 | 1 | 9 | 35 |
| S. America, | | | | 3 | 1 | | 4 |
| New Brunswick, | | | | 1 | | | 2 |
| Isle of Jersey, | | | | 1 | | | 1 |
| Holland, | 4 | 1 | 2 | 1 | | | 8 |
| Hindostan, | | | 8 | | | | 8 |
| Costa Rica, | | | 1 | | | | 1 |
| Nova Scotia, | 1 | 2 | 4 | | | | 7 |
| Bohemia, | 11 | 8 | 21 | | 10 | | 34 |
| Prussia, | 139 | 159 | 9 | | | 15 | 324 |
| Hanover, | 85 | 49 | 1 | | | 13 | 156 |
| Russia, | | | 1 | | | | 1 |
| Switzerland, | 92 | 69 | 2 | | 2 | 17 | 188 |
| Norway, | | | | | 2 | | 3 |
| Austria, | 15 | 11 | | | | 15 | 41 |
| Hamburg, | 37 | 23 | | | | | 60 |
| Baden, | 18 | 14 | | | | 3 | 35 |
| Saxony, | 5 | 2 | | | | 1 | 8 |
| Poland, | | 2 | | | | | 2 |
| Denmark, | 13 | 6 | | | | | 19 |
| Bremen, | 26 | 9 | | | | 19 | 54 |
| Posen, | 3 | | | | | | 3 |
| Mexico, | 1 | | | | | | 1 |
| Waldeck, | 1 | | | | | | 1 |
| Demsted, | 8 | 2 | | | | | 10 |
| Total, | | | | | | | 13,455 |
| Unknown, | | | | | | | 3222 |

CENSUS (CONTINUED.)

| WARDS. | No. Dwellings. | Tenants. | Owners. | Adults. Male. | Adults. Femals. | Children. Males. | Children. Female. | Native Voters. | Nat. Voters. | Aliens. |
|---|---|---|---|---|---|---|---|---|---|---|
| First Ward, | 468 | 259 | 300 | 858 | 778 | 718 | 643 | 110 | 270 | 390 |
| Second Ward, | 599 | 427 | 249 | 1171 | 901 | 822 | 848 | 150 | 347 | 543 |
| Third Ward, | 519 | 330 | 237 | 1222 | 839 | 778 | 775 | 456 | 275 | 254 |
| Fourth Ward, | 353 | 246 | 177 | 970 | 767 | 634 | 716 | 517 | 170 | 105 |
| Fifth Ward, | 287 | 147 | 178 | 595 | 514 | 389 | 458 | 153 | 183 | 110 |
| Sixth Ward, | 149 | 55 | 108 | 328 | 301 | 312 | 340 | 73 | 72 | 69 |
| Total, | 2375 | 1464 | 1249 | 5144 | 4100 | 3653 | 3780 | 1459 | 1317 | 1471 |

The census of Davenport *Township* for 1856, showed a population of 12,821. The above returns show the city to have a population of 16,677. Estimating the inhabitants of the township, outside of the city, to be about 1500, and we have a total of about 18,000, or an increase of fifty per cent in eighteen months.

Of the population of the city, (including a majority of nativities unknown,) fifty per cent are Americans, about twelve per cent Irish, about twenty per cent Germans, and a little less than two per cent English—leaving a balance of sixteen per cent to be divided among unknown and other nativities.

COMPARATIVE ESTIMATE OF POPULATION.

| Year | Population | Year | Population |
|---|---|---|---|
| 1836 | 60 | 1852 | 3,500 |
| 1837 | 150 | 1853 | 4,500 |
| 1840 | 600 | 1854 | 6.000 |
| 1841 | 700 | 1855 | 8,000 |
| 1842 | 900 | 1856 | 11,500 |
| 1850 | 1,848 | 1858 (March,) | 16,677 |

The increase of Cincinnati for twenty years from its formation was from 750 inhabitants to 9,602; of Pittsburg, at the same time, 1,565 to 7,243 ; Louisville 600 to 4,012; New Orleans, 9,650 to 27,658. The greatest increase exhibited by any one of these for any five years was 110 per cent, while that of Davenport for the last five years has been nearly 400 per cent.

# LIST OF OFFICERS

FROM THE DATE OF THE FIRST CHARTER TO THE PRESENT TIME.

1839.—Mayor, Rodolphus Bennett; Recorder, Frazier Wilson; Treasurer, James M. Bowling; Marshal, George Colt.

1840.—Mayor, John H. Thorington; Recorder, Frazier Wilson; Treasurer, James M. Bowling; Marshal, William B. Watts.

1841.—Mayor, Jonathan W. Parker; Recorder, John Pope; Treasurer, James M. Bowling; Marshal, William B. Watts.

1842.—Mayor, Harvey Leonard; Recorder, J. W. Parker; Treasurer, James M. Bowling; Marshal, Gilbert B. McKown.

1843.—(New Charter granted.)—Mayor, James Thorington; Clerk, Jonathan W. Parker; Treasurer, John Evans; Marshal, Jared N. Snow.

1844.—Mayor, James Thorington; Clerk, Levi Davis; Treasurer, John Evans; Marshal, Jared N. Snow.

1845.—Mayor, James Thorington; Clerk, John Pope; Treasurer, John Evans; Marshal, Samuel Lyter.

1846.—Mayor, James Thorington; Clerk, John Pope; Treasurer, John Evans; Marshal, Samuel Lyter.

1847.—Mayor, James M. Bowling; Clerk, James Thorington; Treasurer, ——; Marshal, John Evans.

1848.—Mayor, James M. Bowling; Clerk, James Thorington; Treasurer, John Evans; Marshal, Samuel Parker.

1849.—Mayor, Jonathan Parker; Clerk, James Thorington; Treasurer, John Evans; Marshal, Lockwood J. Center.

1850.—(Charter Amended.)—Mayor, James Hall; Clerk, James Thorington; Treasurer, John Evans; Marshal, L. J. Center.

1851.—(New Charter.)—Mayor, Charles Weston; Clerk, A. F. Mast; Marshal, Patrick Courtney; Treasurer, L. B. Collamer.

*Aldermen*—First Ward, Adam Weigand, Harvey Leonard; Second Ward, Egbt. S. Barrows, Nathanthiel Squires; Second Ward, Ebenezer Cook, Hiram Price.

1852.—Mayor, John Jordan; Clerk, A. F. Mast; Marshal, Samuel Parker; Treasurer, William Van Tuyl.

*Aldermen*—First Ward, Harvey Leonard, Adam Weigand; Second Ward, Nathaniel Squires, John P. Cook; Third Ward, Hiram Price, John Bechtel.

1853.—Mayor, John A. Boyd; Clerk, Richard K. Allen; Marshal, Samuel Parker; Treasurer, Jessamine Drake.

*Aldermen*—First Ward, Adam Weigand, John Weeks; Second Ward, John P. Cook, Joseph Kingerlee; Third Ward, Hiram Price, William Gray.

1854.—Mayor, James Grant; Clerk, B. B. Woodward; Marshal, L. J. Center; Treasurer, L. B. Collamer.

*Aldermen*—First Ward, H. Wilhelme, G. G. Arndt; Second Ward, Chas. J.

H. Eyser, E. A. Gerdtzen; Third Ward, B. Atkinson, D. P. McKown; Fourth Ward—Henry H. Smith, Ebenezer Cook; Fifth Ward, William Burris, A. A. McLoskey.

1855.—Mayor, Enos Tichenor; Clerk, B. B. Woodward; Marshal Samuel Parker; Treasurer, William Van Tuyl.

*Aldermen*—First Ward, G. G. Arndt, Gilbert C. R. Mitchell; Second Ward, E. A. Gerdtzen, Charles J. H. Eyser; Third Ward, D. P. McKown, Austin Corbin; Fourth Ward, Ebenezer Cook, Hiram Price; Fifth Ward, Anthony A. McLoskey, Alfred H. Owens; Sixth Ward, Joseph Lambrite, Samuel Sadoris.

1856.—Mayor, G. C. R. Mitchell; Clerk, Wm. Hall; Treasurer, Samuel Sylvester; Marshal, John H. Taylor.

*Aldermen*—First Ward, James O'Brien, John Schuett; Second Ward, C. J. H. Eyser, Aug. Smallfield; Third Ward—Austin Corbin, James M. Bowling; Fourth Ward, Hiram Price, John Forrest; Fifth Ward, W. S. Kinsey, S. R. Barkley; Sixth Ward, Sam. Sadoris, Joseph Lambrite.

1857.—Mayor, Geo B. Sargent; Marshal, H. W. Mitchell; Clerk, E. Peck; Treasurer, Samuel Sylvester.

*Aldermen.*—First Ward, J. W. Cannon, A. Jennings; Second Ward, H. Ramming, Theo. Guelich; Third Ward, J. M. Bowling, Austin Corbin; Fourth Ward, John Forrest, J. C. Washburne; Fifth Ward, James O'Brien, Geo. E. Hubbell, vice A. LeClaire, resigned; Sixth Ward, Wm. Guy, J. H. Sears.

1858.—Mayor, Ebenezer Cook; Marshal, John Bechtel; Treasurer, Lorenzo Schricker; Clerk, Hallet Kilbourn.

*Aldermen*—First Ward, John M. Cannon, I. P. Coates; Second Ward, Theo. Guelich, Henry Ramming; Third Ward, Austin Corbin, James Mackintosh; Fourth Ward, Thomas H. Morley, John C. Washburne; Fifth Ward, Geo. E. Hubbell, James O'Brien; Sixth Ward, Robt. Christie, J. H. Sears.

# CITY VOTE, APRIL, 1858.

| WARDS. | 1st Ward. | 2nd Ward. | 3rd Ward. | 4th Ward. | 5th Ward. | 6th Ward. | Total. |
|---|---|---|---|---|---|---|---|
| For Mayor, | 236 | 273 | 510 | 414 | 340 | 104 | 1877 |
| For Marshal, | 243 | 287 | 550 | 433 | 355 | 106 | 1974 |
| For Treasurer, | 240 | 276 | 531 | 424 | 353 | 103 | 1927 |
| For Clerk, | 241 | 287 | 545 | 429 | 319 | 104 | 1925 |
| For Alderman, | 228 | 227 | 500 | 412 | 352 | 102 | 1821 |
| Number of Ballots Cast, | 246 | 396 | 558 | 443 | 355 | 106 | 2004 |

# APPENDIX.

Friend Wilkie:—As I am informed you intend in your forthcoming History of "Davenport Past and Present" to give some incidents referring to the Black Hawk War, I will give you, from recollection, a statement of some facts that you may arrange for your book, and put in a shape that will interest your readers.

As I before stated, I carried Gen. Gaines, several officers, and as many U. S. Troops from Jefferson Barracks to Rock Island, in 1831, as I could accommodate on the steamboat Enterprise. I was in the Council Chamber when Black Hawk and his Chiefs and Braves were apparently very near destroying the lives of the U. S. Officers, and every other white man in the Council Chamber. I know the fact, that Gen. Gaines, the officers of the U. S. Army, the Indian Agent, (who was the next year killed by the Black Hawk Band,) Mr. Antoine LeClaire, Indian Interpreter, Mr. George Davenport, Mr. Russel Farnham, and some others, *all* done their duty most humanely to conciliate and reconcile that desperate band of marauders, that separated themselves from the then friendly nation of Indians, called "Sac and Fox," whose principal Chiefs were men of talent, discretion and prudence, and who commanded the respect of officers and traders who had business and intercourse with them.

I know that Gen. Gaines was extremely humane and conciliatory, in 1831, toward Black Hawk and his band, and I know, too, that all the gentlemen I named above, contributed their advice and influence to procure a reconciliation. This disaffected Band had with them a considerable number of Squaws and Pappooses (women and children,) which I know, from conversation at that time with Gen. Gaines, Officcers, Traders, Agent and Interpretor, was a prominent reason, concurred in by all, to induce extraordinary efforts for conciliation towards this Band of inhuman and ill-governed out-laws.

It is a matter of history, that this Band made a Treaty, received valuable presents from the U. S. Government, made promise of *permanent* peace, and returned to their own country in 1831.

In the Spring of 1832, they reorganized with renewed strength from the means they obtained by the Treaty stipulations from the United States, and commenced their work of death and destruction on defenceless inhabitants, at many points, both along the River, and in the interior of the State of Illinois.

I was at Galena with my steamboat Dove in 1832, when two survivors, out of nine, came into Galena, and brought intelligence of the murder of their seven companions, one of whom was the U. S. Indian Agent of the Sacs and Foxes, Mr. Felix St. Vrain, who was a humane and most worthy gentleman, as well as popular Agent with the Chiefs and Indians generally. I knew him well, and in common with all who were acquainted with his character, respectedhim highly.

It happened that Gen. George W. Jones, our present U. S. Senator, who was then in Lead Smelting and Merchantile business some miles from the town, came in that morning, and in a few minutes after, he heard of the probable murder of Felix St. Vrain, his brother-in-law. (The two that came in said that Mr. St. Vrain, when they last saw him, was a quarter of a mile from them, and they heard several rifle shots.) When he mounted his horse to start, I was with him, and begged of him to wait an hour, until some friends could be raised to go with him; and I know, too, that several of his friends tried to prevail upon him to delay until he could have several go with him.

The excitement that morning was intense. The trifling participation I had in the matter gave me knowledge of a fact that is highly creditable to Gen. Jones, and I will state it with the hope that you will make it a matter of history.

Being then intimate with Mr. Jones, I took some interest in detaining him; I think I held the rein of the bridle, and told him it would be rash imprudence for him to go before he procured at least a few companions. He told me he felt it his duty to go immediately. He said to me—"My friend, if I can get to my poor brother-in-law even a few minutes before any one else, to staunch his wounds, and save his life, I will be doing my duty; therefore I will not wait"

Off he went. I started that day for St. Louis; stopped at Rock Island, and called to see my friend, *Major* George Davenport; found him and his family (as all the inhabitants along the river were,) in a state of excitement and dread. His tables and sideboard were covered with powder-horns, cartridges, pistols, &c.; guns in corners, and a swivel at the door.

When he was informed of the probable murder of Mr. St. Vrain, he seemed deeply grieved, evincing generous and laudable solicitude for the wife and children of Mr. St. Vrain, who were residing in the Government Council House on the Island.

Major Davenport and myself went to see Mrs. St. Vrain. We advised her, as there was great danger to her and her family there, to go down on my boat, as they would be safe at St. Genevieve, where her parents and connections lived.

She seemed to know by intuition that her husband was killed. We did not give her even an intimation of the doleful news we had heard, but she seemed convinced that he was killed. The deep affliction of the mother and her children that night was really distressing. The family went to St. Louis with me. When I returned to Galena, I learned that a party of several started in a few minutes after Mr. Jones, but did not overtake him until they were some six miles from Galena. They found the dead body of Felix St. Vrain, I think, some fourteen miles from Galena. The heart was cut out, and head and hands cut off; the corpse was identified by the despatches* and papers that were left undisturbed in his pockets. I thought then, and think still that there are *but few men*, under the circumstances, possessing the courage and magnanimity to act as Gen. George W. Jones acted on that occasion.

The day I arrived at Galena, the news came that daily and nightly murders and depredations were committed by the Black Hawk Band at various points, which created tremendous excitement. Col. Strode had several companies mustered, and proclaimed martial law—which required every able-bodied man to go into service. There was a good supply of patriotic and brave, as well as efficient men there then; hundreds of miners left their diggings, and came into Galena. There were a number, however, who preferred remaining in the town to soldiering. Several that were extremely active and fine healthy looking men, at dancing parties, reported themselves as invalids, and exposed internal and external diseases; some made liberal offers to the Medical Faculty on condition that they should be rejected as *unfit* for service.

Col. Strode pressed my steamboot, crew and self, and we got ready in a few hours.

A short time before we started, my Second Engineer left the boat; I went to see him. He told me he was afraid he might be killed, and did not want to run the risk. I gave him half an hour to make up his mind to go on board, and attend to his duty as an officer of the steamboat Dove, or I would have him put in the ranks of the Army as a Private, with the brand of a coward on him. He immediately went on board, and he and the other Engineer very properly requested plank to be put up to shield them aft of the boilers. We shielded the Pilots from view also by putting plank on each side of the Pilot Wheel House.

On our way down, between Galena and Rock Island, we found Mr. Davidson's house had been attacked the night before. Several rifle shots had been fired into the room that the family occupied. A small block house that they had built the year before, as Mr. Davidson said, "to please the women," saved the lives of that family. Mr. Davidson's was the only house there then; now the flourishing town of Savanna is on that location.

We saw at another point, near where Cordova is now situated, a fire still burning, where the Indians had camped, and the trail where they had traveled, but found no Indians. We returned to Galena, and went up from there to Prairie du Chien, (Fort Crawford.) We heard of Indians being on or near an Island a short distauce above Dubuque, a few hours before we arrived there. Whilst we were in service we had on board a Company of about eighty. It was called the "Spy Company," officers and privates all acted alike, and I think were gentlemen. I have been intimate with, and met many of them from time to time since. They were a choice Company of Pioneers, and acquitted themselves well during the war, and many of them have been since, and are now distinguished gentlemen in this country. I have read several misrepresentations regarding the conduct of the U. S. Government towards the Black Hawk Band, as well as untruthful apologies published to excuse that marauding murderer's party.

Several of the prominent officers in that war have efficiently and honorably filled high places as distinguished Democrats in the Councils of the nation. Instance Governors Reynolds and Dodge, Gen. G. W. Jones, and others.

I had intimate acquaintance with many officers, agents, interpreters, Traders, and Indian Chiefs, from 1827 up to this time, and when opportnnity offered I tried to learn the truth.

Now, when I look back, I cannot call to mind a single instance where there was an act of inhumanity or oppression encouraged by the Administration of the United States, or the Illinois State Government. Nor do I know of a single case of an official or trader giving cause to this Band to commence the war. I do know that thousands of the innocent and unoffending inhabitants of Illinois and Wisconsin were driven from their homes, had their property destroyed, families seriously inconvenienced, and several inhuman butcheries of men who had no part in the war, were committed by those Indians before the United States army made an attack on them. I know that the privations, distress, dread, and intense anxiety of the white inhabitants, caused by the actions and demonstration of this Band of out-laws, were general and wide-spread over the State of Illinois and Territory of Wisconsin, from the Spring of 1831, to the end of the war, which was terminated by the memorable battle of "Bad Axe"—where, by general (and I have reason to believe true,) report, Gov. Henry Dodge, Ex-United States Senator of Wisconsin, gained high honors by his brave and noble conduct in the command of that division of the army. I have frequently heard his officers speak of his admirable military skill. He had, in the war of 1812, acquired an enviable reputation as Captain of a Company of Volunteers from St. Genevive, Missouri.

I could add many incidents of those times that might interest some of your readers, but have

*Mr. St. Vrain was sent from Gen. Atkinson's Army, on Rock River, with Despatches to Galena, with eight escorts.

not spare time to prepare them; what I have written is hastily scratched on the paper from memory, but, nevertheless, I have aimed to state facts.

[By request of the writer of the above, who is a personal friend of Ex-Gov. Reynolds, and also by request of Ex-Gov. Reynolds himself, we append the following account of the Black Hawk War, from "Annals of the West," by Messrs. Perkins and Peck :]

As this portion of Illinois history has been much misunderstood, and consequently misrepresented in several publications, we shall give the facts of the case, but in a very condensed form :

1st. The Sauks and Foxes had no original right, in the Indian sense even, to any portion of Illinois. They were intruders on the country of the Santeaurs and Ioways.

2nd. The head chiefs sold their claim to their lands in Illinois and Southern Wisconsin, to the United States, in 1804.*

3rd. This treaty was violated by all that portion of the united tribes, which committed hostilities against the United States, and joined the British during the war. The portions of the tribes that remained peaceable, re-confirmed the treaty of 1804, at Portage des Sioux, September 13th, 1815. The hostile part of the nation, in 1816, professed repentance for their misdeeds, obtained forgiveness, and the treaty of 1804 was again renewed and re-enacted,

4th. Black Hawk never was a chief; never recognized as such by Indian authority, or by the United States. He was a *brave*, in Indian parlance, gathered around him a small party of disaffected spirits, refused to attend the negotiations of 1816; went to Canada, proclaimed himself and his party British subjects, and received presents from that quarter.

5th. Another treaty was made in full council, "with the chiefs, warriors, and head men of the Sac and Fox tribes," at Fort Armstrong, [Rock Island,] September 3rd, 1822, by the agent of the United States, in which the treaty of 1804, is referred to and ratified. And still another treaty was made by ten regularly delegated chiefs and head men, and Governor Clark on the part of the United States, in Washington City, the 4th of August, 1824. In this treaty they sell, for a valuable consideration, all their title to the northern portion of the State of Missouri, from the Mississippi to the western boundary of that State. At this treaty the United States granted the strip of country between the Mississippi and Des Moines river, to certain half-breeds of that nation. And on all the lands they had claimed *south and east* of this line, they are not to be permitted to settle or hunt, after the first day of January, 1826.

6th. In the treaty of 1804, the Sauks and Foxes were permitted to reside and hunt on the land sold, while it remained the property of the United States.

Writers, and especially Brown, have retained the story of Black Hawk, and by this means misrepresented this whole business. Brown has given Indian speeches, in place of authentic public documents and treaties. Drake, in his "*Book of the Indians*," in many respects a valuable antiquarian work, has made great mistakes.† This work abounds with errors, concerning the causes and the management of the Black Hawk affair.

7th. Another treaty was held at Prairie du Chien, in 1825, with the Sauks, Foxes, Winnebagoes, Chippeways, Sioux, and other North-western Indians. The object was to settle the long existing hostilities among these tribes, in which the United States Government exercised the office of mediator. In 1827, a party of twenty-four Chippeways, on a visit to Fort Snelling, was attacked by a band of Sioux, and eight of their number killed and wounded. The commander at Fort Snelling caused four of the Sioux, who had committed this murder, to be delivered to the Chippeways, by whom they were shot. Red Bird, a Sioux Chief, determined to retaliate, and got defeated. Being derided by his own nation, he resolved to attack the white people, whom he regarded as allies of the Chippeways; and on the 27th of July, two men in the vicinity of Prairie du Chien, were killed, and a third wounded. At the same period hostile demonstrations were made by some Winnebagoes, and Black Hawk's party of the Sauks, in the vicinity of the lead mines, which caused much alarm. About the 28th of July, two keel-boats, conveying military stores to Fort Snelling, were attacked by hostile Sioux, Winnebagoes and Sauks, two of their crew were killed, and four wounded. The party was commanded by Red Bird, but Black Hawk was of the party. General Atkinson marched a detachment of troops into the Winnebago country, captured Red Bird and six other Indians, and committed them to prison in Prairie du Chien, for trial. Red Bird died in prison. A part of the others were convicted and executed in December, 1828.

About this year, the President issued a proclamation, according to law, and the country about the mouth of Rock River, which had been previously surveyed, was sold, and the year following, was taken possession of by American families. Some time previous to this, after the death of old Quashquame, Keokuk was appointed chief of the Sauk nation. The United States gave due notice to the Indians to leave the country, east of the Mississippi, and Keokuk made the same proclamation to the Sauks, and a portion of the nation, with their regular chiefs, with Keokuk at their head, peaceably retired across the Mississippi. Up to this period, Black Hawk continued his annual visits to Malden, and received his annuity for allegiance to the British government. He would not recognize Keokuk as chief, but gathered about him all the restless spirits of his tribe, many of whom were young, and fired with the ambition of becoming "braves," and set up himself for a chief.

Black Hawk was not a Pontiac, or a Tecumthe. He had neither the talent or the influence to form any comprehensive scheme of action, yet he made an abortive attempt to unite all the Indians of the West, from Rock River to Mexico, in a war against the United States.

* Indian Treaties.

† Book v. chapter viii. pp. 141 to 165.

In the memoir he dictated, and LeClaire wrote, he states, "runners were sent to the Arkansas, Red River and Texas—not on the subject of our lands, but on a secret mission, which I am not, at present, permitted to explain." The mission was no secret when the memoir was written. It was to arouse up the Indians to attack the white settlements, through the long line of frontier, at the same time.

Still another treaty, and the seventh in succession, was made with the Sauks and Foxes, on the 15th of July, 1830, in which they again confirmed the preceding treaties, and promised to remove from Illinois to the territory West of the Mississippi. This was no new cession, but a recognition of the former treaties by the proper authorities of the nation, and a renewed pledge of fidelity to the United States.

During all this time Black Hawk was gaining accessions to his party. Like Tecumthe, he, too, had his Prophet—whose influence over the superstitious savages was not without effect.

In 1830, an arrangement was made by the Americans, who had purchased the land above the mouth of Rock River, and the Indians that remained, to live as neighbors; the latter cultivating their old fields. Their enclosures consisted of stakes stuck in the ground, and small poles tied with strips of bark transversely. The Indians left for their Summer's hunt, and returned when their corn was in the milk—gathered it, and turned their horses into the fields, cultivated by the Americans, to gather their crop. Some depredations were committed on their hogs and other property. The Indians departed on their winter's hunt, but returned early in the spring of 1831, under the guidance of Black Hawk, and committed depredations on the frontier settlements. Their leader was a cunning, shrewd Indian, and trained his party to commit various depredations on the property of the frontier inhabitants, but not to attack, or kill any person. His policy was to provoke the Americans to make war on him, and thus seem to fight in defense of Indian rights, and the "graves of their fathers." Numerous affidavits, from persons of unquestionable integrity, sworn to before the proper officers, were made out and sent to Governor Reynolds, attesting to these and many other facts. We have examined these documents, knew, personally, some who subscribed to them, and others from good testimony. Black Hawk had about five hundred Indians in training, with horses, well provided with arms, and invaded the State of Illinois with hostile designs. These facts were known to the Governor and other officers of the State. Consequently, Governor Reynolds, on the 28th of May, 1831, made a call for volunteers, and communicated the facts to General Gaines of this military district, and made a call for regular troops. The State was invaded by a hostile band of savages, under an avowed enemy of the United States. The military turned out to the number of twelve hundred or more, on horseback, and under command of the late General Joseph Duncan, marched to Rock River.

The regular troops went up the Mississippi in June. Black Hawk and his men, alarmed at this formidable appearance, recrossed the Mississippi, sent a white flag, and made a treaty, in which the United States agreed to furnish them a large amount of corn and other necessaries, if they would observe the treaty.

In the spring of 1832, Black Hawk, with his party, again crossed the Mississippi to the valley of Rock River, notwithstanding he was warned against doing so by General Atkinson, who commanded at Fort Armstrong, in Rock Island. Troops, both regular and militia, were at once mustered, and marched in the pursuit of the native band. Among the troops was a party of volunteers under Major Stillman, who, on the 14th of May, was out upon a tour of observation, and close in the neighborhood of the savages. On that evening, having discovered a party of Indians, the whites galloped forward to attack the savage band, but were met with so much energy and determination, that they took to their heels in utter consternation. The whites were one hundred and seventy-five in number; the Indians from five to six hundred. Of this party, twenty-five followed the retreating battalion, after night, for several miles. Eleven whites were killed and shockingly mangled, and several wounded. Some four or five Indians were known to be killed. This action was at Stillman's Run, in the eastern part of Ogle county, about twenty-five miles above Dixon.

Peace was now hopeless, and although Keokuk, the legitimate chief of the nation, controlled a majority, the temptation of war and plunder was too strong for those who followed Black Hawk.

We now quote from the first edition of the Annals, with some emendations:—

On the 21st of May, a party of warriors, about seventy in number, attacked the Indian Creek settlement, in LaSalle county, Illinois, killed fifteen persons, and took two young women prisoners; these were afterwards returned to their friends, late in July, through the efforts of the Winnebagoes. On the following day, a party of spies was attacked, and four of them slain, and other massacres followed. Meanwhile three thousand Illinois militia had been ordered out, who rendezvoused upon the 20th of June, near Peru; these marched forward to Rock River, where they were joined by the United States troops, the whole being under command of General Atkinson. Six hundred mounted men were also ordered out, while General Scott, with nine companies of artillery, hastened from the sea-board, by the way of the lakes to Chicago, moving with such celerity, that some of his troops, we are told, actually went eighteen hundred miles in eighteen days; passing in that time from Fort Monroe, on the Chesapeake, to Chicago. Long before the artillerists *could* reach the scene of action, however, the western troops had commenced the conflict in earnest, and before they *did* reach the field, had closed it. On the 24th of June, Black Hawk and his two hundred warriors were repulsed by Major Demint, with but one hundred and fifty militia; this skirmish took place between Rock River and Galena. The army then continued to move up Rock River, near the head of which it was understood that the main party of the hostile Indians was collected; and as provisions were scarce, and hard to convey in such a country, a detachment was sent forward to Fort Winnebago, at the portage between the

Wisconsin and Fox rivers, to procure supplies. This detachment, hearing of Black Hawk's army, pursued and overtook them on the 21st of July, near the Wisconsin river, and in the neighborhood of the Blue Mounds. General Henry, who commanded the party, formed with his troops three sides of a hollow square, and in that order received the attack of the Indians; two attempts to break the ranks were made by the natives in vain; and then a general charge was made by the whole body of Americans, and with such success that, it is said, fifty-two of the red men were left dead upon the field, while but one American was killed, and eight wounded.

Before this action, Henry had sent word of his motions to the main army, by whom he was immediately rejoined, and on the 28th of July, the whole crossed the Wisconsin in pursuit of Black Hawk, who was retiring toward the Mississippi. Upon the bank of that river, nearly opposite the Upper Ioway, the Indians were overtaken, and again defeated, on the 2nd of August, with a loss of one hundred and fifty men, while of the whites but eighteen fell. This battle entirely broke the power of Black Hawk; he fled, but was seized by the Winnebagoes, and upon the 27th, was delivered to the officers of the United States, at Prairie du Chien.

General Scott, during the months of July and August, was contending with a worse than Indian foe. The Asiatic cholera had just reached Canada; passing up the St. Lawrence to Detroit, it overtook the western-bound armament, and thenceforth the camp became a hospital. On the 8th of July, his thinned ranks landed at Fort Dearborn, or Chicago, but it was late in August before they reached the Mississippi. The number of that band who died from the cholera, must have been at least seven times as great as that of all who fell in battle. There were several other skirmishes of the troops with the Indians, and a number of individuals murdered; making in all, about seventy-five persons killed in these actions, or murdered on the frontiers.

In September, the Indian troubles were closed by a treaty, which relinquished to the white men thirty millions of acres of land, for which stipulated annuities were to be paid; constituting now the eastern portion of the State of Iowa, to which the only real claim of the Sauks and Foxes was their depredations on the unoffending Ioways, about one hundred and thirty years since. To Keokuk and his party, a reservation of forty miles square was given, in consideration of his fidelity; while Black Hawk and his family were sent as hostages to Fort Monroe in the Chesapeake, where they remained till June, 1833. The chief afterwards returned to his native wilds, where he died.

Black Hawk cannot rank with Pontiac or Tecumthe; he fought only for revenge, and showed no intellectual power; but he was a fearless man.

# ERRATA.

Page 252 states that there is no reliable source of coal in this county. This is a mistake—Coal is abundant, as experience and Owens Report both show.

Page 21, omit last word of 13th line.

Page 46, read "Topin" for last word of 4th line from bottom.

Page 104. In 12th line omit "over Platt Smith," and read the same words after "forty-eight" in 18th line.

Page 216, read "fallen" for "befallen" in 16th line from bottom.

www.ingramcontent.com/pod-product-compliance
Lightning Source LLC
LaVergne TN
LVHW010130110826
845151LV00002B/320

* 9 7 8 1 4 2 5 5 3 9 4 5 0 *